This Day in

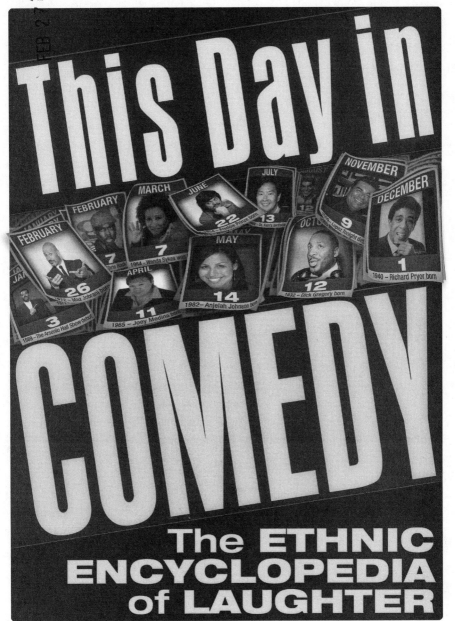

COMEDY

The ETHNIC ENCYCLOPEDIA of LAUGHTER

DARRYL LITTLETON
& FRANK HOLDER

FOREWORD BY **MARSHA WARFIELD**
INTRODUCTION BY **FRANKLYN AJAYE**

This Day in Comedy: The Ethnic Encyclopedia of Laughter
Copyright © 2019 Darryl Littleton & Frank Holder. All Rights Reserved

Published by:
Trine Day LLC
PO Box 577
Walterville, OR 97489
1-800-556-2012
www.TrineDay.com
trineday@icloud.com

Library of Congress Control Number: 2019950245

Littleton, Darryl & Holder, Frank
 – 1st ed.
p. cm.
Includes references
Epub (ISBN-13) 978-1-63424-263-9
Mobi (ISBN-13) 978-1-63424-264-6
Print (ISBN-13) 978-1-63424-262-2
1. Ethnic wit and humor -- United States -- History and criticism. 2. Comedians -- United States -- Biography. 3. Wit and humor -- Social aspects -- United States. 4. Stand-up comedy -- United States -- History. 5. Popular culture -- United States -- History. I. Littleton, Darryl & Holder, Frank. II. Title

First Edition
10 9 8 7 6 5 4 3 2 1

Printed in the USA
Distribution to the Trade by:
Independent Publishers Group (IPG)
814 North Franklin Street
Chicago, Illinois 60610
312.337.0747
www.ipgbook.com

Music played a large role in the survival of the black people in America — that and a sense of humor that just couldn't be enslaved.

– Redd Foxx,
The Redd Foxx Encyclopedia of Black Humor

DEDICATED TO:

Alley Cat
Amazing Grace
Bernie Mac
Big Daddy Fitz
Big Rome
Bobby Law
Cain Lopez
Charlie Murphy
Coolaide
Damon Rozier
Danny Grayson
Della Reese
Denzel Snipes
Dick Gregory
Dijon
Dogface
Ebon Leggs
Freddy Soto
James Hannah
James McNair
Jerry Winn
Jimmy Thompson
Joe Recca

Marilyn Martinez
Michael Ajakwe
Mickey Gordon
Monteria Ivey
Patrice O'Neal
Rasheed Thurmond
Redd Foxx
Reynaldo Rey
Richard Pryor
Ricky Harris
Rip (Tha Playa)
Robin Harris
Rodney Winfield
Sadiki Fuller
Silk Willie Dunn The Bus Driver
Simply Marvalous
Timmie Rogers
T J McGee
Todd Lynn
Tom Webb
Tommy Ford
Vic Dunlop
Yvette Wilson

SPECIAL THANKS

To my life's mentor, my father, William Littleton, Jr., who gave me my sense of humor, tenacity and put steel in my spine. My beacon of hilarity and reason, my wife, Tuezdae Littleton, who keeps my wit razor sharp and my ego in check. My reasons for living, my daughters Darina and Liburti, the two girls I'd have chosen out of two trillion. My mother, Theresa Littleton, for getting me here. My partners in this venture, Frank Holder, Dennis Moore and Kris Millegan for making a dream a reality. Rudy Moreno, Bob Sumner, Dominque Witten, Ajai Sanders, Ray Moheet and Hope Flood for giving it faces. The City of Hope, Huntington Hospital, Dr. Stephen Koehler, Nurse Heidi, Dr Satterthwaite, Askia, 420 Manchester, Herbs of Mexico, Cortney Gee, Rodney Perry, Andrea Rochester, Darxine Jones, Brelon Thomas, 25 King, Wendall Rochester and Thomas Usher for getting me through cancer. Jeff Pancer, Dan Karlok, F. Murray Abraham, Duane Benjamin, Purvis Jackson and Jeff Beasley for getting me through some of the best times of my life. – *Darryl Littleton*

First, I would like to thank God, because without him I wouldn't even be around to make this possible.

I would like to thank Darryl Littleton for the idea of this book and the courage to take it by the horns and to bring me on board to create some comedy history ourselves.

I would like to thank my parents (Frank and Pearl Holder) for making me the man I am today.

I would like to thank my in-laws (Elder Hersey and Pastor Mary Mitchell) for always being supportive and listening to all of my crazy ideas.

Finally, I would like to thank my honey, my wife, Bernadette Holder, who has ALWAYS been my biggest fan and biggest supporter. My honey will make sure I am the last man standing no matter what!

Enjoy!
Frank Holder

CONTENTS

"Bert Williams"

FOREWORD

I love this book!

To say I am honored to be asked to write this foreword is as much of an understatement as it is to say I know how to do it.

I don't.

But, so many artists have similarly stepped out on faith with no blueprint, no network, almost no scholarship, driven by little more than their compulsion to bring laughter and share smiles that just holding this book and knowing it exists gives me confidence as it simultaneously takes a huge step to fix the problem.

As a student, fan and practitioner of comedy, holding an encyclopedia that chronicles and highlights the milestones of this art form I so love is more than a joy.

But as a black woman who all too rarely sees the accomplishments and contributions of "ethnic" comedians, writers, producers, performers, etc., celebrated, it's so much more than that.

When I started doing stand-up back in the early days of black pride, black power and blaxploitation, I would have loved to have an actual encyclopedia to consult for answers to questions I didn't even know I had and to find context for those answers, but no such thing existed.

And as sorely needed as it may have been, I'm sure none of my contemporaries ever even considered the possibility that such a resource ever would exist any more than I did.

So, to have it and go through it is what I imagine any good unnamed, unimagined and unfulfilled longing should be, exhilarating, comforting and "simply marvelous" all at the same time.

Then, see my name and story included leaves me verklempt and frankly, makes me moist.

Your liquidity mileage may vary.

But, if you want to know which one of your favorite comedians won a roast battle, was born, made a movie, or got kicked out of high school for getting pregnant at somebody else's prom 3 years before Roe v. Wade... okay, that last part's not in here.

But if you want to know what happened on your birthday, or your anniversary, or the day after tomorrow in our comedy, this is where you'll find it. And that is a truly wonderful thing.

Thank you Darryl Littleton and Frank Holder for letting me be part of it.

Marsha Warfield

INTRODUCTION

I started in stand up comedy in 1970 when I realized that I would never become a lawyer, as I hated every day of my first and only year at Columbia Law School. It was an act born of desperation as I was bored silly and had stopped attending class, and with the encouragement of my fellow classmates who liked my sense of humor I decided to give stand-up a try. I bombed at an amateur night at the Village Gate in Greenwich Village, and the next day I was back in my law school classes. For two weeks. Even with the devastation of my bombing, I found the study of law more excruciating. So I decided to give stand up another try. But not immediately. I began to study comedians on the talk shows of Johnny Carson, and Dick Cavett, and obsessively listened to the albums of Cosby, Carlin, and Pryor to decipher the secrets of stand up comedy as I began to write my stand up routines. A few months later, I was much better at a hoot night at the famed Bitter End on Bleeker Street, and I officially withdrew from law school, and returned to Los Angeles where I started performing at the then new Comedy Store on Sunset Blvd.

Over the years I looked for books on stand-up comedy and found Phil Berger's *The Last Laugh*, and Larry Wilde's *The Great Comedians* which featured interviews on comedy with the great comedians of that day, and helped my stand up development quite a lot. Years later I actually used *The Great Comedians* as a template for my own book *Comic Insights – The Art of Stand-Up Monology* to try to help and guide fledgling comedians the way that *The Great Comedians* had helped my development. I also bought Gerald Nachman's *Seriously Funny – The Rebel Comedians of the 1950's and 1960* figuring my library of books on stand up comedy and comedians was now complete. Wrong!!!

Sometimes you don't know what's needed or necessary in any profession or endeavor until somebody takes the initiative and creates it. And then when it comes out, you say why didn't somebody think of this before? This is needed. This is necessary. That's was my reaction when Darryl Littleton came out with his *Black Comedians on Black Comedy*. I don't know how or why he thought to do it, but I'm sure glad he did. I knew about Pigmeat

Markham, Timmie Rogers, and Moms Mabley from watching *The Ed Sullivan Show* as a youngster, and Dick Gregory, Nipsey Russell, Bill Cosby, Flip Wilson, and Richard Pryor from watching *The Tonight Show* with Johnny Carson. I went to school with Redd Foxx's daughter Debraca so I knew about him. But that was pretty much my knowledge of the Black comedians who had come before me. So it was quite a treat and delight to read *Black Comedians On Black Comedy* and not only learn about so many others but to also read the interesting analysis and viewpoints voiced by other Black comedians on their comedic work, style, and skills.

Having come up in the giant shadows cast by Richard Pryor, and later Eddie Murphy, I had always felt a bit unnoticed, so it was quite a pleasant surprise to find myself in the book, and see that many Black comedians had noticed and appreciated my writing, style, and approach. I really had no idea that I was being watched in that way by other comedians, and it was very heartening.

What struck me about *Black Comedians* was the amount of meticulous work, and love that went into it's creation. Having written a book myself I know how hard it can be, and I couldn't imagine taking on such a monumental task as Darryl did. Even now I find myself looking through it periodically, and refreshing myself on a particular comedian, and admiring the comprehensiveness of the book about Black comedy and comedians.

And now Darryl and his co-writer Frank Holder have done it again. They have created and written something I didn't know was needed or necessary with *This Day in Comedy --The Ethnic Encyclopedia of Laughter*. So fresh. So novel. So necessary. I don't know how they came up with this idea, but again I'm sure glad they did. You can literally go to any day of the year and find out something interesting about the many great ethnic comedians past, present, and future, as well as tidbits of information about landmark ethnic shows complete with Internet links to both shows and performances. Brilliant! It's a book that hits the sweet spot of being both entertaining and informative, and once again illustrates Darryl and Frank's meticulous research, attention to detail, and sheer love of ethnic comedians and comedy. They are scholars, historians, and curators of ethnic comedy. It's all here. Inspiring. Insightful. Informative.

For comedy lovers, this book is a must have, and it'll have a treasured place in my comedy library.

Now I'm just waiting for the calendar to come out.

Franklyn Ajaye

PREFACE

I've always wanted to see comedy argued in a barber shop the same as sports is discussed. Patrons laying bets down on the who, what and where of comedy milestones. The stars of yesterday brought up to a novice as an example of how that person's generation doesn't know a damn thing about comedy. I always saw comedy as something to debate. Pryor *vs* Chappelle, Goldberg *vs* Mabley, Rodriguez *vs* Lopez or Foxx (Redd) *vs* Foxx (Jamie), the same way it's Jordan *vs* Kobe or Brady *vs* Montana.

This encyclopedia will give you those facts; every day of the year. Movie premieres, sitcom debuts, significant birthdates, network launches, box office grosses, bios, photos, rankings, controversies and monumental occasions are all included. Since comedy is just as legitimate as the other arts and just as entertaining as any sport, its highlights deserve prosperity; canonization for players and plays often unreported.

This Day in Comedy celebrates the comedic accomplishments and significance of African-American, Asian, Latin, First (Native) American and Middle Eastern cultures. Because the melting pot usually simmers light to the top and dark to the bottom, most races are not adequately, much less equally represented in the various mediums. This makes role models new and old hard to find. Artistic heroes and heroines are glorified within their racial group with moniker identifying award ceremonies paying homage to their members primarily because no one else will and that's not fair.

Laughter is for everybody. No group should have a monopoly on it and none does. People laugh at what's funny no matter where it comes from, but it's criminal they're not educated or exposed to the wealth of available gut busting humor all around them. In essence they're being cheated. Comedic inequality leaves the vast majority of the world blissfully ignorant and that's why this book was written. Being ignorant = you've been ignoring. As preservationists we rebuke ignoring and prefer to expose. We'd rather share all that you've been missing; shove it in your face and force you to appreciate it no matter where you're from.

The point is *This Day in Comedy* is like no collection of comedy facts ever compiled and as an added bonus feature, links are provided at the end of each hilariously, informative entry. If you'd like to see that performer you just read about in action – click. Care to check out the sitcom you just read about or the film? There are rare as well as memorable footage to enjoy along with the stories. Comedy is fun to read about and even more so when you can watch it.

So, for the fan, casual or rabid, *This Day in Comedy* will fill your years with a world of laughter that never stops being funny. So, talk trash with confidence. Everything we could come up with so far about ethnic comedy is at your fingertips.

LADIES & GENTLEMEN...

On a daily basis (almost) some comedian or comedy event originates. And here they are...

HARLEM'S HIGH SPOT
APOLLO
125ᵗʰ ST. near 8ᵗʰ Ave • Tel. UNiversity 4-4490

ONE WEEK ONLY BEGINING FRI. JAN 8th

COUNT BASIE
AND BAND

JOE WILLIAMS

REDD FOXX

Eddie "Lockjaw" DAVIS Trio

STUFFY BRYANT | DYERETTES

WED. NITE: AMATEURS | SAT.: MIDNITE SHOW

January

This Day in Comedy...

JANUARY 1, 1997

Former hosts Joe Torry and Martin Lawrence at Def Comedy Jam 25 June 2017.
(*Humor Mill Magazine*)

HBO's *DEF COMEDY JAM* – AIRED ITS LAST EPISODE!

Produced by rap mogul, Russell Simmons, the series had its original run from July 1, 1992 until January 1, 1997. Based on the formula established at the Comedy Act Theater in Los Angeles, California, the show was originally set to have that club's MC, Robin Harris as host. However, after his untimely death Martin Lawrence was tapped for that role and the show went on to defy all odds. Despite its raw, in-your-face barrage of three Black comedians, it not only became must see TV every Friday night; it also changed the comedy landscape in film and television for years. Relative unknowns before their Def Comedy Jam exposure, comedians such as Jamie Foxx, Bernie Mac, Chris Tucker and others dominated the mediums.

The show was criticized for excessive foul language and negative representations of African Americans by letter writers and celebrities like Bill Cosby; at the time known as "America's Dad." However, the public embraced it and it returned on HBO's fall lineup in 2006. The show produced a spinoff called *Loco Slam* and has been spoofed on *In Living Color*, Robert Townsend's *Townsend Television* and *Saturday Night Live*.

https://youtu.be/QyCiunB6mPo

✳ ✳ ✳

11

JANUARY 1, 1964

Adele Givens (2nd from right) w/Miss Laura Hayes, Chocolate, Edwonda White
(Edwonda White Collection)

ADELE GIVENS – BORN!

G ivens got started entertaining at the age of 8 years old at a house par-
ty. She later expanded her audience when she got into stand-up com-
edy and in 1989 became the Grand Prize Winner of the "Royal Crown
Comedy Contest." Givens was the runner up to the "Miller Lite Comedy
Search" the following year (losing out to Bernie Mac). She performed on
Def Comedy Jam and *Comedy Central Presents.*

Circa 2000, Givens, Mo'Nique, Sommore and Miss Laura Hayes toured
as the "Original Queens of Comedy" and taped a concert film. Both were
huge successes. Adele Givens has appeared in the films, *Beauty Shop* and
The Players Club. Givens has guest-starred on *The Hughleys, Moesha, The
Parkers, Martin, Tracey Takes on…* and *The Steve Harvey Show.* Adele Givens went into semi-retirement to care for her ailing husband, Tony, when
he needed a liver transplant (which was supplied by a donor named Jessica), but upon his recovery Givens returned to her sacred public duty as a
national headliner.

https://youtu.be/TGi-ihN4EDA

✳ ✳ ✳

JANUARY 2, 1968

Chris Spencer (The Chris Spencer Collection)

CHRIS SPENCER – BORN IN LOS ANGELES, CALIFORNIA!

Spencer got his start in comedy during the Black Comedy Boom of the early 1990s and developed his act at the Comedy Act Theater and other L.A. and Hollywood clubs. It was his omnipresence on stages which led to his initial film credits. He was prominently featured in *Don't Be a Menace to South Central While Drinking Your Juice in The Hood* from the Wayans clan. Spencer played a militant with an insatiable love for white women. His other movie appearances include *All About You, The Sixth Man, Two Can Play That Game* and *Postal.*

Chris Spencer got his public notoriety from his stint as the host of Quincy Jones' late-night talk show, *Vibe*, launched after *The Arsenio Hall Show* was off the air and the landscape was ripe for a successor. Several personalities threw their reputations in the ring: Magic Johnson, Keenen Ivory Wayans and Jones with *Vibe*. None of those other programs lasted long, but *Vibe* was interesting because Spencer never wanted to do it and when he did the producers never fully had confidence in their hand-picked star. It wasn't long before Spencer was replaced by Sinbad and an even shorter time span for *Vibe* to be cancelled. However, the setback didn't stop the dissed host from finding his place in the sun.

The multi-talented Spencer moved on to other projects, becoming one of the most sought after writer / producers in Hollywood. He was instrumental in the creation of Nick Cannon's *Wild 'N Out* (where he was also a writer). He co-created *Real Husbands of Hollywood* with Kevin Hart and *White Famous* with Buddy Lewis. He has written and

13

produced projects for Will Smith, Tiffany Haddish, Anthony Anderson, Cedric the Entertainer, Steve Harvey, Taraji P Henson and Jamie Foxx, as well as lending his penmanship to the Emmys, BET Awards, MTV Awards and Image Awards.

Spencer's televised credits in front of the camera include *Being Mary Jane, The Jamie Foxx Show, Half & Half, Soul Food* and Cuts. He's also performed on *Jimmy Kimmel Show, The Chris Rock Show, The Arsenio Hall Show, Lopez Tonight, Just For Laughs Gala Special*

Chris Spencer (2nd from R) w/Alonzo Mourning, President Barack Obama and Ray Allen (The Chris Spencer Collection)

and had his own Showtime Comedy Special entitled *The Other Chris.* So Touche.

https://youtu.be/-xXlm-uxqvs

✳✳✳

JANUARY 3, 1989

Arsenio Hall (L) and presidential candidate, Bill Clinton June 8, 1992 (Public Domain)

THE ARSENIO HALL SHOW – DEBUTED!

Hall has the distinction of having two separate late-night shows named after him (not that he even tried to find another title). The first one debuted on January 3, 1989 and took the world by surprise; changing late night's approach and demographics. Once that tsunami subsided Hall came back years later under the same name. That second effort was produced by Tribune Broadcasting and distributed by CBS. It was short lived (September 9, 2013 – May 30, 2014); plagued with poor writing, a changing attitude towards late-night shows and middling support from the media (Brian Williams famously did not mention Hall when listing hosts on the late-night programming grid). That second effort is not Hall's legacy.

The revolutionary late-night talk show created by Hall was known not only for its Black host, but its embrace and influence on pop and hip-hop culture. For decades other late-night entries were the bastion of safe, pre-slumber fare. Hall's show introduced acts like Bobby Brown for more of a late-night party feel. If you were in bed it wasn't for sleeping. Hall had 1992 presidential hopeful Bill Clinton on, who, in a single moment of cool, broke out his saxophone and jammed with Hall's house band known as his "Posse." If you didn't vote for Clinton at least you thought about it. *The Arsenio Hall Show* had his signature "dog pound" of fans barking at the host. He had labels for sections of his audience. He had things that make you go, Hmmmm. His introduction had a long sustained "O" as he stood in the shape of a giant "A." It had style. It was cool. People talked about it the next day. In short, the show was an event.

The initial show was produced by Arsenio Hall's company, Arsenio Hall Communications. After the seasoned stand-up had a run as the warm-up comedian and co-host for Paramount's *Solid Gold* dance series, Hall served as host for 13 weeks on FOX's late-night talk show as a replacement for the fired Joan Rivers. Hall was a hit in the slot and before FOX knew it Hall had made a deal with Paramount for his own late-night show; a show that appealed to a younger audience and sponsors.

The Arsenio Hall Show looked like there was no end in sight and it was in for a run as long and comfortable as the gold standard, *The Tonight Show*. Then all of a sudden the planets in the late-night universe began to collide. First Jay Leno snagged *The Tonight Show* hosting gig over at NBC leaving presumed heir to the Johnny Carson seat, David Letterman, publicly embarrassed. That didn't last long. Letterman wiped the egg off his face and jumped over to a delighted CBS. The one who was not delighted was Hall, who now had to watch CBS affiliates either drop his show or move it to an inconsequential time slot in favor of the golden boy, Letterman. Well, at least Hall had his FOX affiliates, or so he thought. They had instructions to move or drop Hall in favor of the new Chevy Chase late-night talk show. Now Hall was screwed because, even though the Chase show lasted only 5 weeks, most of those FOX affiliates didn't reschedule Hall.

The final death-knell came when Hall booked Louis Farrakhan. The die had already been cast, with affiliate defections, but when Nation of Islam's polarizing leader sat down for an interview the mainstream media declared the questions soft and the scheduling of such a figure questionable and offensive. Hall stood by the interview and was soon off the air. The last episode aired on May 29, 1994.

The Arsenio Hall Show won two NAACP Image Awards for Best Series (1993 & 1995) and two Emmy Awards (1990: Outstanding Sound Mixing for a Variety or Music Series or Special and 1993: Outstanding Technical Direction/Camera/Video for a Series).

https://youtu.be/8fJB1Uxuj6o

* * *

JANUARY 4, 1971

Dominique (The Dominique Witten Collection)

DOMINIQUE (WITTEN)– BORN IN WASHINGTON, DC!

In a profession dominated by men, Dominique is known as "The people's champ." That moniker came from her regular segment on *The Tom Joyner Morning Show*, but it applies to the love her fan base has for her. She's one of them; just good old folks. That type of comedy capital is priceless. It translates and has people rooting for you. It did, when her co-workers at the Brentwood Postal facility encouraged her to take up stand-up comedy. It did, when scouts from HBO's *Def Comedy Jam* sought her out and booked her on their career-changing show, prompting her to relocate to New York. It also did, when Tracy Morgan first saw Dominique and made her his opening act.

Once in the door she roamed around the house known as comedy. Dominique appeared on *Last Comic Standing, Herlarious* (the OWN network), *Black Jesus* on Adult Swim and her big break on the surprise hit, *Chappelle's Show.* That Comedy Central phenomenon catapulted it's host, (Dave Chappelle) and cast of regulars (Charlie Murphy, Donnell Rawlins, Bill Burr, Dominique) to cult status. That not only made Dominique a household face, it put her in the position to knock out audiences with her brand of brutally honest comedy as a major personal appearance attraction worldwide.

https://youtu.be/Fa7kWc3JShg

✳✳✳

January 5, 1906

Fred "Snowflake" Toones (findagrave.com)

Fred "Snowflake" Toones – Born in North Carolina!

Toones was one of the most prolific character actors in Hollywood history of any race. He appeared in over 200 motion pictures in a career that spanned from 1928-1951. His specialty was westerns and he worked for acclaimed directors such as Preston Sturges and with noted cinema stars like John Wayne, Bruce Bennett, Laurel and Hardy and the Three Stooges, just to name a few. His characters often went by Toones' stage name of "Snowflake," but many times he went uncredited.

Fred Toones was part of the old studio system, which meant he was a victim of old-Hollywood stereotyping. Toones' cubbyhole was mostly that of the domestic. He played a porter over 50 times. He also played janitors, elevator operators, doormen, bellhops, stable grooms, valets, butlers, cooks and bartenders. In six of his films Toones portrayed a shoeshine man. The irony of this was the fact that not only did Fred Toones play shoeshiners in the movies, he actually ran a shoeshine stand at Republic Studios.

Some would consider Toones a poor man's Stepin Fetchit, but that characterization would be inaccurate. In the over 200 films Toones made he was only credited in 73 of them. As an uncredited actor those roles were considered bit-player work and he was paid as such. Stepin Fetchit made only 53 films, but he was paid well for all of them. So, even though they played the same roles, Stepin Fetchit became the first Black millionaire movie star and Fred Toones shined shoes on a studio lot.

Fred Toones died on February 13, 1962 in Los Angeles, California.

http://dai.ly/x23dfiv

✳ ✳ ✳

January 5, 1969

Guy Torry (L) w/ Tommy Davidson and Lavell Crawford (*Humor Mill Magazine*)

Robert "Guy" Torry – Born in St. Louis, Missouri!

Torry got his start in comedy in college, then once out, he went to Hollywood. His brother, Joe Torry, had already made the journey and was a successful host of The Comedy Act Theater when Guy arrived. Going by the stage name of Guy T, the younger Torry dug right in and honed his skills as a regular at the popular club. He took his talents and knowledge to The World-Famous Comedy Store and created the institution known as "Phat Tuesday" in 1995. This was the night Black Hollywood was celebrated; on stage in the way of comedians and, out in the audience, in the way of crowds. Celebrities of the moment came to see the celebrities of the future and Torry was the ringmaster. This phenomenal night lasted for a decade, but during that time Torry stayed busy elsewhere.

Guy Torry showed up a lot on the small and big screen. He first appeared in *Family Matters*, then *Martin* (he also wrote for the show and for *Moesha*). Then he got a role in the UPN sitcom, *Good News*. That didn't last long, but so what? He made movies; *Don't Be A Menace to South Central While Drinking Your Juice in the Hood, Life, Trippin, Introducing Dorothy Dandridge, Pearl Harbor*, and his stand-out role as a convict who converts the racist protagonist (Edward Norton) in *American History X*.

As a stand-up, Torry found success on the road. He toured the civilized world and returned to do *Def Comedy Jam* (his brother was the host of that too) and killed it. He was seen on Comedy Central and *The Tonight Show with Jay Leno*. Then Guy Torry became the host of the first outing of the Original Kings of Comedy in 1998. The other comedians were Steve Harvey, Cedric the Entertainer and Bernie Mac. Torry left after that first run to star as a detective in the UPN action series, *The Strip*. That show didn't last long, either. Oh well, he could always do radio, charities, tours, celebrity roasts, film documentaries, guest star on sitcoms, etc., etc., etc.

https://youtu.be/C-7_x64kE1w

✳ ✳ ✳

JANUARY 5, 1974

Pablo Francisco with Haddie Djemal (Instagram)

PABLO RIDSON FRANCISCO – BORN IN ARIZONA!

Beginning his comedy career in Tempe, Arizona, Francisco built his reputation on his frenetic, hyper brand of stand-up. Using a barrage of non sequiturs and a cornucopia of callbacks and sound effects, he became an audience favorite. His forte was impressions – and Francisco counted Keanu Reeves, Ozzy Osbourne, Jackie Chan, Christopher Walken, Danny Glover, Dennis Haysbert, William Shatner, Aaron Neville,

Arnold Schwarzenegger, Jerry Springer, "Tony Montana," Ricky Martin, Chris Rock, Kermit the Frog, Mr. Magoo, Celine Dion and George Clooney as part of his crowd-pleasing expansive repertoire. However, his most famous was Don LaFontaine (aka), "The Movie Voiceover Guy." That characterization put Francisco on the industry radar.

Francisco got recognized and got the work. He was a featured player on *MADtv* in the 1990s. From there the Chilean-American humorist got his own half-hour comedy special on *Comedy Central Presents* in 2000. He toured with Freddy Soto and Carlos Mencia, as "The Three Amigos." Francisco also appeared on *The Mind of Mencia* as "Voiceover Man." He was a perennial on the TV comedy circuit, on shows like *Make Me Laugh, Last Comic Standing, Gabriel Iglesias Presents Stand-Up Revolution* and *Comics Unleashed with Byron Allen.* He did *The Tonight Show* when Jay Leno had it and *Frank TV* when Frank had it.

Pablo Francisco released his comedy album, *Knee To The Groin* in 1998, *Sausage* in 2000, his DVD *Bits and Pieces* in 2004, *Ouch* in 2006 and *They Put it Out There* in 2011.

https://youtu.be/RrwaI2vZpFs

✳ ✳ ✳

JANUARY 6, 1926

Capulina (L) w/Viruta, 1957 (Public Domain)

"CAPULINA" (GASPAR HENAINE PÉREZ) BORN – IN CHIGNAHUAPAN, PUEBLA!

Known affectionately by the nickname, *"El Rey del Humorismo Blanco"* (The King of White Humor), due to his clean, innocent style of comedy, Capulina got his start in show business when he was still innocent.

He was 10 years old and had a small part in the 1936 Fernando de Fuentes film, *Alla en el Rancho Grande*. He won youth acting honors and by 1946 his musical studies began to pay off when Capulina toured Mexico and the USA as a vocalist with the trio Los Trincas.

Capulina's catapult to fame came as a duo. He partnered with Marco Antonio Campos as the team of Viruta and Capulina. They made 26 films together starting in 1951. Initially the pair were compared to American counterparts, Laurel and Hardy. Viruta, the thin one, was smart; Capulina, the fat one, was the fool – but it wasn't long before they carved out their own distinctive on-screen personas. The duo gained fame throughout Latin America. They had their own TV show, *Cómicos y canciones;* a sketch comedy show that included as one of its writers, comedian Chespirito. However, as time moved on Viruta and Capulina made less films together and on their last six they were constantly feuding – feuding about not making enough films. The fighting stopped when Viruta died after his fourth heart attack.

Capulina mourned the untimely death of his partner but believed in the old adage that the show must go on. In his long career, Capulina made 84 movies; 58 of them as a solo act. His formula was simple – his dimwitted character would get into a pickle trying to carry out an easy task and be aided by a celebrity (like pro wrestlers El Santo or Tinieblas, an adventurer, or he'd gain some special power). In any case the results were often hilarious.

Capulina was a national treasure. He released 12 albums, had another television series in 1989 and a tele-novela in 1996. As a comedian he toured until 1997, when he claimed he was too old to keep doing it. That premature prediction became a reality on September 30, 2011 when Capulina died from complications of pneumonia and a gastric ulcer.

His voiceover role in the 2015 film, *Seleccion Canina* was released four-years after his death.

https://youtu.be/j2j7sWkwKj8

✳ ✳ ✳

January 6, 1979

Cristela Alonzo w/ Rudy Moreno at The Ice House (The Moreno Collection)

Cristela Alonzo -Born in San Juan, Texas!

Like many stand-up comics, Alonzo came from a dysfunctional family. It seems her father couldn't keep his hands to himself and her mother got tired of ducking so she left the guy before young Cristela ever even met him. However, she did cross the border regularly to go into Reynosa, Mexico to visit her grandmother from his side. Alonzo's own mother, who'd worked double shifts and raised four children by herself in extreme poverty (the family lived in an abandoned diner for eight years) passed away when Cristela was in her early 20s. They'd been so tight that mother and daughter shared a bed until daughter was 18, ticking off any young boy thinking about sneaking into the diner after lights out.

The next year, the college dropout got a job as an office manager. The office she managed was at the Addison Improv in Dallas, Texas. She started doing stand-up to get past the death of her mother and found a new career. Alonzo moved to Los Angeles, California, hooked up with established comedian, Carlos Mencia and spent the next two years on a bus traveling across country touring. After she got a belly full of that she jumped ship and charted her own course on the college circuit. It was a good fit for Alonzo.

She caught the attention of *LA Weekly* and *Cosmopolitan* magazines as someone to watch and Alonzo didn't disappoint. She appeared on *The Late Show with Stephen Colbert*, *Late Late Show with Craig Ferguson*, *Conan*, *Showtime*, *Last Comic Standing*, *Live at Gotham* and *Gabriel Iglesias*

Presents Stand-Up Revolution. She did voice-over work on Disney's *Cars 3* and the podcast, *Bubble.*

Cristela Alonzo charted her own course again and created (along with producer, Becky Clements) her own TV show, *Cristela.* Alonzo wrote the pilot with her partner, Kevin Hench and ABC picked it up in 2014. That move made Cristela Alonzo the first Latina female to create, produce, write and star in her own network TV show. She'd come a long way from the diner.

https://youtu.be/Fn5cOndgiPA

✱ ✱ ✱

JANUARY 7, 1970

Doug E. Doug (Instagram)

DOUG E. DOUG – BORN IN BROOKLYN, NEW YORK!

Doug got started in comedy at age 17 as a stand-up. His initial break came when he was spotted performing at the Apollo Theater by Russell Simmons. Next thing he knew Doug was writing and starring in *The New Music Report,* a Simmons production. The exposure led to a string of projects.

Doug did movies. His first line on film was in Spike Lee's *Mo' Better Blues.* From there the laughs just kept coming: 1991 – *Hangin' With the Homeboys, Jungle Fever;* 1992 – *Class Act;*1995 – *Operation Dumbo Drop;* 1997 – *That Darn Cat;* 2002 – *Eight Legged Freaks.* The most prominent of these was his role as the happy-go-lucky bobsled racer, Sanka Coffie in 1993's *Cool Runnings.*

ABC aired Doug's sitcom, *Where I Live* in 1993. It was loosely based on his life and he co-produced it, but unfortunately it didn't last long. Fortunately it got the attention of Bill Cosby which got Doug a featured role on Cosby's CBS sitcom, *Cosby.* That lasted for four seasons.

Doug played a number of cards from the deck of comedy. He did animation (the voice of Bernie the jellyfish in *Shark Tale;* Turbo the turtle on *Rusty: A Dog's Tale;* Percy the pet store owner on Nickelodeon's *Little Bill*). He co-wrote, produced, starred in and directed, *Citizen James* forStarz Encore/ BET Movies. He kicked off his YouTube comedy channel, *The Doug Life Show* in 2012.

Doug E. Doug received multiple acting nominations throughout his career. His work in *Hangin'with the Homeboys* was recognized by the Independent Spirit Awards for Best Male Lead in 1992 as well as Supporting Actor for *Cosby* in 1998, '99 and 2000 by the NAACP. In 1994 he got Best Youth Comedian from Young Artist Award for *Where I Live.*

https://youtu.be/2DZoAry851s

* * *

JANUARY 9, 1972

Deon Cole (l) w/ Tony Roberts (*Humor Mill Magazine*)

DEON COLE – BORN IN CHICAGO, ILLINOIS!

Cole began his comedy career in 1993 when a friend bet him $50 he wouldn't go up at an open mic. From there Cole appeared on most of the requisite stand-up shows including BET's *Comic View,* Comedy Central's *Laffapalooza, Showtime at the Apollo,* BBC's *The World Stands Up, Martin Lawrence's 1ˢᵗ Amendment Stand Up* and HBO's *Def Comedy Jam.* He toured domestically, internationally and established a reputation as a comedian who could write; based on the innovative nature of his approach to material. He could also ad-lib which was evident on Nick Cannon's *Wild 'N Out.* Cole's first stand-up special aired on Comedy Central in 2007.

In 2009 Cole's writing ability changed his career. He made an appearance on *The Tonight Show with Conan O'Brien* and soon afterwards received an invitation to become a writer for the show. This made Cole the first Black writer in the history of *The Tonight Show*. O'Brien's tenure was cut short, but he liked Cole and took him on his "The Legally Prohibited from Being Funny on Television" stand-up tour. Once a new deal was in place with TBS, O'Brien brought his late-night antics to a new station and Cole along with him; giving Cole on-air spots to display his comedic abilities. *TV Guide* declared, "A Star is Born" after Cole's commentary pieces kept growing in popularity.

Cole formed a production company and mounted *Deon Cole's Black Box* on TBS. That show was short-lived, but he was liked at TBS and got his role on *Angie Tribeca* when producer, Steve Carell hit it off with Cole and made it clear he wanted Cole on his show. Cole had a similar path to the ABC smash hit, *Black-ish* where Cole's recurring character, Charlie became a breakout character. His on-screen persona fused likeability with maniacal unpredictability which he took to the show's spin-off *Grown-ish*.

During his career Deon Cole has touched as many comedy bases as possible. His distinctive voice earned him narration work. It's also been an asset that gained him admission into the world of speaking engagements, national commercials and guest starring appearances on sitcoms and featured roles in films (*Barbershop 1, 2 & 3*). He's received Primetime Emmy nominations for writing and the WGA Award for Best Comedy/ Variety.

https://youtu.be/CTuP5w4D2tU

* * *

JANUARY 10, 1999

THE PJS – PREMIERED ON FOX!

This controversial stop motion animated sitcom showed life in the projects as each episode dealt with slumlord, Thurgood Stubbs (the voice of Eddie Murphy) and his ways to get out of fixing tenant's dwellings, consuming ghetto grub (including Forties) and his schemes to beat the system. His wife, Muriel (Loretta Devine) is an ole Alabama girl who attended school back in the George Wallace (not the comedian) days and his friends are as lazy as he is. Thurgood's got tenants who hate him, kids who idolize him and crackheads, relatives, in-laws and law enforcement officials who get on his last nerve.

The PJs was created by Eddie Murphy, Larry Wilmore and Steve Tompkins. It was produced by Ron Howard and Brian Grazer's Imagine Entertainment, Will Vinton Studios, Touchstone Television and The Murphy Company. The music was provided by George Clinton and QD3. The show was popular, yet laborious to produce; each installment took no less than two months to complete. In its final season The PJs moved from FOX to the WB. Murphy was AWOL(rumored to be off filming a movie) and replaced vocally by Phil Morris (Mark Moseley, Murphy's voice double is also heard throughout). When that third season was over the sitcom was canceled but aired for a while in syndication. During its 3-year run The PJs won three Emmys and an Annie Award. The PJs aired its last episode on January 8, 2002.

https://youtu.be/lS1SH-aDs74

✱✱✱

JANUARY 11, 1995

Marlon and Shawn Wayans (Public Domain)

THE WAYANS BROS. – PREMIERED ON THE WB!

This sitcom starred real life brothers, Shawn and Marlon Wayans as Shawn and Marlon Williams (why bother?); brothers who live together in Harlem. Their over-the-top, slapstick antics drove the show's comedy. The premise: Shawn "Williams" owns a newsstand (after working for a delivery company) and the duo run it. Their father, "Pops" (John Witherspoon) runs a diner and they all end up working together in a high-rise skyscraper in Manhattan. Security guard, (Anna Maria Horsford) also works in that building. So, the show centered on the building and the apartment and the laughs generated at both.

The Wayans Bros. was produced by Warner Bros. Television along with Baby Way and Next To Last Productions. It was created by the Wayans Bros., Leslie Ray and David Steven Simon. The opening theme was A Tribe Called Quest's Electric Relaxation then changed to a hip-hop beat produced by Shawn & Marlon and Omar Epps. Also featured in the cast during its run were Lela Rochon, Paula Jai Parker, Ja'net Dubois, Jill Tasker and Mitch Mullany. It aired its last episode on May 20, 1999.

https://youtu.be/mX-HaI1kJxM
* * *

JANUARY 11, 1962

Kim Coles (*Humor Mill Magazine*)

KIM COLES – BORN IN BROOKLYN, NEW YORK!

Kim Coles is big on living. She got national acclaim on Season One of *In Living Color* on FOX and then followed it up by playing Synclaire James-Jones for five seasons on *Living Single* on FOX. However, all this living wasn't always the case. Coles was a reserved kid going to Lutheran School and keeping her eyes straight ahead and her arms and legs crossed. Living it up and getting laughs didn't come until high school when things loosened up.

Stand-up comedy is known to make introverts in life, extroverts on stage. It was that way for Kim Coles. She used the mic to tell about her problems and everybody else's. Never mean-spirited, just honest. That authenticity got her plenty film and television work (*Strictly Business, Martin, MADtv, Fraser, The Parkers, My Wife & Kids, One on One, The Soul Man, Baby Daddy* and more). She used her celebrity to compete on television's *Celebrity Mole* and *Celebrity Fit Club*. She also hosted a game show (*Pay It Off*). Of course, more than being a celebrity, Kim Coles is a comedienne and she does what all laugh getters do – hit the road and do some living.

https://youtu.be/YrNJnstNle0

JANUARY 12, 1996

Marlon and Shawn Wayans

DON'T BE A MENACE TO SOUTH CENTRAL WHILE DRINKING YOUR JUICE IN THE HOOD – RELEASED!

Produced by Keenen Ivory Wayans from a Shawn & Marlon Wayans script, this film is a parody of hood flicks. The main celluloid classics from the ghetto to get the spoof treatment are *Menace II Society* and *Boyz n the Hood*. The interweaving storyline of a young black youth delivered by his mother to his father to be raised by a male role model surrounded by questionable role models in the way of friends and the threat of thuggery and hopelessness, gun play and racial insensitivity, sexual promiscuity and self-hatred. It's all there.

This hilarious movie was directed by Paris Barclay and stars Shawn Wayans as Tray that kid dropped off by his mama (Vivica A. Fox) to his Similac smelling daddy (Lahmard Tate). Marlon Wayans is his crazy, 2nd Amendment abusing homeboy; Chris Spencer is the militant with a love-of white meat (women) and Suli McCullough is the requisite hood flick brother in a wheel chair, Darrel Heath channels the brother fresh out of prison who still acts like he's in and Tracey Cherelle Jones has the role as the round away girl everybody has rolled with, but Tray is the latest honoree and newest baby's daddy (as he was informed she was pregnant seconds after their first intercourse). There are acrobatic Korean liquor store owners, overly possessive gang-bangers, weed-smoking, break-dancing senior citizens, black cops who hate black people, a wise neighborhood mailman filled with sage wisdom, horny-hood skanks, hornier hood crackheads and of course – The Man (and a freckly faced one at that).

Though the critics didn't care for it, the ticket buying public approved. On a budget of $3.8 million the film with the title too long to type again made $20,109,115 domestically.

https://youtu.be/JAAhQwcJ20U

✳ ✳ ✳

JANUARY 12, 2000

Mike Epps and Ice Cube

NEXT FRIDAY – RELEASED BY NEW LINE CINEMA!

This sequel to the smash 1995 hit, *Friday* picks up where the original left off. Craig, played by Ice Cube had just defeated the bully on the block, Deebo (Tiny Lister, Jr.) in a street fight. Deebo is arrested, but as he's about to be released word gets out that he's going to come after Craig. So, his father, Willie (John Witherspoon) relocates Craig to live with his "rich" uncle and family away from the hustle and bustle of South Central – Rancho Cucamonga. There, life is initially cool for Craig, kicking it with his cousin, Day-Day (Mike Epps), but reality soon kicks in when Craig discovers his lottery winning relatives are broke by way of taxes to pay.

There's other trouble in the form of neighbors – the Jokers. They turn out to be drug dealers, who Craig turns out to rob of some of their money and is marked. Day-Day loses his job thanks to Craig's involvement in his business. Lives are threatened at gunpoint because Craig poked his nose where it didn't belong. If it wasn't for Willie and "rich" Uncle Elroy (Don "DC" Curry) rescuing Day-Day and Craig there wouldn't have been a third installment.

Next Friday was the first film produced by Cube Vision. It co-starred Kym Whitley, Tamala Jones, Michael Blackson, Clifton Powell, Sticky Fingaz, Jacob Vargas, Justin Pierce, Lisa Rodriguez, Robin Allen, Amy Hill, Lobo Sebastian, Rolando Molina and Nicole Lydy. It was directed by Steve Carr with music by Terrance Blanchard.

On a budget of $11 million, *Next Friday* grossed $57,328,603 domestically and $2,498,725 internationally for a worldwide box office of $59,827,328.

https://youtu.be/YkDll6iRvT0

✳ ✳ ✳

JANUARY 14, 1972

Demond Wilson and Redd Foxx as Lamont and Fred Sanford in *Sanford and Son*, 1972
(Public Domain)

SANFORD AND SON – PREMIERED ON NBC!

Based on the British hit comedy, *Steptoe and Son*, the American version was the brainchild of producer Norman Lear (produced for he and partner Bud Yorkin's Tandem Productions). Starring prolific stand-up comedian, Redd Foxx and actor, Demond Wilson (as the often naïve and combative, but dedicated to his "Pops," Lamont Sanford), *Sanford and Son* was an instant hit for the network and remained so for its entire 6 season run.

A little-known fact is that Lincoln Perry (aka Stepin Fetchit) was originally cast in the part of the junkman in Watts, California with a cantankerous, acid tongue, stubborn nature and a streak of racism against "whitey" (amongst others such as Puerto Rican neighbor, Julio, played by Gregory Sierra and Ah Chew played by Pat Morita), but when the NAACP zeroed in their focus on negative Black images, the shuffling Perry was replaced by Foxx, who owned the part and became a television icon.

The show was so popular it had two spin-offs (*Sanford, Sanford Arms*). Neither garnered the acclaim of the original which was in a class by itself. What made *Sanford and Son* so ground-breaking was its comedic and candid look at Black life. Before it came along there were hardly any Black sitcoms – period. After its success, a slew sprung up in the 1970s (*The Jeffersons, Good Times, What's Happening, That's My Mama, Love Thy Neighbor*) and beyond.

Written by a revolving team of comedians as well as seasoned writers that included Richard Pryor, Paul Mooney and Garry Shandling, the show dealt with St. Louis native, Fred G. Sanford (Foxx), his son, Lamont and their junkyard business. Lamont was always trying to move out and get a life of his own and Fred was constantly guilting him back in with frequent warnings that he'd have a heart attack and go to join Lamont's deceased mother, Elizabeth in Heaven if Lamont were to leave him alone.

The running gags were plentiful: Fred and his get-rich-quick schemes to make "Sanford and Son" a huge financial success, Aunt Esther (played by pioneering comedienne, LaWanda Page) and her attempts to convert the heathen Fred to be the kind of Christian her departed sister would've been proud of, Fred's affection for songstress, Lena Horne (who he finally met in one of the episodes), his gaggle of friends who hung out (comedians, Bubba Bexley, Slappy White, Leroy and Skillet, as well as actor Whitman Mayo as Grady), Lamont's chum Rollo, who was also Lamont's supplier of good times and sexy ladies, Fred's own affection for the ladies (when he wasn't dating his girlfriend, Donna (who Lamont refers to as "the barracuda" because she was not his mother) – he kept them coming to "Casa Sanford"), the cops of the neighborhood, Smitty (Hal Williams) and Swanny (Noam Pitlik) and later Hoppy (Howard Platt); (one Black and one White, who always needed the Black one to translate what was said in ghetto terms by Fred or one of his pals and vice versa – other cops thrown in the mix were Jonesy (Bernie Hamilton) and Percy (Pat Paulsen) and there was Fred's need to refer to Lamont as "you big dummy."

Behind the scenes, Foxx had recruited most of his old friends from the chitlin circuit to portray his on-camera comrades, including Page, who studio heads originally fired for her lack of television etiquette. However, Foxx was not only hilarious, making him indispensable to the program, but he was a loyalist. If she had to go – he had to go, and so LaWanda Page also became a comedy legend with her take on the Bible thumping sister from church who could turn on a dime and thump you upside the head in the name of the Lord.

Sanford and Son was a formula that crossed over effortlessly, to the point of driving its competitor, the seemingly invincible TV mainstay, *The Brady Bunch* off the air. But not all was well when Foxx took a few self-imposed hiatuses in disputes that he wasn't being treated fairly. Rival sitcom star, Carroll O'Conner of the CBS hit and Norman Lear production *All in the Family*, had a window in his dressing room. Foxx did not, and he didn't return until he got one. Foxx made sure he received the same perks and money the other stars of hit shows got at the time and paved the way for better conditions for future Black TV leads.

Sanford and Son received 3 Emmy Nominations for Best Series and Foxx chalked up the same number for best Outstanding Actor. The top-rated show ended its run March 25, 1977.

https://youtu.be/NIK9yffjRK8

✳ ✳ ✳

JANUARY 16, 1998

Guillermo Diaz, Jim Breuer, Harland Williams, Dave Chappelle

HALF BAKED – RELEASED BY UNIVERSAL!

*H*alf Baked is a stoner comedy about the saga of four lifelong friends and their love of weed. From the time they first get high together as middle schoolers, it was all good. Then tragedy strikes while one of the potheads goes on a standard munchies run and is arrested for killing a diabetic police horse with sweet snacks. It's now up to his posse to get him out of the pokey before he gets poked. Fortunately, one of the pals works as a janitor at a place where they test marijuana. Voila! The three amigos would steal the weed, sell it and bail their friend out. It's going to take a lot of dope slinging (the bail is one million, but they only have to come up with $100,000), but they're up to the task. Plus, along the way there's romance and hallucinating.

Directed by Tamra Davis from a Dave Chappelle and Neal Brennan script, *Half Baked* stars Dave Chappelle, Harland Williams, Jim Breuer and Guillermo Diaz. It also features the talents of Clarence Williams III, Tracy Morgan, Rachel True, Tommy Chong, Willie Nelson, Snoop Dogg, Jon Stewart, Bob Saget, Laura Silverman, Steven Wright, Stephen Baldwin, Neal Brennan and Janeane Garofalo.

Half Baked is a cult classic taking in a box office gross of $17,460,020 on a budget of $8 million.

https://youtu.be/HMhUnO2u6qI

✳ ✳ ✳

JANUARY 17, 2014

Kevin Hart and Ice Cube

RIDE ALONG – RELEASED BY UNIVERSAL!

This buddy flick stars Ice Cube as a seasoned cop and Kevin Hart as a high school security guard trying to get his approval so he can marry Cube's sister (Tika Sumpter). The veteran flatfoot's not having it. He doesn't feel Hart is worthy, so he takes him on a ride along to see what Hart's made of. At the same time Cube is trying to catch a ring of smugglers (of passports, not opium, diamonds, coffee grounds, etc.) and will stop at nothing to get them. This means a lot of action: car chases, shoot outs, face slapping, hysterical screaming, multiple subduings, little folks flying through the air, things being destroyed by grenades, double dealings, backstabbings, leg shootings, people being hit in the head with frying pans and a little Michael Vickery.

Based on a story by Greg Coolidge, *Ride Along* was directed by Tim Story and produced by Cube, Will Packer, Matt Alvarez and Larry Brezner. The cast also includes John Leguizamo, Jay Pharaoh, Bruce McGill, Gary Owen, Bryan Callen, Jacob Latimore, David Banner, Gary Weeks, Dragos Bucur and Laurence Fishburne.

The critics turned in mainly negative reviews for the film. The public positively loved it. It not only made $153,262,184 from a $25 million budget (breaking all existing box offices opening records for the month of January), but spawned a sequel (*Ride Along 2*) less than two years from the original's release.

https://youtu.be/5klp6rkHIks

✳ ✳ ✳

January 17, 1957

Steve Harvey (*Comedy the Magazine*)

Broderick Stephen "Steve" Harvey – Born in Welch, West Virginia!

For Steve Harvey it was comedy or bust. After stints as a boxer, mailman, autoworker, insurance salesman and carpet cleaner, Harvey got into standup in 1985 at Hilarities in Cleveland, Ohio. It wasn't overnight stardom. He was homeless for years; sleeping in his car when a gig didn't provide a hotel room for the night and showering at gas stations.

Harvey got a break in 1990 when he became a finalist in the Johnnie Walker National Comedy Search. That got him his job as host of *It's Showtime at the Apollo*. That televised showcase got him his deal to do his first sitcom, *Me and the Boys* in 1994 on ABC. His second sitcom was on the WB, *The Steve Harvey Show* aired from 1996 to 2002 and was a top show in black households.

Steve Harvey's popularity translated when he toured as one-fourth of The Original Kings of Comedy. The quartet of Bernie Mac, Cedric the Entertainer, Harvey and D.L. Hughley (Guy Torry was the fourth member and host before leaving to do a TV show and was replaced by Hughley) toured; packing in history making crowds and setting off a trend that hit other subgroups in comedy, such as The Queens of Comedy, The Original Latin Kings of Comedy, The Latin Divas of Comedy, The Kims of Comedy, Blue Collar Comedy Tour, etc. The pinnacle was when the foursome was recorded by Spike Lee for his concert film in 2000.

The former boxer was out for a knockout. Harvey had his own syndicated radio show. He released his comedy DVD, *Don't Trip, He Ain't Through with Me Yet* and a hip hop and R&B CD. He authored books: *Steve Harvey's Big Time* (also the name of a variety show Harvey hosted on the WB from 2003-2005), *Act Like a Lady, Think Like A Man* and *Straight Talk, No Chaser: How to Find and Keep a Man*. He's hosted award ceremonies (including Miss Universe), appeared in films, launched a clothing line, launched a dating website, hosted *Family Feud*, hosted a self-titled daytime talk show and co-founded The Hoodie Awards (a show recognizing deserving businesses in the black community) along with partner, Rushion McDonald.

Steve Harvey is an 11- time NAACP Image Award winner, a 3-time Daytime Emmy Award winner and he has a star on the Hollywood Walk of Fame.

https://youtu.be/Nd3bLj14VcQ

✳ ✳ ✳

JANUARY 17TH

Darryl Littleton aka D'Militant at The Comedy Union (The Littleton Collection)

DARRYL LITTLETON AKA D'MILITANT – BORN IN LOS ANGELES!

Darryl Littleton began his comedy career writing for *The Tom Joyner Morning Show* and soon afterwards became a regular at the world-famous Comedy Store adopting the stage name,"D'Militant" for his slicing wit and incisive social and political commentary. He was D. L. Hughley's exclusive writer when Hughley hosted BET's *Comic View* and as writer/producer penned material for subsequent hosts Cedric the Entertainer, Sommore, Montanna Taylor and Don "DC" Curry. His writing extended to columns for *Comedy the Magazine* and *Humor Mill Magazine*. Littleton was also a commentator for NPR.

As a stand-up, Darryl Littleton's on camera credits include *The Parent Hood, Townsend Television, HBO's Def Comedy Jam, Comedy Central's Make Me Laugh, SiTV's Latino Laugh Festival, Martin Lawrence's 1stAmendment, Telemundo's Loco Comedy Jam* and *Byron Allen's Comic's Unleashed.* He has toured Europe and Asia performing for the US military and as the host of Katt Williams' "Its Pimpin, Pimpin Tour" (the highest grossing national comedy tour of 2008).

Littleton took his love of comedy and wrote books on the subject. His first, *Black Comedians on Black Comedy*, chronicles the history of African-American comedy. It's taught in universities and was made into the documentary, *Why We Laugh* by director, Robert Townsend. Littleton served as executive producer for the project. He has also published *Pimp Down* (2011), on 21st Century fame and media scrutiny, *Forefathers* (2012), the story of the American Revolution told from a Black perspective, *Comediennes: Laugh Be a Lady*(2012), the history of female comedy which he co-wrote with his wife/comedienne, Tuezdae Littleton, *How to Be Funny: The Essential Comedy Handbook* (2012), a tutorial on the art of laughter, *Black Revenge* (2017) a collection of stories from Black celebrities who were stereotyped and turned the tables on their abuser, and *How to Do Stand-Up Comedy: Preservation of a Dying Art Form* (2018), the title says it all.

Darryl Littleton is the first African-American on the advisory board of the Comedy Hall of Fame and a curator. He has toured the nation as a public speaker lecturing on the historical and social significance of comedy. To that end Littleton produced *Black & Blue: The Laff Records Collection,* a compilation of classic party records from Redd Foxx to Marsha Warfield. As "D'Militant" he's released two comedy albums (*Am I Lying?!, Too Raw for Mainstream*) and won numerous comedy awards including the Bay Area Black Comedy Competition and ABC's *America's Funniest People.* In 2017 he was nominated for an Emmy Award for Writing for his work on the documentary, *Joan Rivers: Exit Laughing* and following a two year bout with cancer, Littleton returned to comedy as an executive for Humor Mill TV.

https://youtu.be/VWGaDgJ_5Vk

✳ ✳ ✳

JANUARY 18, 1975

Sherman Hemsley and Isabel Sanford as George and Louise Jefferson, 1975 (Public Domain)

THE JEFFERSONS – PREMIERED ON CBS!

Created by Michael Ross and Bernie West and developed by Norman Lear, *The Jeffersons* is one of the longest running sitcoms in television history. A spin-off of Lear's cultural milestone, *All In the Family, The Jeffersons* centers around George and Louise Jefferson (Sherman Hemsley and Isabel Sanford), an upwardly mobile Black couple who worked their way out of the working class section of Queens, New York as neighbors to the Archie Bunkers and into a deluxe highrise apartment in Manhattan. This was accomplished through George's expanding dry cleaning business and the show's success was built on great writing, acting and appealing to the times.

When *The Jeffersons* premiered America was in its post-Civil Rights period and all things seemed possible for those who that struggle meant to benefit. *The Jeffersons* showed that if you give a Black man the same financial opportunities as a white man he could end up just as petty, bigoted and greedy as his Caucasian counterpart. George Jefferson was basically a Black Archie Bunker. His wife, Louise was no dingbat, but embodied the solid wife of unwavering morals despite how much money came into her life. They had a maid, Florence (Marla Gibbs),who was also Black and talked Black. Their neighbor, Mr. Bentley (Paul Benedict) worked at the UN as a translator and when the bachelor came home he needed George to walk on his back to keep his spine aligned. *The Jeffersons* also had a son, Lionel, who had a girlfriend, Jenny (Berlinda Tolbert), who had a white father and black mother (Frank Cover and Roxie Roker).

There was a tip happy doorman, Ralph (Ned Wertimer) and George's mother (Zara Cully) who felt George was too good for everything; especially Louise. Outside of his mother, wife and son, George disapproved of these people and that kept the comedy going for 253 episodes. *The Jeffersons* was consistently in the Top 30 of the Nielsen ratings. Even when it was cancelled, the news came as a shock to the cast. Many of them heard about getting the axe through a newspaper article or by a friend telling them. This was particularly upsetting because the end was so much different than the beginning when everybody was so accommodating. Lear had written the part of George Jefferson specifically for Sherman Hemsley and eventually waited until Hemsley finished his theatrical obligations before introducing him as the character on *All in the Family*. That wait took four seasons.

At one point another actor was tried, but the chemistry between Carroll O'Connor (ArchieBunker) and actor Avon Lewis (the "first" George Jefferson) didn't work, according to O'Connor;and they put the physical George back on the shelf. Undaunted, Lear slid George Jefferson into the conversation by writing in George's brother, Henry Jefferson (played by Mel Stewart) and when George Jefferson was finally ready for his close-up, the character of Henry disappeared.

The show also had to adjust to a new Lionel when actor Mike Evans left the show after the first season and was replaced by Damon Evans, who was in turn replaced by Mike Evans until Lionel and Jenny were written out of the show (stated reason – marital problems). The show used the frank language of the 1970s including "nigger" and "honky." George called Tom and Helen Willis "zebras," and everybody called George "short." This was not a politically correct sitcom (until the latter seasons). It spawned one spin-off; *Checking In* starring Marla Gibbs, but it checked out after only 4 episodes and Gibbs was right back in her apron on *The Jeffersons*. The show's theme song *Movin on Up* was composed by Jeff Barry and Ja'net Dubois, who also sang the theme with a gospel choir.

During its 11-season run *The Jeffersons* received 13 Emmy Award nominations for acting with a 1981 win for Isabel Sanford for Best Actress. She was only the second black actress to win this honor (the first was Gail Fisher for Mannix in 1970). *The Jeffersons* aired its last episode July 2, 1985.

https://youtu.be/5bHh8VAb_BQ

***

JANUARY 19, 1955

Paul Rodriguez w/ Brittany Murphy, 2003 (Public Domain)

PAUL RODRIGUEZ – BORN IN MAZATLÁN, MEXICO!

Rodriguez was initially going to be an attorney but decided on comedy instead (though that's not much of a stretch). His career took off quickly with appearances in the films *DC Cab* and *Quicksilver*. If you missed him in either, no problem – he got his own sitcom, *a.k.a. Pablo*; an ABC series meant to pull in the Latin viewing audience. It did for seven episodes before it was canceled. So, it was back to movies (*The Whoopee Boys, Miracles, Born in East L. A., Made in America, Tortilla Soup, Rat Race,* and

Ali), TV guest starring roles (*Tall Tales and Legends, TheGolden Girls, Trial & Error*) and album recordings (*You're in America Now, Speak Spanish*).

Rodriguez was no one trick pony. In 1988 he hosted the epitome of Americana, *The Newlywed Game* for a season. He hosted *El Show de Paul Rodriguez* for Univision from 1990 to 1993. He directed himself in the film *A Million to Juan* and did voiceover work for *King of the Hill, Dora the Explorer* and *Beverly Hills Chihuahua*. His second album, *Cheese and Macaroni* was released in 1997 and he produced and starred in *The Original Latin Kings of Comedy* movie in 2002. In 2009 he did the *Paul Rodriguez: Comedy Rehab* movie and *Paul Rodriguez: Just for the Record*, a comedy documentary in 2011. From 2010 to 2011 Rodriguez hosted two seasons of *Mis Videos Locos* as part of MTV's Latin programming.

Paul Rodriguez's a businessman as well as a comedian. He is part owner of the Laugh Factory in Hollywood and has farming interests in Central Valley. His activism is renowned: charity shows to benefit causes of the Latin community, his 1995 comedy special shot at San Quentin State Prison, and his chairmanship of the California Latino Water Coalition.

Comedy Central ranked Rodriguez #74 on its 2004 list of the 100 Greatest Standups of All Time and he won the NCLR Bravo Awards "Outstanding Performance by a Male in a Variety or MusicSeries/Special" for his work on Latino Laugh Festival in 1996.

https://youtu.be/BY7bZbx8VDU

✳✳✳

JANUARY 19, 1971

Shawn Wayans (Humor Mill Magazine)

SHAWN MATHIS WAYANS – BORN IN NEW YORK, NY!

Even though Wayans hailed from a family boasting comedy pedigree, he learned stand-up by playing small venues in the late 1980s in and around Hollywood. He gained his knowledge of film from studying his brother, Keenen Ivory; particularly on the set of *I'm Gonna Git You Sucka*, where Shawn Wayans had a small part as a pedestrian. So, when FOX picked up Keenen's creation, *In Living Color*, Shawn was ready to contribute to the groundbreaking sketch show and work alongside brothers Keenen, Damon, Dwayne, Marlon and their sister, Kim. He assumed the role of DJ SW-1 (the show's spin master) and later became a featured player.

Shawn was as adept behind the camera as he was in front. He and Marlon created their own sitcom, *The Wayans Bros* which aired on the WB from 1995-1999. It was a popular entry for the new network and gave the brothers clout. Their next move was the big screen. They wrote, executive produced and starred in the 1996 hit *Don't Be A Menace in South Central While Drinking Your Juice in the Hood,* a spoof of hood flicks. Film parodies were good for Team Wayans. Following several guest starring appearances on television (including *Hangin with Mr. Cooper* and voicing the character of Toof for brother, Damon's animated series, *Wayneshead*), Shawn Wayans struck gold with Marlon again as writers and stars of the smash hit, *Scary Movie*; a spoof of horror films. Keenen directed.

They had similar success with the 2001 sequel, *Scary Movie 2* and kept the formula going with *White Chicks* (2004), *Little Man* (2006) and *Dance Flick* (2009).

https://youtu.be/fcStVvA4IHE

✳ ✳ ✳

JANUARY 21, 2005

Aleisha Allen, Ice Cube, Philip Daniel Bolden

ARE WE THERE YET? – RELEASED BY COLUMBIA!

Originally intended as an Adam Sandler project, *Are We There Yet?* was produced by Revolution Studios and stars Ice Cube. In this literal road comedy, Cube plays a kid despising suitor determined to make Nia Long his woman. That means getting along with her two kids who do not like suitors. They terrorize all who've come around with devious booby-traps and at first Cube is no exception. The traumatizing twosome want to see their recently divorced parents get back together and until then all other men are the enemy. However, after volunteering to take them to their pre-planned destination when their real father wigs out, he wins them over, but not before experiencing the journey from Hell. The adorable little tykes get him beat up at the airport, destroy his prized new truck and run off to be with their dad. Once with pops they discover that guy isn't thinking about their mother. He's got a new woman and kid that mathematically is older than their parent's divorce. Hurt and salty they warm up to Cube. If he went through all they put him through and still wants their mother – that's okay with them.

Directed by Brian Levant, *Are We There Yet?* features the talents of Aleisha Allen, Philip Daniel Bolden, Jay Mohr, M.C. Gainey, C. Ernst Harth, Nichelle Nichols, Sean Millington, Henry Simmons and the voice of Tracy Morgan.

Are We There Yet? was not a big hit with critics, but what do critics know when it comes to what the public likes? The film opened #1 at the box office. On a $32 million budget it grossed $97,918,663 worldwide ($82 million domestically and $15,244,265 internationally) and sold 3.7 million DVDs. It was so popular (sorry critics) it spawned a TBS television series in 2010 starring Terry Crews (in the Ice Cube role and Essence Atkins in the Nia Long role). It was nominated for the 2005 Teen Choice and 2006 Kids' Choice Award for Best Comedy and won the BMI Music Film Award.

https://youtu.be/xFvco0kn7bw

✳ ✳ ✳

JANUARY 22, 2003

Dave Chappelle with Chappelle's Show cast member Dominique Witten
(Dominique Witten Collection)

CHAPPELLE'S SHOW – PREMIERED ON COMEDY CENTRAL!

Created by Dave Chappelle and Neal Brennan, this sketch comedy show became legendary. With precursors such as *Rowan & Martin's Laugh-In* and *In Living Color*, *Chappelle's Show* took hard hitting sketch comedy to a new level. The show reflected its times and left no scatological rock unturned. It skewered every topic/person with equal delight and because it was on an up-until-then low rated cable network, Chappelle and many in the cast thought it would be canceled at any moment, so the artists threw everything against the wall and damned if they didn't make them stick.

From the outset *Chappelle's Show* became an instant, bonafide comedy classic. Its star and master of ceremonies, Dave Chappelle would offer up a brief monologue/dialogue with his live audience and then one by one introduce each prerecorded sketch (with an occasional live skit) and wrap it all up with a live performance by a soul or hip-hop artist(s). Season one kicked things off with a sketch about a blind white supremacist who just happened to be Black and when he found out he divorced his wife for being a nigger lover. From there the show piled on. There was the lily-white family circa 1950 who were named The Niggar Family. There was the Racial Draft where races drafted members to other races (Wu Tang Clan got to be Asian for example). Boisterous, yelling Samuel L. Jackson has his own beer that's advertised just like Samuel Adams (complete with Chappelle dressed as Jackson dressed as Adams). Wayne Brady debunked his image as a puedo-Uncle Tom in a skit where he's really gangsta. There were so many: Dave living out the perks of dating Oprah. What if the Internet was a real place? Why is working at McDonalds not good for a young ghetto dwelling person's self-esteem? What happens when keeping it real goes wrong? And of course, there was the joy of "The Playa Haters Ball"; the parody of the notorious annual Players Ball; a flamboyant celebration to pimps everywhere.

The writing was brilliant. Not every skit worked, but their batting average was Hall of Fame caliber. The fan base for *Chappelle's Show* grew quickly and the show gave them the recurring characters they came to love. Lil Jon appeared with an Ivy League accent after Chappelle had played a slightly exaggerated version of Jon. It was all "yeah" and "okay." He had comedy icon and cast member Paul Mooney doing "Negrodamus" where he predicts the future from a Black point of view. Charlie Murphy was featured in "Charlie Murphy's True Hollywood Stories"; based on his real celebrity adventures with Rick James (where footage of the real Rick James was intercut as the funkster attempted to throw shade on the show's version of him) and Prince. There was Tron Carter, the richest man in the world who gained his fortune through reparations and a hot dice game. There was also Tyrone Biggums, the overzealous crackhead, Donnell Rawlings as Ashy Larry (the name says it all), Robot Dancing Man (he does the robot anywhere and everywhere without a word or acknowledgement of anybody by him or them) and many others.

Unfortunately, the show's run ended in controversy. Having broken all existing DVD sales at the time, Dave Chappelle was offered a sweetheart deal in excess of $50 million to keep the romance going. The deal had been made and the advertising juggernaut was in full force. Then the unexpected happened. During a taping Dave was doing a sketch about a Nigger Pixie and a white crew member emitted a laugh that was not so much laughing with Dave as much as laughing *at* him. This changed the comedy paradigm for the artist, who had already expressed dismay about how the show was a 20 hour a day commitment which had taken him away from stand-up comedy which was his first love. Sure, he'd been approached in public settings with non-Blacks using the "term of endearment" word (aka N-word) and had his reservations regarding the lack of public understanding when it came to satire, but this was different. He was now made to feel uncomfortable in his work environment. Dave Chappelle needed to reanalyze the genie he'd let out the bottle. So, he left and went to Africa to chill with relatives; all the while the feces were hitting the fan and after he refused to return to the show if his creative demands weren't met the executives leaped into action.

The third season was dubbed "The Lost Episodes" and aired without the participation of Dave Chappelle. For this abridged version of the show (3 full episodes), cast members Charlie Murphy and Donnell Rawlings were enlisted to act as co-hosts. Chappelle had made it clear that if shows were aired without his okay he would never, ever return. The cast members did not know this. The suits did. So, the die was cast and the lightning in the bottle was extinguished.

Executive produced by Chappelle, Neal Brennan and Michele Amour, *Chappelle's Show* had a cast of comedians and comedic personalities. It featured Bill Burr, Guillermo Diaz, Dominique, Brian Dykstra, Sophina Brown, Drake Hill, Yoshio Mita, Anthony Berry, William Bogert, Randy Pearlstein, Nick Wyman, Amanda Rowan, Drago Ruschinsky, Allen Levy, Max Herman and musician/actor, Mos Def. The guest starring list included Arsenio Hall, Eddie Griffin, Susan Sarandon, Rashida Jones, Jamie Foxx, Joe Rogan, Jim Breuer, Carson Daly, Star, Michael Rapaport and Ron Jeremy. Also seen were musical talents Ice T, Method Man, Redman, RZA, GZA. Q-Tip, De La Soul, Fat Joe, Killer Mike, Anthony Hamilton, Kanye West, Slum Village, Questlove, John Mayer, Cee Lo, Ludacris, Talib Kweli, DMX, Busta Rhymes, Wyclef Jean, Snoop Dogg, Common and Erykah Badu.

TV Guide ranked *Chappelle's Show* as #31 from their list of "TV's Top 100 Shows." The last televised episode aired July 23, 2006.

https://youtu.be/JBC-9k3y1ew

✳ ✳ ✳

January 23, 1996

Brandy Norwood

Moesha – Premiered On UPN!

Originally ordered by CBS, the Tiffany Network got cold feet at the prospect of a sitcom starring a teenage black R&B singer (Brandy Norwood) with a setting in South Central Los Angeles, so they pulled out and gave the new UPN network its first hit and one of the greatest successes in the history of that network.

Moesha centered on the escapades of the title character, her prank playing younger brother (Marcus T. Paulk) and her friends (Yvette Wilson, Shar Jackson, Countess Vaughn, Lamont Bentley). The show tackled issues such as teen pregnancy, premarital sex, drugs, gang violence, racism, parental death and infidelity. On the show Moesha's father, Frank (William Allen Young) is a car salesman and a widower. The latter part is where we get our conflict because he married Moesha's vice-principal (Sheryl Lee Ralph) and Moesha doesn't like it. Additional conflict comes in a pivotal episode when it's discovered that Frank was unfaithful to Moesha's mother and his nephew is actually his son. Moesha moved out and the show got very real.

Created by Ralph Farquhar and written by Sara V. Finney and Vida Spears, *Moesha* featured Fredro Starr as Moesha's love interest and real-life brother Ray J as TV brother, Dorian. Bernie Mac was a recurring character as were Ricky Harris, Kara Brock, Jo Marie Payton, Antwon Tanner, Jon Huertas, Merlin Santana, Jazsmin Lewis, Ginuwine, Olivia Brown, Usher, Lahmard Tate and Master P. The list of guest stars was staggering: Kobe Bryant, Mary J. Blige, Snoop Dogg, Doctor Dre, Faith Evans, Jamie Foxx, Adele Givens, Meagan Good, Robert Guillaume, Bo Jackson, Quincy Jones, Jermaine Dupri, Sanaa Lathan, Lisa Leslie, Marsha Warfield, Kym Whitley, Russell Simmons, Sinbad, A Tribe Called Quest, Lil Kim, Nancy Wilson, Octavia Spencer, DMX, Deion Sanders, Keith Sweat, Shaquille O'Neal, Nia Long, Jessica Simpson, MC Lyte, Shemar Moore, Vanessa Bell Calloway, LeAnn Rimes, Silk, Kellita Smith, Gabrielle Union, Morris Day, Johnny Gill, Boyz II Men, Maureen McCormick, Ja'Net DuBois and Loretta Devine.

Moesha was nominated for almost 40 awards over its six-season run, winning an Image Award for Best Supporting Actress for Countess Vaughn and an Outstanding Youth Actress for Brandy as well as The SHINE Award for Comedy Episode for Brandy. The highly acclaimed series also spun-off the sitcom, *The Parkers*, starring Countess Vaughn, Mo'Nique and Yvette Wilson.

Moesha aired its last episode of May 14, 2001, but its appeal internationally is impressive for an American sitcom. Not only was it syndicated in the UK, but since 2008 it's also been seen in Spain, Italy, Russia, Jamaica, France, Korea, Singapore, South Sudan, India, China, Israel, Australia, Mexico, South Africa, The Netherlands, Kenya, Germany, Nigeria, Ghana, Zimbabwe, Liberia, Brazil, Ireland and Ethiopia.

https://youtu.be/MO0Zl5lB1vU

✳ ✳ ✳

JANUARY 26, 1973

W. Kamau Bell delivering opening keynote at the 3rd Annual Summit on School Climate & Culture (Phil Roeder, Creative Commons Attribution 2.0)

W. KAMAU BELL – BORN IN PALO ALTO, CALIFORNIA!

Few comedians can carry the banner of activist, but Bell is one of them. He doesn't just try to solve the world's ills with a few clever bits. He steps out there. Starting with dropping out of the University of Pennsylvania to go into comedy, he has been one to act on his beliefs.

Once Bell got his stand-up up to par he expanded his new love to include others. He's a founder of Laughter Against the Machine. His material is anti-racism, sexism, ageism and the rest of those manmade maladies that plague all lovers of a free mankind. To that end he's pushed his social/political views in publications, podcasts, on his comedy albums, blogs, stand-up comedy specials, in his book and whenever he hosts anything; whether there's a camera pointed at him or not.

When a camera is pointed at Bell we end up with insightful television like his show, *Totally Biased With W. Kamau Bell*. It was produced by Chris Rock (another radical) and kicked the envelope off the cliff (pushing is way too polite). CNN liked his POV and he hosted *United Shades of America* for them. He sits on the board of two racial think tanks and anti-harassment organizations and personally filed a case against a prejudiced café , won and the place was shut down. That makes Bell an activist who gets things done through any means necessary and if it's through comedy so much the better.

https://youtu.be/yXeQMcleiME

✳ ✳ ✳

JANUARY 27, 1942

John Witherspoon (The John Witherspoon Collection)

JOHN WITHERSPOON – BORN IN DETROIT, MICHIGAN!

Born John "Weatherspoon," he changed his name because of course "Witherspoon" is an obvious improvement. That one was a family discrepancy of which side of the clan was one's preference, but he had other moniker alterations as well. For instance, he also went by the name of "Mexico" John Witherspoon and Johnny Witherspoon. Then again he broke into show business as a male model (he was a "Duke Man" in *Jet* magazine) where aliases' were a necessity, but in the late 60s he drifted into stand-up comedy.

John Witherspoon's onstage persona was accessible and animated. In other words, it was a perfect combination for film and television. His first role was as a youth counselor on an episode of the CBS detective show, *Barnaby Jones*. He went on to guest star in such 70s hits as *Good Times, The Incredible Hulk* and *What's Happening*!! Comedian/Writer, Paul Mooney pegged Witherspoon to be part of the ensemble for *The Richard Pryor Show* in 1977. The show only lasted 4 episodes, but Witherspoon made an impression. He also made a string of guest starring roles: *WKRP in Cincinnati, Hill Street Blues, L. A. Law, You Again? Frank's Place, 227, What's Happening Now!!, Amen, Martin, The Fresh Prince of Bel Air* and as a regular on *Townsend Television*.

Film work has been a constant thread throughout Witherspoon's career. He started out in 1980's *The Jazz Singer* as the emcee and 1986's *Ratboy*, but in 1987 things went into overdrive. Hollywood began making Black films again and Witherspoon was in practically all of them beginning with the Robert Townsend/Keenen Ivory Wayans parody, *Hollywood Shuffle*. After that they just kept coming: *I'm Gonna Git You Sucka,*

Bird, House Party, Talkin Dirty After Dark, The Five Heartbeats, Boomerang, Meteor Man, Fatal Instinct, Murder Was the Case and *Friday.*

The Ice Cube/Chris Tucker blockbuster, *Friday* spawned a franchise and gave Witherspoon his largest role to showcase his talents. In *Boomerang* he popularized in catchphrase "Bang, bang, bang, bang," but in the *Friday* films he was able to utilize all his antics. He played Ice Cube's father; the kind of dad that would call you into the toilet for a family conference/chastising session while he took a dump. Those same hilarious ticks and verbal assaults got a long-term workout back on television on the WB sitcom, *The Wayans Bros.* Witherspoon played father to Shawn and Marlon Wayans (Williams on the show). He ran a café by day, and the attention to him in every scene he stole.

Witherspoon loved stealing scenes. He did it in 2003 on *The Tracy Morgan Show* for all 18 episodes. He did on *Living Single, Black Jesus* and *Black-ish.* He stole them in even more films: *Vampire in Brooklyn, Sprung, Bulworth, I Got the Hook Up, Fakin Da Funk, Little Nicky, Soul Plane, Little Man,* and *A Thousand Words.* He did it when he did voice-overs for animated series, *Wayneshead, The Proud Family, Kim Possible* and *The Boondocks.* He's done it in music videos for Goodie Mob, LL Cool J, Field Mob, Hitman Sammy Sam and Jay-Z, and John Witherspoon always steals the show whenever he tours as a stand-up comedian.

https://youtu.be/EQjP4mLSCMY

* * *

JANUARY 27, 1940

Reynaldo Rey w/ Luenell (The Campbell Collection)

REYNALDO REY – BORN IN SEQUOYAH, OKLAHOMA!

This African-American/Native-American majored in Education, earning a Bachelor of Science degree from Kansas State Teacher's

College. He took that degree to Cleveland, Ohio and taught for seven years. During that period Rey joined the Karamu House Theatre, known for nurturing actors, producers and directors. That's where he began his comedy career. First gig – going on the road with the O'Jays. He later moved to New York, where he became a member of the Harlem Theater Group and appeared in his first of many movies. The next two years found him performing in Asia, Europe and Africa.

Fortune kept shining his way after Rey went to Hollywood. Two months after arriving Redd Foxx caught his show and became his manager for the next 12 years. He opened for Redd in Las Vegas and around the country spending countless hours being schooled by the master on the pitfalls of show business.

This Renaissance man appeared in 52 films and 32 television shows including BET's *Comic View*, 1998–99, 2000-2001, on which he was alternately a judge and then co-host, and on Marla Gibb's sitcom *227* as Ray the Mailman. His filmography includes *Harlem Nights, Friday, A Rage in Harlem, Sprung, Bebe's Kids, White Men Can't Jump, Young Doctors in Love, House Party 3, The Breaks* and *First Sunday*. He recorded three comedy albums and three videos, including his own called *I'm Scared A U* after his rendering of it on *Def Comedy Jam* and the overwhelming response the OG received from the hip hop crowd.

No stranger to the music scene, Reynaldo Rey was also an accomplished song writer having penned the Johnny "Guitar" Watson hit "Superman Lover" amongst others along with being a music publisher, counting the R&B group the Dramatics as clients. He served as host of the Parisian Room, where he introduced some of the top acts in jazz and held court with thunderous laughter in between sets. And unlike many entertainers who make it and leave the stomping grounds that nurtured them, "Red" continued to grace stages in the hood. Sometimes to his detriment; like the time he was mugged exiting the Page Four (a ghetto spot he hosted) after hours and had his proudly displayed diamonds yanked from his fingers. Aside from inconveniences such as getting ripped off by the patrons you just entertained he loved the hood.

The relationship with his adoring public ended on May 28, 2015 after a debilitating stroke a year before, put him down for the last time.

https://youtu.be/OemlBQqG380

✳ ✳ ✳

FEBRUARY

THIS DAY IN COMEDY…

FEBRUARY 4, 1983

Hannibal Buress (The Comedy Hall of Fame Archives)

HANNIBAL BURESS – BORN IN CHICAGO, ILLINOIS!

It can be said that Buress is not the corporate type. When he wrote for old school network NBCs *Saturday Night Live* in 2009, he left in 2010. That same year he got a job writing for the NBC sitcom, *30 Rock* and quit after 6 months. He seemed to work better with the looser constrictions of cable which became evident by his relationship with Comedy Central. He appeared on *The Awkward Comedy Show* special for them. He did stand-up on *Live at Gotham* and *John Oliver's New York Stand-Up Show*. Buress released his second album, (His first was *My Name is Hannibal* from 2010) *Animal Furnace* in 2012. Comedy Central did it as a special and he did an hour-long comedy special for them called *Hannibal Buress Live from Chicago* in 2014. He's on the series *Broad City*, co-host *The Eric Andre Show* and has his own show *Why? With Hannibal Buress*. All on Comedy Central.

This is not to say Buress is exclusive to Comedy Central. He has also been seen on *Louie* and *Totally Biased with W. Kamau Bell* (FX), *Lopez Tonight* and *Conan* (TBS), *Late Show with David Letterman* and *The Late, Late Show with Craig Ferguson* (CBS), *Jimmy Kimmel Live!* (ABC), *The Tonight Show Starring Jimmy Fallon* and *Late Night with Jimmy Fallon* (NBC) and *Russell Howard's Good News* (BBC).

However, what put Buress on the map for many non-comedy aficionados was his bit about Bill Cosby that went viral after being in his set for six months. The routine about the legendary comic dubbed "America's Dad" and his past rape allegations in the face of his better than thou posture took on a life all its own as woman after woman emerged to either reiterate claims of drugging and sexual abuse or level never-before-leveled claims against the iconic comedian. It was a media circus with Buress at the center of the controversy. But being a stand-up comedian meant Hannibal Buress had the distinct advantage of dissecting the situation on stage and incorporate it as part of the act that sucked him into that vortex in the first place.

Hannibal Buress has won Chicago's Funniest Person Award (2007), the Best Performance in a Host Stand-Up/Sketch Comedy Program Series (2011) and the American Comedy Award (2012).

https://youtu.be/xlonY2l3V9c

✳ ✳ ✳

FEBRUARY 5, 1961

Tim Meadows (Instagram)

TIMOTHY "TIM" MEADOWS – BORN IN HIGHLAND PARK, MICH.!

A student of radio and television in college, Meadows got started in improvisational comedy at the Soup Kitchen Saloon and in show business performing in The Second City troupe. Chris Farley was also a member; which was Meadows first contact with his destiny. A short time later he became a cast member on NBCs long running hit sketch show, *Saturday Night Live* and went on to be its longest running cast member for a record 9 seasons (until Darrell Hammond broke that record years later). Meadows played a lot of characters: Michael Jackson, O. J. Simpson, Erykah Badu, Tiger Woods and Oprah Winfrey, but it was his signature persona that got made into a film.

The Ladies Man was extremely popular on a sketch show like SNL. In the theater it bombed. Even though the character of Leon Phelps: a horny radio talk show host prone to say whatever inappropriate thing he wants seemed a natural for audiences always on the hunt for shock value, this flick didn't jolt them enough. Regardless, it was but a minor setback for Meadows. He'd made a lot of friends at *Saturday Night Live* over the years and they showed it by keeping their alumni buddy working. He made appearances in *Mean Girls* (a Tina Fey film), *The Coneheads* (Dan Aykroyd, Jane Curtin, and Larraine Newman), *It's Pat* (Julia Sweeney), *Wayne's World 2* (Mike Myers), *The Benchwarmers* (Rob Schneider), *Trainwreck* (Bill Hader) and *Grown Ups 1 & 2* (Adam Sandler).

Meadows let friends pay him any time to perform, but he also worked for others. No need to feel bad for the guy because over his career Meadows was a regular on *The Michael Richards Show, Lil Bush, The Bill Engvall Show, Glory Dance,* and *Mr. Box Office.* He co-starred on the NBC sitcom, *Marry Me.* He appeared in *Walk Hard: The Dewey Cox Story.* Meadows had recurring roles on *Help Me Help You, Living with Fran, The New Adventures of Old Christine, The Life & Times of Tim, Suburgatory* and *Bob's Burgers.* He'd pop up on *The Colbert Report* and guest starred on *One on One, Everybody Hates Chris, The Office, Reba, According to Jim, Lovespring International, Funny or Die Presents, 30 Rock, The Venture Bros, Comedy Bang! Bang!, The Goldbergs* and *The Spoils Before Dying.*

Like most dedicated entertainers, when not in front of the camera Tim Meadows returns to his roots and continues to perform improv on stages all over the world.

https://youtu.be/kkVqJx04Trg

✳ ✳ ✳

FEBRUARY 6, 1957

Robert Townsend (r) w/ Damon Wayans (Humor Mill Magazine)

ROBERT TOWNSEND – BORN IN CHICAGO, ILLINOIS!

After honing his skills at Chicago's X Bag Theatre; The Experimental Black Actors Guild and studying at Second City, Townsend got his start in comedy at The Improv. He moved to New York to further his education with the Negro Ensemble Company. Then following a string of small stereotypical parts (*Cooley High, Monkey Hustle, American Flyers, Streets of Fire, Ratboy*) and finding rare fulfillment as an actor (he did *A Soldier's Story* with a predominantly Black cast and was chest-fallen when he discovered that might be the only one he would make in his entire career) Townsend co-wrote (with Keenen Ivory Wayans) and directed *Hollywood Shuffle*. This parody of how it is for minority talent in Tinsel Town put the struggling entertainer on the map. The film, financed with Townsend's own funds from acting and his credit cards, was a low budget risk and major box office success. A star was born.

Robert Townsend's initial success allowed him to pursue an aggressive agenda of Black projects. He directed Eddie Murphy's *Raw*. He did *Robert Townsend and His Partners in Crime* for HBO featuring unsung comedians at the time such as Paul Mooney, Franklyn Ajaye, Robin Harris and Damon Wayans, to name a few. Townsend co-starred with Denzel Washington in *The Mighty Quinn*. His next theatrical release was *The Five Heartbeats*, an enduring musical focusing on the trials and tribulations of a fictional 60s R&B singing group. He made *Meteor Man*; about a Black super hero with limited powers. He returned to television with his own variety show on FOX, *Townsend Television* and a few seasons later he created his own sitcom for the WB; *The Parent 'Hood*. He directed *B*A*P*S* with Halle Berry, *Carmen: A Hip Hopera* with Beyoncé and *10,000 Black Men Named George*; also, *Why We Laugh: Black Comedians on Black Comedy*; a documentary on the history of black comedy, *Livin' for Love: The Natalie Cole Story, Holiday Heart, Bill Cosby 77* and others.

Robert Townsend won the Cable ACE Award for *Robert Townsend and His Partners in Crime* and he was the Programming Director for the Black Family Channel.

https://youtu.be/maeDP0R3ju0

✳ ✳ ✳

FEBRUARY 7, 1965

Chris Rock (The Humor Mill Magazine)

CHRISTOPHER JULIUS "CHRIS" ROCK III – BORN IN ANDREWS, SC!

Known universally as one of the premier comedians of his generation and voted #5 on Comedy Central's list of the 100 Greatest Stand-up Comedians of All Time, Chris Rock's road in comedy was paved with boulders. After putting up with enough bullying he dropped out of high school, got his GED and hit the work force in the lucrative fast food industry. He found that not to be a good fit. There had to be something better and because he now prized education he applied its principles in his future vocation.

One of Chris Rock's methods of developing an act is to bring his jokes on stage written down in a legal pad and try out each one before an unsuspecting and involuntary Guinea pig audience. It's that kind of brashness, perseverance and hard work that established him in the many mediums of comedy: film, television, animation, documentaries and theater, but no matter where he used his comedic skills, standup was always the cornerstone of what made Rock so popular. His brand was unapologetic, insightful, bold, opinionated and above all – the unabashed truth.

The career of Chris Rock began in 1984 when he took the stage at New York's Catch a Rising Star. It wasn't long before he got his big break in 1985. It was in his first film – *Crush Groove*, playing "Person Standing Next to Phone during Fight in Club." That didn't do much for his career (nor did a *Miami Vice* guest starring role or a stand-up set on *Uptown Comedy Express*), but when Eddie Murphy caught his act one night, Rock got his real big break. Murphy took Rock under his wing and got him a credited part in *Beverly Hills Cop II*. Rock did his first concert film (*Comedy's Dirtiest Dozen*), some more films (*I'm Gonna Git You Sucka, New Jack City, Boomerang*) a documentary (*Who is Chris Rock?*) and his first comedy album (*Born Suspect*). He was a cast member on *Saturday Night Live,* but he didn't find that to be a great fit so he moved from NBC to FOX to be a player on *In Living Color*, but then it got cancelled. So, Rock made his own vehicle, *CB4*, a parody of the rap scene. It was not a success with the critics and Rock fell into a slump. Hollywood obviously didn't know what to do with him during this period (*The Immortals, Panther, Beverly Hills Ninja, Sgt. Bilko*). He'd even considered quitting. Then he stopped agonizing over what he wasn't getting and went back to his first love – stand-up.

In 1996 Chris Rock was a commentator of the Presidential campaign for Comedy Central's *Politically Correct*. He was nominated for an Emmy for that coverage. It blended man on the street inquisitiveness with current event savvy. Rock was a hit and what happened next catapulted him into another league. *Bring the Pain* on HBO was one of their top comedy specials winning Rock two Emmys and putting him in the fast lane. You know you're hot when you get animated (he played Lil Penny, Penny Hardaway's alter ego for a Nike campaign). After the Year of Rock, he did more HBO specials and albums (*Bigger & Blacker, Roll With The New, Never Scared, Big Ass Jokes, Kill the Messenger*), hosted award shows (*MTV Video Music Awards, BET Awards*), wrote a book (*Rock This*), did films (*Dogma, Lethal Weapon 4, Nurse Betty, Grown Ups, The Longest Yard, Bad Company, Death at a Funeral*), television (*The Chris Rock Show*), animation (*Madagascar series, Osmosis Jones, King of the Hill, Bee Movie*) music videos (Red Hot Chili Peppers, Big Daddy Kane, Johnny Cash) and more Chris Rock films (*Down to Earth, Pootie Tang, Head of State, I Think I Love My Wife, Good Hair* (his doc about hair*) Top Five*).

Rock defied odds. In 2005 when he hosted the 77th Academy Awards he lambasted the hallowed ceremony, the stars and the entire notion of the presentation. Despite this and the fact many members of the Academy were supremely offended he was invited to host again in 2016. His high school experiences were adapted into the successful sitcom, *Everybody Hates Chris* (he executive produced and narrated). Rock produced *Totally Biased with W. Kamau Bell* and *The Hughleys*. In 2011 he was nominated for a Drama League Award for his acting on Broadway in the play, *The Motherfucker with the Hat*. Rock has done the documentaries of others (*Comedian, Torrance Rises, The N-Word, The Aristocrats*), guest starred on sitcoms (*The Fresh Prince of Bel-Air, Martin, The Bernie Mac Show*), popped up in cameos in multiple motion pictures (*Jay and Silent Bob Strike Back, Paparazzi, You Don't Mess with the Zohan*) and directed, *Amy Schumer: Live at the Apollo*.

Chris Rock has been nominated for 19 major awards and won 8, including 3 Grammys, 2 Primetime Emmys. A Kid's Choice Award and a Black Reel Award.

https://youtu.be/tJFS5AFcNtw

✳ ✳ ✳

FEBRUARY 8, 1974

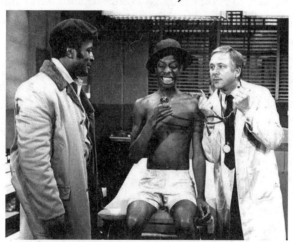

Good Times (l-r) John Amos, Jimmie Walker, William Christopher, 1975 (Public Domain)

GOOD TIMES – PREMIERED ON CBS!

Created by writer Eric Monte (*Cooley High*) and actor, Mike Evans (the 1st Lionel from *The Jeffersons*), *Good Times* was developed by Norman Lear as a spin-off of *Maude* (which was a spin-off of *All in the Family*). The instant hit told the story of the long-suffering Evans family: Florida (Esther Rolle), her husband James (John Amos) and their three children: artistic yet buffoonish JJ (Jimmie Walker), fine as hell Thelma (Bern Nadette Stanis) and mini militant Michael (Ralph Carter), and their life in

59

the projects. They have a drop-in neighbor Willona (Ja'net Dubois) who has an adopted daughter, Penny (Janet Jackson) and they also have a fat building superintendent, Bookman (Johnny Brown). These characters became like the family we loved but didn't want to live with.

Good Times was set in the 1970s and dealt with a lot of issues from that era. Racism, child abuse, drugs, gang violence, police violence and political corruption were all portrayed (sounds like it could be today) and milked for laughs and pathos. James never could keep a job and the family was always in the midst of a crisis, but through it all they had good times. Why? Because they had each other. That dynamic was evident on camera, but behind the scenes there was conflict not scripted. Esther Rolle and John Amos objected to the stereotypical portrayal of the eldest son JJ and pressed their complaints for a more positive direction of the show. The producer's answer to tampering with a hit was to fire them both. Rolle eventually returned, but Amos' character was killed off and the show got new characters to keep the audience and sponsors happy; which they did for a while, but like all good things and times, *Good Times* came to an end.

The last episode aired on August 1, 1979.

https://youtu.be/qfvU-sykrwo

✳ ✳ ✳

FEBRUARY 9, 1955

Marilyn Martinez (c) w/ Ludo Vika, Sully Diaz, Lydia Nicole and Dyana Ortelli as The Hot & Sexy Mamitas (The Nicole Collection)

MARILYN MARTINEZ – BORN IN DENVER, COLORADO!

Martinez got an early start in show business. The youth tap danced to much acclaim on a local TV show. She took acting lessons and began writing polarizing comedy routines; many of them decidedly offensive to some and uproariously hilarious to others.

Martinez was first noticed at the World-Famous Comedy Store in Hollywood. Her in-your-face, raw style was prefect for an era of comedy opposed to being politically correct. She shot from the hip on topics ranging from sex to men to sex with men. Her style was blunt, candid and original. She once said of herself that she was a triple minority: fat, a woman and Hispanic.

Her big break came in the mid-90s when Martinez became a member of the female Latina group, the*Hot and Spicy Mamitas*. She later joined the*Hot Tamales*, which featured Eva Longoria. This led to touring and recording the special the*Original Latin Divas of Comedy*.

When she wasn't on stage, Martinez was making her mark and enhancing each project where she made an appearance. She was seen on the small screen: ABC's*My Wife and Kids*(2001), Starz*1ˢᵗ Amendment Stand-Up*and SiTV's reality show,*Urban Jungle*(2004). She lit up the big screen in*For da Love of Money*(2002) and*Pauly Shore is Dead*(2003).

Marilyn Martinez left behind a grieving husband and a world of comedy fans in the same condition when she passed away on November 3, 2007 of complications of diabetes.

https://youtu.be/QcUPEs7Ri7g

FEBRUARY 9, 1965

Bruce Bruce (r) w/ Cortney Gee (Cortney Gee Collection)

BRUCE BRUCE – BORN IN ATLANTA, GEORGIA!

The name is funny. The hair is funny. And the man known only as Bruce Bruce is hilarious. That's the only obtainable and if you try to mention his real name he'll haul you into an alley and blow your brains out. See, Bruce Bruce (you gotta say both) was raised in The Bluff, one of the toughest areas of anywhere.

When he graduated high school he became a chef, cracking jokes while grilling. He gained a reputation as a funny guy and when he got a job selling for Frito-Lays the corporation had no problem with him doing comedy sets at their corporate events. Bruce Bruce took his jokes to the Comedy Act Theater Atlanta and was soon getting a lot of attention. He went on to host Atlanta's "Uptown Comedy Corner" and the infamous "559" in ATL (it consisted of pimps, hoes and drug dealers who would rather slit a comic's throat with a razor than force themselves to laugh) that was so bad Bruce Bruce had to give a pep talk to comedians the day beforehand so they could get mentally prepared and wouldn't slit their own throats if they got booed by a room packed with killers.

When BET began showcasing comedians from around the country on segment of *Comic View* called "Coast-To-Coast," Bruce Bruce would audition in every club in town to get a spot. Eventually he ended up getting three. He competed on that same show and later became it's host and did that for two seasons. He appeared on HBOs *Def Comedy Jam, Showtime at the Apollo* three times and twice hosted *Coming to the Stage*. Bruce Bruce had his own one-hour "Comedy Central Presents" special and released two comedy DVDs: *Bruce Bruce Live* and *Losin' It: Live from Boston*.

Bruce Bruce plays the mediums. He headlined the 2008 "Just for Laughs Comedy Festival" in Montreal. He also made notable festival appearances at the "Just for Laughs Festival" in Chicago, "Laffapalooza" and the "US Comedy Arts Festival" in Aspen. He's done films: *Idlewild, Larry the Cable Guy: Health Inspector, XXX: State of the Union, Think Like a Man, Top Five, Hair Show, The Wash, Who's Your Caddy?*; music videos: The Ying Yang Twins (who made Bruce Bruce a lyric in their mega hit "Salt Shaker"), Ludacris, Quad City DJs, Outkast and KEM; as well as podcasts: Marc Maron's "WTF," and Bruce Bruce authored the Penguin Publishing's best seller, "Baby James Brown." The rest of the time he just tours, tours and tours.

https://youtu.be/8AIZNJ6KRFo

✳ ✳ ✳

FEBRUARY 9, 1957

Michael Colyar (r) w/Cedric the Entertainer and Edwonda White
(The Edwonda White Collection)

MICHAEL COLYAR – BORN IN CHICAGO, ILLINOIS!

Michael Colyar was born and raised where it was cold. He went to school in the cold, graduated in the cold, went to college in the cold and then high-tailed it to California and became the King of the Beach Comics. Nobody could attract a crowd like him. He would prowl about announcing his upcoming show that will be performed moments from now, steps away . Then once the curious were gathered he'd unleash a barrage of old jokes performed as no one had ever heard them before. Michael Colyar never met a joke he couldn't make into a dazzling experience. To witness him live was akin to how they describe Paul Robeson on stage or Sammy Davis, Jr. in a nightclub. You had to have been there.

Once he was spotted captivating all colors along the Venice Beach boardwalk, he became the buzz of the town and Michael Colyar went Hollywood. He couldn't help it. That's where they were shooting shows and films and he could get further exposure on the hottest stages at the time: The Comedy Store, Improv and Laugh Factory. It was also where he could get the therapeutic release of stand-up. Colyar had been a loyal crack addict, a topic he never shies from, and the more time he was on stage the less time he had to hit the pipe. He spoke of his recovery and made versions of it a staple of his act.

In 2012 he published the book, *A Funny Thing Happened on the Way to the White House, I Knocked on the Door and a Brother Answered.* He's done one man shows ("Michael Colyar's Mama" – 100 City Tour), cartoon voices (*The Princess and the Frog*) and occasionally he's stopped off at the beach.

https://youtu.be/bBxK9uHlAXg

✳ ✳ ✳

FEBRUARY 12, 1956

Arsenio Hall (Humor Mill Magazine)

ARSENIO HALL – BORN IN CLEVELAND, OHIO!

Starting off in entertainment as a child magician, Hall developed the disciplines required to navigate the unchartered waters that would make him a household name. He was the first Black late-night talk show host; having grown up watching legends in the field such as Steve Allen, Jack Paar and Johnny Carson and knowing that's what he wanted to do. However, having no idea that once he did it Hall would put such an indelible stamp on what it meant to be a Black late night host that not only he could surpass it. Nobody could.

Hall's journey began when he moved to Los Angeles to refine his stand-up comedy chops. He did the requisite club circuit and even popped up a few times on *Soul Train*. Then in 1984 he got a break as the on-camera sidekick of talk show host, Alan Thicke on *Thicke of the Night*. It was an instructive opportunity, but unfortunately one that didn't last long. Didn't matter; another break for Hall came in the form of FOX networks failed *The Late Show starring Joan Rivers*. This project was developed specifically to challenge late night king, Johnny Carson and the venerable *Tonight Show* on NBC. The upstart entry couldn't topple the institution and that along with bad blood between Rivers and the show's producers gave an early exit to its title star. The show was renamed *The Late Show* and a series of interim hosts were tried. Nobody hit the right chord, but Hall's brief tenure was the most resonate and he soon got the call to host his own show.

The Arsenio Hall Show was nothing short of a television revolution. Unlike previous late-night talk shows that were designed to lull its viewers to sleep with safe monologues, an orchestra playing standards, banal conversations and advertising targeting the older demographic, Hall threw a party. His band was a hard driving combo that he called his posse. His audience was hyped, not drowsy. Their barking and fist pumping got them labeled "The Dog Pound" and their signature gestures infiltrated pop culture in films (*Pretty Woman, Passenger 57, The Hard Way, Aladdin, Robin Hood: Men in Tights*) countless TV sitcoms and commercials. His guests were not the kind that graced the covers of magazines you'd find at your dentist. He introduced Bobby Brown to late night TV. That alone could've got him cancelled. Hall made a president when then Governor Bill Clinton slapped on some shades and played his saxophone. No amount of church visits could've bonded a white candidate better to a potential Black constituency. That appearance branded Clinton as cool and won him a close election. Whereas, Hall himself was all swagger. His monologues were edgy; interviews probing and fearless. Who else would've booked Louis Farrakhan on their show? Hall was a powerful force; perhaps too powerful. Shaping public opinion is fine as long as the powers that be tell you how to shape it. You got the feeling Hall had cut the strings as soon as the puppeteers weren't looking. Thus, *The Arsenio Hall Show* was cancelled after five years.

The void left by *The Arsenio Hall Show* was gaping. Popular figures were brought in to fill it. Keenen Ivory Wayans and Magic Johnson mounted shows. Both failed – quickly. Music titan, Quincy Jones, spun off from his successful magazine, *Vibe* and envisioned its essence as broadcast entertainment. It tanked with two hosts (Chris Spencer, Sinbad) and it became evident that it was not the amiable personalities presented as substitutes, but that the bar had been raised so high there was no substitution. It was Hall or back to the white guys; white guys who'd gotten increasingly younger and hipper over the years. Once the era of Jay Leno and David Letterman (the last vestiges of the Johnny Carson age) came to an end they were replaced by the effervescent Jimmy Fallon and the grittier Jimmy Kimmel and Stephen Colbert. The landscape changed thanks to Hall. It had altered itself so much that Hall felt it would be a natural fit. He'd resisted a much-requested return due to the fact his friend George Lopez had a late -night show. Could the public really keep track of two minorities on at once? Well, once Lopez got replaced on TBS by non-minority (unless you count the hair style), Conan O'Brien, Hall decided it was time to mount the horse he'd trained again.

Unfortunately, that horse was ornery. The reincarnation of *The Arsenio Hall Show* debuting in 2013 had all the previous elements of its 1989 incarnation: band, hyped crowd, fringe guests and even Hall looking preserved; like he'd been frozen all those years, but it lacked the magic. The spark was gone. It was like returning to an old lover. It would never be the same and before the relationship could be reinvented the suits pulled the plug.

Conventional wisdom has always maintained that careers were marathons, not sprints and Arsenio Hall has always had a career that stayed in motion. He was an animated voice over actor when he did *The Real Ghostbusters* from 1986-87 and other projects. He released the album, *Large and in Charge* under his alter ego Chunky A. He proved to be an accomplished comedy film actor in the movies, *Coming to America and Harlem Nights.* Hall showed the world he was ahead of the curve over most other performers when it came to taking care of business when he won the reality-competition show, *Celebrity Apprentice* and he won it when future president, Donald Trump was the host. Speaking of hosting Hall aptly took over for establishment favorite, Ed McMahon when Hall hosted *Star Search* and he also hosted the *MTV Video Music Awards.* Hall had his own sitcom (*Arsenio*) in 1997 and an action show with Sammo Hung called *Martial Law* in 1999. Hall guest starred on sitcoms and played himself in films, TV shows and commercials.

For his acting expertise, Arsenio Hall won the NAACP Image Award for Outstanding Supporting Actor for *Coming to America* and the 1989 American Comedy Award for the same role. In 1992 he received an honorary Doctor of Humane Letters degree from Central State University, Wilberforce.

https://youtu.be/8fJB1Uxuj6o

✳ ✳ ✳

February 12, 1988

SCHOOL DAZE – RELEASED BY COLUMBIA PICTURES!

This is Spike Lee's second major motion picture following his debut, *She's Gotta Have It*. In *School Daze* the issue is not sexual promiscuity and social morality, but racial identity and division. Its Dark-Skinned Blacks VS Light-Skinned Blacks set in the backdrop of a fictional Historically Black College and its fraternity / sorority culture. It's part comedy, part drama and part musical (but not the corny kind).

Written, directed and featuring Lee, the story is semi-autobiographical from his own college experiences. In the film all his character, "Half-Pint," wants to do is pledge a fraternity and get some girls. Simple, but crossing the burning sands and being made a Gamma Phi Gamma man is not. He has to not only go through the usual hazing, but he's at a Black college and there's discrimination; from one frat to the next based on skin pigment, eye color and hair texture. Then he's got his older cousin who is a militant and fraternally a GDI (Go**amn Independent) played by Laurence Fishburne (back when he was Larry) giving him a hard time about going through that nonsense to be with a group of guys he doesn't even like (led by Giancarlo Esposito, who Fishburne doesn't like). There's conflict and tensions between the local blue-collar Black youth and the "spoiled college boys," jealousy amongst the sisters on both sides of the color line and a faculty that's more clueless than Stacy Dash. But there's nothing to worry about – it's a movie and all this dramedy comes to a head Homecoming weekend when the two rival frats clash and WAKE UP!

School Daze boasts an impressive cast. Tisha Campbell is Esposito's girlfriend. Samuel L. Jackson plays a local homeboy, who doesn't like the college homeboys. Joe Seneca is the President of the college, Ossie Davis the coach and Art Evans an administrator. The rest of the cast is rounded out with Bill Nunn, Jasmine Guy, Darryl M. Bell, Branford Marsalis, Kadeem Hardison, Phyllis Hyman and of course, Joie Lee.

The usually controversial Spike Lee was on his artistic and polarizing ascension during this period and *School Daze* helped fuel his reputation. Behind the scenes he'd housed the light skinned Blacks in better accommodations than the dark-skinned Blacks to add to the tension on the set. It did. The animosity was so great that an actual fight broke out between the two groups of 'actors" and Lee told his crew to keep filming. That fight was in the movie. It vividly demonstrated the realistic relationship dynamics that were themed in *School Daze* and the purity translated, as well as stirred up opposing viewpoints. Whereas mainstream critics found the film frank, honest and revealing; exposing a slice of society they were unfamiliar. The Black colleges on the other hand took exception to Lee's use of real-life language used in those colleges to describe language used in those colleges. They resented his portrayal of racial separatism and during filming Morehouse, Spelman and Clark Atlanta University kicked him off their campuses. Filming had to be completed at nearby Morris Brown College.

School Daze was the inspiration for the NBC sitcom, *A Different World.* It also spawned a number one hit on Billboard's R&B chart (*Da Butt*) and featured the Phyllis Hyman song, *Be One.* On a budget of $6.5 million *School Daze* grossed $14,545,844.

https://youtu.be/uLT3Qu76-bw

✳ ✳ ✳

FEBRUARY 15, 2005

NEVER SCARED – RELEASED BY DREAMWORKS/GEFFEN!

This was Chris Rock's fourth album and fourth HBO special simultaneously. *Never Scared* was taped at Washington DC's DAR Constitution Hall March 24-26 in 2004. Once it aired on HBO, the DVD version dropped August 31st. The 25-track album came out six months later offering the jokes and added bonus of recorded music, parodies and skits. Rock intertwines the themes of "Tip Your Hat to Whitey" and "Thug Radio" throughout the CD and collaborates with rapper Lil' Jon on "Get Lower." It's a hilarious roller coaster ride of comedy.

Never Scared won the Grammy Award for Best Comedy Album in 2006.

https://youtu.be/s6X0Qqxx3f0?list=PL98292C7E7A908D0E

✳ ✳ ✳

FEBRUARY 16, 1992

Jess Hilarious (Instagram)

JESSICA "HILARIOUS" MOORE – BORN IN BALTIMORE CITY!

Jess Hilarious, as she's come to be known, was part of the wave of Internet comics that sucker punched traditional comedy in the forehead. Social media replaced the old school way of agents schlepping out to clubs to spot up & rising talent. Thanks to everybody having at least a camera in their phone and an account to post whatever your imagination could conjure, new comedy stars were being created by producing short, and (excuse the pun if you want) hilarious content. Moore's specialty was celebrity gossip and her field of battle was Instagram. Her *Jess with the Mess* segment amassed over 3 million followers, making her a certified sensation.

No need to leave anything on the table. Moore climbed up on the stand-up stage and started packing the house. Up to this point the formula for newbie Internet draws had been for them to put butts into the seats while a seasoned professional stand-up comedian closed the show, but as experience on stage was built up in a short amount of time due to demand it was obvious to anyone noticing that the novelties were becoming the real thing.

Hollywood loved this new way to sell an old product and the red carpet was soon rolled out. Moore was a regular for Season 9 of Nick Cannon's *Wild N Out*. Her appearance on HBO's *All Def Comedy* exposed her to a wider audience and her co-starring status on FOX's *Rel* (Lil Rel's self-titled sitcom) presented her weekly to the network TV crowd.

Moore joined the controversy club when she posed naked with her infant son, Ashton and caused social media to almost crash behind the volume of comments. Beyoncé had gotten away with it, but comics aren't singers. Moore even got flak from other comedians and wasted no time in giving as good as she got, and shutting it down. It was an Internet exchange that gave her additional street cred by showing that even though she hadn't been in comedy long she'd been Black for a while. End of backlash.

Moore was the first celebrity to win the BET social award for "Clapback."

https://youtu.be/2tKcrt40W9Y

✳ ✳ ✳

February 18, 2011

Martin Lawrence, Brandon T. Jackson

Big Momma's House 3: Like Father, Like Son – Released by 20th Century Fox

Martin Lawrence once again plays FBI agent, Malcolm Turner in this sequel to the sequel to the original. This time out Lawrence has to go undercover as an old woman to protect his stepson, who saw a murder. Naturally the step-son (Brandon T. Jackson) has to dress up like a female too and they hide out in an all-girls school. The stepson falls for one of the girls. One of the workers (Faizon Love) falls for Big Momma. They blow their covers. The gang of killers catch up to them and just as they are about to kill the duo somebody (in this case Love) come in just in the nick of time to save the day. Yay!

Big Momma's House 3 was critically panned. There was more than one Razzie Award nomination. However, on the upside, Faizon Love's performance was heralded, and the film was shot for less than the two previous offerings from the franchise. This was due to being shot in Georgia and Lawrence taking less money.

Budgeted at $32 million, *Big Momma's House 3* grossed $83,915,414 worldwide.

https://youtu.be/3G6ypC7bg6M

✳ ✳ ✳

February 19, 1963

Joey "CoCo" Diaz (r) w/ Corey Holcomb at Serra's, 2009 (The Littleton Collection)

Joey "CoCo" Diaz – Born in Havana, Cuba!

Diaz is one tough customer. He grew up as an only child. That's tough. He was raised in New Jersey. That's tough. Both of his parents were dead before he got out of high school. Wait, it gets tougher. He alternately lived with four different generous families until he got in so much trouble with drugs and crime that Diaz wound up in prison. Now are you ready for the toughest part? Joey Diaz did stand-up comedy behind bars for convicts and then had to stay there to hear their critiques. It doesn't get any tougher than that. No comic wants to hear that crap. You want to leave after the show.

Once he saw the movie *Punchline* (where Tom Hanks and Sally Fields play stand-up comics) Diaz realized being a professional stand-up can't be that hard and took a comedy course in Colorado. He worked up an act, debuted it on June 18,1991, won some local competitions, got some experience as an opening act and then moved to Los Angeles to make it in the bigtime. That had to work. He was running out of options and didn't want to wind up back in Colorado working as a doorman, selling roofing or worse – back in stir because somebody poked the big bear with the wrong stick. Joey had a temper.

Joey Diaz also had a lot of untapped talent. Once it was unleashed the beast devoured everything in sight. After a CBS pilot he got from being spotted doing stand-up in Seattle didn't get picked up, he got his first movie (*BASEketball*) and didn't stop making them: *The Longest Yard, Analyze That, Spider-Man 2, Grudge Match, 18 Fingers of Death, American Gun, Taxi, Dickie Roberts: Former Child Star,* his personal favorite, *The Dog Who Saved Christmas* and a plethora of others.

Diaz didn't ignore television either and felt obliged to show up often. He appeared in *NYPD Blue, Law & Order, Cold Case, Murder 101, I'm Dy-*

ing Up Here, Brooklyn Nine-Nine, ER, Mad-TV, Frank TV, My Name is Earl, How I Met Your Mother, Everybody Hates Chris and a whole lot more. He also showed off in televised stand-up performances on BET's *ComicView, 1st Amendment* and *The Payaso Comedy Slam.*

Another thing about Joey Diaz besides talent was his impatience. He didn't wait for work to come to him. He created vehicles for himself. He had his own very popular podcast, *The Church of What's Happening Now* (with co-host Lee Syatt) and made regular appearances on his good friend's show, *The Joe Rogan Experience.* Felicia Michael's had turned Diaz onto the podcast world when she asked him to join her as a co-host on her podcast, *Beauty & Da Beast.*

In 2012 Diaz even did a documentary about what else – Joey Diaz. It was aptly named, *Where I Got My Balls From* and was a tribute to the people who helped him when times were bad. Not to mention that he has released 13 comedy specials so far and played Roman, the Butcher in the video game *Mafia III.* How's that for tough?

https://youtu.be/NeoTlsfMQEU

✳ ✳ ✳

FEBRUARY 20, 1984

Trevor Noah (r) w/ Mohamed Salah and Hasan Minhaj (Instagram)

TREVOR NOAH – BORN IN JOHANNESBURG, SOUTH AFRICA!

Initially known in America as Jon Stewart's successor on *The Daily Show,* Noah has always carried more weight than most. When his Swiss/German father and Xhosa/Jewish mother ended their illegal relationship due to apartheid (she was jailed, and he moved back to Switzerland), Noah was raised by his mother and grandmother. That is until his mother married, got divorced and then was shot in the face by her jealous ex for getting engaged to another man. Noah was also threatened with death and moved from Johannesburg to Los Angeles, California in 2011.

Prior to relocating Noah had made his mark in Africa where themes of race were basic to his material. He broke onto the public scene at the age of 18 in 2002 starring on the South African soap opera, *Isidingo*. He hosted his own radio show (*Noah's Ark*) on YFM, a leading youth radio station; hosted an educational show on SABC2; a gossip show, and a sports show on SABC 1 and a dating show called *The Amazing Date*. Noah hosted the South Africa Film and Television Awards, *The Axe Sweet Life* (a reality competition show), his own show, *Tonight with Trevor Noah* and he was a spokesperson for one of the largest cellular providers in South Africa, Cell C. He's performed all over South Africa, toured with Gabriel Iglesias and taped multiple standup comedy specials. He was the first South African comedian to perform stand up on *The Tonight Show* in 2012 and the first to appear on *The Late Show with David Letterman* in 2013. He's been the subject of a documentary, a Roast Master on Comedy Central and a recurring contributor on *The Daily Show*.

So, when Comedy Central announced Jon Stewart's replacement in March 2015 they were confident the seasoned Trevor Noah was ready. Yet despite the fact the takeover wasn't going to happen until September, the internet was abuzz about how Stewart was irreplaceable and that this guy Noah had no right to be in a successor conversation. Haters trolled YouTube looking for incriminating evidence to support their case and he had some. They uncovered several jokes of his that did not work. Social media was aghast. A comedian who has bombed before. Unheard of! He was called anti-Jewish even though he is part Jewish, but fortunately the network ignored the firestorm and Noah made his debut. His self-described politically progressive style fit right into *The Daily Show* mindset. Though it took a moment for the audience to get used to the new host, Noah drew his crowd to him and the long running signature program kept bringing in viewers. So much for irreplaceability.

Trevor Noah speaks more than a half dozen languages fluently and has won the 2012 South African Comic's Choice Comic of the Year Award and the 2015 MTV Africa Music Award for Personality of the Year.

https://youtu.be/y3jlR6k_wo0

✳ ✳ ✳

FEBRUARY 21, 1979

Jordan Peele, 2014 (Public Domain)

JORDAN PEELE – BORN IN NEW YORK, NY!

Who Knew? Very few souls living when *Get Out* was released would've imagined it coming from the mind of half a popular TV sketch comedy team. Yet after 9 years of nursing an idea and bringing it to fruition, Jordan Peele had changed the game not only for science fiction fans and the Black community's appreciation for Sci-Fi, but he shifted the Tectonic plates on racism in the arts. With the help of his sometime partner, Keegan-Michael Key introducing the script to the right power broker, Peele was able to direct a masterpiece and Hollywood had to stop gerrymandering skin color and canvass the color of success. *Get Out* exceeded all box office expectations, set BO records (grossed $255 million on a $4.5 million budget) and won an Oscar to boot. Maybe there was something to this diversity thing.

Maybe there was something to this guy Jordan Peele. It's easy to say a comic's a comic, but not all comics are created talented, or smart. Peele was a fan of teamwork early on. He dropped out of college to form his first comedy duo with Rebecca Drysdale, who would later write on *Key & Peele*. He was regular at The Second City and Boom Chicago. Then came *Mad TV*, where Peele got to shine as a variety of characters, many with the other Black guy on the show, Key. After 5 seasons, Peele left.

Jordan Peele stayed busy doing mainly low-profile projects until *Key & Peele* came along for Comedy Central. Their success was of its time. In an era when going viral was just on the cusp, these guys had practically every sketch they did going viral. They were web giants before the ribbon was even cut on the new lane. A year after the show left the airwaves, they starred in their first film together, *Keanu,* about a cat. It was a hit.

Suffice it to say, Jordan Peele became a big man on campus. His choice of future projects will only be limited by his amount of time in a day as a human. As a result of his Orson Welles-like Tinseltown freedom, he retired from performing (unlike Welles) to concentrate strictly on creating. Two more prominent being *Us,* another Sci-Fi film and a highly acclaimed reboot of *The Twilight Zone.*

It would be easier to list the accolades withheld from him. That smattering of small potato name organizations don't matter anyway. So here we go with the esteemed whose awards he has: American Comedy, Primetime Emmy, Writer's Guild, Director's Guild, Gotham Independent Film, Independent Spirit, Satellite, L A Film Critics Association, Critic's Choice, National Board of Review, Peabody and of course that Oscar.

https://youtu.be/bDJKtoj_HCk

✳ ✳ ✳

FEBRUARY 21, 1929

Roberto "Chespirito" Gomez Bolanos (findagrave.com)

ROBERTO GÓMEZ BOLAÑOS, AKA "CHESPIRITO" – BORN!

Highly regarded as one of the most recognized Spanish-language comedians of the 20th Century, Chespirito gained international renown for being the creative force behind the television hits, *Chespirito* (1968), *El Chavo del Ocho* (1973) and *El Chapulin Colorado* (1973). He wrote, directed and starred in each. His shows were so popular that *El Chavo del Ocho* still receives viewership of over 91 million.

Born in Mexico City, Chespirito got his stage moniker writing plays and film dialogue. It means "Little Shakespeare." The artist of many hats was discovered as an actor while waiting in line for a job as a writer. He initially wrote and starred in children's comedy shows where he was able to introduce a variety of enduring characters for Mexican network, *Televisa*. Those shows aired in 124 countries.

Chespirito's influence was felt throughout the artistic community. Matt Groening, creator of *The Simpson* said "Bumblebee Man" was a take-off of a character on Chespirito's *El Chapulin Colorado*. Chespirito was an accidental composer. He began writing music as a hobby and developed into an accomplished composer. He's written songs for film, television and theater. The prolific talent published three books and received numerous awards; both from the creative community as well as national honors.

https://youtu.be/WrBo-MK-yWk

＊＊＊

FEBRUARY 21, 1978

Kumail Nanjiani w/ Emily V. Gordon
(Creative Commons Attribution 2.0 Generic - Cropped)

KUMAIL NANJIANI – BORN IN KARACHI, PAKISTAN!

Nanjiani is a classic example of good things happening no matter what. He lived in Pakistan until he was 18 years old. Then Nanjiani came to the United States, learned the customs of a foreign nation while attending the University of Iowa, pulling a double major in philosophy and computer science. Naturally after all that he became a stand-up comedian. That should've been the end of it. Jack swapped his hard-earned knowledge that was expected to be cashed in the marketplace and traded it for a handful of magic promises from comedy agents, bookers and groupies.

Good thing Nanjiani had talents and a good dose of common sense. He applied the first rule of writing: Write about what you know. So, he wrote about himself. However, before he made his mark in 2017 and became the talk of the town, he did a lot of other projects kicking things off in 2008 on *Saturday Night Live*. During a James Franco hosted episode Nanjiani played an Indian Reporter – uncredited.

From such explosive beginnings Nanjiani went forward. He's been on podcasts (*Harmontown, TV Guidance Counselor Podcast*) and hosted them (*The X-Files File, The Indoor Kids* with Ali Baker and later his wife, Emily V. Gordon after Baker jumped ship). He's voiced video games (*The Walking Dead: Season Two*) and animation (*Animals, Aqua Teen Hunger Force, Penn Zero: Part Time Hero, Archer, Trip Tank, Bob's Burgers, Adventure Time, Ugly Americans*). Nanjiani has had guest starring roles (*Portlandia, Veep, Broad City*), recurring roles (*Newsreaders, Adventure Time*), and regular roles on series (*Franklin & Bash, The Melt Down with Jonah & Kamail, Silicon Valley*). He's done commercials (Old Navy), movies (*The Kings of Summer, Sex Tape, Hot Tub Time Machine 2, Central Intelligence, Life as We Know It, Fist Fight*) and a Comedy Central comedy special, *Beta Male* (2013). Busy guy.

Now back to 2017. That was the year Nanjiani wrote his own ticket. He co-wrote, *The Big Sick,* where he played himself and hired an actress to play his wife. Well, at least his wife was the other co in co-wrote about the story of their relationship (you needed somebody who remembered the facts). Their creation was hailed as one of the top films of 2017 and thanks to *The Big Sick* Nanjiani won the Kanbar Award for Storytelling and the Independent Spirit Award for Best First Screenplay, the San Diego International Film Festival Auteur Award and a box office gross of 40 million making it the third highest grossing film of that year.

https://youtu.be/iGh1aO1skNc

✳ ✳ ✳

FEBRUARY 23, 1983

Aziz Ansari at the 71ˢᵗ Annual Peabody Awards Luncheon Waldorf-Astoria May 21, 2012
(Photo Credit: Anders Krusberg / Source: Aziz Ansari)

AZIZ ANSARI – BORN IN COLUMBIA, SOUTH CAROLINA

Taking a different career path than his gastroenterologist father, the versatile Ansari got his start in comedy while still in school at the New York University. He performed in clubs in New York and furthered his comedic education at the Upright Citizen's Brigade Theatre. To date he has headlined several national tours and released four comedy CD/DVDs. He takes the approach of talking about his own personal experiences, so no other comedians can steal his act or bits. He's performed at such prestigious venues as Madison Square Garden and Carnegie Hall.

His television credits include *Uncle Morty's Dub Shack, Reno 911!, Scrubs,* MTV's *Human Giant,* which he created as a vehicle for himself, HBO's *Flight of the Conchords,* and NBC's *Parks and Recreation.*

He created *Master of None* for Netflix and formed a strong relationship with MTV (he hosted the MTV Movie Awards in 2010) and Comedy Central which yielded many of Ansari created projects and collaborations.

Ansari has worked in numerous films such as *Funny People, I Love You, Man. Get Him to the Greek, Observe and Report* and *30 Minutes or Less.*

Ansari is also an author with his first book *Modern Romance: An Investigation* which dropped in 2015. It's about dating and was co-written with Eric Klinenberg, an actual sociologist.

He has done voice-over work as the recurring, Darryl on *Bob's Burgers,* Mub in *Epic,* Martin in *The Ventura Bros.,* Billy Billions in *Ben 10: Omniverse,* DMO in *Adventure Time,* Charles in *Animals* and on music videos ("Otis" by Jay-Z and Kanye West). In the latter, he played himself (as in the film, *This Is the End, Comedy Bang! Bang!* and the animated feature, *Ice Age: Continental Drift)*

Ansari has earned numerous industry nominations and has won the Variety Power of Comedy Award, a Critics' Choice Television Award and a Primetime Emmy Award for Outstanding Writing.

https://youtu.be/JbCnmuLw54g

✳ ✳ ✳

FEBRUARY 24, 1969

Edwin San Juan (Moreno Collection)

EDWIN SAN JUAN – BORN!

When San Juan was coming up in comedy there weren't a passel load of clubs catering to the Asian audience. So, the Filipino funny man cut his teeth in Latin clubs and bars alongside comedians such as Gabriel Iglesias, Felipe Esparza and Jeff Garcia. It was the perfectly rough circuit to get polished and he did. Soon he was doing USO shows and headlining nationally. So, San Juan was a seasoned pro when he gained notoriety as the creator and Executive Producer of *SlantED Comedy*, a showcase of Asian American stand-up comedians televised on Showtime.

As a standup comedian, San Juan appeared on all available shows. He was seen on *Comics Unleashed with Byron Allen, Comedy Central's Live at Gotham's, BET's Comic View, Live from Hollywood, Latino Laugh Festival, Que Loco, Inside Joke, Latino 101, International Sexy Ladies Show* (ummm), *Loco Comedy Jam, Comics without Borders, The Payaso Comedy Slam* and *Destination Stardom*.

Edwin San Juan appeared in the 2010 film, *I'm Not Like That No More* with Paul Rodriguez and he was the grand champion on the UPN show, *Talent Agency*. He later moved to Nevada to become the resident comedian at the Las Vegas Live Comedy Club and in 2015 San Juan won Las Vegas Weekly's "Best Comedian on the Las Vegas Strip."

https://youtu.be/cMf_xD4azHI

✳ ✳ ✳

FEBRUARY 26, 1933

Godfrey Cambridge (Public Domain)

GODFREY MACARTHUR CAMBRIDGE – BORN IN NEW YORK, NY!

If his parents had had their way, Cambridge would've become a doctor. He attended Hofstra College where he studied medicine for three years, then woke up one morning, dropped out and became an actor. That was probably a dramatic moment remembered by all who witnessed, but then the reality of being a struggling actor set in. Cambridge found himself doing less acting and more job bouncing. He was an ambulance driver, a gardener, bead-sorter, cab driver, popcorn bunny maker, airplane cleaner, New York Housing Authority clerk and judo instructor.

Cambridge's hard work to keep food in his belly paid off. He took his bartending skills from real life and played a bartender in his first play, *Take a Giant Step*. It was off-Broadway, but in 1957 he made it to the big time. He debuted in the original production of Herman Wouk's *Nature's Way*. Four years later Cambridge earned an Obie Award for his work in *The Blacks: A Clown Show*. A year later he received a Tony nomination for his work in the original version of Ossie Davis' *Purlie Victorious* in a cast that included Ruby Dee, Helen Martin, Beah Richards, Alan Alda, Sorrell Booke and Roger C. Carmel. His performance in 1965's *A Funny Thing Happened on the Way to the Forum* was lauded as well. Cambridge proved himself to be an accomplished actor.

Godfrey Cambridge was also good on film. He played a government agent in *The President's Analyst* (1967); a cab driver in *Bye Bye Braverman* (1968); a white racist who turns black in *Watermelon Man* (1970); a line-crossing cop in *Cotton Comes to Harlem* and its sequel *Come Back Charleston Blue* (1972) and a gay gangster in Pam Grier's *Friday Foster* (1975). In 1970 he financed and produced the graphic anti-drug film, *Dead is Dead*, where actual addicts were shown shooting up and going through withdrawal. Cambridge also appeared in the films, *The Busy Body, The Biggest Bundle of Them All, The Biscuit Eater, Beware! The Blob* and *Whiffs*.

Godfrey Cambridge made his presence known on television. He guest-starred on *Car 54 Where Are You?*, *The Dick Van Dyke Show*, *I Spy*, *The Phil Silvers Show* and in *Night Gallery* playing a comedian who appeals to a genie to get his career back on track. Steven Spielberg directed that episode which co-starred Tom Bosley. Cambridge also did underwear commercials for Jockey.

Standup comedy was another Cambridge strength. In 1965 Time magazine recognized him as being one of the top four most celebrated Black comedians in the nation along with Dick Gregory, Nipsey Russell and Bill Cosby. Cambridge was universally accepted with a brand of comedy that though truthful, sarcastic and incisive, was unifying. He made appearances on *The Tonight Show* and was one of the country's top earning nationally headlining standup comedians. In a career spanning several decades he released four albums; all from Epic Records.

Godfrey Cambridge died on November 29, 1976 in Burbank, California of a heart attack. It happened while he was filming *Victory at Entebbe*, a movie where Cambridge was portraying brutal dictator, Idi Amin. When the news was made public Amin was quoted as saying Cambridge's death was "punishment from God." Godfrey Cambridge was 43 years old.

https://youtu.be/k6Pf8p3Md3o

✳ ✳ ✳

FEBRUARY 26, 1972

Maz Jobrani (The Maz Jobrani Collection)

MAZIYAR "MAZ" JOBRANI – BORN IN TEHRAN, IRAN!

Jobrani was part of the Middle-Eastern comedian boom that came to the forefront after the 9/11 terrorist attacks to bring a better understanding of the misunderstood culture in America. He adopted the nickname, 'The Persian Pink Panther' and focused his material on race relations and tolerance. He took his stand-up act on the road with the touring group, "The Axis of Evil." They were so popular they had a special on Comedy Central.

Funny is funny and with an ever-growing platform and fan base Jobrani could take advantage of other media opportunities. He's appeared on television shows: *The Tonight Show with Jay Leno, Talkshow with Spike Feresten, Still Standing, The Late Late Show with Craig Ferguson, Cedric the Entertainer Presents, The Colbert Report, Malcolm in the Middle, Whitney, The West Wing* and *CBS's Superior Donuts*(as a regular).

Jobrani has also racked up an impressive film resume in *The Interpreter, Friday After Next* and *Dragonfly*. He's used radio to his advantage as well on NPR, *WTF with Marc Maron* and his own podcast, *All Things Comedy*.

https://youtu.be/KEe7nYTw_Ik

✱✱✱

FEBRUARY 26, 1968

DeRay Davis (Humor Mill Magazine)

DERAY DAVIS – BORN IN CHICAGO, ILLINOIS!

DeRay Davis is a regular guy who works regularly. Since moving to Los Angeles from his native Chicago, he put it in starting with a competition win to get people's attention and then impressive work on stages throughout Hollywood. He caught the right eyes and was booked on the Cedric the Entertainer Tour. He also got a plum gig at the Improv in Hollywood as the regular weekly host. The club was so set on their choice they changed the name of their regular Monday night show to "MonDeRays."

Davis became a regular in Ice Cube's *Barbershop* films as Ray-Ray, the Hustle Guy. He was a regular on the Damon Wayans sitcom, *My Wife & Kids* as RJ. He was a regular headliner on *Shaq's Comedy All-Stars*. Davis was a regular on television shooting sets (*Reno 911, Empire, Entourage*); comedian shows (BET's *Comic View, Nick Cannon's Wild N Out, The Big Black Comedy Show*); music videos and album recordings(Kanye West, Three 6 Mafia, Lil Flip, Chris Brown) and movie sets (*The Fog, Scary Movie 4, Semi-Pro, 21 Jump Street, All Eyez on Me*).

Davis has also used his hosting skills to expand the cultural dialogue. He's the host of *Hip-Hop Squares*. That reimagining of an old standard was created and narrated by DeRay's regular old friend, Ice Cube.

https://youtu.be/FZegO4_KDGI

✳ ✳ ✳

March

This Day in Comedy...

MARCH 1, 1939

Rodney Winfield (l) w/Hope Flood, J. Anthony Brown and Wan Dexter at The Townhouse in Inglewood, CA (The Hope Flood Collection)

RODNEY WINFIELD – BORN IN ST. LOUIS, MISSOURI!

Winfield was a comedy enigma. Anyone who witnessed him perform stand-up comedy live will never forget it. The man was brilliant in style (he sported a yachting cap), material and delivery. He was the kind of comedian other comedians refused to follow. His renown was well known in the comedy circles, but not so with the public. He once said of himself that big name comics won't let him open for them because if you put him in front of any huge audience he'd bring the house down, but if you put his name on the marquee nobody would show up.

Winfield's anonymity wasn't always the case. Rodney Winfield was a comedy pioneer. Long before *Star Search, Last Comic Standing* and *America's Got Talent*, former *Today Show* host, Dave Garroway had gone around the country scouting out talent to introduce to the nation and make them stars. Rodney was one of those next-big-things on *The CBS Newcomers* in 1971, but the show went nowhere and rapidly fell into the annuls of obscurity. The Pentagon couldn't even find it on radar. So, it was back to the grind for Rodney Winfield.

He began his ebb and flow career opening up for Richard Pryor, The Temptations and the O'Jays. His style was frank, honest and bluntly to the point. Audiences loved him. It was Rodney Winfield who wrote the joke, "If you follow an ugly person home an ugly person is going to open the door." Heard that one before? Well, now you know where it came from.

He made sure to tell that joke in the film, *Talkin Dirty After Dark* starring Martin Lawrence in 1991. He confided to a number of friends that he expected more to come from that film as far as career opportunities. It disappointed him that stardom had alluded him when he was so damn funny. However, disappointment was not resignation. Rodney Winfield also appeared in *Dead Presidents* and *Survival of the Illest*. He voiced a character playing cards in the animated feature, *Bebe's Kids* and went on HBO's *Def Comedy Jam* and destroyed.

Comedy was his constant companion and friend, and Rodney Winfield loved doing it (and we loved watching him do it) until he passed away on February 9, 2009 in St. Louis, Missouri due to kidney failure.

https://youtu.be/gmoG_C0RJ78

✳ ✳ ✳

MARCH 1, 2000

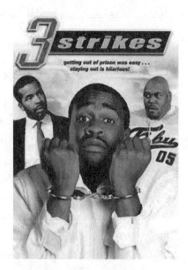

3 STRIKES – RELEASED BY MGM!

Written and directed by DJ Pooh, *3 Strikes* stars Brian Hooks as a guy caught up in the system. Hooks gets out of jail after a year for his second offense as he discovers there's a new three strikes law. If he goes down one more time it's for a minimum of 25 years. No problem. He has no intention of ever going back inside. He's a new man. Changed life. This is what he tells JJ, a guy who picked him up instead of his real friend. So as JJ, the substitute pick-up ride, listens to this tale of personal revelation, the cops pull up behind them and this forces JJ into an inconvenient admission. Seems the pick-up car was stolen and now JJ has to have a gun battle with the cops. Next thing Hooks knows – it's on!

3 Strikes is a full-on chase film. Hooks spends most of his time alluding the cops in hopes of proving his innocence. In the meanwhile, JJ has been apprehended, taken to the hospital with a buttocks wound (he's hung in a sling with his bandaged ass hiked up in the air), raped by a gay janitor and vows to pin the crime all on Hooks when the cops come asking. Hooks, during this time, makes a deal to get a tape with JJ admitting wrongdoing. All he has to do is go to bed a woman he does not want to go to bed with. That's all, but it turns out it doesn't matter. Hooks is caught and through the miracle of movie storytelling he is only found to be in violation of his parole, goes to jail for 30 days and gets out because the prison was overcrowded.

3 Strikes co-stars David Alan Grier, Faizon Love, N'Bushe Wright, Antonio Fargas, E-40, DJ Pooh, George Wallace, Meagan Good, Mo'Nique, De'Aundre Bonds, Phil Morris and Vincent Schiavelli. Cameos are made by Mike Epps, Anthony Anderson, Jerry Dunphy and Big Boy. The film was poorly received by critics but was nevertheless profitable. On a budget of $3.4 million, *3 Strikes* pulled in $3,684,704 in its opening weekend for the #12 spot and an eventual box office take of $9.8 million.

https://youtu.be/GDFqdXToYxE

✳ ✳ ✳

MARCH 2, 1956

Angel Salazar w/Kool Bubba Ice (Instagram)

ANGEL SALAZAR – BORN.

Salazar once said that if he had a dollar for every time somebody said to him, "Chi Chi, get the YaYo" he'd be a millionaire. It was the immortal line in 1983's *Scarface* uttered by Al Pacino's drug kingpin character, Tony Montana to Salazar's henchman during a drug deal gone wrong. That single instructive phrase to grab the almost forgotten cocaine came after a hail of gunfire in an iconic scene that made Salazar a pop culture fixture. Not bad for a Cuban-American comedian in an era when few Latin comedians were on the mainstream radar.

Angel Salazar was 27 years old when *Scarface* made him a hot commodity. He was a seasoned stand-up comedian, whose style was raw, interactive and manic. Like most ethnic comics he talked about being ethnic; punctuating punchlines as well as set ups with his catch phrase, "Sheck it out." During his career Salazar opened for the Beach Boys, Billy Ocean, Van Halen, the Miami Sound Machine and Whitney Houston. He also appeared on *Last Comic Standing* and had numerous HBO specials.

Prior to *Scarface* Salazar had a productive film career going. He had roles in *Boulevard Nights, Walking Proud, Where the Buffalo Roam* and *A Stranger is Watching*. After *Scarface* he stayed right on track with appearances in *The Wild Life, Sylvester, Hot to Trot, Punchline* (w/Tom Hanks), *Maniac Cop 2, Carlito's Way* (w/Al Pacino again), *Vote For Me, Harlem Blues, Rose Woes and Joe's, Made In Brooklyn, Trust Me, Crumble* and *The Last Gamble*. Angel Salazar liked popping up in documentaries, too such as 2002's *Comedian* and *The Latin Legends of Comedy* featuring Joey Vega and JJ Ramirez in 2006. Though mainly Salazar liked doing stand up and would take year-long extended breaks from films to hit the road and just be a comedian.

https://youtu.be/1o_boUVZo30

***

MARCH 5, 1954

Marsha Warfield (The Marsha Warfield Collection)

MARSHA FRANCINE WARFIELD – BORN IN CHICAGO, ILLINOIS!

A night at comedian Tom Dreesen's place changed phone company employee Marsha Warfield forever. Prompted by her friend, Evelyn, Warfield went up on the open mic and got laughs and got hooked. A career in comedy seemed a foreign idea, though. There were no relatable role models. She was from a different mold than Moms or Lawanda Page. How do you become a working stand-up? When she met Elayne Boosler it became clear. Warfield said the way was paved for her and others thanks to trailblazers such as Elayne along with Judy Tenuta, Sandra Bernhard, Diane Nichols, Shirley Hemphill and Shelly Pryor. Outside of Phyllis Diller these women knew of no other stage comediennes and it wasn't like they were having tea with Phyllis daily, so they made their own rules. In the case of Marsha Warfield those rules worked.

Warfield got her break when comedian and Richard Pryor collaborator, Paul Mooney picked her when he assembled a cast of virtual unknowns for *The Richard Pryor Show* in 1977. She was blunt, sexy and uncompromising. The powerhouse comedienne had made her mark on the stand-up comedy circuit and Mooney knew she'd be equal to the task of writing and perform-ing with the red-hot Pryor. At that time Pryor was the comedy god. Or as Warfield once said, "God takes second billing as far as Richard was con-cerned." So, there were high expectations. She didn't disappoint as Warfield and the rest of the cast made an indelible impression in the four short epi-sodes they had on network television. However, the failure of the show left her depressed with thoughts of quitting comedy. That was until she won the prestigious San Francisco National Stand-Up Comedy Competition in '79.

By the time she gained fame on the NBC hit sitcom, *Night Court* Warf-ield was seasoned and had a reputation of reliability. Though short on act-ing experience, her deadpan, straight delivery to bailiff counterpart, Rich-ard Moll was as good a team as comedy gets, and nobody in television gave a better cynical look. The Chicago native embodied Roz to critical and fan approval and had viewers in stitches from 1986-1992.

Warfield pulled double duty in 1990. She was so popular NBC slotted her with a self-titled day time talk show where she and guests discussed hot topics of the day and got a load of laughs along the way. Her show was easy going and lasted for two seasons. Of course, it didn't stop there. Following her run on *Night Court* Warfield kept up her AFTRA status on the sitcom, *Empty Nest* playing Dr. Maxine Douglas from '93-'95. She did major films (*D. C. Cab, Mask, Caddyshack 2*), television guests spots (*Family Ties, Riptide, Cheers*) and of course stand-up.

Then in 1995 tragedy struck. After her house was totaled in the Northridge earthquake, Marsha's mother and her sister died within three months of each other. Not long after her "lifestyle" caught up with her so she took time to regroup. By the time she returned to the scene a lot of time had passed in show biz terms and newer faces had stepped in to fill the void. She eventually moved to Las Vegas. From there she kept her presence known via social commentary on sites and remained a living inspiration to a whole generation of comediennes who followed in her footsteps. Marsha Warfield returned to the standup comedy stage in 2015 and became a Las Vegas mainstay.

https://youtu.be/PvDJvuCmDpE

MARCH 6, 1963

D L Hughley, 2017 (Humor Mill Magazine)

DARRYL LYNN "D. L." HUGHLEY – BORN IN LOS ANGELES!

Hughley's life arc goes from gangbanger to *Los Angeles Times* employee to top standup comedian. The comedy part got its start in clubs in L.A. including the Comedy Act Theater and Miss Wiz, where Hughley was house host. He got early recognition and landed a late-night talk show on local based K-CAL, but it was short lived due to his hot competition – Arsenio Hall premiered that same season. The setback didn't have time to breathe before Hughley was pegged to be the first host of BET's standup showcase, *Comic View*. He remained there for two seasons (1992-1993) then moved on to tour.

In 1998 D. L. Hughley made his next foray into television on his own self-titled sitcom, *The Hughleys,* originally airing on ABC, where it was broadcast for two seasons. The show then moved to UPN as Hughley was gaining fame for his contribution in the Original Kings of Comedy in 2000. He replaced Guy Torry, who'd moved on to star on a TV action drama. The tour featuring Hughley, Cedric the Entertainer, Steve Harvey and Bernie Mac was a cultural phenomenon, packing arenas across the country, being made into a hit concert documentary directed by Spike Lee and spawning a cottage industry of copycats all being packaged as royalty and touring under that brand.

Once *The Hughleys* ended its run in 2002, D. L. Hughley got traction as a political commentator. He had a Comedy Central program, *Weekends at the D.L.* and hosted *D.L. Hughley Break the News* on CNN. Hughley was also a correspondent for NBC's *The Jay Leno Show*. He competed on *Dancing with the Stars* and held down his own radio shows. He released a comedy album (*D.L. Hughley: Notes from the GED Section*) has had recurring roles (*Studio 60 on the Sunset Strip, Scrubs*), guest-starred (*Fresh Prince of Bel Air, The Parkers*), hosted award shows (*BET Awards*), done voice-overs (*Inspector Gadget*) films (*The Brothers, Soul Plane, Scary Movie 3, Spy School*) and wrote books (*I Want You to Shut the Fuck Up: How the Audacity of Dopes Is Ruining America, How Not to Get Shot and Other Advice from White People, Black Ma, and White House: An Oral History of the Obama Years*).

https://youtu.be/w8FL5EiChx8

∗∗∗

MARCH 6, 1984

A.K.A. PABLO – PREMIERED ON ABC!

On paper *a.k.a. Pablo* had everything going for it. It was executive produced by respected and successful TV icon, Norman Lear. It starred hot, young (at the time), hilarious Latin comedian, Paul Rodriguez. It had a strong cast: Joe Santos, Hector Elizondo, Katy Jurado, Martha Velez, Alma Cuervo and Mario Lopez. It also had one other thing – it stunk. TV Guide ranked it #45 out of "50 Worst Shows of All Time." Obviously it could've been worse, but why quibble?

Beyond its critical flaws viewing audiences weren't interested in the exploits of a struggling stand-up comedian (as they were with *Seinfeld*) to tune in. And so, the hook came out and snatched *a.k.a. Pablo* off the air on April 10, 1984 after 6 episodes were broadcast. That's why this is a short entry.

https://youtu.be/vnDbassftIA

✳ ✳ ✳

MARCH 6, 1964

Yvette Wilson w/producer, Bob Sumner (Priscilla Clarke of PC & Associates)

YVETTE WILSON – BORN IN LOS ANGELES!

To live and die in L.A. was more than a movie or a string of lyrics on a Tupac jam. It was what bubbly and loveable Yvette Wilson did by passing unexpectedly and suddenly in the town of her birth and fame. Let's first start at the beginning. Like probably half the comics who ever existed, Wilson first got on stage on a dare (in her case a bet) and kept doing it. She honed her skills under the tutelage of Robin Harris at the Comedy Act Theater in L.A. in the late '80s and early '90s. She got seen and got work.

Following a spot on *Def Comedy Jam* and a few episodes in sketches on *Uptown Comedy Club* and FOX's *In Living Color*, Wilson got her first major TV exposure on ABC's *Thea*, starring Thea Vidale. Over the next several years she appeared in the films, *Poetic Justice, Blankman, House Party 3, Friday* and *Don't Be a Menace to South Central While Drinking Your Juice in the Hood*. Then she got steady employment, a co-starring part on the UPN sitcom, *Moesha* starring Brandy. Wilson rode that pony for four seasons and then jumped over to the spin-off, *The Parkers* starring Mo'Nique for another five seasons. The character of Andell Wilkerson was very good to Wilson. Two hundred and four combined episodes of good.

Cervical cancer is the official cause of Yvette Wilson's death on June 14, 2012 in L. A. Her last film role had been in the 2005 movie *Ganked*. At the time of her passing she had kidney disease and required a transplant that would cost $25,000. Her husband, record producer, Jerome Harry, set up a website to raise the needed funds. When she succumbed 56% of the required money had been pledged.

https://youtu.be/W2QILr2UJ1o

MARCH 7, 1964

Wanda Sykes (Public Domain)

WANDA SYKES – BORN IN PORTSMOUTH, VIRGINIA!

Raised in the Washington, DC area, Sykes was an NSA (National Security Agency) contracting specialist before getting into comedy. After five years of that day job she tried her hand at being funny in 1987 at the Coors Light Super Talent Showcase. She honed her skills for five more years (while still working for the NSA) until in 1992 she moved to New York. Sykes got a gig there working for Hal Leonard Publishing as a book editor. At night she'd step out and do comedy. One evening she got a break which led to Sykes opening for Chris Rock at the famed Caroline's Comedy Club. In 1997 she joined Rock's writing staff on *The Chris Rock Show* for HBO, where she also appeared on camera. In 1999 she won an Emmy as part of that writing team.

Further success followed Sykes. She's done theater (*Annie*), films (*Pootie Tang, Monster-in-Law, My Super Ex-Girlfriend, Evan Almighty, License to Wed, Down to Earth, Nutty Professor II: The Klumps*) and plenty of television (*Curb Your Enthusiasm, The New Adventures of Old Christine* (as friend, Barb Baran), *The Drew Carey Show, Chappelle's Show, Mad TV, Will & Grace, Alpha House, Real Husbands of Hollywood* and *Black-ish*). Sykes has also done voice-overs for animated features (*Over the Hedge, Barnyard, Brother Bear 2, Rio, Ice Age: Continental Drift, Ice Age: Collision Course*), television (*Bubble Guppies, Futurama, The Simpsons*) and did a voice for the televised puppet show, *Crank Yankers.*

Wanda Sykes had her own sitcom, *Wanda at Large* on FOX in 2003 and one on Comedy Central, (*Wanda Does It*). She also debuted her hour-long standup special, *Tongue Tied* on Comedy Central in 2003. In 2006 she did her first HBO special, *Wanda Sykes: Sick & Tired.* It was nominated for an Emmy Award. She did her second for HBO in 2009, *Wanda Sykes: I'ma Be Me.* Also in 2009 she hosted her own late night talk show, *The Wanda Sykes Show* on FOX. Sykes has hosted *Premium Blend* on Comedy Central and was a sports correspondent on HBO's *Inside the NFL.* In 2004 she published the best-selling book, *Yeah, I Said It.*

In 2014 Wanda Sykes co-produced the languishing NBC standup comedy competition show, *Last Comic Standing* and brought it back to its previous prominence. She has written for *The Keenen Ivory Wayans Show, The 74th Annual Academy Awards,* The Downer Channel and of course every show she was ever on or hosted.

Wanda Sykes was active in the anti-gay bashing campaign, "Think Before You Speak" and has been an outspoken advocate for LGBT rights. She performed as part of Cyndi Lauper's Tour for that cause. In 2009 she was the first openly LGBT person as well as the first African-American female to be a featured entertainer at the White House Correspondents' Association Dinner.

Sykes was named by *Out* magazine as number 35 on their Annual Power 50 List. She was one of the 25 Funniest People in America by *Entertainment Weekly* in 2004 and ranked by Comedy Central as #70 on their list of the 100 Greatest All-Time Standups. In 2001 Sykes won the American Comedy Award for Outstanding Female Stand Up Comic, the 2003 Comedy Central Commie Award for "Funniest TV Actress," the 2010 GLAAD Stephen F. Kolzak Award and the Activism in the Arts at the Triumph Awards in 2015.

https://youtu.be/nIBx1eMhzHQ

✳ ✳ ✳

MARCH 8, 2002

ALL ABOUT THE BENJAMINS – RELEASED BY NEW LINE CINEMA!
Teaming Ice Cube and Mike Epps up again, this action comedy is about diamond thieves and the tale of tracking them down. Cube is a bounty hunter, Epps a criminal. They pair up to get the crooks and a winning lottery ticket Epps needs to retrieve. There's plenty of running, multiple shoot outs, some murders, a kidnapping, a tasing, a neck breaking, several escapes, a lot of yelling, scenes of mild torture, a boat crash, along with various chases, some searching, plotting, planning, handcuffing and conniving.

All About the Benjamins was directed by Kevin Bray and produced by Ice Cube and Matt Alvarez. It featured Eva Mendes, Roger Guenveur Smith, Tommy Flanagan, Carmen Chaplin, Anthony Michael Hall, Bob Carter and Bow Wow. The critics hated the film. They thought it was crude and offensive with way too much violence. The fans loved it because of everything the critics hated.

On a budget of $15 million, *All About the Benjamins* grossed $26,306,533 at the box office.

https://youtu.be/VNINLCCZ8lg

✳✳✳

MARCH 9, 1990

HOUSE PARTY – RELEASED BY NEW LINE CINEMA!

Written and directed by Harvard alumni, Reginald Hudlin and based on his award-winning student film, *House Party* stars rappers, Kid and Play as two buddies out for a good time. That prospect becomes reality when Play announces his parents are leaving for a while and he's going to throw a party at the house. His friend Bilal (Martin Lawrence) will be the DJ and the only thing that can stop them is Kid's Pops (Robin Harris), who has banned him from going out and being a parent himself he just might make trouble. The only other thing is a threesome of thugs out to get Kid which is definitely trouble.

Well, Kid gets past his Pops and sneaks out. Then he gets past the thugs, who don't get past the cops and get arrested several times while trying to get Kid, who is busy avoiding all manners of obstacles to get to the party. When he finally makes it there it's crackin. After showing off his dance moves with Play, Kid hooks up with Sharane (A. J. Johnson), but really wants to be with Sydney (Tisha Campbell). As in most movies the love situation works itself out so well that Kid and Campbell are about to have sex, but his condom is too old and besides he's got to get going. Campbell's parents come home, and Kid is back on the streets running to avoid trouble. Too late. The cops catch him and throw him in jail. His friends bail him out and he sneaks into his house just in time for Pops to catch him and whoop his butt with a belt.

House Party is a comedy classic. Besides great music provided by Marcus Miller and Lenny White, the film was a critical and box office success.

On a budget of $2.5 million the film grossed $26,385,627. It spawned four sequels (two theatricals, two straight to DVD) and the soundtrack released on Motown Records was also a hit reaching #20 on the Top R&B/Hip-Hop Albums chart.

Produced by Reginald's brother, Warrington Hudlin and partner, Gerald T. Olsen, *House Party* featured the talents of Paul Anthony, Bow-Legged Lou and B-Fine (from Full Force), Darryl "Chill" Mitchell, Kelly Jo Minter, BeBe Drake, George Clinton and John Witherspoon.

House Party was the last film appearance of pivotal and influential stand-up comedian, Robin Harris, who passed away nine days after its release.

https://youtu.be/vudUSoBp_2s

✳ ✳ ✳

MARCH 12, 1959

Luenell (The Campbell Collection)

LUENELL CAMPBELL – BORN IN TOLETTE, ARKANSAS!

Luenell cut her comedy teeth in Oakland, California in clubs like The End Zone and Sweet Jimmies. During the Black Comedy Boom of the early 90s she was seen on local cable station, KSBT on *Soul Beat*, an interview show, and received standup television exposure with hilarious appearances on BET's *Comic View*. She toured internationally entertaining troops and domestically cracking up audiences from coast to coast.

National notoriety was gained when Luenell toured twice with Katt Williams, the latter being the third largest comedy tour of 2006 (behind Larry the Cable Guy and Dane Cook). She was also featured in the concert film of that tour, *American Hustle*. Her breakthrough film role had her mistaken for the real thing and not an actress. That too-real-for-the-audience part was as girlfriend to Sacha Baron Cohen in the smash hit, *Borat*. However, there were other films: *So I Married an Axe Murderer* (1993), *The Rock* (1996), *Never Die Alone* (2004), *Spring Breakdown* (2009), *All About Steve* (2009), *Head Case* (2009), *Hey Luenell* (2009 TV movie), *35 and Ticking* (2011) and *Budz House* (2011).

Luenell has the distinction of being seen in three films that made it to #1 at the box office. The year was 2012 and the movies were *Think Like A Man*, the animated *Hotel Transylvania* (where she was heard) and *Taken 2*, with old tough guy, Liam Neeson. That same year she also appeared in *That's My Boy, C'Mon Man* and *Mac & Devin Go to High School*.

Television has also been a friend to Luenell. She had roles in *Nash Bridges, The Tracy Morgan Show, The Tony Rock Project, Californication, The Boondocks, Laugh Out Loud Comedy Festival, Funny or Die Presents, the Middle, Breaking In, It's Always Sunny in Philadelphia* and *Comedy Underground*.

Luenell has toured extensively as a top headliner and appeared prominently on *Snoop Dog's Bad Girls of Comedy* and *Stand-up In Stilettos*.

https://youtu.be/8B1TTvji96E

✳✳✳

MARCH 12, 1931

Billie Thomas (Buckwheat) 1937 (Public Domain)

WILLIAM "BILLIE" THOMAS, JR. (BUCKWHEAT) – BORN IN LA!

Although Thomas is synonymous with the groundbreaking Black character (of *Our Gang / Little Rascals* fame {1934-1944}), the original Buckwheat was a little girl, played in 1934 by Carlena Beard and later by Willie Mae Walton. Thomas was around during this time, but only as a background character. Even when Thomas took over the part in 1935 Buckwheat remained a girl; in dress and hairstyle. He didn't make Buckwheat masculine until 1936 and Thomas wore trousers from then on out.

Thomas is the only child actor to appear in all the *Our Gang* comedies once they moved to MGM. He always felt Buckwheat's treatment was equal to that of the other kids on the series; the white kids. However, various protest groups over years felt differently and the character carried a stigma from its inception. Despite this, Buckwheat was popular with fans. Along with his running buddy Porky, he'd gleefully mangle the English language in the tradition of early Black entertainers. The fact was both children had speech impediments, but their malady was perfect for comedy. Where would we be without the catch-phrase, O-TAY?

Once the series ended, Thomas went into the Army and upon his return (with Honors) he had no interest in performing again. He was offered parts as many of the gang kids were, but he couldn't see himself going through the rigors of a Hollywood actor's life. Instead he learned film editing and made a career behind the scenes.

Though Thomas tried to live a quiet life, the character remained steeped in controversy whenever Black images were examined. Eddie Murphy's famous take-off of Buckwheat brought down the ire of George McFarland aka "Spanky," who felt it reduced beloved Buckwheat into a mere stereotype. Whereas there were others who attempted to capitalize on the public's fuzzy recollection of the iconic child star. The ABC newsmagazine show *20/20* ran an interview in 1990 with Bill English, a man who claimed to have originated the Buckwheat character. Once again the grown up Spanky stepped in to set the record straight. McFarland let it be known that Thomas had been dead for over 10 years and that English was a fraud. A producer from *20/20* was forced to resign and Thomas's son sued. While all these shenanigans were transpiring the real Buckwheat (Billie Thomas) had passed away on October 10, 1980 and was buried in Inglewood Park Cemetery in California.

https://youtu.be/DjW0dk2_fgk

✳ ✳ ✳

MARCH 15, 1980

Redd Foxx and Reynaldo Rey in *Sanford*, 1981 (Reynaldo Rey Collection)

SANFORD – PREMIERED ON NBC!

Redd Foxx left his hit NBC show, *Sanford & Son* in 1977 and went to ABC to do a variety show that only lasted 4 months. Since they were in the basement in network ratings, NBC jumped at the chance to get Foxx back in the role of Fred G. Sanford and so *Sanford* was born. It aired minus Demond Wilson (who refused to return) and lasted two shortened seasons. The show was a mid-season replacement in the 1979-80 season and the 1980-81 season.

The ill-fated incarnation centered around Fred and his new partner, Cal (Dennis Burkley), a Southern white guy with a big heart and gut who Lamont had worked with on the Alaska Pipeline and who he sent to stay with Fred. Aunt Esther and Rollo were still around, but that was the only magic left from the first time we met Fred Sanford.

The show was yanked and retooled, showing back up with Rollo and many new characters. This retooled version was scrapped faster than some of the junk in Sanford's yard. *Sanford* went off the air July 10, 1981.

https://youtu.be/ZExyQSAZ0E4

✳ ✳ ✳

MARCH 17, 1927

Rudy Ray Moore as Dolemite (The Donald Randell Collection)

RUDOLPH FRANK MOORE (AKA DOLEMITE) – BORN IN FORT SMITH, ARKANSAS!

Moore was known as the "Godfather of Rap" based on his numerous comedy albums featuring dirty rhymes and jokes. He went by the stage name of Dolemite, a character in his films who was part-pimp, part gangster.

Moore got his start as a preacher in Milwaukee. He expanded his flair for entertaining as a dancer/singer in nightclubs, known by the name of Prince DuMarr. His Army buddies changed that name to the Harlem Hillbilly when Moore shipped out to Germany as part of their entertainment troupe. He sang country songs with an R&B feel. He also got turned onto comedy. Once out of the Army he moved to Los Angeles, got back in nightclubs and got discovered. Dootsie Williams recorded Moore's songs under five different labels from 1955-1962. In 1959 Moore recorded his first comedy album, *Below the Belt*, followed by *The Beatnik Scene* (1962) and *A Comedian Is Born* (1964). He was making a living, but not living it up.

Then came Dolemite. He'd heard stories about the character from a guy while Moore was working at a record store in 1970 and decided to become that character for his own persona. He recorded the comedic tales in natural settings; like his own home with friends over drinking and getting high as Moore told jokes, sang songs and did nasty rhymes. He was an immediate hit.

Moore was one of the titans of "party records"; recordings labeled XXX by most of their distributors. Many of these albums were sold under the table at record stores and had to be given to the patron in a brown paper bag so the suggestive covers of naked women were obscured. In rapid succession Moore released *Eat Out More Often*, *This Pussy Belongs to Me* and *The Dirty Dozens*.

It was through those recordings that he was able to finance his first film, *Dolemite* (1975). That low budget hit became known as one of the greatest Blaxploitation films of all time and spawned sequels: *The Human Tornado, The Monkey Hustle, Petey Wheatstraw: The Devil's Son-in-Law* and *The Return of Dolemite*. Moore was ghetto fabulous and traveled extensively as Dolemite as his stage act and his fans adored him. He could do no wrong with them. On the road his merchandise sales often tallied more than the fee he received to perform.

As the years wore on, Rudy Ray Moore remained active. His popularity endured as rap artists; especially Snoop Dogg credit rap to Moore. It was his raw edged rhymes accompanied by music in the background that lent itself to his pioneer status. Even in his later years he was so revered rappers sought his collaboration on their tunes and he's featured in many from Big Daddy Kane to 2 Live Crew.

Rudy Ray Moore was prolific. He released over 30 records, appeared in almost 20 films and lent his talent and expertise to other artists until he passed away on October 19, 2008 in Akron, Ohio from complications of diabetes.

https://youtu.be/Voxp3ckwJZ0

✳ ✳ ✳

MARCH 19, 1894

Moms Mabley, 1968 (Public Domain)

JACKIE "MOMS" MABLEY (LORETTA MARY AIKEN) – BORN IN BREVARD, NORTH CAROLINA!

Mabley adopted a persona of an older person when she was still very young. This might be because when she was even younger everybody was telling her what to do. Her father told her to marry an old man she hated. The old man she hated told her to do everything she hated. And the town sheriff who raped her told her not to tell. It was time to do some telling of her own. She became the voice of wisdom on stage and audiences responded.

Moms became known as a crusader for social justice and her comedy reflected it. A star of the Apollo Theater in the 40s and 50s, Mabley was making in excess of $10,000 per week. She rose to national prominence in the 1960s and punctuated a lengthy career, which included 20 comedy LPs, with a hit recording of "Abraham, Martin & John" in 1969 becoming the oldest artist to ever have a Top 40 Hit at age 75.

History records Moms Mabley as the first female stand-up comic. Whoopi Goldberg made a documentary about this pioneer to hold her up as an inspiration and a yardstick. Mabley's took advantage of every medium at her disposal; no small task when you consider the obstacles of her era. She was in five films, nine stage plays, four television appearances, recorded 24 comedy albums and performed countless times.

Unfortunately, all good things must come to an end and the true legend took her journey home on May 23, 1975 after a fatal heart attack.

https://youtu.be/vM880a92rgo

✷✷✷

MARCH 20, 1987

HOLLYWOOD SHUFFLE – RELEASED BY SAMUEL GOLDWYN!

Produced, directed, and co-written by Robert Townsend, this film is a satirical attack on Hollywood's systematic stereotyping of Blacks in the media. Townsend financed the indie with his own credit cards and used the storyline of a struggling Black actor interspersed with vignettes to illustrate his point. There are scenes of slavery, popular films, movie reviewers and more as Townsend's character's imagination lets us in on his conflict in being an underused and often degraded minority in the world of entertainment.

Hollywood Shuffle is about Bobby Taylor (Townsend) having to decide to take a cooning part in a Black gang film. His grandmother is against it. His mother supports him, but she is also against cooning. His co-workers and boss couldn't care less if he coons or not. They don't think he'll ever make it as an actor anyway and he needs to keep his mind on his job at Winky Dinky Dog. They're wrong. He gets the coveted role and finds out he can't do it. It's too much cooning. So, he takes his grandmother's advice and gets a job working for the post office. He does a commercial for USPS.

This comedy classic was co-written by Keenan Ivory Wayans and co-produced by Dom Irrera, *Hollywood Shuffle* features Anne-Marie Johnson, John Witherspoon, Brad Sanders, Helen Martin, Eugene Robert Glazer and Paul Mooney.

The film was a critical and box office success. It won the 1987 Deauville Film Festival Grand Special Prize Critics Award and Coup de Coeur LTC Award for Robert Townsend and made $5,228,617 on a $100,000 budget.

https://youtu.be/msbo6TiwA5A

❊ ❊ ❊

MARCH 22, 1971

Keegan Michael Key (r) w/ Jordan Peele at 2014 Peabody Awards
(Public Domain WikiCommons 14471841627.jpg)

KEEGAN-MICHAEL KEY – BORN IN SOUTHFIELD, MICHIGAN!

Growing up bi-racial has its challenges. One has to navigate two opposing worlds and cultures. Keegan-Michael Key had to plot his course through even more. He was adopted by a white mother and Black father because his biological white mother and Black father couldn't hang. Keep up!

Keegan not only didn't run away or blow up the house he actually went to school and excelled. Upon graduation (with a Master of Fine

Arts), Key made his comedy bones at Second City (Detroit and Chicago) then got with *MADtv* and stretched his comedic chops by doing dozens of impressions. He mocked politicians, athletes, singers, rappers, movie stars and other comedians. Originally he and his eventual partner, Jordan Peele, were pit against each other so the show wouldn't have to have two Black guys in the cast, but they were both so good together as well as separately, *MADtv* had two Black guys in the cast.

Key stayed for 6 seasons, with Peele leaving before him. They reteamed to make magic together again later for Comedy Central and the fit was perfect. In *Key & Peele*, the duo had their thumbs on the pulse of the ever shifting public and weekly they'd press down on it until they heard screams. The sketches were inventive and hilarious, making the men, Keegan-Michael Key and Jordan Peele, the hottest comedy team in America even though technically they weren't a team.

The show, *Key & Peele* ran for 5 seasons. During that time, they introduced a wide variety of unforgettable characters. One of those will be harder to forget because he made political history. Key's "Luther" showed up at the 2015 White House Correspondents' Dinner and using his anger translation expertise, said what lame-duck, President Barack Obama was thinking. The assembled gathering of journalists and stuffed-shirt (and skirt) politicos forced grins and chuckles as Key yelled blunt and barely veiled truths and insults at them. It was good TV.

Good TV and comedy's what Key's about. He performed the stand-out role in Netflix's, *Friends From College*. He co-starred on the CBS show, *Gary Unmarried* and the USA Network comedy *Playing House*. Key was recurring on *Reno 911* and *Fargo* (along with Peele). His guest-starring roles are too numerous to list without a scroll and so are his other deeds, like movies. He's made a ton of them and the demand for his services show no sign of waning. Key has done commercials, podcasts, animated voices and made his Broadway debut in a Steve Martin comedy, *Meteor Shower.*

On top of everything the guy is benevolent. He's a founder of the Michigan's Planet Ant Theatre and the co-founder of the Detroit Creativity Project, a group that teaches young children improv skills to help with their social skills. Before you start singing, "For He's a Jolly Good Fellow," there's more.

Keegan-Michael Key has won a Peabody Award, an American Comedy Award and a Primetime Emmy. Now you can sing.

https://youtu.be/G6NfRMv-4OY

✳ ✳ ✳

MARCH 24, 1995

MAJOR PAYNE – RELEASED BY UNIVERSAL PICTURES!

Written by and starring Damon Wayans, this satire of military films is a hilarious remake of an old 1955 Charlton Heston film, *The Private War of Major Benson*. Didn't try to hide that fact either. Wayans' character name is Major Benson Winifred Payne. Directed by Nick Castle, *Major Payne* co-stars Karyn Parson, Orlando Brown, Albert Hall, William Hickey, Michael Ironside and Steven Martini.

In the film Wayans plays a veteran of the Marines who has hit the glass ceiling. After a big deal drug mission, he is still passed up for Lt. Colonel, so he gets an honorable discharge and retires mentally from fighting anymore battles for the Corps. Once out he joins the cops. That lasts as long as it takes him to knock out a domestic violence suspect on his first call. Payne is put in jail. Fortunately, a friend bails him out and arranges for him to instruct youngsters at a military school; youngsters with disabilities, like deafness and heart conditions.

Payne's new job is to train the cadets. He overzealously treats them like hardened grown men and soon gets the wrath of the cute lady school counselor. Payne doesn't care – he wants his new recruits to win the Military Games that hasn't been won by the school ever. They are always last. Well not again if Payne can help it. He tells his troops that he wants that trophy. So, they sneak over to the school that has it and tries to steal it, but Payne drops a dime on them and the cadets from the rival academy ambush his boys.

After their defeat Payne makes a deal. If his guys can win the trophy legit, he will leave. They go all out in their training to accomplish that goal. It looks like they're ready, but Payne gets called back into the service to go to Bosnia. Morale is down, but the boys compete anyway. Even though he's gone anyway, they're fired up to win. However, Payne feels he let them down and returns just in time to root his squad on to victory and they … win. Throughout the experience Payne himself has gotten more sympathetic, but not totally. In the final scene when a new blind recruit mouths off Payne shaves him and his seeing-eye dog bald.

Major Payne got mixed reviews, but was an audience pleaser coming in at #2 on its opening weekend and taking in a worldwide gross of $30.1 million.

https://youtu.be/5UNJodUl5KY

* * *

MARCH 25, 2005

GUESS WHO – RELEASED BY 20TH CENTURY FOX!

This comedy remake of the classic Sidney Poitier film, *Guess Who's Coming to Dinner*, stars Bernie Mac, Ashton Kutcher and Zoe Saldana. Directed by Kevin Rodney Sullivan it tells the story of a Black father who discovers his daughter is in love with a white guy. Mac (the Black father) doesn't like it. He tries to take Kutcher (the white guy) to a hotel, but they're all full and so he allows Kutcher to sleep in his basement and to make sure he stays there, Mac sleeps with him. Meanwhile Mac is having Kutcher investigated to dig up some dirt to discredit him in Zaldana's (the daughter) eyes.

The occasion of Mac and Kutcher ever meeting is Mac's 25th wedding anniversary. Zaldana wants to surprise the family with her engagement announcement. It was such a surprise that Mac ends up running Kutcher off by exposing him as a liar. Turns out Kutcher quit his job and didn't tell Zaldana. Busted trust, but when Mac finds out that the reason Kutcher quit was because his boss didn't approve of interracial relationships, he tracks him down and brings Kutcher back to Zaldana. And cut!

Written by Peter Tolan and Jay Sherick, *Guess Who* got mixed reviews. The cast, which also included Sherri Shepherd, Hal Williams, Judith Scott, Kel-lee Stewart, Ronreaco Lee, Lawrence Hilton-Jacobs, Niecy Nash and Mike Epps, got positive notices, but by 2005 the topic of interracial love was hardly the searing hot button it was in 1967 when the original was made. Regardless, on a $35 million budget the film grossed $68,915,888 domestically and $32,950,142 internationally for a grand total of $101,866,030 worldwide.

https://youtu.be/6Ww5vMKWDuM

* * *

MARCH 26, 2003

WANDA AT LARGE – PREMIERED ON FOX!

Created by and starring comedienne, Wanda Sykes, this sitcom ran for two seasons. It was initially a 6-episode interim show for FOX. The premise was Sykes is a stand-up comedian doing correspondence work for a political talk show. She's not particularly their cup of tea and her bosses (Ann Magnuson and Phil Morris) barely tolerate her and her antics. While trying to ignore them, Sykes juggles her domestic life with her sister-in-law (Tammy Lauren) and her two kids (Robert Bailey, Jr. and Jurnee Smollett).

The show was set in Washington, DC and premiered after FOX's mega-hit, *American Idol.* Following a second season renewal and a decline in ratings, *Wanda at Large* was moved to the Friday night death spot of 8:30 P.M. and aired its last episode on November 7, 2003.

Wanda at Large was nominated for the BET Comedy Award for Outstanding Comedy Series and a Teen Choice Award for Choice Breakout Show. Wanda Sykes received nominations for Best Actress by the BET Awards, Teen Choice and Satellite Awards.

https://youtu.be/9A9oBQnAVsk

* * *

MARCH 27, 2015

GET HARD – RELEASED BY WARNER BROS.!

This buddy comedy starring Kevin Hart and Will Ferrell was the directorial debut of Etan Cohen. The critics savaged it, but as usual what do critics know when it comes to popular taste? The film about an accused white-collar criminal tutored by a guy who said he spent time behind bars raked in $90.4 million domestically, $21.3 million internationally for a worldwide total of $111.7 million on a $40 million budget.

Ferrell plays a hedge fund manager with an ideal life. He's engaged to his boss' daughter and has a bright future. He's cheap which is evident by the two-dollar tip he gives his car washer, (Hart), but during a party Ferrell is arrested for embezzlement and given 30 days to get his affairs in order before going to prison for 10 years. Naturally he freaks out. He cuts off his ankle monitor, then tries to swoop up his fiancée to run away with him, but the cops bust him again and as they're taking him away he asks Hart how did he deal with prison? Of course, Hart would have to know – he's Black. Hart is also crafty. He makes a deal to instruct Ferrell on how to survive for $30,000. Deal!

The normally scary Hart puts the unsuspecting and scared Ferrell through the rigors of penitentiary life. He pepper sprays him, mad dog faces him, gets him into fights at the park and has a mock prison riot to toughen him up (where Ferrell gets stabbed in the forehead with a home-made shiv). Thinking his once future father-in-law is on the up and up Ferrell tells him he's getting help and he'll be okay. That was the wrong thing to say to the actual embezzler. Ferrell's almost pappy thinks Ferrell is onto him and tells his hit man to take care of Ferrell immediately.

Meanwhile Hart has been convinced that Ferrell is no criminal and certainly not tough, so they go in another direction. Hart tells Ferrell he has to learn how to give head or be killed. They even go to a gay hang out, but Ferrell can't go through with the fellatio. So, Hart tries to get Ferrell into his cousin's gang, that way he'll be protected in prison. No luck. Next they try a white supremacist gang, but Ferrell is not a convincing racist and the bigots try to kill him thinking he's a cop. With time running out Hart and Ferrell figure it was the father-in-law. They get his computer records and have him dead to rights. Ferrell's fiancée was also in on it and the hitmen are about to handle him and Hart when the US Marshals show up because Ferrell's ankle monitor went off. After a short hitch behind bars for having an unregistered gun (Ferrell had it hidden up his butt – "kestering") he is released without incident. Ferrell's almost pappy didn't fare as well in the joint. Speaking of – in the end, Hart gets his carwash business and Ferrell gets his life back. Yay!

Get Hard also features the talents of Craig T. Nelson, Alison Brie, T. I., Edwina Findley, Shad Gaspard, Paul Ben-Victor, Ron Funches with Jimmy Fallon and John Mayer as themselves. Christophe Beck composed the music. The screenplay was done by Jay Martel, Ian Roberts and Etan Cohen from a story by Martel, Roberts and Adam McKay.

https://youtu.be/lEqrpuU9fYI

✳ ✳ ✳

MARCH 28, 2001

MY WIFE AND KIDS – PREMIERED ON ABC!

This sitcom starred Damon Wayans, who plays an old school dad in a new school world. So, he resorts to becoming a smart aleck dad; teaching his kids lessons in life sometimes at their own expense. The modern world says you can't whoop kids, but nothing said anything about everything else you can do to them. Hard lessons in the house of hard knocks.

Wayans goes through some tough lessons himself. In the final episode he wants to have sex with his wife (Tisha Campbell-Martin), but she doesn't want to get pregnant again. So Wayans vows to get a vasectomy. He gets cold feet and tells her he got it anyway. When she finds out she is livid, so Wayans goes to get one for real. The kicker is he returns to find out she's pregnant anyway.

Produced by Touchstone Television, *My Wife and Kids* was co-created by Wayans and Don Reo. The supporting cast included George O. Gore II as the only son; an underachieving son at that. The middle daughter was played by Jazz Raycole the first season and by Jennifer Freeman for seasons 2-5. The final episode aired on May 17, 2005.

The youngest daughter was played by Parker McKenna Posey. Noah Gray-Cabey had the role of Posey's friend/boyfriend. Megan Goode played Gore's girlfriend and Andrew McFarlane was boyfriend to Freeman. Recurring characters were Ella Joyce, Lester Speight, Liliana Mumy, DeRay Davis, Brian Holtzman, Todd Lynn, Katt Williams and Sean Whalen.

My Wife and Kids was a huge hit in syndication; broadcast in Argentina, Australia, Austria, Belgium, Brazil, Canada, Croatia, Egypt, Estonia, Finland, France, Germany, Hungary, Italy, India, Israel, Ireland, Latvia, Malaysia, Mexico, The Netherlands, New Zealand, Norway, Pakistan, The Philippines, Poland, Portugal, Russia, Saudi Arabia, South Africa, South Korea, Tanzania, the United Kingdom, Venezuela and Zimbabwe.

The sitcom received numerous awards during its run. It won the AS-CAP Award for Top TV Series; The BET Award for Outstanding Lead Actor in a Comedy Series (Wayans) and Outstanding Lead Actress in a Comedy Series (Campbell-Martin); Family Television Award for Best Comedy Series, People's Choice Awards for Favorite Male (Wayans) and Favorite Comedy Series; a Prism Award for TV Comedy Series Episode and Young Artist Awards for Noah Gray-Caney and Jessica Sara for a guest starring role.

https://youtu.be/IGx2Yg1akJw

✳ ✳ ✳

MARCH 28, 1997

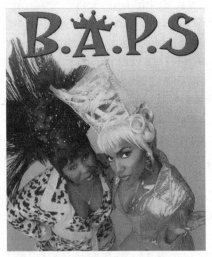

B*A*P*S (Instagram)

B*A*P*S – RELEASED BY NEW LINE CINEMA!

Directed by Robert Townsend and written by Troy Beyer, *B.A.P.S* stars Halle Berry and Natalie Desselle-Reid as Decatur, Georgia waitresses trying to come up. They want to open up the first combination beauty shop/soul food joint and go make a music video in Los Angeles, California to raise the money. Since we are talking about Halle Berry (no matter how ghetto they tried to make her look); they instead wind up in Beverly Hills at a sick old millionaire's mansion helping his butler (Ian Richardson) take care of him and living the life of Black American Princesses (thus the title).

However, the girls are ghetto, but they're not skanks. So, once they see how other gold-diggers are trying to financially abuse the old rich guy (Martin Landau), they decide to pump the brakes themselves and look after him on the real. Of course, when he finally dies he leaves them half his money. So, they're ghetto, but not "ignant."

B.A.P. S. features comedians Bernie Mac, Faizon Love, Rudy Ray Moore, Pierre and Anthony Johnson. It was panned by critics and audiences weren't too enthusiastic either. The film grossed a grand total of $7,338,279 on a $10 million budget, but we are talking about Halle Berry. She got nominated for Best Actress by the Acapulco Black Film Festival.

https://youtu.be/cHPpnwYVV8s

∗∗∗

MARCH 30, 2005

BEAUTY SHOP – RELEASED BY METRO-GOLDWYN-MAYER!

This spin-off of Ice Cube's *Barbershop* franchise stars Queen Latifah as Gina, a character introduced in 2004's *Barbershop 2*. The plot in this installment has Latifah moving from Chicago to Atlanta to give her daughter a better life and so she can attend a private music school. Latifah is a great hair stylist but is driven away from her home salon by her jealous boss (Kevin Bacon) so she opens her own shop. It's a shop of misfits: old ornery customers, new dumb and lazy stylists and a rapper wannabe (Lil JJ) who's always filming himself.

Eventually things start to look up. Latifah's old clients return to her, her old boss' clients come her way and the new people start to trust her and give up some business. Then the jealous ex-boss sends in a guy to destroy Latifah's business. It almost works at a crucial time, but thanks to Latifah's loyal employees it all turns out right. That also means Kevin Bacon gets paid a visit by some folks from the shop who give him a proper shaving.

Beauty Shop was directed by Billie Woodruff and co-stars Alfre Woodard, Alicia Silverstone, Andie MacDowell, Mena Suvari, Della Reese, Paige Hurd, Octavia Spencer, Keshia Knight Pulliam, Golden Brooks and Djimon Hounsou. It also features the comedy talents of Adele Givens, Sherri Shepherd, Laura Hayes and Sheryl Underwood with cameos by LisaRaye McCoy, Birdman, Kimora Lee Simmons and Wilmer Valderrama.

On a $25 million budget, *Beauty Shop* earned $37,245,453 at the box office.

https://youtu.be/MmN4tdA-2Qg

✳ ✳ ✳

GREENSBORO COLISEUM

SUN. 8:30 P.M. NOV. 12

ADMISSION $2.50 - $3.00 - $3.50 - All Seats Reserve

n Sale: Coliseum Box Office - Greensboro Record Center - Ronnie's Hobby Shop, Main St., Burling
Reznick's Downtown and Thruway Shopping Center in Winston-Salem

WEAL Radio presents

Supersonic Attractions present

"MOMS AT THE U.N."

MOMS MABLEY

"I stayed away too long"
SOLOMON BURKE
"TAKE ME"

"I HAD A DREAM"
JOHNNIE TAYLOR
"Got to love somebody baby"

JIMMY HUGHES
"GOODBYE MY LOVER GOODBYE"..."IT WAS NICE"

MITTY COLLIER
"watching and waiting"

BETTY HARRIS
"CRY TO ME"

FANTASTIC FOUR
"YOU GAVE ME SOMETHING"

THE PRECISIONS
"IF THIS IS LOVE"

PEG LEG MOFFETT

BILL MURRY
M.C.

Johnny JONES
and

KING CASUALS BAND

APRIL

THIS DAY IN COMEDY…

APRIL 1, 1994

Tia & Tamera Mowry w/Darina Littleton and unknown (Littleton Collection)

SISTER, SISTER – PREMIERED ON ABC!

Starring the Mowry Twins (Tia & Tamera), this sitcom also lived two lives. Starting out as a mid-season replacement on ABC it was cancelled by the network when the show didn't perform up to its ratings standards in the second season. The fact the network changed its time slot might've had something to do with it, but it didn't matter. The newly founded WB stepped in and slotted it on their schedule. There it caught its stride.

The show was about identical twins separated at birth and adopted into two very different situations. After 14 years they discover each other and reunite. They're now one big happy family with one twin's father (Tim Reid) and the other's mother (Jackee Harry) under the same roof.

Naturally there's an annoying neighbor who stops by unannounced; this time it's in the form of Marques Houston. The boyfriends who come along later are played by RonReaco Lee and Deon Richmond. Other characters included Tahj Mowry as cousin, Tahj, Brittany Murphy as their best friend, Dorien Wilson as a boyfriend to Jackee Harry and Sherman Hemsley as Tim Reid's daddy.

Sister, Sister was created by Kim Bass, Fred Shafferman and Gary Gilbert. A device used early on had the girls breaking the fourth wall often and talking to the audience. That was tapered down once the show moved to the WB and was eliminated altogether by the series final season. *Sister, Sister* won an Emmy Award for Outstanding Lighting Direction (Electronic) for a Comedy Series for George Spiro Dibie; four acting Image Awards for The Mowrys and Jackee Harry; three Kids' Choice Awards for acting for the Mowrys and a Young Artist Award for Marques Houston. It aired its final episode May 23, 1999.

https://youtu.be/T4JcOZJi5JQ

✳ ✳ ✳

APRIL 2, 1997

SMART GUY – PREMIERED ON THE WB!

This spin-off of *Sister, Sister*, stars Tahj Mowry, real life little brother to *Sister, Sister* stars, Tia and Tamera Mowry. On this show, Mowry plays a child genius (photographic memory, speaks multiple languages, etc.), who went from the 4th Grade to the 10th grade and all the adjustments he has to make in his new life. He now attends the same high school as his older brother (Jason Weaver) and sister (Essence Atkins), which they're not crazy about. For one – they're not as smart as him (at least his older brother isn't anyway – he's the dumb one, sis is smart). After that there's no reason for a second reason they don't like it.

Set in Washington, DC, the sitcom was created by Danny Kallis and produced by de Passe Entertainment. Omar Gooding plays Tahj's older brother's underachieving friend and John Marshall Jones has the role of the trio's single parent father. Kyla Pratt also has a recurring role.

During its three-season run (the show ended on May 16, 1999), *Smart Guy* was nominated for 7 major awards including American Cinema Foundation, Humanitas Prize, NAACP Image, Young Artist and Young Star Award. Four of those nominations were for Tahj Mowry's acting.

https://youtu.be/sf0goBbPQoo

✳✳✳

APRIL 3, 1961

Eddie Murphy (Public Domain)

EDWARD REGAN "EDDIE" MURPHY – BORN IN BROOKLYN!

When his father, Charles, an amateur comedian, died when Murphy was young, Eddie Murphy and his older brother Charlie found themselves in a foster home for a year because their mother had fallen ill. It was that time, Murphy later said, that helped form his sense of humor. His mother, Lillian, later remarried after regaining her health and reunited the family and young Eddie began performing skits he'd written around the age of 15.

Murphy's writing skills came in handy in 1980 when he landed a featured player spot on *Saturday Night Live* during the show's bleak period. It was Murphy's infusion of signature characters (Buckwheat, Gumby, Mr. Robinson, and James Brown) that admittedly kept the show afloat while the era creator/producer, Lorne Michaels was absent.

During and after his tenure at *SNL*, Murphy stretched his stand-up muscles. He released his first album, *Eddie Murphy* in 1982, *Delirious* in 1983 and *Raw* in 1987. However, Murphy virtually abandoned stand-up when his film career took off, starting with 1982's *48 HRS*, co-starring, Nick Nolte. It was a hit as were his next two films, *Trading Places* with Dan Aykroyd and *Beverly Hills Cop* (Murphy's first starring vehicle).

With a trifecta like that out of the box, Murphy was a certified movie star. So naturally they dug up one of his early duds and tried to capitalize on his success and momentum. The dud was *Best Defense*, starring Dudley Moore. Murphy had a small part boosted up in the marketing to be a big part (they dubbed him "Strategic Guest Star"). The main part was

Murphy himself said it was a terrible flick and went back to making hits. Murphy was originally slated to be the 4th Ghostbuster, a part written specifically for him by Dan Aykroyd for the box office hit, *Ghostbusters,* but when scheduling conflicts occurred the part of Winston Zeddemore went to Ernie Hudson.

Few things slowed Murphy down in the early days. Similar to the way he saved, *SNL* from financial ruin, he did the same for the dollar strapped Paramount Studios. Thanks to Murphy the studio came back to profitability. He cranked them out for that studio and others: *The Golden Child, Beverly Hills Cop II, Boomerang, Another 48 Hrs, Vampire in Brooklyn* (co-written with brother, Charlie), *Harlem Nights* (where he wrote, directed and starred alongside, Richard Pryor and Redd Foxx), *Life, Mulan, Dr. Dolittle,* the *Shrek* saga, *Daddy Day Care, The Haunted Mansion* and *Bowfinger* (with Steve Martin).

With haters seeping out of every pore of the entertainment industry, it's no surprise Murphy was criticized for playing multiple parts in his films (*Coming to America, The Nutty Professor, The Klumps,* etc), a practice he rightfully defended since it was an homage to one of his comedy idols, Peter Sellers, who did it in many of his films, most notably *Dr. Strangelove.*

However, with such massive successes there were statistically bound to be failures; especially in a collaborative field such as film. And when Eddie Murphy had a bad film it was always reported as the end of his career. The list of laugh-stoppers included, *Beverly Hills Cop III, Metro, I-Spy, Holy Man* and *The Adventures of Pluto Nash* (rated as one of the worse films ever made with a worldwide box office take of $7 million to prove it).

The film adapted from the Broadway smash hit, *Dreamgirls* was a turning point in Murphy's career. He played a dramatic part which required singing and was rewarded for the stretch. He won the Golden Globe, SAG and Broadcast Film Critics Association awards for his performance and was nominated for a Best Supporting Actor Oscar. He left the auditorium when he lost the Academy Award to Alan Arkin. They said the shocker of a loss was because of his film *Norbit,* in which Murphy played multiple parts, one being a fat woman some found offensive. Any excuse.

Eddie Murphy also sang ... seriously. He did background vocals for songs released by his buddies, The Bus Boys. He released "Boogie in Your Butt" and had hits with "Party All the Time" which was produced by Rick James and "Put Your Mouth on Me." Murphy recorded, "I Was a King," a duet with Shabba Ranks and the reggae song, "Red Light" with Snoop Lion in 2013.

Comedy Central ranked Eddie Murphy #10 on its list of the 100 Greatest Stand-ups of All Time. Box-office takes from Murphy's films make him the 5th-highest grossing actor in the United States. His films have made over $6.6 billion worldwide and he was awarded by the John F. Kennedy Center, the Mark Twain Prize for American Humor in 2015.

https://youtu.be/w1TKGtai7og

* * *

APRIL 3, 1975

Aries Spears performing at The Peppermint Lounge, 1992
(Courtesy of APJ Photos) Source: Bob Sumner

ARIES SPEARS – BORN IN CHICAGO!

Silent film legend, Lon Chaney was billed as "The Man with a Thousand Faces." Aries Spears might have just as many voices. We just haven't had the time to hear them all yet, but the stockpile is daunting. One person having the range to do Martin Luther King, Jr., Chaka Khan, Redd Foxx, Shaquille O'Neal, Louis Farrakhan, Missy Elliot, Malcolm X, Little Richard, Snoop Dogg, Bryant Gumbel, Isabel Sanford, Oscar De La Hoya, DMX, Wayne Brady, Robert DeNiro, Jay-Z, Arnold Schwarzenegger and a myriad of others is pretty dope. That talent was on full display on *MADtv* from 1997-2005 as well as his original characters, such as Belma Buttons, a BET co-host of a BET show and Dollar Bill Montgomery, a full host of a *Politically Incorrect* ghetto parody. Many of these creations were flushed out in Spears head early on.

Spears mother was a jazz singer so he moved around a lot. He found himself in New Jersey going to school and getting into fights. Expulsion only further implanted in his mind that school wasn't for him and maybe something else was. He started doing stand-up at the age of 14 in clubs in New York that would let him on their stage. One was the Uptown in Harlem where he busted his comedy cherry doing impressions of Jack Nicholson and James Brown. From there he was a comedy addict.

Aries Spears loaded up his resume. He did *Def Comedy Jam* and *Showtime at the Apollo*. Then he bounced to the West Coast and got his Hollywood on. He was hired to do a recurring role on the NBC smash hit, *A Different World*. In between he squeezed in *The Adventures of Brisco County, Jr.*, *Crosstown Traffic* and *Soul Train*. He appeared in *Malcolm X, Home of Angeles, The Pest , Jerry McGuire* and had the co-starring role opposite musical superstar, Glenn Frey, in the extremely short-lived (canceled after one episode) CBS misfire, *South of Sunset*. Oh well, when you're a comedian, you can only do one thing when another fails – back on the road and for Spears a destination course to his time on *MADtv*.

After his time on *MADtv*, Aries Spears enjoyed a life of doing stand-up, animated films and television voice-overs, early morning radio show interviews, and displaying his many other impressions such as Don King, Gerald Levert, Paul Mooney, Al Roker, Jesse Jackson, Mother Love, Al Pacino, Sylvester Stallone, LL Cool J, Ray Charles, 50 Cent, Michael Jackson, Allen Iverson, Queen Latifah, Eddie Murphy...

https://youtu.be/eNaZwBMvIf8

✳ ✳ ✳

April 3, 1950

Miss Laura Hayes (Tuezdae Littleton Collection)

Miss Laura Hayes – Born in Oakland, California!

The Bay Area produced a true Queen of Comedy when Laura Hayes got ahold of a microphone. Her former experience as a store booster prepared her for how to steal the laughs out of bar crowds with their arms folded. Hayes got so good with a take charge, but loving style that the up-coming, BETs *Comic View* found a place for her on stage in a mock kitchen for the sole purpose of interacting with the show's host. In 1994 that was Cedric the Entertainer and the gimmick was that Laura had a crush on Ce-dric. The following season Sommore was the host and the new dynamic to involve a man had the show's writer/producer, Darryl Littleton (comedian, D'Militant), make entrances as a delivery guy with a crush on Laura.

Since *Comic View* aired twice a day, six days a week, Laura became a household name. She had a recurring role on *Martin* as Cole's mother. Then BET gave her a show of her own. *The Blackberry Inn* (originally enti-tled *Nuthin But a Woman* in season one) was a comedy soap opera where Laura owned a hotel. The plot was basically all the wacky characters who worked there trying to have sex with the hotel guests. Your typical soap opera. It pushed the envelope in its first season, but in season two the "brains" behind the festivities put everything into over-drive: sex with-out ambiguity and innuendo, double entendre, eye-popping, mugging, speeded up camera shots, jiggling cleavage, gawking, ogling, cartoony sound effects anchored in wholesale buffoonery and cooning. Laura quit.

Hayes went back to acting. She appeared in *The Parent 'Hood, I've Got the Hook-Up, That's Life, The Hughleys* and *King of Queens*. She also got back to doing stand-up and her re-entry into the market place got her placed on the brainchild of comedy producer, Walter Latham, "The Queens of Comedy Tour." Hayes hosted the mammoth outing consisting of Adele Givens, Sommore and Mo'Nique. They made history, not only on the tour, but the film that followed that was released on January 27, 2001.

Things were going fine until an unfortunate incident changed it all. While on the road, a promoter refused to pay Miss Laura her money and the en-suing argument resulted in a stroke and Laura being whisked to the hospi-tal. When she regained consciousness, she retired from stand-up comedy. The year was 2002. Since then she has worked exclusively as an actress. Her credits are extensive: *The Parkers, Whose Making tha Rules, Beauty Shop, Mal-colm in the Middle, All of Us, The Sarah Silverman Program, Meet the Browns, Shadow Hills, The Sea of Dreams, Whatcha Cookin', Act of Faith, Mann & Wife, Little Bitches* and she was a series regular as Mabel on *In the Cut*.

Miss Laura Hayes has produced and directed several short films and remains a mainstay in Black culture.

https://youtu.be/ik4iQe153yo

✳ ✳ ✳

April 3, 1961

T.K. Kirkland (T K Kirkland Collection)

T.K. KIRKLAND – BORN IN NEW JERSEY!

An alumni of the famed Comedy Act Theater, Kirkland cut his teeth in the House Robin Harris Built. His experience served him well when the Black Comedy Boom erupted and frank, raw comedians like Kirkland were in high demand. His style was all about oral sex and how he like to give it and all the different ways he liked to give it. Needless to say, it was a very popular act with the ladies and guys picked up some pointers as well, making T.K. Kirkland the number one underground comic on the circuit before the title was even coveted.

Kirkland took full advantage of his status and gift of gab. He talked so well he became superstar, Eddie Murphy's opening act. Things were going great until Kirkland's fingers got itchy and next thing you know Eddie Murphy's expensive Rolex (is there any other kind?) wrist watch was missing, and so was T.K. Kirkland. Charlie Murphy tracked him down and retribution was dealt out. However, a similar incident happened when Kirkland was arrested for allegedly pilfering jewelry from rap mogul, Russell Simmons's not-so-humble abode.

He walked away from both ordeals with only minor injuries and no regrets. Kirkland admitted he liked to steal, and he went right back to working. He was a presenter at the "Soul Train Comedy Awards." He appeared in the film, *Strays* with Vin Diesel, *The Champagne Gang* and *Good Brutha Bad Brutha.* Kirkland performed on BET's *Comic View,* at Laffapalooza, and the documentary *Phunny Business: A Black Comedy.* And last we heard he was sticking audiences up for big laughs.

https://youtu.be/dwySXR3KlBg

✳ ✳ ✳

APRIL 4, 1968

James Hannah (r) w/ Ricky Harris (*Comedy the Magazine*)

JAMES HANNAH – BORN IN CHICAGO!

James Hannah was a writer's writer. He left his native Chicago after a stint as quality control monitor for All Jokes Aside, Chicago's premier Black comedy club. James would listen to each act and then offer notes to improve that performer's set. Whether they liked it or not most comedians tried his tweaks and found that James Hannah knew comedy. Once he'd established himself as a joke doctor he took his skills to Hollywood beginning as a staff writer for *The Steve Harvey Show* and from there the dominoes fell: *My Wife & Kids, Cedric the Entertainer Presents,* Chris Rock's, *Never Scared, Weekends at the DL* and Tyler Perry's, *House of Payne* as well as penning material for some of the top comedians in the industry.

Hannah was also a comedian's comedian. His lists of credits include, *Def Comedy Jam, Comic View, Bad Boys of Comedy, Laffapolooza, One Mic Stand and Martin Lawrence's First Amendment.* He was a yardstick and an uncompromising comedy personality. His *Truthpaste* on social media was an online hit as James sounded off on subjects many would go nowhere near. He was bold, fearless and scathing.

James Hannah's influence was evident in his era. Many Chicago comedians, such as Deon Cole credit Hannah with getting them into comedy by example and in some cases by writing out their first successful bits and teaching them the art. His work ethic was legendary. While most staff writers pander to series stars, James would tell them that they were not funny and then show them how to be. He was a blunt, brutally honest, unparalleled humor mechanic.

James Hannah died from an aneurysm on February 10, 2014, but his comedic phrasings will live on forever.

https://youtu.be/jIk92uLiIuk

✳ ✳ ✳

APRIL 6TH

Latin Kings of Comedy, Alex Reymundo and Joey Medina at the premiere of Latin Palooza, 2006
(Joey Medina Collection)

ALEX REYMUNDO – BORN IN ACAPULCO!

Raised in Texas, Reymundo worked the Booming Latin comedy circuit as a stand-up in the 90s. He appeared on P. Diddy's *Bad Boys of Comedy* and was one of *The Original Latin Kings of Comedy* with Paul Rodriguez, Cheech Marin, Joey Medina and George Lopez on Showtime and Comedy Central.

Reymundo moved into production. He hosted and produced *The Latin Divas of Comedy* featuring Marilyn Martinez, Sara Contreras, Sandra Valls and Monique Marvez. He also produced *The Payaso Comedy Slam*. In 2007 his one-hour comedy special, *Alex Reymundo Hick-Spanic: Live in Albuquerque* premiered on Comedy Central. In 2008 it won the ALMA award for "Outstanding Comedy Special"

Reymundo has appeared in the films, *The Movement* (2002*),* *El Matador* (2003) and *Permanent Vacation* (2007); on television on *Latino 101,* where he was Alex Reymundo and he lent his vocal talents to the video game, *Cars* in 2006. In 2009 he appeared in *Red-Nexican* once again as Alex Reymundo.

Alex Reymundo's brother-in-law is Blue Collar comedian, Ron White and they tour together.

https://youtu.be/AisGWg1qtPo

✳✳✳

APRIL 7, 1995

Martin Lawrence and Will Smith in 'Bad Boys' (Instagram)

BAD BOYS – RELEASED BY COLUMBIA PICTURES!

Starring Will Smith and Martin Lawrence, this buddy flick is Michael Bay's directorial debut. The story centers around two narcotic detectives in Miami, Florida on a case. After $100 million of their seized heroin is stolen from the police vault, Internal Affairs suspects it was an inside job and the narcotics division has a week to recover the missing drugs or they're going to be shut down. Smith enlist one of his informants (Karen Alexander) to see what she can find out on the streets about a recent big robbery. Alexander and her friend, (Tea Leoni) pose as escorts for a baller's party. Things go south, and Alexander and the baller are killed. Leoni manages to escape but will only tell her tale to Smith. Unfortunately, he's away when she calls into the station, but Lawrence is there and the police captain (Joe Pantoliano) talks him into impersonating Smith (since Leoni never met him) so she will cooperate. Lawrence does, and they meet up.

The conflict arises because Lawrence is married to a jealous wife (aren't they all), and has to now live Smith's life for a while until they can bust the thieves. Smith returns to find out he now has to live Lawrence's life. The problem is that Smith is a happy bachelor with all kinds of women stopping through; women Lawrence has to kick out, so he can continue his investigation and stay faithful to his wife. Needless to say, Smith is not happy living at Lawrence's house. Meanwhile the thieves realize Leoni saw the murder and now they're after her. The chase is on, but after a series of near-death experiences and multiple gun fights, the criminals are killed, order is restored and Lawrence cuffs Smith and Leoni up together so he can go explain to his wife why he's been running around with a white woman.

Bad Boys was produced by Don Simpson and Jerry Bruckheimer. It featured the talents of Theresa Randle, John Salley, Michael Imperioli and Marg Helgenberger. Originally it was written for Jon Lovitz and Dana Carvey. Then once the script was retooled, Arsenio Hall was approached to play the Will Smith role. Hall later admitted turning down that part was the worse career mistake he ever made.

Though it received mixed reviews, *Bad Boys* was a commercial success. On a budget of $19 million it made $65,807,024 domestically and $75,600,000 internationally for a worldwide box office gross of $141,407,024.

https://youtu.be/uwgbgg0XWL4

✳ ✳ ✳

APRIL 7, 1965

Bill Bellamy (Humor Mill Magazine)

WILLIAM "BILL" BELLAMY – BORN IN NEWARK, NEW JERSEY!

If you've ever heard the expression, "Booty Call" you know the work of Bill Bellamy. Whether he invented the term or took it from the streets (as most pop culture is) and popularized it on a national platform (*Def Comedy Jam*) doesn't matter. He owns it. This makes him an indelible part of pop culture.

Bellamy backed up a world-known phrase with a lot of funny and versatility. He became a creature of MTV, hosting and doing VJ duties on *MTV Beach House, MTV Jamz* and a number of others. He stayed in the youth lane with appearances on *Kenan and Kel* as well as doing the voice for the title character in *Cousin Skeeter* on Nickelodeon. He was in the movies *Any Given Sunday, Fled, How to be a Player, Love Jones* and *The Brothers*.

Bellamy was congenial and made a good television host. He held down the festivities on NBC's *Last Comic Standing* and TV-One's *Who's Got Jokes*. His other comedy duties have included traveling everywhere he can as a goodwill ambassador for booty calls.

https://youtu.be/01H6Xbzz4F0

✳ ✳ ✳

APRIL 8, 1998

THE PLAYERS CLUB – RELEASED BY NEW LINE CINEMA!

Ice Cube made his directorial debut in this comedy starring LisaRaye, Bernie Mac, Faizon Love, Jamie Foxx, Terrance Howard, Charlie Murphy, Alex Thomas, A. J. Johnson, Dick Anthony Williams, Monica Calhoun, Tiny Lister, Adele Givens, Michael Clarke Duncan and John Amos.

The story is centered on LisaRaye, who narrates. She tells how as a young, single-mother-to-be she had a put-your-foot down argument with her father and moved out of the house. She subsequently got a job as a shoe store employee barely making ends meets. Then she meets up with a couple of girls who set her straight. Why be that sexy and not get paid for it? She needs to be stripping.

LisaRaye reluctantly gets into the stripping game, working at the Players Club and pulling in undeclared cash. It's all good until her younger cousin gets a job stripping. This relative is soon doing more than stripping. She's getting drunk and doing private parties. LisaRaye knows how wild those private parties can be from personal experience and tries to warn her cousin, who doesn't want to hear it. She's going where the money is. All the while the club owner, (Bernie Mac) has his own problems. He owes $60,000 to a gangster and his time is up. He's beat up and thrown into the trunk of his car. If two crooked cops hadn't shown up and arrested him that would've been it. Once Mac is out of jail retribution takes place on both sides.

During all the club drama, LisaRaye seeks some normalcy by dating the DJ. She discovers that her cousin has been tricked into doing a private party thinking there would be other strippers there. It turns out she is the only stripper and she ends up beaten and raped by the guest of honor who was told she was "that" kind of girl. LisaRaye and the DJ (Jamie Foxx) go

131

to see her and then proceed to the club where Foxx holds a gun on the two strippers who got LisaRaye's cousin ambushed while LisaRaye fights one of them furiously. After beating her down and quitting, LisaRaye knocks the other in the jaw as she and Foxx exit. Their timing is perfect, because just then the gangster and his henchmen shoot up the club and destroy it.

The epilog is that the cousin gets a job at the shoe store then moves back home to live with her mother. LisaRaye and Foxx are a happy couple (He's a top DJ on the radio station and she's a reporter). Bernie Mac was killed by the gangsters. The two strippers that were beat down go work at a new strip club and Bernie's henchmen go to Freaknik.

On a budget of $5 million, *The Players Club* grossed $23,047,939 domestically and $213,546 internationally for a worldwide box office take of $23,261,485.

https://youtu.be/BM_rc2rO-E0

* * *

APRIL 10, 1968

Orlando Jones (Instagram)

ORLANDO JONES – BORN IN MOBILE, ALABAMA!

After getting turned onto entertaining by playing a werewolf in a haunted house in high school, Orlando Jones graduated and got serious. He and fellow comedian, Michael Fechter formed a successful production company, Homeboy's Productions and Marketing, with Michael Jordan being one of their clients. From there Jones got a writing gig for NBC's *A Different World* and a small part on the sitcom as well. He next formed a relationship with the new FOX network. Jones wrote for *Roc*, appeared on *Herman's Head* and co-produced *The Sinbad Show*. Though audiences might best remember him as one of the original cast members on FOX's sketch comedy show, *MADtv*.

With limited sketch comedy experience, Jones relied heavily on his comedy writing and producing skills to cement his stature. He created memorable characters (Dexter St. Croix, Reverend LaMont Nixon Fatback) and provided spot-on impressions (Danny DeVito, Eddie Griffin, Ice Cube). After two seasons he left to do movies and racked up an impressive resume of comedies as well as dramas (*In Harm's Way, Sour Grapes, Woo, Office Space, Magnolia, Drumline, The Replacements, Bedazzled, Double Take, Biker Boyz, The Chicago 8* and more).

Despite big screen achievements, Orlando Jones never strayed far from television. A series of commercials for 7-Up put Jones on the national map for over two years and he took advantage of it. He hosted an HBO special, got his own talk show, guest starred on popular sitcoms (*The Bernie Mac Show, Girlfriends, Everybody Hates Chris*) and had a leading role in an ABC crime drama. He's appeared in documentaries (*Looking for Lenny*), done voice-over work for cartoons (*The Boondocks, Yuletide in the 'hood, Father of the Pride, The Adventures of Chico & Guapo, King of the Hill*) and performs stand-up nationwide.

https://youtu.be/oeioGyTgoiA

✳ ✳ ✳

APRIL 11, 1965

Joey Medina (The Medina Collection)

JOEY MEDINA – BORN IN THE BRONX!

Medina has called himself his own job fair. He worked in fields ranging from Domino's Pizza to police officer (because girls like men in uniform) to boxer (where he won state championship), but it was comedy that kept his interest. It was the fact it entered his life when he was in the rare position of having no job. He also had no home at the time because his wife had kicked him out of it. So, he sought solace at Laff's Comedy Club in Tucson, Arizona, but instead of just a few laughs to forget about his miserable life, Medina found a new life. He observed the comedian on stage and thought – I can do that … and he did.

Joey Medina's credits are expansive. Besides appearing on multi-cultural standup comedy showcases, such as BETs *Comic View* and *Que Locos!* he toured internationally entertaining US troops. Medina financed his first film, *El Matador* using credit cards and favors. It won best film, directing and acting awards at the 8th Annual East L. A. Chicano Film Festival. His Showtime special *Joey Medina: Taking Off the Gloves* was also highly acclaimed. He toured with the Original Latin Kings of Comedy (with Paul Rodriguez, Cheech Marin, George Lopez and Alex Reymundo) and released his comedy CD, suggestively titled, *Below the Belt.*

Medina built a solid track record as a prolific producer. He's overseen almost a half dozen films by using the philosophy learned from his first endeavor – sell to a distributor first – then make the film. He's also produced, *Latin Palooza* for television as well as producing, writing and hosting SiTv's *Circumsized Cinema.* He produced and directed *Cholo Comedy Slam* and hosted his own morning radio show in Los Angeles, for station KXOL 96.3FM.

https://youtu.be/xq4ygQ7AIGk

✳ ✳ ✳

April 13, 1999

Martin Lawrence and Eddie Murphy in Life (Instagram)

Life – Released by Universal Pictures!

Starring Eddie Murphy and Martin Lawrence, *Life* is the second time the duo worked together, and the last time Murphy did an R-rated film. The film dealt with two mismatched men thrown together by bad circumstances. Joined by perception they're both accused of murder when they're in the wrong place (a back alley) at the wrong time (after a man is killed) and get pinned with a crime that gets them sentenced to life in prison in the South; meaning a life of hard labor.

The story of Murphy and Lawrence is told by an old inmate (Obba Babatunde), who spent many of those years with them. He weaves the tale about how they were reluctant allies trying to initially get out through court appeal. That is until Lawrence tries to gain his freedom without including Murphy, who Lawrence views as a component to drag him down. Before entering prison Lawrence was on his way to get a job working for a reputable bank. Murphy was a small-time hustler. For his betrayal Lawrence loses his girl (Sanaa Lathan) on the outside trying to help him. She leaves him for the lawyer working on his appeal. So, life it is. That's when Lawrence decides to join Murphy in his schemes to escape through not-so-legal methods.

The years pass slowly. During their stay the pair meet various inmates who die one by one over the years including prison staff (Nick Cassavetes, Erik Begnal, Brent Jennings). The survivors grow old together, through escape attempt after attempt, punishment after getting caught after punishment. Then one day they are old enough to be assigned to work for a local big shot (Ned Beatty) as domestic help in his home. All is well until the bigshot goes hunting with another visiting bigshot, who turns out to be the murderer responsible for their incarceration. A confrontation occurs, and the old murderer is killed by the bigshot in defense of his workers. A pact is established between the three. The bigshot would release them the next day, but he died, and it was back to prison for them.

As the story is told two young inmates (Heavy D, Bonz Malone) are burying two bodies. They think it must be Lawrence and Murphy who reportedly were burned up in a prison fire. The old narrator smiles knowingly. That's because those two old rascals (90 years old each) had escaped and the final scene has them taking in a live game at Yankee Stadium after so many years of denial from such a basic treat. Now we all smiled.

Life was directed by Ted Demme and written by Robert Ramsey & Matthew Stone. The cast consisted of comedians: Bernie Mac, Guy Torry, Miguel A. Nunez, Jr., Anthony Anderson; actors: Bokeem Woodbine, Clarence Williams III, Michael Taliferro and Barry Shababa Henley as well as musical legend, Rick James.

Life received mixed reviews and was considered a box office failure. On a budget of $80 million *Life* grossed $75,576,029 worldwide. Regardless it was nominated for a NAACP Image Award for Outstanding Motion

Picture, an Academy Award for Best Makeup and won a BMI Film & TV Award for Most Performed Song from a Film.

https://youtu.be/7R_vTEEyxoo

✳ ✳ ✳

APRIL 14, 1963

Buddy Lewis w/ Lady Tuezdae at the Sundance Film Festival, 2009
(The Littleton Collection)

ROLAND "BUDDY" LEWIS – BORN IN GARY, INDIANA!

Some comedians get into comedy and remain comedians. Others get into comedy and clutch everything that comedy encompasses. That's Buddy Lewis. After graduating from Howard University, he worked as a stand-up at novelty joints like the Natural Fudge Café in Hollywood and clubs like The Comedy Act Theater in the hood. He was a founding member of The Comedy Act Players, the improv group that warmed-up the audience before Robin Harris took the stage at the Comedy Act. Lewis went on the stand-up tours and all the stand-up shows TV made available (*Comic View, Def Jam, 1ˢᵗ Amendment, Laffapalooza, Comic's Unleashed*).

When Buddy Lewis wrote he not only penned for himself, but headlining stars (D.L. Hughley, Jamie Foxx) as well as sitcoms (*Tyler Perry's House of Payne*), award shows ("Essence Awards," "Vibe Awards," "Espy Awards") and films (*Compton Christmas Tree*).

The main thing though is when called upon to act just about any competent comic can say lines and not embarrass themselves, but Buddy Lewis actually acts. Not just guest-starring roles (*Reno 911, That's So Raven, The Parkers, Martin*) where take after take can correct a flub. Or films (*Black Dynamite, The Chosen One, The Brothers, Woo*) where the same principle applies.

No, this man does full length stage plays (*The Fabric of a Man, Pearl*) and has taken home the NAACP Theatre Award for Best Supporting Actor two years in a row (on plays written by David E. Talbert and Debbie Allen respectively). Sorry, but few comics have legitimate acting trophies. Then in his spare time he co-created the Jay Pharaoh sitcom, *Black Famous* and is the self-proclaimed "World's Greatest Comic Golfer." He even produced a vlog saying so. Thus, when Buddy Lewis is called on to produce ...

https://youtu.be/pnZZ3EBX3bM

APRIL 15, 1990

IN LIVING COLOR –PREMIERED ON FOX!

The relationship between FOX network and the Wayans family started off fine. Following his back-to-back box office successes of *Hollywood Shuffle* and *I'm Gonna Git You Sucka*, Keenen Ivory Wayans was approached to do a show for the network. He said he wanted to create a variety sketch comedy show. They said fine. He said he wanted Black cast members. They said fine. Then when the show blew up based on the formula set up by Keenen and his co-creator, brother, Daman Wayans, FOX wanted to step in and run the creative side and to the Wayans that wasn't fine.

In Living Color was a golden goose for FOX. Kicking off with a quick snappy welcome from Keenen the show featured the Fly Girls, a group of house dancers choreographed by Rosie Perez and that was a spring board for the careers of Jennifer Lopez and Carrie Anne Inaba. The sketches showcased the talents of Damon Wayans, David Alan Grier, Jim Carrey, Kim Wayans, Tommy Davidson, Kim Coles, Shawn & Marlon Wayans, Kelly Coffield and T'Keyah Crystal Keymah. Jamie Foxx came on in the third season. It was an amazing cast which created indelible characters such as Homey D. Clown, a fully made up circus dweller with a nasty attitude; The Homeboys Shopping Network, two thieves selling boosted goods on public access TV; Ugly Wanda, Jamie Foxx as a disgusting chick; Venus D'Milo, Jim Carrey as a disgusting chick; Fire Marshal Bill, Jim

'In Living Color' cast (Instagram)

Carrey as a disgusting fire marshal with the catchphrase, "Lemme show ya something" and Men on Film, two flamboyantly gay movie critics.

Wayans dream of a variety show had to include musical acts. There were plenty. Live performances were rendered by Queen Latifah, Monie Love, Public Enemy, Kris Kross, Eazy-E, Tupac, Mary J. Blige, 3rd Bass, Father MC, En Vogue, Us3, Gang Starr, MC Lyte, Onyx, Arrested Development, Leaders of the New School and Jodeci. There were guest stars and recurring players: Rodney Dangerfield, Chris Rock, Marc Wilmore, Barry Bond, James Brown, Peter Marshall, Ed O'Neill, Reggie McFadden, Sherman Hemsley and Biz Markie. The show also had powerhouses behind the scenes: a solid comedy writing team headed up by Paul Mooney, and Heavy D and the Boyz performed the opening theme.

From the very first show, *In Living Color* was praised for its rawness, inventiveness and edgy point of view. For two seasons it enjoyed immense popularity and public adoration. That's about the time the tampering comes in and FOX was no different. With a proven winner in their laps they decided to stand up for their right to do the show their way. Big mistake. In those latter seasons executive interference was too much for the Wayans and they walked. The once brilliant television landmark went off the air on May 19, 1994.

Over its five-season run, *in Living Color* amassed 2 Image Awards (Outstanding Variety Series. Outstanding Comedy Series), a PGA Most Promising Producer in Television (Keenen Ivory Wayans), A People's Choice Award, a Primetime Emmy and a TV Land Award for Groundbreaking Show.

https://youtu.be/pGt87ffkTEU

✳ ✳ ✳

APRIL 16, 1965

Martin Lawrence (Humor Mill Magazine)

MARTIN FITZGERALD LAWRENCE – BORN IN FRANKFURT, WEST GERMANY!

Martin Lawrence almost became a boxer. He was a Mid-Atlantic Golden Gloves contender and was eyeing a professional career until an eye injury put a stop to those plans. His plan B turned out to be suitable for some of those same principles he'd learned in boxing and it wasn't long before Lawrence knocked out some obstacles and chalked up an impressive record.

He found his gym in New York at the Improv. His first big bout was on the CBS competition show, *Star Search*. He fought his way to a title bout, but he was robbed. Didn't matter. He got a good look and landed a part on the ABC rebooted sitcom, *What's Happening Now!!* After it was canceled he played journeyman comedian/actor until he got another break in Spike Lee's big screen smash hit *Do the Right Thing*. Lawrence was now in demand. He appeared in *House Party* (which became a franchise), *Talkin' Dirty After Dark* and *Boomerang*.

Lawrence really showed what he could do when he was selected to host *Def Comedy Jam* on HBO. It was a smash hit and Lawrence was now TV's latest champ. He not only defended his title week after week he went into another division when he got his own self-titled sitcom which was a giant hit on FOX. Lawrence followed in the tradition of playing multiple roles in a project. He did it on *Martin*, performing as his female neighbor, Shanaynay and other assorted characters. While doing the sitcom, Lawrence wrote, starred in and directed *A Thin Line Between Love and Hate*.

When *Martin* ended Lawrence went back to the big screen in a string of hits: *Nothing to Lose, Bad Boys* (another franchise) *Life, Blue Streak, Big Momma's House* (also became a franchise), *Wild Hogs, Welcome Home Roscoe Jenkins* and *Death at a Funeral.* In 2014 Lawrence partnered with another TV standard bearer, Kelsey Grammer on the show *Partners.*

Despite his early brand of raunch (he's banned from life from appearing on *Saturday Night Live* after making over the top remarks about female genitalia and hygiene) he's done family content. Lawrence did the voice of an animated character in *Open Season* and starred in Disney's *College Road Trip.*

Martin Lawrence has released two stand up albums and several specials. A multiple acting award nominee, Lawrence has won two NAACP Image awards and a BET Icon Award.

https://youtu.be/0Ct54XPPnN8

✷✷✷

APRIL 18, 1904

Pigmeat Markham Chess Records Mr. Vaudeville LP (Public Domain)

"PIGMEAT" MARKHAM (DEWEY MARKHAM) – BORN IN DURHAM, NORTH CAROLINA!

Markham got his nickname from a risqué routine where he's boasting. A lot about Markham was risqué. His material was loaded with it and in an age of prudes and Bible-Thumpers, he was considered quite a wild fellow. That means he was funny as hell and that kept him working.

Starting out in burlesque, Markham was a blackface minstrel and soon found himself in Bessie Smith's Traveling Revue when he was still in his teens. He invented the "Truckin'" dance that was all the rage in the early 1930s and played the role of Alamo, the cook on *The Andrews Sisters Show* for radio.

In the 1950s, Markham was the unofficial King of Comedy. He played the Apollo Theater more than any other performer. He was practically a regular on Ed Sullivan's *Toast of the Town*. He was in demand at the best venues and even had an international hit record, "Here Comes the Judge," which had a resurgence when the NBC sketch show, *Rowan & Martin's Laugh-In* used the line during a Sammy Davis, Jr. guest skit appearance. The image of Sammy's wacked out judge strutting about proclaiming "Here Comes the Judge" was such a hit that the producers invited the originator on the show to do it and Markham became an overnight celebrity to a new generation.

Over the course of his long career, 'Pigmeat' Markham released nineteen comedy albums and seven singles. He appeared in race films, vaudeville and the top variety shows on television. He was an old school comedy legend who lived to watch comedy go new school and embrace many of his creations. DJ Hollywood, universally known as the "First Rhythmic Rapper" and creator of hip hop, counts his influences as radio disc jockey, Frankie Crocker, The Last Poets and Pigmeat Markham. The rapper says he got his style from Markham's recording of *Here Comes the Judge*. Other rappers, such as Kool Moe Dee confirmed Markham's signature routine as rap's genesis. Pigmeat Markham was the last of his era and that era ended when he left us on December 13, 1981.

https://youtu.be/MK7j-gmSBzo

✳ ✳ ✳

APRIL 18, 2013

CHEECH & CHONG'S ANIMATED MOVIE – RELEASED!

This cartoon version of legendary stoner comedians Cheech Marin and Tommy Chong was directed by Branden and Eric D. Chambers. The full-length film was written by Cheech and Chong and starred their voices. It was released on Blue Ray five days later and is their only film on that format.

Cheech & Chong's Animated Movie is a collections of their famous album routines in animated form. Classics such as Sgt. Stedanko, Afghanistan, Earache My Eye, Ralph & Herbie, Trippin' in Court, Acapulco Gold, Dave's Not Here, Sister Mary Elephant, Let's Make a Dope Deal and others all get the drawn-up treatment. Tying them all together is a cartoon body crab desperately trying to get high off of Tommy Chong's THC ridden scalp.

https://youtu.be/817P98hewyg

✳✳✳

APRIL 19, 1982

Ali Wong (Instagram)

ALEXANDRA "ALI" WONG – BORN IN SAN FRANCISCO, CA!

Wong had a Chinese-American father and a Vietnamese mother, so naturally when she went to UCLA she majored in Asian-American Studies along with a bunch of white kids. Theater was her gateway art to stand-up. That cherry was busted at Brainwash Café after graduation at the age of 23. From there Wong moved to New York where she was hitting stages up to nine times per night.

The intense and enviable work paid off. Soon after being named one of the "10 Comics to Watch" by Variety in 2011, Wong appeared on the *Tonight Show, John Oliver's New York Stand-Up Show*, and *Dave Attell's Comedy Underground Show*. She appeared on *Chelsea, Lately* and was a cast member on *Are You There, Chelsea?* on NBC. She's been on VH-1 (*Best Week Ever*), MTV (*Hey Girl*), the big screen (Oliver Stone's *Savages, Dealin' With Idiots, Father Figures*) and on *Inside Amy Schumer*. She's done voiceovers (*Ralph Wreaks the Internet, OK K.O.! Let's be Heroes, BoJack Horseman, Animals, Angry Birds*) Wong even landed a gig writing for *Fresh Off the Boat* which has been on since 2015 and began work as a series regular on *American Housewife* in 2016.

However, what put Ali Wong in the pop culture conversation were her Netflix specials. Her first one, *Baby Cobra*, was released on Mother's Day 2016 and displays a 7-month pregnant Wong ripping the Neptune Theater in Seattle. It made her a star. So naturally her second special, *Hard Knock Wife* displayed a 7-month pregnant Wong ripping the Winter Garden Theater in Toronto. Obviously Wong likes shooting her specials with a silent partner.

https://youtu.be/oItPQRZ3xpI

✳ ✳ ✳

APRIL 19, 1999

The Boondocks (Public Domain)

THE BOONDOCKS – NATIONAL DEBUT!

The original syndicated comic strip was created by animator, Aaron McGruder. It began as a daily for the online music site Hitlist.com in 1996 and then on The Diamondback. The latter paid McGruder $30 per strip; a boost from the usual compensation of $13. The high wages weren't the problem with The Diamondback. They omitted running the strip and refused to run an apology after making it look as though it was McGruder's fault. So he pulled *The Boondocks* from The Diamondback in 1997, the same year it made its first appearance monthly in the hip hop magazine, *The Source*. It wasn't long before the popular strip was scooped up by Universal Press Syndicate and became a coast-to-coast hit. Satirizing popular culture and racism *The Boondocks* is seen from a black point of view.

The strip was plagued with controversy. McGruder was unyielding in his attacks on Black culture and many of its absurdities. Targets such as BET music videos, Whitney Houston's drug problems, Larry Elder, Cuba Gooding, Jr. and politicians were ripe for ridicule. McGruder spared no one. The chief protagonist was the character of Huey, a pint-sized radical in a little boy's body. He was too young to have learned how to bite his tongue. He and his brother Riley were moved out of South Side Chicago to a neighborhood surrounded by white folks. They're with their World War II veteran grandfather who thinks Huey is too militant and Riley is too materialistic (he wants to be a gangsta). They live next to an interracial couple and their mixed and mixed up daughter, Jazmine, who likes Huey. There's a standard issue friend of Huey's named Michael who's just as crazy as Huey, but with a dash of humor. Rounding out the principle characters is Uncle Ruckus, a blatant Uncle Tom who hates everything Black (including himself) and loves everything white (including Ronald Reagan). The teachers and the principal have a similar dilemma – they love white but fear black and rely on old stereotypes (some from Blaxploitation flicks) to figure out how to handle the two Black brothers.

During the course of its run, other artists helped illustrate *The Boondocks* to keep things on schedule as McGruder's schedule became more and more crammed with commitments, but he always had his hand in the final product. Nevertheless, internal battles came to a head when McGruder put the strip on a six-month hiatus, so he could work on the TV version. *The Boondocks* premiered as a fully animated cartoon on Cartoon Network's Adult Swim in late 2005. McGruder made his announcement in early 2006 about the temporary suspension. Well, after seeing some papers use provided reruns and others opting to move onto other strips, Universal Press cut their losses and informed papers that they shouldn't count on a timely return and they canceled *The Boondocks* September 25, 2006.

https://youtu.be/6mV_i32m9Vo

✱✱✱

APRIL 22, 1961

COMEDIAN BYRON ALLEN BUYS
WEATHER CHANNEL FOR $300M

BYRON ALLEN – BORN IN DETROIT, MICHIGAN!

Allen began doing stand-up comedy as a teenager. His interest in show business began during his childhood, when he would accompany his mother to NBC studios in Burbank where she worked as a publicist.

At age 14, Allen put together his first stand-up routine and began appearing on amateur night at comedy clubs throughout the Los Angeles area. Comedian Jimmie Walker saw Allen's stand-up act and was so impressed that he invited the 14-year-old comedian to join his comedy writing team alongside promising young comedians Jay Leno and David Letterman. At age 18, Allen made his television debut on *The Tonight Show Starring Johnny Carson*. Allen holds the distinction of being the youngest standup comedian ever to have performed on the show.

Watching Allen's network television debut were the producers of NBC's *Real People*, who were so taken with his comfortable, relaxed style that they made him an offer the very next day to co-host the show. And while Allen was getting his feet wet as a television personality, he was also learning the ins and outs of television production. The business of advertising and syndication, he learned in the trenches by personally calling station owners, programming directors and advertisers, one-by-one and market-by-market from his dining room table.

Mr. Allen's foray into television production began in Los Angeles in 1993 when he founded Entertainment Studios with the launch of his first series — *Entertainers with Byron Allen*—a weekly, one-hour series profiling the current stars of film and television. Entertainment Studios produces, distributes, and sells advertising for 32 television series, making it the largest independent producer/distributor of first-run syndicated programming for broadcast television globally.

Among the company's top programs are: Emmy-winning *Cars.TV*, Emmy-nominated *America's Court with Judge Ross* and *We the People With Gloria Allred, Comics Unleashed, ComedyTV, Beautiful Homes & Great Estates, Pets.TV, Recipe.TV, Career Day* and *The Young Icons*. His company also made its first foray into scripted programming, producing two weekly primetime sitcoms: *The First Family* and *Mr. Box Office*.

In 2009, Allen became the first television entrepreneur to own and launch a portfolio of six 24-hour HD television networks simultaneously. The six networks are Pets.TV, Comedy.TV, Recipe.TV, Cars.TV, ES.TV, and MyDestination.TV. Then in 2018 Allen spent 300 million and bought The Weather Channel and so it wasn't too lonely on his way to the pinnicle, in 2019 Byron Allen joined the Sinclair Broadcast Group, Inc as an investor in a 9.6 Billion dollar sports channel deal that gave Allen interest in 21 sports channels coast-to-coast. Not bad for a child comic.

https://youtu.be/-Gj0Eh1kTUs

* * *

APRIL 22, 1967

Sherri Shepherd (Humor Mill Magazine)

SHERRI SHEPHERD – BORN IN CHICAGO, ILLINOIS!

The Comedy Act Theater in Los Angeles, California should've had a Wall of Fame. Just about every comic working the microphone in the late 80s and early 90s hit that stage hosted by legendary comedian, Robin Harris. It was practically a comedy school and Sherri Shepherd was one of its graduates. She took her knowledge she obtained from that training ground and others and staked her claim. She hit the cabaret circuit and was so fine-tuned she made an immediate impression and the next stop was Hollywood sound stages.

Shepherd became known as the actress you didn't want to see when you showed up for an audition. She nailed practically each one she tried out for and built an impressive resume quickly as a series regular on *Cleghorne, Suddenly Susan* and *Less Than Perfect* plus scores of guest starring roles way too many to mention (seriously – look it up). Her filmography is no joke either where she's played everything from animated characters to herself.

Most got a gander at Shepherd as the co-host of the ABC morning chatfest, *The View*. Television news pioneer, Barbara Walters created and led an ensemble of women from different political ideologies (Whoopi Goldberg, Joy Behar, Elisabeth Hasselbeck,) and threw them daily bones to pick over. America's housewives and the unemployed tuned into to watch the feathers fly as the panel grilled or fawned over (Prince) every guest from politicians looking for votes to celebrities seeking forgiveness for a public gaffe. Whatever the case, the ladies of *The View* had power and leverage. Episodes went viral and even guys and the employed started tuning in.

In 2007, Shepherd made history by simply by being put on the same show as Goldberg. Two Black women hosting as network show was "monumental," in the words of Shepherd quoting Goldberg. What was also huge was public reaction to some of Shepherd's controversial views on evolution, religion, voting and race identification. She was part of a chemistry that hit the mark called ratings and did it until 2014.

Following her tenure at *The View* (she did some guest co-hosting in 2015-2016) Sherri Shepherd kept busy. She had her own self-titled show then went back to playing roles that weren't billed as "Herself" on TV and in film. Shepherd hosted games shows and competed on them. She wrote the book *Permission Slips: Every Woman's Guide to Giving Herself a Break* and co-authored *Plan D: How to Lose Weight and Beat Diabetes*. She's produced stage productions and appeared in the Broadway production of *Cinderella*.

Another responsibility of Sherri Shepherd's is polishing up her many awards: Daytime Emmy Award for Outstanding Talk Show Host(s), Boston Society of Film Critic's Award for Best Ensemble cast (*Precious*), two NAACP Image Awards for Outstanding Talk Series, Gracie Award for Leading Actress in a Comedy Series (*Sherri*), and The Braveheart Powerful Women on Hollywood Award.

https://youtu.be/P_N66WKEPME

✳ ✳ ✳

APRIL 23, 1961

George Lopez (The Moreno Collection)

GEORGE LOPEZ – BORN IN MISSION HILLS, CALIFORNIA!

Deserted by his father at 2 months old and his mother at 10 years old, Lopez was raised by his grandmother and step-grandfather. He forged his standup material from race and Mexican-American culture in particular. He made a name for himself with this formula on Latin and mainstream comedy stages. Then after years of ping-ponging successes and failures, Lopez got his career changer.

At the turn of the Century, movie star actress, Sandra Bullock got a thirst for diverse television. She saw a void in Hispanic representation and went to Lopez to do something about it. If she would lend her name and influence to getting a show about Hispanics greenlit, would he star in it? Duh. Not only did George Lopez star in *The George Lopez Show*, he also co-created, wrote and produced it as well. The show was a huge hit for ABC, which had previously received flack for a lack of racial programming. The show ran from 2002-2007 and was a surprise and sustaining hit when it went into syndication. However, Lopez had some choice words for the network's president, Steve McPherson, claiming his sitcom had been given the axe to make TV more-white again. *The George Lopez Show* was replaced by *Cavemen*, a sitcom about cavemen. It was cancelled after 13 episodes.

During his time on the sitcom, Lopez took advantage of his increased profile. He was a cast member on HBO's *Inside the NFL*. He starred in the Disney Christmas film *Naughty or Nice* and in the Robert Rodriguez directed *The Adventures of Shark Boy and Lava Girl*. Lopez garnered accolades for his performance in the HBO drama, *Real Women Have Curves*, receiving the Audience Award for 2002. He was honored with the 2003 Imagen Vision Award, the Latino Spirit Award and was selected as *Time* magazine's "Top 25 Hispanics in America" in 2005.

Also, during the taping of *The George Lopez Show*, its star had a medical emergency. Doctor's informed Lopez that his genetic condition now required an immediate kidney transplant. In stepped his wife, Ann to provide the much-needed organ. Lopez took this life saving blessing to his sitcom in an episode highlighting the threatening affliction.

In 2009, following a couple of years of guest starring and road work, Lopez was back in front of a television audience in a night-time talk show, *Lopez Tonight* on TBS. His show ran for a year undisturbed until 2010 when it was moved back in the time slot, so Conan O'Brien's show could premiere and occupy Lopez's time frame, a move Lopez himself supported. In 2011 *Lopez Tonight* was cancelled, the same year Lopez and Ann's divorce became final.

In 2014 George Lopez signed up to star in a sitcom for FX called *Saint George*. Under the network's agreement a new show had to hit a certain ratings threshold in its first 10 episodes to get a back order of an additional 90. *Saint George* wasn't so blessed and got cancelled in 2014. In March of 2016 TV-Land debuted the sitcom, *Lopez*.

George Lopez has stretched his tentacles creatively. He has co-written his autobiography, became the annual MC for the Playboy Jazz Festival (replacing first perennial host, Bill Cosby) hosted award shows, appeared at the 2009 Inaugural celebration, and collected a plethora of humanitarian awards. All during that time he's also toured as a top standup comedian working on a powerhouse lineup cosisting of Eddie Griffin, D.L. Hughley, Cedric the Entertainer and Charlie Murphy, whose adventures were televised until Murphy passed away in 2017.

https://youtu.be/ikr-QGhndz4

* * *

APRIL 24, 1964

Cedric the Entertainer at Def Comedy Jam 25 (Humor Mill Magazine)

CEDRIC ANDERSON KYLES (CEDRIC THE ENTERTAINER) – BORN IN JEFFERSON CITY, MISSOURI!

Cedric walked through the comedy door with an established work ethic. He'd been a claims adjustor for State Farm and a substitute teacher. How hard could standup comedy be? Beginning right before the Black Comedy Boom in the early 1990s, he'd already grasped his persona and how to "entertain" an audience by working on the chitlin circuit throughout the Mid-West and Down South on runs like Creative Entertainment one-niters, Comedy Zones, Punchlines and other assorted repeated named clubs.

In 1993 he got a major break. After foregoing the advice to concentrate on HBO's *Def Comedy Jam,* Cedric put all his efforts (and at the time the bulk of his new hot and tested material) into a BET *Comic View* appearance where the bigger payoff was hosting that show for a season. All he had to do was beat out over 50 other comics in a city not his own. In 1994 he succeeded first host, D. L. Hughley and the ratings were great. Cedric's price went up and his notoriety skyrocketed.

Next break came from Steve Harvey. In 1996 Cedric was tapped to play Steve's buddy on *The Steve Harvey Show* on the WB. The role of Cedric Robinson gained Cedric numerous Image Awards. Then it was off to the movies. Cedric got a deal and got busy. In rapid succession he appeared in *Ride, Big Momma's House, Kingdom Come, Serving Sara, Barbershop, Ice Age, Intolerable Cruelty, Barbershop 2: Back in Business, Johnson Family Vacation, Lemony Snicket's A Series of Unfortunate Events, Be Cool, Man of the House* and *The Honeymooners.*

During this busy period Cedric took time out to go on tour. "The Original Kings of Comedy" consisted of Bernie Mac, Steve Harvey, Cedric and Guy Torry (as show host). On the second leg of this ground-breaking black comedy tour playing to packed arenas, D.L. Hughley was added (Guy Torry had left to do a TV series) and Steve Harvey took over the hosting duties. Director, Spike Lee filmed it and the tour set the new template of what the public expected for their hard-earned dollars: familiar faces with proven track records individually; now combined to equal an entertainment bargain. Every sub-group and gender and race picked up on it and everybody was some type of royalty before they set foot on a stage.

Cedric made more movies (*Code Name: The Cleaner, Talk to Me, Welcome Home Roscoe Jenkins, Street Kings, Cadillac Records, Larry Crowe, A Haunted House, Top Five*) and went back into television, guest starring and more. He had the short-lived variety show, *Cedric the Entertainer Presents.* He hosted *Who Wants to be a Millionaire* and starred in his TV-Land hit, *The Soul Man* (co-starring Niecy Nash) simultaneously. He's had HBO Comedy Specials, voiced animated films (*Madagascar, Planes* and TV's *The Proud Family* and *The Boondocks*) and did the Broadway revival of David Mamet's *American Buffalo.* He toured with Hughley, along with Eddie Griffin, Georege Lopez and Charlie Murphy. In 2018 he was a regular on Tracy Morgan's *The Last OG* on TBS and starred in *Neighbors* on CBS as well as continuing to be a patron of standup comedy by fronting comedy tours introducing newer or unsung acts.

https://youtu.be/ggRw0gqqzIA

✳ ✳ ✳

APRIL 24, 1967

Ajai Sanders w/ Ralph Harris (The Ajai Sanders Collection)

AJAI SANDERS – BORN IN TRENTON, NEW JERSEY!

Sanders credits iconic actress Diahann Carroll as a major influence. This was well before actually working with the legend on the blockbuster NBC sitcom, *A Different World*. After cutting her comedy teeth doing stand-up at the Comedy Act Theater, under the tutelage and guidance of stand-up master, Robin Harris, Sanders was now a series regular. She'd worked her way up from a small guest-starring role as Gina Deveaux and credits the show's director, Debbie Allen as the reason and counts her as a mentor.

Allen's eyes weren't the only ones who saw Sanders' abilities. In the 90s and up into the 21st Century if the sitcom was Black, Sanders was going to show up. *Martin, Hangin with Mr. Cooper, Fresh Prince of Bel-Air, The Wayans Bros, The 'Parent' Hood, Moesha, Are We There Yet?* and *The Jamie Foxx Show* all got a dose. However, she never strayed far from her comedy roots and stages a long running show called "That Time of the Month" where some of the hottest comediennes in comedy perform.

https://youtu.be/x4PCnqpS1Rc

✳ ✳ ✳

April 26, 1995

Ice Cube and Chris Tucker in 'Friday' (Instagram)

Friday – released by New Line Cinema!

This was rapper, Ice Cube's first foray into comedy and he and co-writer, DJ Pooh knocked it out of the park. The story of a day getting high was a box office success and made co-star, Chris Tucker a movie star. Directed by F. Gary Gray (his first film), Smokey (Tucker), a low-level weed dealer has to pay the dope man (Faizon Love) $200 later that night and he's just kicking it getting high with his newly unemployed buddy Craig (Cube) until he can figure out how he's going to do it. That's pretty much it with the rest being the hilarious antics that situation is bound to set up.

All the neighborhood characters are there. You've got the crackhead (A J Johnson) always looking to get some money for the sole purpose of hitting the pipe; the Pastor (Bernie Mac) who's always lurking around to lay "hands" on the sisters in need of "hands"; the unattended to or horny wife (Kathleen Bradley) who the Pastor lays his "hands"; the husband of the unattended wife (Tony Cox) who catches the one he said vows with and the guy they might've said them in front of involved in "hands" laying; the fine-girl-in-the-ghetto (Nia Long) who Craig likes; the hood bully (Tiny Lister) who whoops you and takes your stuff or vice-versa; the poot-butt (D J Pooh) who gets his stuff taken from the bully and the girl named Felicia who begs so much you've got to tell her "bye" (Angela Means).

All fun and games aside Smokey is in a life or death situation. If he doesn't come up with $200 – it's curtains. Death for Craig, too by association. With his life on the line, Craig starts packing a pistol and gets caught by his dad (John Witherspoon) who tells him to fight with his hands, not a gun. Good advice, but it seems meaningless later when confronting the bully, but he gives the fists thing a try and is losing – badly. So, Craig tries more than his fists – things like a brick and wins. Smokey steals the unconscious bully's money and pays his dealer; the crackhead gets his shoes and *Friday* spawned sequels.

Chris Tucker and Ice Cube in *Friday* (Instagram)

Friday also featured the talents of Anna Maria Horsford, Regina King, Yvette Wilson, Reynaldo Rey, Paula Jai Parker, Ronn Riser, Terri J. Vaughn, WC, Meagan Good, Michael Clarke Duncan, Vickilyn Reynolds and LaWanda Page. On a budget of 3.5 million the film grossed $24,467,564 domestically and $748,354 internationally for a total worldwide box office gross of $28,215,918.

https://youtu.be/dxduMVVnrvU

∗ ∗ ∗

APRIL 27, 1984

CHEECH & CHONG'S *THE CORSICAN BROTHERS* – RELEASED BY ORION PICTURES!

The Alexandre Dumas classic gets the Cheech Marin and Tommy Chong treatment in response to Nancy Reagan's "Just-Say-No-To-Drugs campaign. She used them as poor societal role models and so they made a movie where they never mentioned weed or the smoking of it. Take that, marijuana prude.

The plot takes place in old France and revolves around a rock band (where Cheech and Chong are members) who play music nobody in the village wants to hear and the villagers pay them to stop and leave. Before departing fully, a gypsy tells Cheech and Chong the story of the brothers who tried to overthrow an evil member of the monarchy. Once the story ends the music resumes without complaint.

Other actors involved were more or less related to Cheech and Chong (Shelby Chong, Robbi Chong, Rae Dawn Chong and Rikki Marin) or they were Edie McClurg, Kay Dotrice or Roy Dotrice. This was the duo's sixth film and it grossed $3,772,785.

https://youtu.be/LTgZhdirHKo

✳✳✳

MAY

THIS DAY IN COMEDY...

MAY 2, 1986

JO JO DANCER, YOUR LIFE IS CALLING – RELEASED BY COLUMBIA PICTURES!

Richard Pryor stars in and directed this take on his own life. Starting once he's set himself on fire freebasing cocaine, his spirit leaves his hospital bed-confined smoldering body to relive his existence and see where he went wrong. Up from his youth raised in a brothel to his early struggling stand-up days on the chitlin circuit, the film hits all the major beats of the legendary entertainer's true story.

Jo Jo overindulges once he makes it. Sound familiar? Then again, it's hard to overindulge before you make it because – how? Anyway, Pryor's character overdoes it with women, drugs and his own ego. After he's made his journey through his life, Jo Jo returns to the hospital and climbs back into himself; hopefully a better and more enlightened man.

Jo Jo Dancer, Your Life is Calling is the only film Richard Pryor ever directed. It co-starred Paula Kelly, Carmen McRae, Billy Eckstine, Debbie Allen, Art Evans, Diahnne Abbott, Barbara Williams. Michael Ironside and Wings Hauser. The film was written by Paul Mooney, Rocco Urbisci and Pryor with music by Herbie Hancock. It made $18,034,150 at the box office.

https://youtu.be/yPnPJyQsZ7o

❊❊❊

MAY 3, 1977

Jeff Garcia w/ Thea Vidale (The Littleton Collection)

JEFFREY "JEFF" GARCIA – BORN IN LAPUENTE, CALIFORNIA!

Garcia got started in comedy early – age 15. A few years later he was working steadily in clubs and bars on the Latin circuit in Southern California such as The Wild Coyote. He became a popular club host and in-demand headliner. Known as a quick wit with a strong stage persona, he soon got the attention of mainstream establishments and the industry. Garcia performed on televised standup showcases and toured nationally as well as overseas.

The masses got the biggest Jeff Garcia impact through his voice. Garcia was the voice of Buster the Dog in 1999's *Toy Story 2*. Then he got the role that gained him fame – Sheen Estevez in *Jimmy Neutron: Boy Genius*. The film was nominated for an Academy Award and when it crossed over to television he remained in the Neutron world through its various phases and specials. He also did *Planet Sheen* on Nickelodeon. Garcia has played Pip the Mouse in *Barnyard,* Rinaldo in *Happy Feet* and the Baby Fish in *Finding Nemo*. He was Tipa Bat in *Rio* and a spoonbill in *Rio 2*. He's also voiced numerous video games for Nicktoons including one for *Happy Feet* and *SpongeBob SquarePants.*

However, Jeff Garcia's more than just a funny voice. His face is too, and has been seen in 3 *Strikes, Caroline in the City, Dangerous Minds, Something to Sing About, Mr. Box Office, Transformers: Robots in Disguise* and *Clone High*.

Garcia has done radio with the KMRK-FM 96.1 Wild Wake Up Crew. He performed a half-hour special on *Comedy Central Presents* and hosted *Latin Comedy Fiesta Volume 1*. In 2004 he won the Annie Award for Outstanding Voice Acting in an Animated Television Production.

https://youtu.be/4gtQ6cxUong

✳✳✳

MAY 5, 1965

A.J. Johnson (*Comedy the Magazine*)

A. J. JOHNSON – BORN IN COMPTON, CALIFORNIA!

Famed stunt man and founder of the Black Stuntman's Association, Eddie Smith, was the father of A. J. Johnson. All that rough and tumble lifestyle and talk must've sunk in because Johnson started his comedy career as a comedy heckler. He'd fall through clubs in the hood and talk trash to whoever was on stage from the back of the room. The crazy part was that he was funnier than the so-called professionals he was challenging so it wasn't long before it was suggested he stop getting laughs for free and become what he had been ridiculing – a comedian.

Johnson took to comedy like a dog to a fire hydrant. He's best known as Ezel in the hit 1995 movie *Friday* and playing Eazy-E in music videos. However A.J. Johnson has the distinction of being in every hood TV show ever aired (*Martin, South Central, The Parent 'Hood, The Jamie Foxx Show, Malcolm & Eddie* and *Moesha*) and every hood flick ever seen (*House Party, House Party 3, Players Club, Def Jam's How to be a Playa, Menace II Society, I Got the Hook Up, I Got the Hook Up 2, Woo, O, Hot Boyz, Repos, Roscoe's House of Chicken & Waffles, Hoover Park, Dark Angeles, Rising to the Top, Hittin It!, Baller Blocking, Sweet Hideaway, Lethal Weapon 3, Panther, The Great White Hype* and *B*A*P*S*).

He deserves a Hoodie Award.

https://youtu.be/7YClnIj2Qac

✳ ✳ ✳

May 7, 1939

Dap Sugar Willie 'The Ghost of Davy Crockett album, 1973 (Laff Records)

Dap Sugar Willie (Willie James Anderson) – Born!

There's always been a discrepancy as to where Dap Sugar (a moniker relating to how well he dressed) came from. Some say he was born in Johnston, South Carolina. Others say Philadelphia, Pennsylvania. Well, one thing that's indisputable is that he was damn funny. As part of the party record artists, Dap Sugar's style was raw and dirty. Audiences around the country devoured his stand-up and his LP *The Ghost of Davy Crockett* released by Laff Records in 1973 presents him at his best.

Dap was a polished stage performer but gained his wide spread notoriety through the small screen. He was a recurring character on the CBS hit sitcom, *Good Times*, known as Lenny, a ghetto fixture who always had everything you need, and if he didn't he could get it. He also appeared on *The Jeffersons, CHiPS, Sanford and Son* and the 1986 feature film, *Wildcats*, as a guy in the pool hall.

The rigors of living on the road is the death of a lot of comics and Dap Sugar was no exception. After doing a cross country tour with the Marvelous Entertainment show, "I Need A Man," he fell ill and was hospitalized until he passed away on October 24, 1994 in Los Angeles, California.

https://youtu.be/AZ9c52gTBDY

✳ ✳ ✳

MAY 9, 1987

EDDIE MURPHY'S *UPTOWN COMEDY EXPRESS* – PREMIERED!

Taped Live at the Ebony Showcase Theater in Los Angeles as part of the *On Location* series, this 1-hour comedy special was produced by Eddie Murphy Productions and featured stand-up and sketch performances by up & coming comedians Chris Rock, Marsha Warfield, Barry Sobel, Arsenio Hall and Robert Townsend. The quintet portrayed night club employees with the MC played by Ray Murphy (Eddie Murphy's Uncle Ray).

Directed by Russ Petranto, *Uptown Comedy Express* was written by Ilunga Dell, Margaret Oberman and the five featured comedians. There are uncredited cameos by Jasmine Guy, Paul Mooney, Magic Johnson, Gladys Knight and Eddie Murphy as audience members. Mark Corry and Clint Smith were the producers of the special and played servers on the show. Eddie Murphy was executive producer with musical guests; Eddie Murphy favorites – The Busboys.

https://youtu.be/GmxTJ88u34I

✳✳✳

MAY 13, 1949

Franklyn Ajaye (Comedy Hall of Fame Archives)

FRANKLYN AJAYE – BORN IN BROOKLYN!

Dubbed "The Jazz Comedian" by his admiring peers for his improvisational comedic style, Ajaye was always more artist than fame seeker. A contemporary of mega-star, Richard Pryor, Ajaye shunned the confining and debilitating effects of stardom after witnessing firsthand those effects had on Pryor the man and comedian. Ajaye disdained being put under the show biz microscope. He just wanted to be funny and get paid for it. Hanging out at comedy clubs when he wasn't working or with comics he wasn't working with wasn't his style.

Ajaye had dropped out of college to become a comedian. His original goal was to become a lawyer, but all that flew out the window when he gave stand-up a try at the encouragement of classmates who thought he was funny. Thus, law was history and after giving himself a crash course in the art of levity he was ready to pass the comedy test. Ajaye's first national recognition was on *The Flip Wilson Show* in 1973, the same year he released his first comedy album, *Franklyn Ajaye, Comedian*. In 1974 he debuted on *The Tonight Show Starring Johnny Carson* and dropped his second LP, *I'm a Comedian, Seriously*.

Franklyn Ajaye's known as a strong influence among the generations that followed him. He was smart, insightful and above all funny in a broad range of mediums. There were movies: *Sweet Revenge, Car Wash, Convoy, Stir Crazy, The Jazz Singer*, starring Neil Diamond, *Hysterical, Get Crazy, Fraternity Vacation, Hollywood Shuffle, The Wrong Guys, The 'Burb, The Yakuza* and *Bridesmaids*. Television: *Barney Miller, Partners in Crime, Deadwood, The Greenroom*. Albums: *Don't Smoke Dope, Fry Your Hair* (1977), *Plaid Pants and Psychopaths* (1986) and *Vagabond Jazz & the Abstract Truth* (2004) and the book *Comic Insights: The Art of Standup Comedy*.

In 1997 Ajaye got tired of the whole crazy scene and went south. So south he ended up in Australia, where he stayed. He made occasional trips to the United States for comedy work, but other than that he made his final pilgrimage to the land he would call home following the 2012 election cycle when Ajaye saw just enough and stated, "…as long as America's going in this direction, I'm going in another" and he left for good; carving out a comfortable niche for himself in Sydney, and Melbourne in particular by appearing on the shows, *The Panel* and *Thank God You're Here*. He also mounted one man shows in his new home at the Melbourne International Comedy Festival: "Nothing But The Truth," Talkin Vagabond Jazz," and "Vagabond Jazz & The Abstract Truth."

Franklyn Ajaye has retired from comedy, but is a two-time Emmy nominee for Outstanding Writing in a Variety Series for his work on *In Living Color* and *Politically Incorrect*.

https://youtu.be/QnRCr3HRDto

✳ ✳ ✳

MAY 14, 1982

Anjelah Johnson (r) w/ Vanessa Fraction (The Fraction Collection)

ANJELAH NICOLE JOHNSON – BORN IN SAN JOSE, CALIFORNIA!

Johnson began performing as a Pop Warner cheerleader when she was age eight. This led to winning the Oakland Raiderettes Cheerleaders Rookie of the Year Award. When a friend hit her with the old cliché, "you ought to go to Hollywood" – Johnson did. She took a writing class, studied improv and started running her own shows. She got good fast and got to work.

Following a guest appearance on the short-lived UPN show, *Love, Inc.*, Johnson was cast on *MADtv* on FOX. She did a wide variety of characters, but her breakouts were My Linh/Tammy, the Vietnamese nail shop employee and Bon Qui Qui, the music star who used to be a rude fast food employee. The latter was so popular that Johnson released a studio album as Bon Qui Qui and has appeared in music videos as the character. The interesting thing – she wrote those characters herself because of the writer's strike at the time was limiting the number of skits the show's writers could issue out.

Johnson stayed active. She's been on *Ugly Betty* and *Lopez Tonight* (the TBS George Lopez late-night talk show). She was a spokesperson for Taco Cabana and lent her voice talents to the animated features, *Marmaduke* and *The Book of Life*. Johnson was featured in the films, *Alvin & the Chipmunks: The Squeakquel, Our Family Wedding, Enough Said, Moms' Night Out* and *The Resurrection of Gavin Stone*.

As far as stand-up so far Anjelah Johnson has three stand-up comedy specials (Comedy Central's *Anjelah Johnson: That's How We Do It* then *Homecoming Show* filmed in San Jose, California and *Anjelah Johnson: Nothing Fancy* filmed in Southern California, both on Netflix).

Johnson is of Mexican and Native American descent and in 2008 she was nominated for an ALMA (American Latino Media Arts Award) for Outstanding Female Performance.

https://youtu.be/4iKU_lbpLCc

✳ ✳ ✳

MAY 16, 1967

Sommore (Humor Mill Magazine)

SOMMORE (LORI ANN RAMBOUGH) BORN IN TRENTON, NJ!

A Catholic school graduate, Sommore's original path was business administration, which she studied at Morris Brown College in Atlanta, GA, but somewhere in there, comedy became her business. The comedy community first took notice when she came from nowhere and won the prestigious Birdland Comedy Competition in California. Her next major victory was becoming the first female host of BET *Comic View* in 1995.

Her successful tenure on *Comic View* established her as one of the top stand-ups in Black comedy. She quickly landed guest-starring sitcom roles (*The Hughleys, The Parkers*) and appearances on *Def Jam, Oprah Winfrey, The Tonight Show, Comics Unleashed* and *Nick Cannon's Wild N Out*.

In 2001 Sommore toured internationally, as ¼ of the Original Queens of Comedy and starred in the film and best-selling comedy DVDs. The other Queens were Miss Laura Hayes, Adele Givens and Mo'Nique. Other films included *Friday After Next, Miami Tail, Soul Plane, Something New and Dirty Laundry*. She's done comedy specials, kicked knowledge in documentaries (*Why We Laugh*) and roasted Flavor Flav.

Sommore won Celebrity Fit Club on television, hosted *Love & Hip Hop: Atlanta* and tours regularly as a top stand-up and comedy attraction.

https://youtu.be/jgkcc9gctjk

✳ ✳ ✳

MAY 18, 1950

Gerry Bednob (r) w/ comedian, impressionist, actor and voice-over artist, Greg Eagles
(Greg Eagles Collection)

GERRY BEDNOB – BORN IN TRINIDAD AND TOBAGO!

Bangladeshi is how Bednob describes his act and people know exactly what he's talking about. The Indo-Trinidadian has a gift of being instantly likeable as soon as he touches the microphone. With an easy-going, accessible manner, Bednob charms his audiences and lulls them into a false sense of knowing what's coming next before he cuts left and leaves them surprised and rolling with laughter.

A regular at the Comedy Store in the important days, Bednob was a hilarious stereotype breaker. Hollywood took notice and his talents were allowed to shine in a variety of projects. He appeared in *The 40-Year-Old Virgin, Friday After Next, Furry Vengeance, Encino Man, The Five-Year Engagement, Walk Hard and Zack and Miri Make a Porno*. He had recurring roles on the TV programs, *Wilfred, Undeclared* and *Playing House*. Bednob guest starred on *Seinfeld, The Wonder Years, Mad About You* and *George Lopez*. Gerry Bednob co-starred in *Free Radio as* Bling Bling Shelton on VH-1 and keeps raking up more projects as we type.

https://youtu.be/Cy4PO5rbYho

* * *

MAY 19, 1983

Michael Che (r) w/ Colin Jost at Citi Field in New York, October 12, 2015 (Public Domain)

MICHAEL CHE – BORN IN MANHATTAN!

C he packed in a lot of work in a short amount of time. He started doing stand-up comedy in 2009, putting in multiple sets per night. Three years later he was on *Late Night with David Letterman* and *John Oliver's New York Stand-Up Show*. The following year *Variety* announced Che as one of "10 Comics to Watch"; whereas *Rolling Stone* went one better and named him "One of the 50 Funniest People." That same year he got on the writing staff of the NBC sketch show institution, *Saturday Night Live*, starting as a guest writer then in the blink of an eye he was promoted to regular writer. The following year he became a correspondent for another comedy institution. This time it was *The Daily Show* on Comedy Central. His segments received universal praise from critics. That was the same year Michael Che replaced Cecily Strong on *Saturday Night Live's* long running feature, "Weekend Update," becoming the first Black man to occupy the chair (next to Colin Jost). He also appeared in the Chris Rock film, *Top Five* that year and that was just the first five years in the career of Michael Che.

The rest of Michael Che's career so far has been pushing the envelope on his stand-up comedy special (*Michael Che Matters*), co-hosting the 70th Primetime Emmy Awards (with Jost), collecting awards of his own (two Writer Guild of America Awards for Comedy/Variety-Sketch Series) and keeping his schedule packed.

https://youtu.be/37G0D6s0J8s

✳ ✳ ✳

MAY 21, 1962

Gilbert Esquivel (The Moreno Collection)

GILBERT ESQUIVEL – BORN IN PARMA, IDAHO!

Esquivel's parents were migrant workers who kept the family traveling. Eventually they settled down in Pacoima, California, where young Gilbert became a gangbanger. When he figured out his quality of life aspects would be low based on his lifestyle choice he decided to pull a 180 and get his positive on. He began going to church to hang out with a girl he liked and ended up accepting Jesus as his savior. Next step towards his salvation – he became a comedian. Many of his first bits revolved around his gang life experiences. Why not? It was universal. Who didn't know a gangbanger?

Gilbert Esquivel found work easily after winning a high-profile comedy competition at the oldest comedy club in Southern California, The Ice House, his first year as a comedian. He came in during the comedy boom and took advantage of the television available. He appeared on a multitude of shows including *Que Loco* and BET's *Comic View* (the first Latin to reach the semi-finals) as well as performing nationally in clubs, prisons and colleges. His comedy style appealed to all audiences; which was evident by his rousing reactions at the Apollo Theater and Caesar's Palace.

Esquivel is one of the country's leading Christian Comedians even though he doesn't classify his comedy by that label. He views himself as a Christian doing comedy. Either way, he's a funny role model for the nation's youth. That's the goal. To show kids it's more fun to laugh and live a positive life than to cause misery and end up behind bars or under a tombstone.

https://youtu.be/H8OELh0sRgo

✳ ✳ ✳

MAY 24, 1938

Tommy Chong (r) w/ Cheech Marin, 1972 (Public Domain)

TOMMY CHONG – BORN IN EDMONTON, ALBERTA!

His mother was an Irish-Scotch waitress and his father was a Chinese truck driver. With a set up like that what else would Tommy Chong be but a comedian? However, that would come later. Chong's first love was music. Once he found out playing guitar could get him laid – he played. He was in a soul group called "The Shades." They were successful enough to record a single, open a club and rename themselves. Things were rolling until Chong felt they should rename themselves again. This time to "Four Niggers and a Chink." Some felt it lacked appeal and they changed the name again.

In 1965 the group signed with Gordy Records (a subsidiary of Motown) under the name, Bobby Taylor & the Vancouvers. Chong got fired for getting to a gig late, but Berry Gordy rehired him once Chong told him he'd rather be a Berry Gordy than work for a Berry Gordy and quit. Then he got his wish to be a bigshot when he met Vietnam War draft dodger Cheech Marin in Vancouver.

Cheech & Chong were the comedy duo of the 70s and 80s. Their weed smoking humor captured an entire generation of young, pot-puffing counter-culturalist who consumed all the Grammy winning pair pushed at them and they pushed plenty. The public got hit with 11 albums, 12 singles, 7 movies and over a dozen side projects, including *Born in East L. A.* (which starred only Cheech) before Cheech split and went solo in 1985. They did some reunion stuff later, but for now Tommy Chong was back on his own.

Chong languished for awhile before landing the recurring roles of Leo, the hippie on *That 70s Show* and Carl, the hippie on *Dharma and Greg*. Chong also began an online drug paraphernalia site, selling bongs and other items for weed smokers. His son, Aris ran it and it got busted by two government sting operations. Tommy Chong was drug through the legal process which ended in him being given 9 months in prison. Many felt his celebrity status was used against him and protests were mounted.

During his confinement he convinced his cellmate, Jordan Belfort to write his story and thus introducing the world to "The Wolf of Wall Street." Chong had a documentary done on his time behind bars and court tribulations called *a/k/a/ Tommy Chong* (close to 10,000 copies were seized in a government raid) He lost a gig in an Off-Broadway production, *The Marijuana-Logues* because members of the audience were smoking weed during the performances and this violated Chong's probation. In 2012 he was diagnosed with prostate cancer and attributes his hemp oil treatment to curing him. He was later diagnosed with colorectal cancer and went right back to cannabis for relieve and longevity. Obviously it worked because he competed on ABC's *Dancing with the Stars* in 2014 with professional dancer Peta Murgatroyd and made it to the semi-finals. Tommy Chong was the oldest contestant to have done so. Wonder if it had anything to do with the weed.

https://youtu.be/j1L3eqTpU4E

✳ ✳ ✳

MAY 26, 1970

COTTON COMES TO HARLEM – RELEASED BY UNITED ARTIST!

Based on the Chester Himes novel this Ossie Davis directed hit starred Godfrey Cambridge and Raymond St. Jacques. It was co-written by

Davis and Arnold Perl and the theme song (which was sung by Melba Moore) was also written by … Ossie Davis. Oh, and by the way *Cotton Comes to Harlem* marks the screen debut of Calvin Lockhart, Judy Pace, Cleavon Little and Redd Foxx as a junk dealer.

The story revolves around a back-to-Africa movement and $87,000 in stolen cash. Seems the crooks stuffed their loot into a bale of cotton and dumped it on the streets during their high-speed getaway. Two Harlem detectives are assigned to find the cash, but everybody else who heard about it feels it's their obligation and duty as well and the citywide hunt is on. There are shoot outs, more car chases, sexy women, gangsters and a whole lot of jive talking. It was considered a Blaxploitation film. What would you expect?

Cotton Comes to Harlem boasts an impressive cast of 1970's character actors: Theodore Wilson, Don "Bubba" Bexley, John Anderson, Eugene Roche, J.D. Cannon, Lou Jacobi, Emily Yancy, Dick Sabol and Mabel Robinson. Produced on a budget of $1.2 million the film grossed $5.2 million making it one of the most commercially successful films starring Blacks in Hollywood history and it spawned the sequel,*Come Back Charleston Blue* (which was not written, directed or theme song composed by Ossie Davis).

https://youtu.be/ZYjkAkJNBNM

✳ ✳ ✳

MAY 27, 1916

Willie Best (r) w/ Dudley Dickerson in 'Dangerous Money' (1946) (Public Domain)

WILLIE BEST – BORN IN SUNFLOWER, MISSISSIPPI!

Death is a good career move. Had Willie Best and his ilk passed away as youngsters, the newly "woke" public of the Civil Rights Era might've forgiven their youthful folly. Best would not have had to see his legacy as one of the top Black performers on film stripped away and picked apart like a rancid carcass. He was a king. Why didn't they remember? They once ran to get his autograph and now they ran in the other direction with disgust on their faces at the sight of him.

All he did was make movies. At first he was just a stage performer paying his dues like everybody else on the circuit. One day he got lucky and a man from a studio saw him. Next thing he knew, Best was standing in front of a camera and acting with silent screen superstar, Harold Lloyd in 1930's, *Feet First*. Life was great. Best got screen credit which was rare for bit players,; especially Black ones. Sure, they billed him as "Sleep N Eat," but that was his stage name. Later they'd bill him as "Willie Best" and he was the best. Next to Stepin Fetchit (Lincoln Perry), Best was Hollywood's top Black coon ... I mean actor. At one time the term "coon" was not as reviled as in modern days.

Best made over 100 films and by all accounts he was good in all of them. Bob Hope called him "the best actor I know" and Hal Roach called Best one of the greatest talents he ever met. Let's not think this was Hollywood hyperbole – Best was good. He just excelled in a backwards time when the only way to evolve film comedy for minorities was to sacrifice a few truly wonderful performers, so the mainstream could even get used to seeing non-white faces 30 feet tall.

To list all of Best's films would be a waste as would listing the icons of the era he worked with. The main thing is this man moved from stage to screen to television and packed a wallop in each medium. He only ended up on TV because of a drug bust. Most Black men would've been jailed for knowing how to spell "drug" in those days, but Best was still given the opportunity to work. Real big punishment – you're on TV. This is a testament to how good he was. A good actor saves studios money in re-takes. Best must've been good.

However, money seemed to be an issue. His last screen appearance was in 1955 on the show, *Waterfront*. He died 7 years later at the Motion Picture Country Home in Woodland Hills on February 27, 1962 at the age of 45 and was buried by the Motion Picture Fund.

https://youtu.be/CVZ7k8flGKA?list=PLqDGO1xGeU-5KKy29WWpxwRGyEFXgI4JK

✳ ✳ ✳

MAY 27, 1998

I GOT THE HOOK-UP – RELEASED BY MIRAMAX FILMS!

This was a pure Master P production. As No Limit Records' first film he co-wrote it, co-produced it, did some of the music and co-stars in this tale of two merchandise-is-in-their-van hustlers who come up when a mistake is made. Thanks to dumb luck they (Master P and A.J. Johnson) now have a fleet of erroneously delivered cell phones in a mobile phone hungry hood. Eureka! Of course, whenever there's new money to be made, local gangsters always want their cut and whenever there's criminals the authorities get involved and in the movies that usually means the FBI to make it seem even more important.

I Got the Hook-Up features the acting talents of Ice Cube, C-Murder, Tiny Lister, Mystikal, Mr. Serv-On, Fiend, Mia X and Snoop Dogg. Also getting their thespian on was Sheryl Underwood, Tangie Ambrose, Helen Martin, Joe Estevez, Richard Keats, Gretchen Palmer, Anthony Boswell, Frantz Turner, Harrison White and John Witherspoon.

The film was directed by Michael Martin and distributed by Dimension Films. The soundtrack made it to #1 on the *Top R&B/Hip-Hop Albums* and #3 on the *Billboard* 200. On a budget of $3.5 million, *I Got the Hook-Up* grossed $10,317,779 at the box office.

https://youtu.be/sHHL5nVpJ0w

✳ ✳ ✳

MAY 28, 2004

SOUL PLANE – RELEASED BY METRO-GOLDWYN-MEYER!

Labeled as a comedy, *Soul Plane* became known as a disaster film and the first major casualty of the "DVD Bootleg Era." The flick was out on the streets before the premiere. At the box office it lost money big time, but out-of-the-trunk-of-cars it was a resounding hit. Everybody saw it – liked it or not. Based on a popular comedic premise of the time about "what if there was a Black airline?," *Soul Plane* misses none of the stereotypes prevalent during that period.

In Kevin Hart's first starring movie role, he plays the guy who owns the Black airline. After digesting some bad stroganoff and getting the bubblies on a standard airline, Hart is stuck in a malfunctioning toilet while his dog is sucked through the jet engine. So he sues and uses his newfound fortune to buy, what else? – his own airline. Dice hanging from the rearview mirror in the cockpit, malt liquor being served, a disco, a casino, a strip club, a hot tub, spinners and hydraulics are welcome additions for the predominantly Black patrons. The white fliers consists of one family and before the flight ends the wife (Missi Pyle) is turned on by brothers, the daughter is intent on screwing a brother, the little boy (Ryan Pinkston) goes wigger and dad (Tom Arnold) hooks up with security guard, Mo'Nique.

Hart's airline (departing out of Malcolm X Terminal) is fine until they take off. The pilot (Snoop Dogg) is scared of heights and has to fly low. Doesn't matter for long because he "dies" after taking some mushrooms that didn't agree with him. Now it's up to Hart to land his own plane and with the help of a flight attendant (Sophia Vergara) he pulls it off. Yay!

Soul Plane was directed by Jessy Terrero and written by Bo Zenga and Chuck Wilson. It co-starred D.L. Hughley, Method Man, Loni Love, K.D. Aubert, Sommore, Queen Latifah, John Witherspoon, Lil Jon, Ying Yang Twins, Richard T. Jones, Brian Hooks, Bernie Mac, Arielle Kebbel, Gary Anthony Williams and Godfrey. On a budget of $16 million, *Soul Plane* took in $14,190,750 in the US and $631,596 overseas for a worldwide box office take of $14,822,346.

https://youtu.be/-GlwowBL_bY

✳ ✳ ✳

MAY 29, 1963

Earthquake (Humor Mill Magazine)

EARTHQUAKE – BORN IN WASHINGTON, DC!

Actor, Voice-Over Artist, Radio Personality and stand-up comedian, Earthquake is the name used to guard his secret identity as a regular person, (Nathaniel Stroman), which is only known to his bank and dry cleaners. Under his persona of Earthquake, Stroman shot comedy specials for HBO, appeared in the Kevin Smith film, *Clerks II* and the movie *Longshots*. On the TV front, Earthquake had a recurring role in *Everybody Hates Chris* and he supplied to voice of Root the Rooster in the film and video of *Back at the Barnyard.*

The stage moniker was coined by his mother. Seems she had tried to avoid having this child. She'd used the diaphragm and condoms, but Nathaniel came into the world anyway. So, she decided to name him after a natural disaster and he's been wrecking house ever since. However, before he pursued his destiny, Quake was sidetracked with the more pressing business of living. His mother raised him in a poverty-stricken part of town. It wasn't until after lunch was served at school that Quake had the strength to concentrate on his studies. Meaning he was a half-ass student because he could focus for half the day. His report card was sprinkled with "F"s.

Regardless of his academic failings, Earthquake showed promise as a cut-up. He was the class clown always getting laughs out of the other kids. When he thought about it later in life it upset him that none of his teachers had the vision or forethought to point him in the direction of a performer.

Without clear-cut guidance Earthquake enlisted in the Air Force right out of high school. He stayed there for eleven years, where he saw the world and got out of his mother's house and the corruptive neighborhood where it sat. The military looked like the snug fit Earthquake had been searching for. He'd found his niche in life and was content to be a career military man. Then the Gulf War hit and the last man you would've ever suspected became a conscientious objector. Earthquake refused to fight in a war aimed at killing brown people and taking their resources. He was dishonorably discharged.

Prior to letting his convictions point him in his own direction, the military had given Earthquake an option he'd never considered. There was a talent show, "Tops and Blues." He entered it and was bitten. Once out of the service he dug into comedy, gigging in dinky clubs and holes-in-the-wall, until he was good enough to ask for and receive money for his services. He also contributed to *Steve Harvey's Morning Show* (radio). Before long he had his own spot – The Uptown Comedy Corner in the Buckhead District of Atlanta, Georgia. The hottest talent in Black comedy came through his club. This gave him much needed exposure and he opened up two more clubs: one in Dallas the other in Atlanta.

Earthquake took advantage of the Black Comedy Boom of the early 1990s and was seen on the major stand-up shows of the day; most notably, BETs *Comic View* and HBO's *Def Comedy Jam*. His performance on the latter was so well received that he was recruited to be on the "Def Comedy Jam Tour." From there his career blossomed.

Touring was the hot ticket for comedians during the boom and Earthquake was no exception. Besides, the "Def Jam Tour" he also joined the "Latham Entertainment Presents Comedy Tour" in 2002. In 2005 he did "About Goddamn Time," the All-Star Def Comedy Jam in 2007 and TBS's Comedy Festival Lollapalooza in 2008. Earthquake was the main attraction on Shaq's All-Star Comedy Jam Special in 2009 and in 2011 he popped up on TV One's *Way Black When*. 2013 saw Earthquake make a high-profile appearance on ABC's *The View* as a favorite of co-host, Whoopi Goldberg and also a return to radio. He was full time on station WBLS during the weekdays until his departure in 2016. In 2018 he opened up *Quake's House* on Kevin Hart's LOL Radio on Sirius XM and became the show everybody talked about in the barber shop (so you know everybody was talking about it). And the saga continues...

https://youtu.be/qUNNI7TLGSg

✳ ✳ ✳

May 30, 1902

Lincoln Perry aka Stepin Fetchit, 1959 (Public Domain)

Stepin Fetchit (Lincoln Theodore Monroe Andrew Perry) – Born in Key West, Florida!

He was billed professionally as "The Laziest Man in the World," so much so that when he ended his shows he'd have another man come out on stage and lift up Perry's arm to wave good-bye to the audience. Fact is, he was one of the most accomplished men of his generation. Under the moniker of Stepin Fetchit, Lincoln Perry became the first Black movie star, film millionaire and the first Black actor to get an on screen credit. He was the first with a five-year studio contract and one of the first to have an on-screen romance with a Black woman in a non-Black film. Perry made 44 movies in 12 years and was in the first studio film with an all-Black cast (*Hearts of Dixie*). Lincoln Perry opened the doors in Hollywood for every Black performer who followed. Of course, when one blazes a trail they're also the ones who get stuck, pricked, lacerated and slapped in the face by stubborn and unforeseen obstacles.

Stepin Fetchit was branded a coon. This label wasn't imposed in the 1920s and 30s, when he had Black and white movie goers rushing out to his films to share a collective laugh at one individual despite his color or race. Nobody frowned or turned up their noses when Perry and his good friend, Will Rogers (the first recognized stand-up comedian) were making block-buster flicks together and palling around off-set. The backlash caught up to Perry later when America as a whole began to examine its own history and Stepin Fetchit was deemed a stain on the tapestry of the nation. He and his ilk represented a time the country would much sooner forget.

Perry made films that in hindsight (and for some in real time) disgraced Black people and created harmful images of buffoonery and subservient behavior. His dimwitted antics did not set well particularly with the NAACP. They didn't grasp what his audiences of the time did; that his persona was a throwback to the trickster archetype from slavery days. Perry was simply playing the put upon servant who faked ignorance of how to use tools or do a job so somebody else would end up doing the work (preferably the white man). Such characters developed in Africa through griots (storytellers).

Perry used the prankster persona in real life a well. Though he owned acres of property in costly California with limousines and Asian servants, Perry was still thought to be just a lucky fool. Well, the supposed idiot was also an accomplished writer for the well-read publication, *The Chicago Defender.* He even fooled the studios by having two telephones. One he'd answered in his buffoon persona the other he would answer as the intelligent, Lincoln Perry.

The man later known as Stepin Fetchit got started in show business at 12 years old. Since his mother wanted him to be a dentist to the point of having him adopted by some guy with a white jacket, dental instruments and a sign in the door, Perry waited for his opening (probably when the dentist had his face in somebody's mouth) and ran away to join the carnival. He broke in as a singer and tap dancer. From there he developed into a comic and managed a carnival. He merged into vaudeville, films and stardom.

Naturally, hubris took over. Perry was in uncharted territory. No Black man has ever breathed this rarified air and in 1940 he walked away from his lucrative career because he wasn't making as much money as his white movie star counterparts. Another factor was his out-of-control lifestyle of drunken and drug-induced club-hopping up and down Central Avenue with a couple of his chauffeurs and Perry's penchant for the company of underage females (16 was his preference). The man was a PR nightmare.

Stepin Fetchit languished for years in obscurity as the studios merely replaced him with his type – Willie Best and Mantan Moreland. Meanwhile Perry still had outgo, but there was no income. He'd stooped to working county fairs with midget (I mean "little people") acts. So, he officially swallowed his pride and returned to motion pictures in 1945, but it wasn't the same. Stepin Fetchit was no longer a star and had to settle for cameo roles. In the next eight years he only made 8 films. Times were so bad that in 1947 he filed for bankruptcy with only $146 in the bank.

The rest of Perry's days were a steady downward spiral. In 1968 his son went on a rampage of violence, shooting 20 people on the Pennsylvania Turnpike, killing four (including his wife) before turning his carbine rifle on himself. There was talk of a conspiracy and that the young man was set up, but in any case this was a hardship for Perry. After making only three more films (one a TV flick) he had a stroke in 1976 which ended his film career and he was forced to move into the Motion Picture and Television Country House and Hospital where he passed away on November 19, 1985. The stated cause was heart failure. However, Lincoln Perry had expired long before that date.

People in general, but especially Blacks had turned their backs on Perry long ago. In the Civil Rights era of defiance and pride which gave a raised finger to the traditions of old (the trickster) his own race grew to hate the very sight of this white man's nigger. America was embroiled in a revolution it could not ignore and there was no room for sentimentality for such a loathsome character, but it was the 1968 CBS special, *Black History: Lost, Stolen or Strayed*, written by Andy Rooney (he got an Emmy for it) that shined the burning hot light on the Black experience and Perry. He was blamed for betraying his race and being a negative image who's works should be banned and never spoken of again. He was a disgrace to all mankind, a smear on our collective humanity and should pay a stiff penalty for his odious and repulsive deeds by being forever shunned and reviled. Society has no choice but to rebuke him and cast him from our memories for the remainder of Earth's history and beyond. The narrator advocating this posture in that damning broadcast was comedian, Bill Cosby.

https://youtu.be/5qALvc-MIDY

✳ ✳ ✳

MAY 31, 2002

UNDERCOVER BROTHER – RELEASED BY UNIVERSAL PICTURES!

Eddie Griffin stars as the title character that was created by John Ridley. Undercover Brother has but one purpose – stick it to the Man. Based on the hit Internet sensation, the film centers on the renegade's recruitment into B.R.O.T.H.E.R.H.O.O.D., an organization formed specifically to stick it to the Man. Seems the Man has been trying to make blackness look bad and has a mind-altering drug floating around the hood. It makes Black leaders and celebrities in the community go all coon and somebody has to put a stop to it.

Griffin infiltrates the Man's criminal organization, but soon loses himself as he is under the influence of a deadly white woman (Is there any other kind?) sent by who else? The Man. Before long, *Undercover Brother* is an out & out Tom. Despite the pigment of his skin – he's been converted into a white boy. It takes a bold, soul sister to get him back in touch with his blackness and B.R.O.T.H.E.R.H.O.O.D. has one of those. Griffin is back to Black and the white girl follows him to that side. She's a traitor to her own (Surprised?). In a climatic plot to get James Brown to coon Griffin disguises himself as Brown and blows the case wide open (as they say in movie review speak) and goes off into the sunset with the sistah.

Directed by Malcolm D. Lee, *Undercover Brother* was well-received by the critics. It won a Black Reel Award for Best Film Song and one for the film itself by the Washington DC Area Film Critics Association Awards. The movie featured Chris Kattan, Dave Chappelle, Chi McBride, Gary Anthony Williams, Neil Patrick Harris, Aunjanue Ellis, Denise Richards, Billy Dee Williams, Jack Noseworthy and James Brown. Written by Michael McCullers and co-executive produced by Ridley, the music was provided by Stanley Clarke. On a budget of $25 million *Undercover Brother* earned $41.6 million.

https://youtu.be/ubV3t9_CwDc

✳ ✳ ✳

WANTED

— LIVE AND UNCENSORED —

RICHARD PRYOR

★ ★ ★ ★ ★ ★ ★ ★ ★ ★ ★

CHICAGO
AUDITORIUM THEATRE

SEPT 28, 1978

SHOWTIME : 8:00 P.M. TICKETS : $15.00 • $20.00 • $25.00

JUNE

THIS DAY IN COMEDY...

June 1, 1961

Mark Curry (Humor Mill Magazine)

Mark G. Curry – Born in Oakland, California!

Once Curry had put in time as an up & coming stand-up comedian on the Bay Area circuit in rough clubs and bars like The End Zone and Sweet Jimmie's, he was ready for the visual mediums where cameras captured if you were really funny or not and kept it on record. His first outing was the Martin Lawrence film debut, *Talkin' Dirty After Dark* in 1991. It must've impressed the right people because 1992 became Curry's breakout year.

A year after his first film Mark Curry found himself doing two television shows. He took over as host on the syndicated hit, *Showtime at the Apollo*. At the same time his ABC sitcom, *Hangin' with Mr. Cooper* premiered. On that show Curry played a retired NBA baller who is now a substitute teacher when he is not teaching gym. During and following "Cooper's" successful five season run, Curry appeared in the motion pictures, *Panther*, *The Fanatics*, *Switchback* and *Armageddon*; and guest starred on *Living Single*, *The Jamie Foxx Show* and *Martin*.

After the turn of the century things kept rolling. Mark Curry had a recurring role on *The Drew Carey Show*. He played Carey's boss. On the Holly Robinson-Peete vehicle, *For Your Love*, he played a doctor and hosted the Comedy Central show, *Don't Forget Your Toothbrush*. Curry did movies for the Disney Channel and a few seasons later he hosted *Animal Tails* and then *Coming to the Stage*.

In 2006 tragedy struck. While doing laundry (the butler must've been off that day) Mark Curry was burned over 20% of his body when an aerosol can accidently fell behind a water heater and exploded. During a lengthy recuperative period, excruciating pain and being placed in a medically induced coma for several months, Curry contemplated suicide. It was the intervention of fellow comedians, Sinbad and Bill Cosby that kept Curry's mind right and put him back on track. He got it together and went back to work.

In November 2008 Mark Curry returned with a stand-up routine on the Comedy Central special, *Laffapalooza* hosted by Tracy Morgan. The following year, Curry found himself as host of *FoxxHole Live* on Satellite Radio Sirius. He toured with Earthquake, Sommore, Tony Rock and Bruce, Bruce under the title, "The Royal Comedy Tour" followed up with "Sommore's Standing Ovation Comedy Tour" featuring Tommy Davidson and Bill Bellamy. Curry co-starred opposite Sheryl Lee Ralph in the Bounce sitcom, *One Love* and had the role of Marcus on the Scott Baio comedy series, *See Dad Run* for Nick at Nite for 2012-2015.

Mark Curry has appeared in music videos and continues touring as a stand-up comedian.

https://youtu.be/HArLGNjQjC0

✳✳✳

JUNE 2, 1971

Jo Koy autographing his CD for a Marine at Camp Pendleton (Public Domain)

JO KOY – BORN IN SPANAWAY, WASHINGTON!

Though Koy began his career in 1994 he is considered a pioneering comedian in the Filipino community. The product of a European-American father in the Air Force and a pure Filipino mother, Jo Koy was a military baby. Once Koy graduated high school, the family moved to Las Vegas, Nevada where he took up stand-up comedy after handling a little formality like dropping out of college.

Koy developed his act at Catch a Rising Star at the MGM Grand Hotel and Casino. With his confidence built he rented the Huntridge Theater and hustled his own show. A Los Angeles talent agent got a load of Koy and booked him on his first national TV spot: BET's *Comic View*. The urban circuit agreed with Koy and he also appeared on *Laffapalooza* and won on *Showtime at the Apollo*. He toured internationally performing for the troops and then became a cable television favorite. Koy was a regular on the VH1 series of *I Love the 70s, 80's and 90's*. He was on Tru TV's *World's Dumbest* and *New Millennium* and *Chelsea Lately* starring Chelsea Handler. He also has the distinction of being one of the rare breed of comedian to receive a standing ovation on *The Tonight Show* starring Jay Leno.

Koy's career has not been without controversy. He was derailed for a while after making an anti-gay slur while the cameras were rolling. This faux pas forced Koy to issue a public apology. On the flip side his philanthropic organization, the Jo Koy Foundation does shows for charity, donating the tickets sales proceeds to The Children's Hospital of Orange County.

Koy has toured with Carlos Mencia, done commercials for AMP'D Mobile Phone, been a semi-regular on *The Adam Carolla Show*, had his own Comedy Central special and won the prestigious Gemini Award; one of Canada's highest honors.

https://youtu.be/X0Ny6BAac9o

✱ ✱ ✱

JUNE 5, 1981

NICE DREAMS – RELEASED BY COLUMBIA PICTURES!

Directed by Tommy Chong this was Cheech & Chong's third film. *Nice Dreams* is the simple story of two weed-heads who pretend to sell tasty confections out of their ice cream truck, but they're really pushing weed. What else do you expect from weed-heads? Their goal is to make a lot of money, buy an island, get high and play music all day surrounded by beautiful girls. Thanks to a free stash unwittingly provided by their pot growing neighbor who lives below them – our boys are on their way. The money rolls in.

Obviously, whenever there's weed flowing the cops show up. They're onto the boys and are on their tails, but these are movie cops meaning they don't know squat and screwing up is the reason they're in the movie. While one cop (Stacy Keach) smokes the weed himself in an undercover ploy, his partners arrest the weed growing neighbor and not the weed selling ice cream truck drivers. After a series of misadventures including cocaine snorting, bad check passing, an attempted threesome, a released crazy husband, naked hotel scaling, a visit to a mental institution, straitjacketing, LSD popping and a lizard man spotting our heroes become male strippers to fulfill their broken dream. The End.

Nice Dreams featured the talents of Paul Reubens, Sandra Bernhard, Evelyn Guerrero, Tony Cox and Timothy Leary. The film made $37 million at the box office.

https://youtu.be/YRd1REDjJNo

✳ ✳ ✳

JUNE 8, 1923

George Kirby, 1964 (Public Domain)

GEORGE KIRBY – BORN IN CHICAGO!

Kirby got his beginning in show business at the Club DeLisa on the South Side of Chicago. He cut a record as a stand-up blues singer in 1947 for Aristocrat Records. His easily accessible style and warm demeanor made him a favorite among other performers. It also made Kirby an unwitting pioneer for Civil Rights in entertainment when singer, Bobby Darin insisted Kirby open for him during his first run at the famed Copacabana, a club not known for allowing non-headlining "Negros" to perform or be in the show room. Darin and Kirby changed all that. The club forever changed its racist policy in the name of humanity and commerce.

Throughout Kirby's career he had mixed audiences. Since he was an impressionist few could find division in laughing at familiar voices. He had universal appeal, doing impressions of white icons like John Wayne, Clark Gable and Walter Brennan and not just Black performers like Nat King Cole (who he nailed). Kirby was innovative in his choice of targets. He did female singers such as Ella Fitzgerald and with a singer's range and dexterity to pull it off flawlessly.

Television was a friend to Kirby as he worked across the board. He appeared on *The Ed Sullivan Show*, *The Dean Martin Show*, *The Temptations Show*, *The Jackie Gleason Show*, *Rowan & Martin's Laugh-In*, *Perry Como's Kraft Music Hall* and *The Tonight Show starring Johnny Carson*. Kirby had his own show for a short time and was a regular on *The Kopycats*, a show with impressionists such as Frank Gorshin, Marilyn Michaels, Charlie Callas, Fred Travalena and Rich Little acting out famous scenes doing the impressions of those actors. Kirby was riding high.

The success for impressionists was tenuous. Like magicians at the turn of the 20th Century, the day of the public's rapt attention to the novelty art form cooled and acts like Kirby were left staring out at more tables and chairs than patrons. Gigs dried up and Kirby, a functioning heroin addict began dealing to make up the lost income. This led to a loss of freedom. Kirby was busted and sent to prison for 42 months on a plea bargain. His career never did recover to its former glory, as he was a repeat offender and his health was failing. He was diagnosed with Parkinson's disease and died of it in a Las Vegas nursing home on September 30, 1995.

https://youtu.be/qxayIx8bjfM

✳ ✳ ✳

JUNE 8, 1973

Shappi Khorsandi (The Shappi Khorsandi Collection)

SHAPARAK "SHAPPI" KHORSANDI – BORN IN TEHRAN, IRAN!

In her first book, *The Beginner's Guide to Acting English*, Khorsandi says she was called a "terrorist." Naturally, she's a stand-up comic from Iran. Terrorist might be one of the lighter heckles levied her way and we're sure the heckler wasn't trying to say her jokes were the bomb. Considering she's from a family of comedians what's a little cliché slight anyway? Her brother, Peyvand and father, Hadi were both comedians. As a matter of fact, it was the hijinks of Hadi and an anti-regime poem he wrote that forced the family to flee from Iran and settle in London, England.

After earning her degree in Drama, Theatre and Television at the former King Alfred's College, Khorsandi got into the family business of stand-up. She learned her craft at Joe Wilson's Comedy Madhouse and was a hit at the Melbourne Comedy Festival, later being nominated for a Chortle Award for Best Breakthrough Act. Khorsandi made her presence known on BBC Radio 4 on a slate of programs and also hosted her own. She's done television: *Rove, Live at the Apollo, Michael McIntyre's Comedy Roadshow, Friday Night with Jonathan Ross, 8 Out of 10 Cats, I'm a Celebrity … Get Me Out of Here,* has an online column, did game shows, published two books and lends her time and talent to many worthy causes.

Like her father before her, Shappi Khorsandi is political as well. She is a proclaimed friend and supporter of Labour. She is also the president of the British Humanist Association, which promotes people to live good lives without religious or superstitious beliefs. And you call that terrorism?

https://youtu.be/hgTZ0VY0dYk

* * *

JUNE 8, 1958

Everybody came to see a young Keenen Ivory Wayans (wearing shades) (APJ Photos)
Source: Bob Sumner, Omar Epps to the far right

KEENEN IVORY WAYANS – BORN IN HARLEM!

This son of a devout Jehovah Witness stepped out on faith when he walked away from Tuskegee University and his engineering scholarship a semester prior to his graduation to become a comic. As fate (or providence) would have it, he met Robert Townsend when he did his first set at the Improv in New York. They drove across country together to Hollywood. Wayans got a part on the show, *For Love and Honor*. A year later his traveling buddy Townsend got back to him with an idea.

Hollywood Shuffle was a satirical take on the problems Black actors have keeping their dignity in Hollywood. The pair co-wrote the script and Townsend directed it. With that money he made from the surprise hit plus the dough he got for writing Eddie Murphy's, *Raw*, Wayans made his own breakout motion picture, *I'm Gonna Git You Sucka*, a parody of Blaxploitation flicks of the 1970s. It was a hit and the new FOX network approached Wayans about doing his own show. He chose the variety format and *In Living Color* was born.

From the jump network executives were terrified at some of the concepts Wayans had in mind and bit their collective nails until the show's premiere and it became an overnight ratings bonanza. On Monday morning everybody was talking about how funny the show had been that Sunday night. With a cast of virtual newcomers (Tommy Davidson, Kim Coles, David Alan Grier, Damon Wayans, Kim Wayans, T'Keyah Crystal Yemah, Kelly Coffield and Jim Carrey. Shawn Wayans served as the show's resident DJ. Later Jamie Foxx signed on), comedy genius, Paul Mooney as the top writer and the Fly Girls dancers with the choreography of Rosie Perez (Jennifer Lopez came aboard on Season 3), the party got started in 1990 and didn't stop until 1994.

After severing his ties with FOX, Wayans made a series of films. He starred in *Low Down Dirty Shame* (which he also wrote and directed) and *Glimmer Man*. He produced, *Don't be a Menace in South Central While Drinking Your Juice in the Hood*. Then he took time off to host a self-titled late night talk show in 1997. Once that wrapped he directed the first 2 *Scary Movies* (conceived by his brothers, Shawn and Marlon), produced and directed, *White Chicks, Little Man and Dance Flick*. All family affairs. All extremely profitable.

Keenen Ivory Wayans has the awards to show it was worth the drive from New York. He's received two Image Awards, a PGA, People's Choice, TV-Land and a Primetime Emmy.

https://youtu.be/PRuZ54UCrm8

✳ ✳ ✳

JUNE 9, 1980

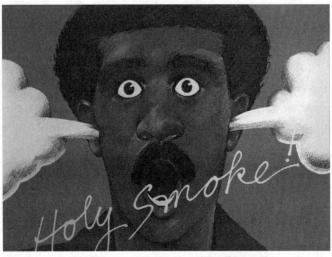

Richard Pryor's Holy Smoke! LP (Laff Records)

RICHARD PRYOR – SET HIMSELF ON FIRE!

In an incident fraught in mystery and conflicting versions, the end result was that one of the greatest comedians of all time was in critical condition with second and third degree burns over 50% of his body. It was the culmination of days of uninterrupted freebase cocaine use during a break while filming *Bustin' Loose*. In the pre-crack era of hitting the pipe,

Pryor had been ingesting virtually pure coke into his system and at one point made an almost fatal decision. He poured 151 proof rum all over his body and lit himself on fire. The immediate result was Richard Pryor running down Parthenia Street from his Los Angeles residence in plain sight, being rescued by police and taken to the hospital. The aftermath was a circus.

While Pryor laid prone in the hospital fighting for his life the spin doctors went to work. His friend and business partner at the time, former NFL superstar running back Jim Brown, insisted it was an accident. His daughter, Rain, claimed it was drug-induced psychosis. Of course, there were other theories – there was an explosion, a faulty lighter, a mistake. Then came the truth from the horse's own mouth. Pryor had tried to commit suicide.

Following six weeks of recovery at the Herpolscheimer Burn Center at Sherman Oaks Hospital, Pryor went back to work and made the incident the gift that kept on giving. Two years later he joked about it in his concert special, *Richard Pryor: Live on the Sunset Strip*. That was supposed to have been his final performance. Instead, the seemingly recovered artist shot *Richard Pryor: Here & Now* one year later. Three years after that he released his directorial debut, *Jo Jo Dancer, Your Life is Calling* and centered the film on the 1980 freebasing episode and his bio.

Almost ending his life did not slow Pryor down that much. After the attempt, he made over a dozen more films and released several new records. However, multiple sclerosis did put a crimp in his style. Once he was diagnosed with the crippling disease the downward slide was steady. He still appeared on stage, but in a wheelchair usually pushed by long-time friend and writer, Paul Mooney. Pryor's speech was impaired and some days were better than others as far as hearing him talk. The decline stopped on December 10, 2005 when Richard Pryor passed away at the age of 65 years old.

https://youtu.be/bjD4PHojNBU

✳ ✳ ✳

June 10, 1895

Hattie McDaniel (Pixabay)

Hattie McDaniel – Born in Wichita, Kansas!

Hattie McDaniel followed her brother, Sam into show business. He was a minstrel and she honed her songwriting skills on his show. Next she inadvertently became a pioneer when she landed a spot on radio as Hi-Hat Hattie, the maid who often got out of line. This made McDaniel the first African-American female to perform on radio.

Historical achievements were fine, but the radio show paid so little McDaniel had to get a job as a real maid to pay the bills. Nevertheless, she didn't let a little hard work stop her dream. She sang on the local radio station in Denver and recorded several records for Okeh Records and Paramount Records in Chicago. Then the stock market crash of '29 hit and all that came to a screeching halt. McDaniel was forced to work as a bathroom attendant and waitress at Club Madrid in Milwaukee, where she was eventually allowed to take the stage and perform.

In 1931 McDaniel moved to Los Angeles where she found radio work and appeared in a number of uncredited film parts. In 1934 she joined the Screen Actors Guild and got parts as maids. During this period the Black community lashed out at McDaniel for taking maid roles. No matter how sassy the maids she played were, Blacks didn't like it. Then came the casting process for the much publicized *Gone with the Wind*. With the help of friend Clark Gable (they'd worked on a film together previously and he wanted her for the part), McDaniel got the coveted role.

However, getting the role was one thing, being able to watch her work at the premiere was another. *Gone with the Wind* made its debut in Atlanta, Georgia. None of the Black actors from the film were invited to attend. As a matter of fact, they were expressly told not to attend. Clark Gable heatedly refused to go under those circumstances. That is until McDaniel pulled him to the side, thanked him for his friendship and loyalty, but informed him that she wasn't surprised and he needed to go to promote the film. She'd make the Hollywood premiere. Reluctantly Gable relented and made the journey to Georgia.

For her troubles, Hattie McDaniel was the first African-American to be nominated for an Academy Award and the first to win (for Best Supporting Actress). In her speech she graciously thanked the Academy for the honor, and sporting pulled back hair laced in gardenias, expressed her gratitude and thanked God. Many in attendance were moved to tears.

Following *Gone with the Wind*, McDaniel played other maid parts in films starring Bette Davis, Humphrey Bogart and worked under the direction of John Huston. She always turned in fine performances and received glowing reviews. However, by the late 1940s the place for domestics on screen was becoming passé. Regardless, McDaniel stayed busy on radio and later in television starring in *Beulah* (for both mediums), where she earned $2,000 per week. She'd taken over from Ethel Waters after the first season of the show, but after discovering she had breast cancer, McDaniel had to bow out and was herself replaced by Louise Beavers.

When Hattie McDaniel died on October 26, 1952 from breast cancer at the age of 57 it was her wish was to be buried in the Hollywood Cemetery, but that wish was denied by the owner, Jules Roth because Black people were not allowed there. So she found a final resting home at Rosedale Cemetery. Then in 1999 the Hollywood Cemetery reversed its decision under new owner Tyler Cassity, but it was too late. The family refused to have her remains moved, so to make amends Cassity built a memorial at the Hollywood Cemetery in McDaniel's honor.

https://youtu.be/gPJVFLv3_v8

***

JUNE 11, 1976

Felipe Esparza (Troy Conrad Photography)

FELIPE ESPARZA – BORN IN SINALOA, MEXICO!

Esparza wasn't born in East L. A., but he was raised there and those experiences are the basis for his material. His comedy is raw, unflinching and filled with universal cultural references. You don't have to be Latin to know what's he's talking about even though that's what he's talking about. With his signature wild hair and infectious catchphrase, "What's up, fool," Esparza got immediate attention as soon as he jumped into comedy.

Esparza received television exposure in record time. Within a year and a half of telling his first joke he was on Showtime; on the "Diamonds in the Rough" segment. From there he went on to appear on Showtime's *Comics Without Borders, Byron Allen's Comic's Unleashed,* Comedy Central's *Premium Blend,* BET's *Comic View, Russell Simmons Presents Stand-Up at the El Rey* and *Que Locos* on Galavision. On the latter program, he made more showings than any other comedian in the show's history. The culmination of all this TV hopping was his 2010 win on NBC's *Last Comic Standing.* In 2011 Showtime aired his special, *They're Not Gonna Laugh at You.*

He was featured in two films in 2009, *The Deported* co-starring Nick Turturro, Paul Rodriguez and Talia Shire as well as *I'm Not Like That Anymore,* a movie based on Esparza's stand-up and also co-starring Rodriguez (playing Esparza's father). In 2014 he launched his hit podcast on the All Things Comedy Network entitled what else? – "What's Up Fool?"

In 2014, Esparza was in a Honda ad campaign to sell more Hondas to the Latin market. The way he did the commercial was to make fun of ads that try to sell products to the Latin market. He also did some ads with comedienne, Lauren Lapkus for Target Mobile services. In 2017 HBO broadcast his stand-up comedy special, *Translate This.* Its success allowed

Felipe Esparza to tour to even larger audiences than before and sell out more shows. That's what's up, fool.

https://youtu.be/JdNtl5T9CoY

* * *

JUNE 11, 1987

Jimmy O. Yang (Instagram)

JIMMY O. YANG – BORN IN HONG KONG!

Mike Judge, an alumnus, gave the commencement speech when Jimmy O. Yang graduated from the University of San Diego in California. Of course, this was after Yang had lived in Hong Kong until his family immigrated to the US and put him in good schools, culminating in this moment. Yang used his degree in economics and got a gig at Smith Barney. Then he came to his senses and got a career instead of a job. He became a comedian.

Yang made a strong debut. His first televised stand-up set was on *The Arsenio Hall Show*. From there he did a lot of TV. Within two years he was guest-starring on *2 Broke Girls, Agents of S.H.I.E.L.D, It's Always Sunny in Philadelphia, New Girl, Criminal Minds*, had a recurring role on *Things You Shouldn't Say Past Midnight*.

Mike Judge came back into Yang's life with another recurring part. Judge was show runner of *Silicon Valley*, the HBO comedy and Yang developed into a series regular. More guest-starring parts (*Battle Creek, Those Who Can't, Broken, Another Period*) including animated voices for *The Simpsons* and *American Dad*; films (*Crazy Rich Asians, Life of the Party, The Happytime Murders*) and naturally a book. *How to American: An Immigrant's Guide to Disappointing Your Parents* tells the tale of how a young immigrant ticks off his parents by trying to go Hollywood. Yang launched a stand-up comedy tour of the same name. Oh, and by the way, the foreword of that book was written by none other than, who else – Mike Judge.

https://youtu.be/RJt35XkrFUo

* * *

JUNE 12, 1977

Lil Duval (Instagram)

LIL DUVAL (ROLAND POWELL) – BORN IN JACKSONVILLE, FL!

Powell adopted the name "Lil Duval" to honor his stomping grounds of Duval County. He then dropped out of high school, moved to Atlanta and became a comic. After bouncing around from one Peachtree Street to another, Duval ended up at the Uptown Comedy Corner, Atlanta's premier comedy club. He honed his skills and got marketable, so much so that he was scooped up by Cedric the Entertainer's road manager to join Ced on his 2001 Budweiser comedy tour. Then Cedric liked him so much he invited Lil Duval to be on his TV special, *Cedric the Entertainer: Starting Line-Up.*

Lil Duval stayed on his steady grind to success. On *Coming to the Stage,* he was a finalist. He put together a nice relationship with MTV2, appearing as a regular on *Guy Code* and *Hip-Hop Squares* and continuing that relationship when he hosted *Ain't That America*, a video show. He performed on BETs *Comic View* several times as well as working in a lot of films (*Stomp the Yard 2: Homecoming*, *Scary Movie 5*, *School Dance* (where he starred as "Bam-Bam"), *Grow House*, *Meet the Blacks* and *Meet the Blacks 2*). Along the way he found time to drop two comedy DVDs (*Dat Boy Funny*, 2003 and *Put Your Hands on Me*, 2005)

His musical dance card was also full. Lil Duval has appeared in music videos with Ludacris, T. I., Yung Joc, E-40, Lil Jon, the Eastside Boyz, Yung L. A., Big Kuntry King, Wale, Plies, Young Dro, Yo Gotti, Hotstylz, Young Jeezy, D J Drama, D4L and Meek Mill.

Lil Duval released his first music video, "Wat Dat Mouf Do?" with Trae tha Truth in 2014 and then in 2018 he collaborated with Snoop Dogg and Ball Greezy to come up with "Smile, Bitch" better known as "Living My Best Life." That tune hit so hard it fell into the Billboard Top 100 topping off at #56 with everybody bumping it from grandkids to grandparents.

Now that sounds like a good life.

https://youtu.be/QFFdSR6U_kc

✳ ✳ ✳

JUNE 13, 1962

Alonzo Bodden (The Alonzo Bodden Collection)

ALONZO BODDEN – BORN IN QUEENS, NEW YORK!

Prior to achieving any type of comedy notoriety, Bodden worked on the assembly line at Lockheed and McDonnell Douglas moving heavy equipment. This was big man work; which is probably why little has ever been said about Alonzo Bodden and hecklers. He was just another working comedian with day job experience and a few films under his belt (*8 Guys, Bringing Down the House, The Girl Next Door*) when he got his national break.

Last Comic Standing, the NBC ratings darling was entering its third season. Bodden had been a runner up on Season 2 and 3 was billed as the "Battle of the Best" with top contestants from seasons 1 & 2 competing. When the 2004 competition was done Alonzo Bodden had won out over Geoff Brown, Corey Holcomb, Rich Vos, Tammy Pescatelli, Gary Gulman, Ralphie May, Tess, Jay London, Todd Glass, Tere Joyce, Rob Cantrell, ANT, Jessica Kirson, Sean Kent, Dat Phan, Cory Kahaney, Dave Mordal, John Heffron and Kathleen Madigan. The prize was $250,000 (not the talent contract and televised special awarded to the previous two season's winners). The winning episode also wasn't broadcast with the hoopla of the previous two seasons.

Regardless, Bodden made the most of it. He released his comedy DVD *Tall, Dark and Funny* in 2005. That same year he returned to *Last Comic Standing* as a celebrity host along with Kathleen Madigan and ANT. He made more films (*Scary Movie 4, National Lampoon's Totally Baked A Potumentary* and *Why We Ride*); appeared on all available late-night shows (*The Tonight Show with Jay Leno, The Late Late Show with Craig Kilborn, Late Night with Conan O'Brien*) stand-up showcases (*It's Showtime at the Apollo, Make Me Laugh, Comedy Central Presents*) and guest starring opportunities (*Angel, Californication*). As a car and motorcycle enthusiast, Bodden was a natural to host several automotive driven shows: Speed TV's *101 Cars You Must Drive* and *America's Worst Driver*. Alonzo Bodden has been a panelist on BBC America and Game Show Network, a co-host on WGN America, a recurring guest on NPR and *The Adam Carolla Show* and done voice-overs on *Power Rangers: Lightspeed Rescue, Masked Rider* and *O'Grady*.

https://youtu.be/kWHLQjHNjk4

***

JUNE 14, 1968

Faizon Love (l) w/ Derrick Ellis (The Ellis Collection)

FAIZON LOVE (LANGSTON FAIZON SANTISIMA) – BORN IN SANTIAGO DE CUBA!

The offspring of a Naval father, Love moved around a lot. His main stomping grounds were Newark, New Jersey and San Diego, California. He got into stand-up comedy and got good in clubs like Maverick Flats and The Comedy Act Theater. Coincidently he made his film debut as the voice over of the latter club's host, Robin Harris in the motion picture based on Harris' routine, *Bebe's Kids*. Harris passed away suddenly of a heart attack as his career was on a fast ascension and Love was there to lend his vocal talents for the project. From then on we heard less of Love and saw more of his face and the rest of him.

Faizon Love has amassed an impressive array of hood flicks and mainstream films throughout his career. His first film appearance was in Robert Townsend's *Meteor Man* followed up with *Fear of a Black Hat* and his signature role as Big Worm in *Friday*. The year was 1995; the same year he signed up to co-star in the Townsend sitcom, *The Parent 'Hood*. That gig lasted until 1998, but Love kept busy as the time passed. He was seen in *Don't be a Menace in South Central While Drinking Your Juice in the Hood*, *A Thin Line Between Love and Hate*, *B*A*P*S**, *Money Talks* and *The Players Club*.

Once *The Parent 'Hood* was canceled, Love stayed on the set. He made *3 Strikes*, *The Replacements*, *Made*, *Mr. Bones*, *Blue Crush*, *Wonderland*, *Elf*, *Idlewild*, *Who's Your Caddy?*, *The Perfect Holiday*, *Animal*, *Torque*, *Couples Retreat* and *Big Momma's: Like Father Like Son* just to name a bunch. He also did TV: *My Name is Earl*, *Real Husbands of Hollywood*, *Black-ish* and more voice-overs: *Grand Theft Auto: San Andreas*, *Ice Age: Dawn of the Dinosaurs*, *Zookeeper*. He appeared on "Freaky Thangs" from Ludacris and "Put Yo Hood Up" by Lil Jon & The East Side Boys. Love starred in the theatrical version of Thornton Wilder's classic, *Our Town* and did commercials for Boost Mobile.

https://youtu.be/1ChbeGbwJtk

✳ ✳ ✳

JUNE 19, 1960

Marga Gomez (Instagram)

MARGA GOMEZ – BORN IN NEW YORK, NEW YORK!

Robin Williams is quoted as saying of Gomez, "Amazing! She's like a lesbian Lenny Bruce." High praise from a comedy master about a future one. The Puerto Rican/Cuban American got her started in San Francisco at legendary spots such as the Valencia Rose Cabaret. Once proficient, she toured everywhere there was a stage: universities, cruise ships, night clubs and political events.

Gomez put it in. She has a comedy recording entitled *Hung Like a Fly*. She has appeared on *Out There* (Comedy Central), *Comic Relief* (HBO), *Latino Laugh Festival* (Showtime) and the documentary, *Laughing Matters* (PBS). She has almost a dozen theater pieces that have been produced Off-Broadway, nationally and internationally. Selections of her plays have been published in anthologies and Gomez has performed in *The Vagina Monologues* with the likes of Rita Moreno. She has also been commissioned as a playwright by the Mark Taper Forum.

Marga Gomez won a GLAAD Award for Off-Off-Broadway theater and is the recipient of Theater LA's "Ovation Award."

https://youtu.be/DZtJ76Apv3A

✳✳✳

JUNE 21, 2002

JUWANNA MANN – RELEASED BY WARNER BROS!

Starring Miguel A. Nunez, Jr., *Juwanna Mann* is a comedy about the re-demption of a bad boy professional basketball star. In the big league he's one of the best, but can't stay out of trouble and after going off once too often (stripping on court) Nunez is banned. In an instant his entire house of cards crumbles. He loses his house, cars, friends, girl and life. Nunez is forced to go live with his no nonsense aunt. Those arrangements smack him in the face that he can't live like that so he resorts back to the only thing he knows – basketball. He dresses up like a female to play women's pro ball.

The gender swapping plan works wonders. Nunez becomes a star in the women's league with all the perks that come along with it including a male groupie (Tommy Davidson) hell bent on getting some. Nunez has his hands full trying to avoid that one and tries to get his hands full of his teammate with the big booty (Vivica A. Fox), but can't because he's supposed to be a girl – remember? Meanwhile Fox is dating a rapper (Ginuwine) who's cheating on her. Oh, drama!

The redemption part is coming up. Nunez learns to be a better player (team work) and a better person thanks to his experience. Too bad it had to blow up in his face. When the women's team played their championship game it was at the same time Nunez (the male version) was having a hearing to get reinstated. He chose to play ball and not let his team down, but during play his wig comes off and the jig is up. Now he has nothing again until Fox and the other girls vouch for his renewed character and all's well that ends well. He got his career back and the girl.

Juwanna Mann was written by Bradley Allenstein, produced by Bill Gerber and directed by Jesse Vaughan. It co-starred Jenifer Lewis, Kevin Pollak, J. Don Ferguson, Kim Wayans, Lil' Kim and real league players (Cynthia Cooper, Rasheed Wallace, Teresa Weatherspoon, Vlade Divac, Katy Steding, Muggsy Bogues, Jeanne Zelasko, Dikembe Mutombo). The movie was not well received by the critics or the public. On a budget of $15,600,000 the film grossed $13,802,599 at the box office.

https://youtu.be/LfGnspMWpUY

* * *

JUNE 22, 1954

Freddie Prinze (Public Domain)

FREDDIE JAMES PRINZE, SR. – BORN IN NEW YORK, NY!

Born Frederick Karl Pruetzel, the Puerto Rican/German was raised in a mixed neighborhood and took those diverse experiences to the stage as a comic. Prinze dropped out of school in his senior year, altered his Germany heritage to Hungarian and introduced himself to audiences as a "Hungarican" in New York comedy clubs like Catch A Rising Star and The Improv. He adopted the stage name of "Prinze" as a compromise to his original wish moniker of being the "King of Comedy." Since that title was already taken (by Alan King) he settled for being known as the prince.

1973 was the year of Freddie Prinze. He made a memorable appearance on *Jack Paar's Tonite* as the show was making its swan song and at the end of that year Prinze made history on *The Tonight Show starring Johnny Carson*. After his rousing stand-up set he was bestowed with every young comedian's dream – he was invited to sit down on the couch and chat it up with Johnny. Wow!!! This was on his very first appearance. He knocked it out of the park on *The Midnight Special* right after that and the industry took notice.

Freddie Prinze was cast by NBC to star in their new sitcom, *Chico and the Man*. His co-star was veteran entertainer, Jack Albertson. The show was another NBC hit and Prinze was another NBC star; that carried perks. Prinze was hired numerous times for *The Dean Martin Roasts* (Muhammad Ali, Sammy Davis, Jr.), starred in the TV movie, *The Million Dollar Rip-Off* and since they liked him, NBC signed Prinze to a five-year deal worth $6 million. He also dropped his comedy album, *Looking Good*, during this time.

The career side of Freddie Prinze's life was outwardly ideal and it was assumed his personal life was as well. He was rich, had a new bride and a healthy baby son (future actor Freddie Prinze, Jr.). What wasn't known outwardly was that Prinze suffered from depression and was addicted to drugs. This put a strain on his erstwhile perceived storybook existence and the marriage ended abruptly following an arrest (Prinze was driving under the influence of Quaaludes). So, with his wife and child out of his life Prinze sunk further into a depressed funk and on January 28, 1977 he put a revolver to his head and committed suicide; dying 33 hours after the fatal wound. He left a note behind blaming no one but himself. He also left an unfulfilled promise and a legacy of brief comedy brilliance.

The life and times of Freddie Prinze have been explored in a book (*The Freddie Prinze Story*) and film (*Can You Hear the Laughter? – the Story of Freddie Prinze*). In 2004, the Hollywood Walk of Fame recognized his contributions with a star for Prinze on Hollywood Boulevard.

https://youtu.be/VT3mDGtk5RE

✳ ✳ ✳

JUNE 22, 1987

Jerrod Carmichael (l) w/ Amber Stevens West, Lil Rel, Tiffany Haddish, Loretta Devine and David Alan Grier (Instagram)

JERROD CARMICHAEL – BORN IN WINSTON-SALEM, NC!

Experience never played much into the life of Jerrod Carmichael. He moved to Los Angeles, California to become a stand-up comedian before he'd actually ever tried stand-up. Growing up poor he didn't have time to plan things out. Life had been a series of improvisations and things had worked out so far. He was still alive. So away he went.

Something or someone must've told him he was funny, because his no experience necessary policy was working out. He lost his comedy virginity at the World-Infamous Comedy Store. It didn't kill him so he kept working clubs in L. A. then he went to Montreal and showcased at the Comedy Festival. He was heralded for his work in the film, *Neighbors* and got a gig on the show, *The Goodwin Games*.

For a guy with little experience he was doing fine. He created his own self-titled, semi-autobiographical sitcom and NBC said "yes." *The Carmichael Show* had a plum spot and lasted until creative differences ended a good thing, but it wasn't all bad. The show introduced the mass public to Tiffany Haddish and Lil Rel Howery. Carmichael might've left his own show, but he executive produced *Rel* on the FOX network. He also produced and directed the stand-up special of Drew Michaels for HBO and appeared in the Jay-Z musical video, *Moonlight*. If all this comes from a guy that has no idea what he's doing, just think what would happen if he did.

https://youtu.be/j5qEovgLEys

✳ ✳ ✳

JUNE 22, 1970

Freddy Soto (The Moreno Collection)

FREDDY SOTO – BORN IN EL PASO, TEXAS!

Soto broke into comedy at the top: he was a limo driver for the legend, Richard Pryor. Before long he was on his way downhill – he became the doorman at the World-Famous Comedy Store. Next thing you know he changed up again. Soto became a national headliner.

Things moved fast. Soto toured with Pablo Francisco and Carlos Mencia as "The Three Amigos" in 2001 and 2002. He cranked out two comedy specials; one for HBO the other for Comedy Central. Soto appeared on *The Late Late Show with Craig Kilborn* and *The Tonight Show with Jay Leno*. He also had a role in the Adam Sandler film, *Spanglish*. Everything was going fine and then tragedy struck.

Freddy Soto died on July 10, 2005. He had performed a set at the Laugh Factory, went to a friend's house, fell asleep and never woke up. Four months later, the coroner's report stated the cause of death was a combination of alcohol, fentanyl (a morphine-like substance) and Xanax. He was 35 years old.

https://youtu.be/71dR_kd6_BQ

✳ ✳ ✳

JUNE 23, 1968

Corey Holcomb w/Shayla Rivera at Serra's, 2009 (The Littleton Collection)

COREY HOLCOMB – BORN IN CHICAGO!

Known for his caustic wit and brutal honesty when it comes to contemporary relationships, Holcomb began in comedy with the assistance and encouragement of established comedian, Godfrey. He gained a grass roots following through appearances on standup based shows: *Def Comedy Jam, Comic View, Wild 'n Out* and *Last Comic Standing*. He performed on *Shaq's All-Star Comedy Jam* and released several comedy specials (*Corey Holcomb: The Problem is You, Comedy Central Presents: Corey Holcomb* and *Corey Holcomb: Your Way Ain't Working*).

Holcomb played the mediums. He guest-starred on sitcoms: *Everybody Hates Chris, Half & Half, Tyler Perry's House of Payne* and had a regular role on *Black Jesus*. His film credits include *Dance Flick, Like Mike, Baggin', Who's Watching the Kids, Think Like a Man Too* and *The Wedding Ringer*. He provides the voice of Robert Tubbs on *The Cleveland Show* and has his own internet show, *The Corey Holcomb 5150 Show*.

https://youtu.be/Vro9-ay2Mbw

***

JUNE 24, 1979

Mindy Kaling w/ B J Novak from 'The Office' (Instagram)

MINDY KALING (VERA MINDY CHOKALINGAM) – BORN IN CAMBRIDGE, MASSACHUSETTS!

Raised by Hindu parents from India, Kaling didn't fit the typical mold. She was a student of Latin from the time she was in the 7th grade, who studied the classics at Dartmouth and got into comedy via an improv troupe around campus. With thirst for the creative and a hunger to move forward, she created a comic strip for the college's paper while working as an intern on *Late Night with Conan O'Brien*.

After graduating with a bachelor's degree in playwriting, Kaling moved to Brooklyn and did stand-up. She toured with future *Office* cast mate, Craig Robinson as well as solo, but gave up stand-up because of the time required for the craft. Besides the house MCs were always mispronouncing her last name of "Chokalingam" and making fun if it which is why she changed it to "Kaling" in the first place (the change of Vera to Mindy came from her parent's desire for her to have a nice, perky American name and since Mork & Mindy was on TV…). Anyway, instead of grinding it out in comedy clubs and on the road she took a job working as a production assistant on the psychic show, *Crossing Over with John Edward*; a gig she hated, but hey – she was in New York. That upside proved advantageous when she had a surprise Off-Broadway hit in the form of a play she co-wrote/co-starred with college friend, Brenda Withers, called *Matt & Ben*. It was a project they penned to entertain themselves about a fantasized version of the relationship between famous screenwriting buddies Matt Damon (Withers) and Ben Affleck (Kaling) and how they came to write their Academy Award winning script *Good Will Hunting*. Time magazine named it one of the "Top Ten Theatrical Events of the Year."

Fortune kept grinning Kaling's way soon after when a spec script she'd written landed her the job that opened the doors. Producer, Greg Daniels thought Kaling a fresh, original voice and hired her to help him adapt the British hit comedy, *The Office* into an American version. At age 24 she attacked the assignment with gusto and by the time the sitcom wrapped, Kaling had written over 20 episodes (as the only female on the staff) making her the most prolific writer from that staff and earning her multiple Emmy nominations. On camera she had established herself as a new pioneering comedy face in the role of office employee, Kelly Kapoor.

All this *Office* success led to a few well-deserved perks. At the end of season seven, Kaling resigned for season eight with a stipulation she'd get full Executive Producer credit. She also made her directorial debut and a development deal for a future project which she exercised following the cancelation of *The Office*. That future project came to be known as *The Mindy Project*; where she acts, produces and writes. It originally aired on FOX and was picked up by Hulu once FOX cancelled it.

Surprisingly Kaling recites more than her own words. She made her acting film debut in *The 40-Year Old Virgin*. Other movies have included *Unaccompanied Minors, License to Wed, Night at the Museum: Battle of the Smithsonian, No Strings Attached, The Five Year Engagement* and *This is the End*. On the small screen she guest-starred on *Curb Your Enthusiasm* and *The Muppets* (as herself). She did voice work on *Wreck-It-Ralph, Despicable Me* and *Inside Out* and figured with so much going on she'd write her memoirs; which she did in 2011 and then a second autobiographical tome in 2015. That's not all – she wrote a blog under the name Mindy Ephron (imagining herself as a long-lost Ephron sister) because she's trippy like that.

It's her level of trippiness that's propelled Kaling into the circle of reliable and emerging industry darlings. Throughout her career Mindy Kaling has received numerous award nominations; taking home three SAG Awards, two Gracie's, an Asian Excellence Award, a Critic's Choice Television Award, A Satellite Award, plus a Reader's Choice Award. In 2013 *Time* magazine recognized her as one of the 100 most influential people in the world.

https://youtu.be/nT_i0a2pBkU8

✳ ✳ ✳

JUNE 25, 1947

Jimmie Walker backstage at 'Martin Lawrence's 1st Amendment Stand-Up' taping, 2010
(The Littleton Collection)

JAMES CARTER "JIMMIE" WALKER, JR. – BORN IN THE BRONX!

Walker initially got into show business through radio. Thanks to the federal program, SEEK (Search for Education, Evaluation and Knowledge) he was able to get into radio engineering at station WRVR and later became a radio personality on R&B station KAGB 103.9 FM in Inglewood, California. He got started in stand-up in 1969 and following appearances on *Rowan & Martin's Laugh-In* and *The Jack Paar Show*, Walker was plucked up by a casting director to be in the next big Norman Lear sitcom for CBS.

Good Times was an instant hit and earned Walker two Golden Globe nominations for Best Supporting Actor. A spin-off from *Maude* (which was spin-off from *All in the Family*) the show was about Florida Evans, a maid married to James Evans, a chronically unemployed father of three: a teen-age daughter, a young militant son and a buffoon. The part of JJ didn't start off that way, but once producer John Rich latched onto the catchphrase "Dy-no-mite," he mandated Walker utter it at least once an episode; the die was cast.

The eldest son of the Evans clan stole the show with his increasingly over-the-top antics and before long the two stars (Esther Rolle and John Amos) and many in the Black public turned against the tone of the character, the show and by association – Walker. There were defections and in its waning days the smash about a struggling Black family in the projects turned into the JJ show as Walker and a skeleton cast held things together before they completely fell apart and *Good Times* was canceled.

However, before those times ceased, Walker got busy. He released a comedy album titled, "Dy-no-mite!" on Buddah Records. He co-starred in the Sidney Poitier directed theatrical comedy, *Let's Do It Again* along with Bill Cosby and John Amos (the father on *Good Times*). Walker also starred in the TV movie *The Greatest Thing That Almost Happened* with James Earl Jones. His other film credits include *Rabbit Test, The Concorde: Airport '79* and *Airplane*. He starred in two other sitcoms; the short lived, *At Ease* (1983) and *Bustin' Loose* (1987). Jimmie Walker hawked product on commercials, guest-starred on sitcoms and yukked it up on game shows. He later went back on radio with his right-wing brand of conservative comedy (Ann Coulter, anyone?), wrote his autobiography, *Dy-no-mite! Good Times, Bad Times, Our Times – A Memoir*, and continues to tour as a stand-up comedian.

https://youtu.be/nqIUedSr0LI

***

JUNE 26, 1988

King Bach (l) w/Justin Hires (Humor Mill Magazine)

KING BACH (ANDREW B. BACHELOR) – BORN IN TORONTO!

When the video sharing service Vine existed, King Bach was its emperor. Nobody had more followers (17 million and 6 billion loops) or cache than he and thanks to his phenomenal success a new branch of comedy spread across the landscape – Internet comedy. Funny people could now produce their own content and post it for direct delivery to the public. Who needed a manager who worked for you half the time when you could create your own exposure and take the world by storm or sputter on your own terms? King Bach was ruling the world.

The King's early life had prepared him to claim his kingdom. His skits were well crafted fast-paced funny comedy mixed with rapidly performed athletics. No problem. He competed in the high jump at Florida State and graduated with a business management degree, which accounts for him having business savvy. Next stop was the New York Film Academy, so he knew how to present a visual story and to top it off he studied with the legendary improvisational group, the Groundlings. So, he had the chops to pull off the skits like a seasoned pro.

Internet stardom led to Hollywood opportunities. Bach signed with the powerhouse agency, UTA and got right to work. He had recurring roles in *House of Lies*, *Wild N Out* and *The Mindy Project*. Bach was a series regular on *Black Jesus* and was featured in the film parody *Fifty Shades of Black*. He guest starred on *Key & Peele, Angie Tribeca* and *The Soul Man* and had fun popping up in Bart Baker music videos parodies impersonating Big Sean, Pharrell and Tupac. Bach also appeared in the film, *We Are Our Friends*, playing a fictionalized version of himself.

And more subjects flocked to the kingdom.

https://youtu.be/yf0Q9Tq2WXc

* * *

JUNE 26, 1998

DR. DOLITTLE – RELEASED BY 20TH CENTURY FOX!

This PG-13 movie marketed as a family film was based so loosely on the Hugh Lofting children's book series that the only thing used was the name and the skill of the lead character. In this second filmed version (the first starred Rex Harrison in 1967 and bombed miserably), Eddie Murphy plays the title role of a guy who can not only understand when animals talk, he can talk back to them and they understand him. The fact he's an actual doctor makes this just slightly less weird to the people in his life.

The plot revolves around Murphy, who as a child (Raymond Matthew Mason/Dari Gerard Smith) knew he had the gift to communicate with animals, but his father didn't care for his son sniffing the backsides of humans as way of saying hello and had an exorcist exorcise the gift outta him. That traumatic experience leaves the young Murphy with no memory of being so awesome and he grew up to be bland like most. Then one day a standard issue movie bump on the head causes the adult Murphy to regain his gift and it freaks him out. At first he thinks he's crazy, but after he befriends a dog, who turns him onto a suicidal tiger, who Murphy tries to save along with any animal that needs saving and he's caught giving CPR to a rat, his business partner thinks he's crazy. That suspicion gets Murphy committed to an insane asylum.

While in the padded room Murphy gets in touch with his inner disdain for talking animals and upon his release he wants nothing to do with any of them including the suicidal tiger who still hasn't offed himself yet. Well, Murphy's youngest daughter thought it was cool her dad could talk to animals and tells this to her grandfather; the same guy that hired the exorcist. Murphy overhears this and hooks up with the dog so they can save the tiger. Of course, they do, with the help of all available animals who thwart the attempts of the authorities to stop Murphy. The climax being the tiger just needed an operation to ease some pain, it was a complete success and Murphy is a hero and nobody thinks he's crazy.

Dr. Dolittle co-stars Ossie Davis, Raven-Symone, Kyla Pratt, Kristen Wilson, Peter Boyle, Oliver Platt, Jeffrey Tambor, Richard Schiff, Paul Giamatti and Pruitt Taylor Vince; with vocal talent provided by Chris Rock, Norm MacDonald, Ellen DeGeneres, Jenna Elfman, Albert Brooks, Gilbert Gottfried, Hamilton Camp, Julie Kavner, John Leguizamo, Jonathan Lipnicki, Brian Doyle-Murray, Paul Reubens and Garry Shandling.

Written by Larry Levin & Nat Mauldin and directed by Betty Thomas, *Dr. Dolittle* received mixed reviews from the critics, but plenty of love from the public. On a budget of $70.5 million, the film grossed $144,156,605 domestically and $150,300,000 abroad for a worldwide box office take of $294,456,605 and that was enough to justify four sequels: *Dr. Dolittle 2, Dr. Dolittle 3, Tail to the Chief* and *Million Dollar Mutts.*

https://youtu.be/ozMmf9Yi7TM

* * *

JUNE 27, 1970

Ahmed Ahmed (Ahmed Ahmed Collection)

AHMED AHMED – BORN IN HELWAN, EGYPT!

When it's said Ahmed was born in Egypt it sounds very exotic. Truth is he was one month old when his parents moved him to Riverside, California. Things didn't get exotic until he moved himself to Hollywood when he was 19. That's where he went to kick his stand-up and acting career into gear. He became a regular at the World-Famous Comedy Store; getting much needed exposure and plenty of looks by industry.

Ahmed's film credits include *Virtuosity, Executive Decision, Swingers, Don't Mess with the Zohan, The Onion Movie* and *Iron Man*. He has guest-starred on *Roseanne, JAG, Girlfriends, Tracey Takes On* ... and popped up *The View* and *Punk'd*. He was also a regular on *Sullivan & Son*. His other televised comedy appearances include *I Am Ahmed Ahmed, Wild West Comedy Show: 30 Days and 30 Night in the Heartland, Hey Hey It's Saturday* and *Tough Crowd with Colin Quinn*. On those he played himself, even though throughout his career Ahmed has played characters named Ahmed three times.

Ahmed Ahmed was seen in the PBS America at a Crossroads documentary, *Stand Up: Muslim American Comics Come of Age*. He also appeared on the front page of the *Wall Street Journal* and *Newsweek*. In 2004 Ahmed attended the Edinburgh Festival in Scotland and won the 1st Annual Richard Pryor Award for ethnic comedy. He's known for the "Axis of Evil Comedy Tour" and the "One Arab, One Jew, One Stage Tour," where he and Rabbi Bob Alper performed together right after 9/11 until 2004 in the name of unity and interfaith harmony.

https://youtu.be/Iu81NDXNaNM

✳ ✳ ✳

JUNE 28, 1996

Jada Pinkett and Eddie Murphy in The Nutty Professor (Instagram)

THE NUTTY PROFESSOR – RELEASED BY UNIVERSAL PICTURES!

This was considered an Eddie Murphy comeback film. It wasn't the first or the last. After his first slump; the unholy trilogy of *The Distinguished Gentleman, Beverly Hills Cop III and Vampire in Brooklyn*, Hollywood was ready to remove Murphy's name plate from his studio parking space until the 1963 Jerry Lewis remake got made. Hollywood had to be quiet until the next slump from the mega-star.

In this updated version Murphy plays the portly Professor Sherman Klump, a genius with a weight loss formula. It makes him develop a slim, toned, wild and crazy alter ego who gets the unknowing Klump in plenty of real time trouble. Originally based on Robert Louis Stevenson's *Strange Case of Dr. Jekyll and Mr. Hyde*, Klump's dilemma is that the alter ego, once controllable, takes over. The climax occurs when Klump regains his life and banishes the thin man.

The Nutty Professor co-starred Jada Pinkett, Dave Chappelle, Larry Miller, James Coburn, Jamal Mixon, John Ales and Montell Jordan as himself. Eddie Murphy displayed his versatility by playing his entire family; his father, mother, grandmother and brother as well as a Richard Simmons parody character. The film deservedly won an Oscar for Best Makeup. Tom Shadyac directed and Jerry Lewis was one of the executive producers.

The critics loved the film and so did the ticket buying public. On a budget of $54 million, *The Nutty Professor* earned $273,961,019 at the worldwide box office. Murphy even received a Golden Globe nomination for Best Actor. This so-called lightning in the bottle fluke even spawned a sequel (2000's *Nutty Professor II: The Klumps*). The comeback was complete and the string of flops was over; that is until *Showtime*, *The Adventures of Pluto Nash, I-Spy, Daddy Day Care, The Haunted Mansion*…

https://youtu.be/7IrB1OE9Blo

* * *

JUNE 28, 1932

Pat Morita, 1971 (Public Domain)

NORIYUKI "PAT" MORITA – BORN IN ISLETON, CALIFORNIA!

Morita has the distinction of starring in the first American network sitcom focusing on an Asian lead character (*Mr. T and Tina*). The year was 1976 and the network was ABC. The show didn't last, but that wasn't on Morita. He'd proven himself back in 1975 with a featured role as Matsuo "Arnold" Takahashi on the hit sitcom, *Happy Days*, starring Ron Howard and Henry Winkler. Prior to that he was Ah Chew, Lamont Sanford's friend on the NBC blockbuster sitcom, *Sanford and Son* in 1974. He played that role until 1976.

However, before all that Morita got his start telling jokes for customers at his family's restaurant after World War II. This was following years wrapped up in body casts and undergoing one spinal operation after another. When he was finally released from the hospital at age 11 he was whisked to an internment camp to join his family. Not much to laugh at, but Morita, now known as Pat, kept it pushing. He worked as a data entry clerk for the state until he went into stand-up in the early '60s. They called him The Hip Nip. He played night clubs and was a member of the improv troupe, The Groundlings.

Morita's work in front of the camera began in 1967 with a part in the Julie Andrews comedy, *Thoroughly Modern Millie*. From there he appeared in a succession of comedies (*The Shakiest Gun in the West, Evil Roy Slade, Every Little Crook and Nanny, Where Does it Hurt? Cancel My Reservation*). He also had a recurring role on the Alan Alda television comedy, *M*A*S*H*. Morita played a South Korean Army Captain.

Once *Mr. T and Tina* was abruptly canceled in '76, Morita performed his *Happy Days* character of Arnold on the sitcom, *Blansky's Beauty's* in 1977. He revived the character again on *Happy Days* in 1982. In 1984 Morita gained movie stardom as Mr. Kesuke Miyagi in the *Karate Kid*. He was nominated for the Academy Award for Best Supporting Actor. He went on to star in three sequels as well as *Karate Dog* in 2004.

Morita stayed busy. In 1987 he starred in *Ohara* for ABC. Another short-lived show, but Morita hardly noticed. That same year he wrote and starred in the World War II film, *Captive Hearts*. He starred in the Nickelodeon series, *The Mystery Files of Shelby Woo* and *Talk to Taka*. He had a recurring role on *The Hughleys* and guest starred on *Married With Children*. Morita did animation voice-overs (*Mulan, SpongeBob SquarePants*, and *Robot Chicken*) and music videos (Alien Ant Farm's "Movies"). Until his passing (November 24, 2005), he was busy working on independent films, industrials and feature length motion pictures (many released posthumously).

https://youtu.be/j-uAumH1DFc

JUNE 29, 1988

Eddie Murphy and Arsenio Hall in 'Coming to America' (Instagram)

COMING TO AMERICA – RELEASED BY PARAMOUNT PICTURES!

Reuniting Eddie Murphy and director John Landis, the comedy is about African crown prince, Akeem Joffer, from the fictional nation of Zamunda, who comes to the United States in the hopes of finding a bride. The film co-stars Arsenio Hall, James Earl Jones, Shari Headley and John Amos.

Following a negative press screening in New York, Paramount cancelled all press screenings of the film. Their concern proved to be unfounded as the film was a

Shari Headley and Eddie Murphy in *Coming to America* (Instagram)

commercial box-office success, both domestically and worldwide, grossing $288,752,301, making it the highest earning film that year for the studio and the third-highest grossing film at the United States box office.

Coming To America was nominated for two Academy Awards for Best Costume and Best Makeup. The soundtrack also did well. Two singles ("Coming to America" and "Come into My Life") were released and the song, "That's the Way It Is" went to the top ten in the UK.

It seemed the only downside was the 1990 *Buchwald v. Paramount* civil suit. Humorist Art Buchwald claimed the film's idea was stolen from his 1982 script treatment; a treatment Paramount had optioned from him, with John Landis attached as director and Murphy as the lead, but after two years in development, the studio dropped the project in 1985. Then in 1987, Paramount began working on *Coming to America* based on a story by Murphy. Buchwald won for breach of contract and settled out-of-court.

https://youtu.be/-R1h2Df3Nrc

JUNE 30, 1956

David Alan Grier performing in Iraq 2007 (Public Domain)

DAVID ALAN GRIER – BORN IN DETROIT!

Grier has received acclaim since he graduated from the Yale School of Drama. His maiden voyage role was in the Martin Charnin directed

Broadway musical, *The First*. He played Jackie Robinson and won the The-atre World Award. He later performed the role of James "Thunder" Early in *Dreamgirls* and was nominated for a Tony Award. Then Grier took his winning ways to film in 1983 and won the Venice film Festival's Golden Lion Award for Best Actor in Robert Altman's, *Streamers*. He was nomi-nated for an Image Award for *Damon* and *Life with Bonnie* and a Satellite Award nomination for the latter. He received his second Tony nomina-tion for his performance in David Mamet's 2009 Broadway production, *Race* and his third for *Porgy and Bess*, where he played Sportin' Life. Grier was also in *A Soldier's Story* on stage (to accolades) and again in the Nor-man Jewison film.

After working with Keenan Ivory Wayans in his theatrical hit, *I'm Gonna Git You Sucka*, Grier was hired as a cast member for Wayans FOX sketch show, *In Living Color*. There, he displayed his comedic chops. He played a variety of characters imagined (the shop teacher Al MacAfee, the bluesman Calhoun Tubbs, flamboyant film reviewer Antoine Merriweather) and real (Al Sharpton, Ray Charles, Clarence Thomas, Ike Turner, Joe Jackson).

Once *In Living Color* ended, Grier starred in the *Preston Episodes, DAG, My Wife and Kids, Dream On* and *Damon*. He had recurring roles where he played a reverend on *Martin,* the principal on CBS's *Bad Teacher* and he hosted *Premium Blend* on Comedy Central. His film credits include *Boo-merang, Blankman, In the Army Now, Jumanji, Tales from the Hood, McHale's Navy, 3 Strikes, Stuart Little, Bewitched Dance Flick* and *Tyler Perry's Peeples*.

Grier was so multi-faceted he returned to Broadway in *A Funny Thing Happened on the Way to the Forum* and in 2009 he published the book, *Barack Like Me: The Chocolate Covered Truth*. He appeared regularly on Adam Carolla's *Loveline*, but was controversially banned under Dr. Drew Pinsky's regime. He premiered his comedy special, *The Book of David: The Cult Figure's Manifesto* on Comedy Central and was a recurring performer on the station's *Crank Yankers*. In 2008 Grier hosted *Chocolate News*, a hilarious spoof on a TV news magazine show. It was raw and offensive and it was canceled after one season. In the year 2015 he introduced the character of Joe Carmichael on the NBC sitcom, *The Carmichael Show*; that was the same year he performed in the Live version of *The Wiz* play-ing the Cowardly Lion.

Comedy Central ranked the grossly underrated David Alan Grier # 94 on their list of the 100 Greatest Stand-Ups.

https://youtu.be/OKEFmpS-oP4

✳ ✳ ✳

JUNE 30, 1974

Tony Rock w/ Hope Flood (Hope Flood Collection)

TONY ROCK – BORN IN NEW YORK, NY!

Upon becoming a professional comedian, Tony was chiefly known as Chris Rock's younger brother. However, that turned around as Tony made a name for himself in a number of projects. At the turn of the century, Rock hosted the game show *Can You Tell?* For Oprah Winfrey's Oh! Oxygen network and was a correspondent for *BattleBots* on Comedy Central.

Since then he's made appearances on *The Howard Stern Show* and *The D'Angelo Show*; co-starred as Dirk Black on the UPN/CW sitcom, *All of Us* and the Chris Rock sitcom, *Everybody Hates Chris* in the recurring role of uncle Ryan. Tony has also hosted TV One's, *The Funny Spot.*

In 2008 Tony starred in his own sketch comedy show called *The Tony Rock Project* for MyNetworkTV from 2008 to 2009. He was featured in *Think Like a Man*, hosted *Apollo Live* on BET and *All Def Comedy* on HBO.

https://youtu.be/UGIn7qNDLrU

✳ ✳ ✳

JULY

THIS DAY IN COMEDY…

JULY 1, 1992

Eartha Kitt and Eddie Murphy in *Boomerang* (Instagram)

BOOMERANG– RELEASED BY PARAMOUNT PICTURES!

This Eddie Murphy vehicle was directed by Reginald Hudlin. Murphy plays a womanizing ad executive who meets his match in the form of new colleague, Robin Givens. She gives him the same sex 'em and diss 'em attitude Murphy has been dishing out for years and he doesn't like it, but he's sprung. Once respected by all, he is now humiliated at work, embarrassed in front of his boys (Martin Lawrence, David Alan Grier) and a disgrace to himself. The absurd part is he's loved by Halle Berry, but opts for Robin Givens; until he opens his eyes (literally) and takes his ass home to Halle.

Boomerang co-stars Eartha Kitt, John Witherspoon, Bebe Drake-Massey, Geoffrey Holder, Grace Jones, Chris Rock, Jonathan Hicks, Tisha Campbell and Lela Rochon. It was produced by Brian Grazer and War-rington Hudlin with music by Marcus Miller. The screenplay was written by Barry W. Blaustein and David Sheffield based on a story by Eddie Murphy. On a budget of $42 million *Boomerang* grossed $131,052,444 at the worldwide box office.

The film was nominated for the BMI Film & TV Award and the MTV Movie Award.

https://youtu.be/UD_gJShgozE

***

221

JULY 1, 1947

Shirley Hemphill (r) w/ Fred "Rerun" Berry, Ernest Thomas and Haywood Nelson in *What's Happening!* (Instagram)

SHIRLEY ANN HEMPHILL – BORN IN ASHVILLE, NC!

Hemphill wanted to be a stand-up so badly she sent her tape to Flip Wilson personally and he personally responded. They met and he encouraged her to get on the circuit and pay her dues. She followed that sound advice and after moving to L.A. and putting in some time at clubs like the Comedy Store she was noticed by the right casting person and got a guest part on *Good Times*. She was so good Norman Lear, the show's producer, offered Hemphill her own show; a spin-off. She turned him down and instead won the part of "Shirley" on the ABC sitcom, *What's Happening!!* The role of the smart mouthed diner waitress suited her comedic skills and spot on timing perfectly, but due to cast and contract problems the show was canceled after three seasons.

Hemphill parachuted out with her own sitcom, *One in a Million*. In it she played a cabbie who inherits a fortune from one of her fares. It was short-lived. So, she went back and did a new version of her old sitcom, renamed, *What's Happening Now!!* featuring a young talent, Martin Lawrence. It also lasted three seasons and once the revived version expired Hemphill went back on the road as a stand-up. She'd also make guest appearances on television (*The Love Boat, Martin, Pryor's Place, The Sinbad Show, Linc's, The Wayans Bros.*) and films (*CB4* and *Shoot the Moon*).

The Laugh Factory regular performed stand-up on *The Tonight Show with Johnny Carson* and A&E's *An Evening at the Improv*, as well as, *Black Comedy Showcase* and *Black Comedy Tonight*, both on BET. She was busy touring when she fell ill forcing her off the road and into her house. Never fond of a pity party, Hemphill changed her number so she wouldn't have to talk to her friends as she wasted away in seclusion. She refused surgery and was discovered by her gardener when he peeked through the window and found her lifeless on the floor. Hemphill died on December 10, 1999 of a heart attack brought on by renal failure in West Covina, California at the age of 52.

https://youtu.be/NRmCG3ZOpkc

***

JULY 4, 1914

Timmie Rogers (The Timmie Rogers Collection)

TIMMIE ROGERS (TIMOTHY JOHN ANERUM) – BORN IN DETROIT, MICHIGAN!

Rogers was known as the Jackie Robinson of Black Comedy because he opened the door for other performers such as Dick Gregory by insisting on not wearing blackface, donning a tuxedo and standing firm with his convictions. His comedy was clean, topical and political. His catchphrase was "Oh Yeah!" and Timmie Rogers starred in US television's first Black prime-time show *Uptown Jubilee* on CBS in 1949 and opened for Latin sensation, Carmen Miranda.

At the age of eight, he began earning money by dancing on the street. Rogers ran away from home at age 12 and became a dishwasher. He also learned nine languages by learning those of the other dishwashers. He later recorded in French and German. A job cleaning ashtrays led to a job at that ballroom dancing onstage. He became part of the vaudeville dance team, Timmie & Freddie in 1932. They dissolved in 1944.

Rogers found work as a recurring guest star on *The Jackie Gleason Show* and worked with Gleason for over forty years. Rogers wrote, "If You Can't

Smile and Say Yes," recorded by Nat King Cole. He also wrote songs for Carmen McRae and Sarah Vaughn. In the late 50's he recorded the hits, "Back to School Again" and "I Love Ya, I Love Ya, I Love Ya."

Timmie Rogers made appearances in sitcoms in the 60s and 70s including *Sanford & Son* and *Good Times*. He's featured in the oral history book, *Black Comedians on Black Comedy* and in 1993 Rogers was inducted into the National Comedy Hall of Fame.

Rogers passed on December 17, 2006 of undisclosed causes at the age of 92.

https://youtu.be/rlm53CiComo

✱✱✱

JULY 4, 1971

Al Madrigal (Instagram)

AL MADRIGAL –BORN IN SAN FRANCISCO, CALIFORNIA!

Madrigal grew up in the real world; the multi-cultural one. He's a Mexican who hung out with his Korean neighbor, Margaret Cho as a kid. He went to a Catholic school and learned French (since he doesn't speak enough Spanish). Then he went to work in human resources firing people and almost every race under the sun wanted to kill him.

Since he didn't want to literally die young Madrigal got into stand-up comedy where the deaths are more figurative. No worries though. Madrigal got major love at the Montreal Just For Laughs Festival and won Best Comedian at Aspen's U. S. Comedy Art Festival. The result was a talent holding deal with CBS, two highly acclaimed stand-up specials on Comedy Central and one on Showtime.

Al Madrigal popped up all over. He's done *The Tonight Show, Jimmy Kimmel Live!, The Late Late Show with Craig Ferguson, Conan* and a bunch of pilots and short-lifers. Of the latter, there was *The Ortegas*, a series that was shot, but dropped from the FOX network schedule before a single episode aired. There was the CBS clunker, *Welcome to the Captain*, a series that aired for five episodes before it wore out its welcome and got yanked. There was *Gary Unmarried* on CBS. It lasted 2 seasons. Yay! He finally caught a break on NBC in the show *About a Boy*. He was nominated for Best Supporting Actor by the Imagen Awards. And then came cable TV.

Madrigal got a dream role on an ensemble program that's all about comedians. Executive produced by Jim Carrey for Showtime, *I'm Dying Up Here* showcases a group of talented comedians of today (Erik Griffin, Andrew Santino, Brad Garrett and Madrigal) portraying composites of talented comedians from the 1970s Hollywood Comedy scene. It's gritty, seedy and a true representation of what that dog-eat-puppy age was all about. Madrigal plays a gritty, seedy Mexican comic named Edgar.

Al Madrigal is a comedian of his time. He worked as a satirical news correspondent on *The Daily Show with Jon Stewart*. He co-founded the comedy podcast network, *All Things Comedy* along with Bill Burr. They help comedians control and protect their own content as well as host scores of comedy podcasts. Naturally Madrigal has co-hosted podcasts himself with Maz Jobrani, Chris Spencer and Aaron Aryanpur and then later one with Burr. He's done film, voice-overs and years and years of French.

https://youtu.be/l8xHMpDaG6k

***

July 5th

Hope Flood (The Hope Flood Collection)

FICA (Females in Comedy Association) Founder, Hope Flood – Born in Benton Harbor, MI!

Flood began her comedy career in the early 1990s. She appeared on BETs *Comic View*, were she was featured in her own special. Always an executive as much as a performer, Hope Flood co-founded BASH (Blacks About Social Happenings); a promotion group dedicated to producing quality comedy shows in the community. From there she branched off into publishing with her comedy magazine, *Comedy the Magazine* and its follow up *Comedy 2000*.

She appeared in the John Singleton film, *Baby Boy* and has toured internationally as a headliner. In 2011 she founded FICA (Females in Comedy Association) and presented the first of its kind comedy convention solely for comediennes. Amateur females from all over the country were able to learn from veterans in the field and be showcased at some of Los Angeles, California's most prestigious comedy clubs. She currently runs the Comic Rocks Annual Convention.

https://youtu.be/pm9NLBTk_yw

✳ ✳ ✳

July 6, 1979

Kevin Hart (Creative Commons Attribution)

Kevin Darnell Hart – Born in Philadelphia, PA!

Hart got his big break in comedy in 2000 when Judd Apatow cast him in a recurring role in *Undeclared* following of series of amateur comedy competition wins. He was off and running with parts in the films *Paper Soldiers*, *Scary Movie 3*, *Soul Plane*, and *Little Fockers*.

In 2008 he released his first stand-up album *I'm a Grown Little Man*. He cranked it up with performances in *Think Like a Man*, *Grudge Match*, *Ride Along* and *About Last Night*. He dropped two more comedy albums and starred as himself in *Real Husbands of Hollywood*.

Raised by his single mother, Hart used his ability to make people laugh to deal with the family problem of having a cocaine addicted father he hardly ever saw. Hart got into professional comedy after performing at an amateur night at The Laff House in Philadelphia under the name of Lil Kev. After an early period of rough shows along with having chicken wings thrown at him, Hart entered comedy competitions throughout Massachusetts. That was the turning point.

Hart is truly a 21st Century comedian. He has a game available through iTunes called "Little Jumpman." His Facebook page, Twitter account, and YouTube channel are all connected to and accessible through this app. Most overseas fans of Hart discovered him on YouTube.

Kevin Hart has hosted various ceremonies. Hart first hosted the *2011 BET Awards* then the *2012 MTV Video Music Awards* (with the help of a referral by friend, Judd Apatow). Hart has hosted two episodes of *Saturday Night Live*. He starred in *Central Intelligence, Get Hard, Jumanji* and *Night School,* making him one of the biggest box-officw draws of his era. Then Kevin Hart added a tentacle when he became a media mogul with Sirius XM LOL Radio, playing comedy content and hosting a show with him and the Plastic Cup Boys and broadcasting the Earthquake show, *Quake's House.*

https://youtu.be/AiW-7YTx78g

* * *

JULY 6, 1951

Charlie Hill (Instagram)

CHARLES ALLAN "CHARLIE" HILL – BORN IN DETROIT, MI!

Hill left school to become a comedian. He was attending the University of Wisconsin-Madison, studying speech and drama. He'd gotten into the Broome Street Theatre Group and then he just packed up and moved to Los Angeles. He became a regular at the Comedy Store in Hollywood. From there it didn't take him long to get work.

Charlie Hill's first television appearance was on *The Richard Pryor Show*. He was the first Native-American comedian to perform on *The Tonight Show with Johnny Carson*. Hill made numerous appearances on *Late Night with David Letterman* and Hill grew old enough to do *The Tonight Show with Jay Leno*. He was a writer for *Roseanne* on ABC and guest starred on *The Bionic Woman, The Golden Girls* and *Moesha*.

Hill toured all over the world and was often interviewed for documentaries dealing with being an Oneida-Mohawk. He appeared in almost a half dozen documentaries including the 1999 Sandra Osawa directed PBS documentary, *On and Off the Res' with Charlie Hill.* He was an award show host (*First Americans in the Arts Awards*) and an awards show winner (Hill won the 2009 Ivy Bethune Tri-Union Diversity Award).

On December 30, 2013 after an extended fight with lymphoma, Charlie Hill passed away in Oneida, Wisconsin. He was 62 years old.

https://youtu.be/545t5SvcyDo

***

July 6, 1948

Brad Sanders (Brad Sanders Collection)

Brad Sanders – Born in Chicago, Illinois!

Sanders was the head writer for ground-breaking DJ, Tom Joyner. Known as "The Fly Jock," Joyner was the first Black millionaire DJ. He flew from Chicago to Dallas daily to do both shows and he was also smart. He put Brad Sanders in charge of his comedy writing team.

Sanders had enjoyed plenty of success on his own in radio. He was responsible for "The Clarence Update" and "Tyrone on the Phone," both very popular soap opera features for the radio and they led him into syndication on a ground floor level. Sanders became a millionaire thanks to his deal.

Once he went to work with Joyner, Sanders ran a crew of gag men/writers that included Larry Wilmore and his brother, Marc, Buddy Lewis, Greg Eagles, Joey Gaynor, Mary Boyce (gag lady), Doug Starks, Joe and Guy Torry, as well as a first-time writer, Darryl Littleton (whom Sanders mentored). This bunch created raucous and outrageous character driven comedy content (it's where the comedy persona of "D'Militant" was hatched) for years until Joyner changed his direction, but not the man who charted the course behind the scenes.

Brad Sanders and Darryl Bohanan on the set of their pilot 'Bo-Sand' (Brad Sanders Collection)

Sanders transitioned seamlessly to Joyner's new female-friendly format. Brad Sanders already had an enormous fanbase from his soap opera updates, so he fused them into "It's Your World," the instant hit with the Joyner audience. The writing staff was now primarily women (Myra J, Jedda Jones, the holdover, Mary Boyce and others) with Sanders at the helm. He had a true talent for theater of the mind (aka radio) and another solid accomplishment under his belt.

Prior to radio success, Sanders dabbled in television. He and partner, Darryl Bohanan shot the TV-pilot "Bo-Sand" as the team of Bohanan & Sanders. As a solo act Brad Sanders appeared as "Ghetto Man" on the Hanna Barbara special *Legends of the Superheroes*, who could do all the super feats of other heroes, but he confined his activities to the hood. Sanders did guest spots on *The Bold & The Beautiful*, *Reed Between the Lines* (where he played the president), *The Donny & Marie Show*, *The Richard Pryor Show*, *Frank's Place*, *Soul Train*, *The NAACP Image Awards* and *The Young & the Restless*.

He was featured in films. Brad Sanders played "Batty Boy" in the Robert Townsend breakout movie, *Hollywood Shuffle*. He was seen in *Tequila & Bonetti*, *Brewster's Millions*, *The Incredible Hulk: Ultimate Destruction*, *Fear of a Black Hat*, *The Last Stand*, *G. I. Joe: The Movie* and did a voice for the animated feature film based on the routine by comedian, Robin Harris, *Bebe's Kids*.

Sanders did the web-series, "Clarence Weekly Wrap-Up" and "Inside the News." He was nominated for a Daytime Emmy Award for Outstanding New Approaches – Daytime Entertainment.

https://youtu.be/qICz-4q4VhM

* * *

JULY 6, 2005

"MIND OF MENCIA" – PREMIERED ON COMEDY CENTRAL!

Starting off with an initial order of ten episodes, *Mind of Mencia* caught fire and got a second season order. Comedy Central timed the release of the first season DVD with the premiere of that second season. The show's creator, comedian, Carlos Mencia put together a slate of memorable characters (Punji, the Hindu storekeeper who attacks customers flaws, Carlosaurus Rex, a Barney & Friends parody with Carlos dishing out advice to kids on adult issues like sexuality and death, and Judge Carlos with the star playing a judge who gets help from the ghost of Johnnie Cochran) that kept Comedy Central chugging along in the awkward period following the abrupt departure of *Chappelle Show*, the cultural phenomenon of Dave Chappelle that basically put the network on the 21st Century map. And when he left sent it and it's PR team into freefall. *Mind of Mencia* was the parachute it needed.

Mind of Mencia lasted four seasons. Its regular players were Brad Williams, Joseph Mencia, Ray Payton and Carlos. The guest that appeared was a diverse who's who of the era: Dave Attell, Josh Blue, Frank Caliendo, Gabriel Iglesias, Bobby Lee, Robin Williams, John Witherspoon, Peter Boyle, Edge, Cheech Marin, Method Man, Gene Simmons, Daniel Tosh, Tracy Morgan, Mario Lopez, Jamie Kennedy, Aries Spears, Three 6 Mafia and more.

The show left the air on July 23, 2008 because Mencia did not want to do a fifth season.

https://youtu.be/uls5I5vpDLw

✳ ✳ ✳

JULY 9, 2006

Director Rusty Cundieff, Susan Sarandon and Dave Chappelle (as Lil Jon) during a break in a never aired "Lost Episodes" sketch (Rusty Cundieff Collection)

COMEDY CENTRAL – AIRS CHAPPELLE SHOW: THE LOST EPISODES!

Despite its namesake host abandoning the show that made him a comedy icon, the network Dave Chappelle put on the map broadcast skits from the unaired, incomplete 3rd season and dubbed them "The Lost Episodes." They were a result of Chappelle fleeing after hearing a too hard laugh at one of his racial remarks. It was one of those laughs that only a comedian can distinguish as not laughing with me, but at me.

In his permanent absence, Charlie Murphy and Donnell Rawlings served as hosts. When asked about his attitude towards such an unprecedented move, Rawlings response was, "I'm a loyal person, but I know as a professional I have to keep my career going, and I felt it was an opportunity for me, for people [to] see what I do as funny ... without knowing what Dave Chappelle's agenda is, the reason why he left, with no communication saying, 'Hey guys, I feel this way. I would much rather you not be part of this process.' Had I had a conversation with Dave like that then there's a possibility that I would reconsider me hosting it."

https://youtu.be/WIneIwPFN78

* * *

231

JULY 12, 1971

Loni Love (Humor Mill Magazine)

LONI LOVE – BORN IN DETROIT, MICHIGAN!

Love got into stand-up comedy during her college days. She won a $50 competition and then had to wrestle with the decision to pursue her dream of being an electrical engineer; a goal she'd labored towards since working the assembly line putting doors on the 1993 Oldsmobile Cutlass; the reason she was at Prairie View A&M. Her well-thought-out plan consisted of her getting her degree and diving face first into a career that would offer her a lifetime of job security and substantial benefits or she could give all that up and become a comic who'd probably be broke for the first half-a-decade and have to sleep on other comic's couches and on floors or worse – hook up with some guy who's no good to make the journey take even longer. Hey, she won a $50 competition. What was so hard to decide?

Loni Love compromised. She got a job at Xerox as an engineer and at night worked the club circuit; becoming a regular at Hollywood's Laugh Factory. On her eighth year at Xerox, Love quit do to comedy fulltime. In 2003 she won the jury prize for best stand-up at the US Comedy Arts Festival. She got work on VH1 as a talking head on their series "I Love the 2000s" and other decades. She came in as runner-up on *Star Search*. The competition was so tight, judge Naomi Judd said loudly and emphatically that "Loni should've won" once the winner, John Roy's name was announced. In 2009, *Variety* magazine and Comedy Central named Love one of the "Top 10 Comics to Watch" and she ended up as a sidekick to Chelsea Handler on *Chelsea Lately*.

Loni Love has performed on *The Tonight Show with Jay leno* and joked it up on Byron Allen's *Comics Unleashed*. She has appeared in the films, *With or Without You, Soul Plane, Bad Asses, Paul Blart: Mall Cop 2, Bad Asses on the Bayou, Gunshot Straight* and *Mother's Day*. Her television guest roles have included *Girlfriends, Cuts, Phineas and Ferb, Chocolate News, Whitney* and *American Dad*. She had recurring parts on *Kickin' It* and *Ned's Declassified Survival Guide*, was a series regular on *Thick and Thin* and hosted *Premium Blend*.

In 2008 Love covered the inaugural of Barack Obama for CNN. She dropped her first comedy special, *America's Sister* on Comedy Central in 2010 and her first book, *Love Him or Leave Him But Don't Get Stuck With The Tab* in 2013.

Loni Love's been a co-host on the daytime talkfest, *The Real* since 2013.

https://youtu.be/4vpYr0GE6ZI

* * *

JULY 12, 1937

Bill Cosby, 1965 (Public Domain)

WILLIAM HENRY "BILL" COSBY JR. – BORN IN PHILADELPHIA, PA!

After failing the 10th grade due to too much class clowning, Cosby later earned his equivalency diploma and was awarded a track scholarship to Temple University. While bartending at a Philadelphia club to earn money, he used his ability to make people laugh on his customers and saw his tips increase.

Cosby left Temple to pursue a career in comedy, receiving his first national exposure on NBC's *The Tonight Show* in 1963, which led to a recording contract with Warner Bros. Records, who, in 1964, released his debut LP *Bill Cosby Is a Very Funny Fellow … Right!*, the first of a series of comedy albums dealing with his specialty – childhood recollections. The family themes were universal and Bill Cosby was a hit.

TV came knocking in 1965 the form of a co-starring role on the 1960s espionage show *I Spy*. Working with white actor Robert Culp, it was the first black-and-white television duo and initially stations in Georgia, Florida, and Alabama refused to air it. Regardless, Cosby won three consecutive Emmys for Outstanding Lead Actor in a Drama Series.

During this period Cosby recorded six comedy albums and also sang. In 1967 he had a hit record, "Little Ole Man (Uptight, Everything's Alright)," selling over a million copies. In 1968 Cosby left Warner Brothers to record on his own label, turning down a five-year, $3.5 million renewal contract in the process.

Tetragrammaton Records was founded by Cosby, his manager Roy Silver, and filmmaker Bruce Post Campbell. It signed British heavy rock group, Deep Purple and cranked out some films, records, Cosby's television specials and a Fat Albert cartoon special before folding in 1970.

Cosby returned to TV in 1969 with *The Bill Cosby Show*, with Cosby playing a PE coach. The show featured veteran Black performers Lillian Randolph, Moms Mabley, and Rex Ingram, but only lasted two seasons. Cosby blamed that shortness on his dispute with NBC about use of a laugh track which he refused to use. After *The Bill Cosby Show* left the air, Cosby was a regular for two seasons on the PBS series *The Electric Company*.

In 1972, he came back with a variety series, *The New Bill Cosby Show*. It lasted one season, but his simultaneous offering on Saturday morning show, *Fat Albert and the Cosby Kids*, based on Cosby's specialty – childhood recollections was a hit and some schools use it as a learning tool. Its creator was bestowed with honors and degrees not based on academic achievement, but life experience.

Bill Cosby made movies. Some were good (*Uptown Saturday Night* (1974) and *Let's Do It Again* (1975) with Sidney Poitier. Some were mediocre (*Mother, Jugs & Speed* (1976), costarring Raquel Welch and Harvey Keitel; *A Piece of the Action* and *California Suite*). Others were just plain lousy (*Leonard Part 6* {Cosby even told people not to go}, *Ghost Dad*). Back to TV, where in 1976 he did *Cos,* an hour-long variety show that barely lasted a season. Family projects for ABC filled the gaps until he struck gold in 1984 with the revolutionary sitcom, *The Cosby Show,* depicting a rich Black family. It became the highest rated sitcom of all time and was one of only three shows to ever rank #1 for five consecutive seasons. Bill Cosby became known as "America's Dad."

While the iron was hot Cosby produced the *Cosby Show* spin-off sitcom *A Different World.* In 1992 when *The Cosby Show* went off the air, Bill Cosby went into overdrive with a revival of the Groucho Marx game show *You Bet Your Life* (1992–93), the TV-movie *I Spy Returns* (1994) and *The Cosby Mysteries* (1994). From 1996 to 2000 he starred in the CBS sitcom *Cosby* and hosted *Kids Say the Darndest Things* from 1998 to 2000. Not to mention, *Little Bill,* for Nickelodeon in 1999.

May 2004, Bill Cosby became an activist. While receiving an award at Constitution Hall, Cosby made remarks critical to modern Black culture and its priorities and lack thereof. He called for more parental responsibility. A lot of Blacks were offended and he faced harsh criticism, which lingered.

In October 2014, comedian Hannibal Buress' criticized Cosby for "talking down" to young Black men and capped it off by saying "you rape women." That particular performance of a bit he'd done many times before before went viral resulting in a media firestorm and leading to a turn of public opinion about "America's Dad."

A new NBC show for Cosby scheduled for 2015 was scrapped. TV Land pulled reruns of *The Cosby Show* due to accusations by over 40 women of drug facilitated sexual assault. During this period Cosby maintained his innocence (despite mounting evidence of guilt) and remained active as a touring stand-up comedian performing at theaters throughout the United States.

Nevertheless, in September of 2018 William H. Cosby, Jr. was sentenced to 3-10 years in prison. As soon as the sentence was imposed he was taken immediately into custody, whisked out of the courtroom and sent off to live his new existence.

https://youtu.be/UEwPy31vWZ8

✳ ✳ ✳

JULY 12, 1959

Charlie Murphy (l) w/ brother, Eddie Murphy (Humor Mill Magazine)

CHARLES QUINTON "CHARLIE" MURPHY – BORN IN BROOKLYN!

Charlie Murphy got started in comedy after a short jail stint as a minor, followed immediately by a six-year stint in the US Navy. During this period his younger brother, Eddie had become a star and when Charlie came to town the first thing casting agents wanted was an Eddie Murphy look alike. They soon found out after a lot of four-letter words, that Charlie was nobody's look alike. He didn't have to be – he was funny.

Murphy took comedy seriously and got into stand-up, working out in small spots to hone his craft. However, there was no need to squander his in born celebrity so while getting good enough to use the title of "stand-up comedian," Murphy acted in films: *Harlem Nights, Mo Better Blues, Jungle Fever, CB4, King's Ransom, The Players Club, Roll Bounce, Night at the Museum, Paper Soldiers* (which he wrote), *Norbit* (which he co-wrote with Eddie), *The Perfect Holiday, Lottery Ticket, Meet the Blacks* and others. He wrote songs for the hip hop group, K-9 Posse and was the executive producer of their debut album and his television credits include *Martin, One on One, Wild 'n Out, Are We There Yet?* and *Black Jesus.*

Charlie Murphy became a public celebrity when he was featured on *Chappelle's Show.* He tapped into the public's thirst for Hollywood gossip with his *Charlie Murphy's True Hollywood Stories,* where he would regal the audience with pre-taped sketches of his adventures with stars, most notably

Rick James and Prince. The show was a surprise hit and Murphy was credited as part of the reason for its success. So, when Dave Chappelle left his own show and Comedy Central made the decision to broadcast the remaining footage without Chappelle's participation, it was Charlie Murphy and fellow cast member, Donnell Rawlings who got the call to host those shows. They came to be known as *The Lost Episodes,* but the only thing lost was the opportunity for more *Chappelle's Show.* It was over and Murphy moved on.

Charlie Murphy toured the nation as a stand-up comedian – solo (with opener Freez Luv) and as part of packaged celebrity comedian tours (Eddie Griffin, George Lopez, D L Hughley and Cedric the Entertainer was the last such outing). Murphy had his own sketch comedy show on Crackle called *Charlie Murphy's Crash Comedy* and a Comedy Central standup special, *Charlie Murphy: I Will Not Apologize.* Besides his work in front of the camera and on the road, Murphy has been heard providing voices for *The Boondocks, Thugaboo and Grand Theft Auto.* And he not only wrote *Paper Soldiers* and *Norbit,* Murphy also penned *Vampire in Brooklyn,* which starred his brother Eddie and Angela Bassett.

On April 12, 2017 Charlie Murphy passed away after a lengthy bout with Leukemia.

https://youtu.be/Ege_zAtGjJU

✳ ✳ ✳

JULY 13, 1969

Dr. Ken Jeong (r) w/ Rudy Moreno (The Moreno Collection)

DR. KENDRICK KANG-JOH "KEN" JEONG – BORN IN DETROIT!

Dr. Ken Jeong is a show-off. First thing – the man is a real doctor. He graduated high school at age 16, completed his undergraduate studies at Duke (1990) and then obtained his M.D. degree in 1995; the same year he won the Big Easy Laugh Off. He'd been working on his stand-up act the whole time and as luck or fate would have it, Improv founder, Budd Friedman and NBC CEO Brandon Tartikoff were judges and told Dr. Ken to move to L. A. immediately. He did and performed regularly at the Improv and Laugh Factory at night. For his day job, Dr. Ken simply became a licensed doctor in California and set up his practice at Kaiser Permanente in Woodland Hills.

Dr. Ken made the rounds on television. He guest-starred on *The Office*, *Girls Behaving Badly* (he was a regular), *Entourage*, *MADtv*, and *Curb Your Enthusiasm*. However, it was the part of Dr. Kuni in the Judd Apatow filmed comedy, *Knocked Up* that changed the trajectory. He was now in demand, but personally scared to make that leap of faith. Being a doctor sure does pay the bills and it's not like they just handed him a degree. It was hard work. Plus, acting's so flakey. Hot today, the next day people are looking at you in disgust. It was his wife who convinced him to go for it. Medicine wasn't going anywhere. Besides, she's a licensed physician.

So he went for it. Dr. Ken has appeared in *Pineapple Express*, *Step Brothers*, *Role Models*, *All About Steve*, *Zookeeper*, *Transformers: Dark of the Moon*, *Pain & Gain*, *Big Momma's: Like Father Like Son*, *Rapture-Palooza* (he played God), *The Goods: Live Hard, Sell Hard*, *How to Make Love to A Woman*, *Ride Along 2*, *Couples Retreat* and the *Hangover* trilogy. He received critical acclaim for his part of Ben Chang on NBC's *Community* and the fans loved him too. For that role he was nominated for the 2010 Teen Choice Award for "Male Breakout Star."

Dr. Ken has done commercials (Adidas), hosted award shows (*2011 Billboard Music Awards*) and showed people how to stay alive (American Heart Association 2011 Hands Only CPR PSA campaign). He's done animated voices for the *Despicable Me* franchise, *Birds of Paradise*, *Penguins of Madagascar*, *Norm of the North*, *American Dad*, *Robot Chicken* and *Turbo*. Then he got a chance to show off again by creating, writing and being the executive producer of his own show for ABC, *Dr. Ken*.

Jeong has won the Streamy Award for "Best Guest Appearance" (*Burning Love*).

https://youtu.be/LgQ1JnhV9pI

✳ ✳ ✳

JULY 13, 1946

Cheech Marin (The Moreno Collection)

RICHARD ANTHONY "CHEECH" MARIN – BORN IN LA!

Marin is a pioneer of stoner comedy along with his partner, Tommy Chong. Together they made up the team of Cheech and Chong. The name Cheech came from chicharrons. Why? Because when Mexicans get high they satisfy the munchies with – chicharrons. (We don't make up the stereotypes we only report them). Marin's dad was a cop, but when the possibility that the Vietnam War could enter into the world of young Cheech, he hightailed it up to Canada to avoid the draft; where he met Chong, who was a resident. Chong was a musician who'd had a band with a couple of hits records and had opened a popular night club in Vancouver. The problem was the more business got into Chong's musical career the less it was a career. When he met Marin in 1968 the timing was ripe.

Cheech and Chong were a cultural phenomenon; catching lightning in a bottle by being on the crest and sometimes leading the love-of-cannabis movement. They came along between the Summer of Love and Woodstock and were to weed what Snoop Dogg is to weed, but before him. The stand-up comedy material they performed on stage talked about smoking weed. The albums the released talked about smoking weed. The movies they made (except for one) showed them smoking weed. It was branding at its best.

Even a good high comes to an end and thus Cheech and Chong broke up in 1985. They'd made seven films (Chong directed four of them) and recorded eight albums; the most popular being 1978's *Up in Smoke*. There had been creative differences and Marin was itching to jumpstart a solo acting career so it was time; even if it wasn't it became time.

Cheech Marin's breakout film was *Born in East L. A*. It was a hit and he went on to appear in *Fatal Beauty, The Shrimp on the Barbie, Ghostbusters II, Tin Cup, A Million to Juan, Desperado, The Great White Hype, Christmas* with *The Kranks, Once Upon a Time in Mexico, Far Out Man, From Dusk Till Dawn, Spy Kids* and *The Book of Life* just to name several. On the television front Marin co-starred on the *Golden Palace, Nash Bridges* with Don Johnson, *Judging Amy* and Rob Schneider's *Rob*. He had a recurring role on *Lost*, hosted *Latino Laugh Festival* and did a slew of guest-starring on sitcoms.

Marin became a noted voice-over artist. He's been featured in *The Lion King, Oliver & Company, Car, Car2, It's Tough to Be a Bug* and *Beverly Hills Chihuahua, Blazing Dragons, South Park, Dora the Explorer, Hoodwinked, Ferngully: The Last Rainforest, Pinocchio, The Simpsons* and *Cheech & Chong's Animated Movie.*

Cheech Marin is a prime example of reinvention. The former counter-culture comedian has been on mainstream game shows competing against mainstream celebrities. The former munchies man was on a reality show on the Food Network of all places; cooking, not eating. His career did so much of a 180° that Marin, once a tutu wearing, mind-altered rocker released two children's albums and a book based on his wholesome creation, *Cheech, The School Bus Driver.*

https://youtu.be/c-B0Siwgyz4

✳ ✳ ✳

July 13, 1979

Chris Rock's *Bigger & Blacker* – Released by DreamWorks!

The album is a melding of studio-recorded comic sketches, featuring Ol' Dirty Bastard, Biz Markie, Gerald Levert, Ali LeRoi, Wanda Sykes, Kaz Silver, Horatio Sanz, Ice Cube, Kali Londono, Don Newkirk, Kate Wright, and Nneka Kai Morton as well as live stand-up comedy tracks recorded for the HBO special that premiered on July 10th of that same year at the Apollo Theater in Harlem. That show was directed by Keith Truesdell with Slick Rick opening for Rock with "The Show."

The live stand-up highlighted Rock's social commentary with bits harpooning gun control, President Clinton, homophobia, racism, black leaders, and relationships.

Bigger & Blacker won the 1999 Grammy Award for Best Spoken Comedy Album.

https://youtu.be/vez6KHV_3Jk

* * *

JULY 14, 2006

LITTLE MAN – RELEASED BY COLUMBIA PICTURES!

This film is a labor of love by the Wayans Family. Keenan Ivory Wayans co-produced it, co-wrote it and directed it. Brothers Marlon and Shawn Wayans co-produced it, co-wrote it and co-starred in it. And in the pivotal co-co-co-starring role of the Officer Wilson – Damien Dante Wayans. Other non-Wayans members of the cast are David Alan Grier, Molly Shannon, Uriel Garcia, Brittany Daniel, Lochlyn Munro, Kelly Coffield, Dave Sheridan, Fred Stoller, Alex Borstein, Rob Schneider and John Witherspoon.

The story revolves around a dwarf of a jewel thief who heists a priceless diamond (aren't they all in the movies? There's never a retail price) and before getting busted with it he stashes it in the purse of an innocent citizen (Kerry Washington) and now has to get it back. Retrieving means going to her home, discovering she and her husband (Shawn Wayans) want a baby and masquerading as a baby to get inside.

Once in Wayans does his best to find the diamond, but his attentive parents are always in his face. He tries to get help from his partner in crime (Tracy Morgan), but he's already been approached by the local gangster

(Chazz Palminteri) who knows the score and wants the priceless diamond. And as if that wasn't enough, none of the couple's friends or relatives think Wayans is an adorable baby. Maybe not, but when everything swirls out of control it's baby Wayans who saves himself, his "parents" and gets the gangster jailed.

All ends happily ever after. The baby Wayans (now an admitted criminal) gets to hang out with the couple and play games in the park with his "parents," who now have a newborn who looks like daddy and not Baby Wayans (who also got some booty from the wife).

The critics didn't care for *Little Man*, but when have the Wayans ever cared about critics. Bottom-line – on a budget of $64 million *Little Man* grossed $101.595,121 million at the worldwide box office.

https://youtu.be/x9STUnqrE_c

✳ ✳ ✳

JULY 14, 1893

Spencer Williams (r) w/Alvin Childress as "Amos 'n Andy" respectively 1951 (Public Domain)

SPENCER WILLIAMS – BORN IN VIDALIA, LOUISIANA!

Spencer Williams lived his teen-age years in New York, working as a call boy for Oscar Hammerstein while being mentored as a comedian by Bert Williams. By 1923 Spencer Williams was in Hollywood getting bit parts in films like Buster Keaton's comedy classic, *Steamboat Bill, Jr.*

In 1929, Williams created the dialogue for a series of comedy films featuring all-Black casts. That developed into him creating *The Melancholy*

Dame, the first Black talkie. Despite being an innovator, the Depression hit Spencer Williams like everybody else and he struggled; getting uncredited parts in well regarded films such as 1931's smash hit *Public Enemy.*

Spencer Williams didn't care for unemployment so he expanded his range of skills. Besides being an actor and writer, Williams was also a sound technician, an assistant director, a casting director, supervisor for recording sessions and by 1931 a co-founder of Lincoln Talking Pictures Company; making movies and news reels. Self-financed, Williams built most of the equipment including a sound truck.

Williams was a driving force behind race films; those all-Black cast independents made for Black audiences in segregated theaters. Initially he got roles in all-Black Westerns and moved into writing. He wrote the Western, *Harlem Rides the Range* and the horror-comedy, *Son of Ingari.* He utilized his growing experience to integrate into directing. At the time the only other Black director was the renowned Oscar Micheaux. Williams traveled throughout the South showing his films.

Spencer Williams first major success (and some say his masterpiece) was 1941's *The Blood of Jesus* produced by his own company, Amnegro, on a $5,000 budget using non-professional actors. It is recognized as the most successful race film ever made.

His subsequent films did not garner the critical nor financial success. He found himself in another career rut. After a series of directing mediocre race films patterned after Hollywood movies, Williams left Dallas and returned to the real Hollywood and his future as Andy in the immensely popular *Amos 'n Andy*; except instead of being on radio it was the television version.

Amos 'n Andy was the first U.S. television program with an all-Black cast, running for 78 episodes on CBS starting in 1951. It co-starred Alvin Childress as Amos and Tim Moore as the Kingfish. As should've been expected the show was met with controversy; complaints of stereotypical portrayals by the NAACP, who filed a federal court injunction to halt its premiere. That was that. It soon met the inglorious fate of early cancellation in 1953. Following the show's demise, the cast took it on the road, but CBS considered that a violation and the tour was halted.

Williams bumped around awhile longer, but eventually retired and lived off his military pension. Spencer Williams died of a kidney ailment on December 13, 1969.

https://youtu.be/nOh6jVGC4zc

✳ ✳ ✳

JULY 15, 1968

Eddie Griffin (Comedy the Magazine)

EDWARD "EDDIE" GRIFFIN – BORN IN KANSAS CITY, MI!

After high school, he enrolled as a biological engineer at Kansas State University, but left after only three months. He found comedy and moved west to Hollywood where he became a regular at the World-Famous Comedy Store and attracted the attention of Andrew "Dice" Clay, who hired Griffin as his opening act. He gained wide spread popularity following his *Def Comedy Jam* appearance where he parodied Michael Jackson on crack. Other successes followed as well as film and television roles.

Eddie Griffin has starred in *Meteor Man, Deuce Bigalow: Male Gigolo, Undercover Brother, John Q, Norbit* and many others. From 1996-2000 he co-starred in the hit UPN sitcom, *Malcolm & Eddie*, along with Malcolm Jamal Warner.

Griffin was ranked #62 on Comedy Central's list of the 100 Greatest Stand-ups of All Time. He toured with D.L. Hughley, Cedric the Entertainer, George Lopez and Charlie Murphy; their on-stage antics and chemistry captured for a mini-series. Griffin is also renown as a headlining tourist attraction in Las Vega, Nevada.

https://youtu.be/9tzrnwoSpeo

✳ ✳ ✳

JULY 15, 1976

Gabriel Iglesias (l) w/ Alfred Robles, George Lopez (Moreno Collection)

GABRIEL IGLESIAS KNOWN PROFESSIONALLY AS "FLUFFY" – BORN IN SAN DIEGO!

Like most successful comedians, Iglesias came from a poor background. He was raised by a single mother along with his five siblings in Section 8 housing. When he was old enough to work he got a job at a cell phone company. When he thought about giving comedy a try of course his family tried to talk him out of it. Stay at the job for security. Don't risk it. Where will you be able to get another job at a cell phone company? He tried to do both and like most successful comedians, failed. Comedy requires concentration. So, in 1997 he left his job, lost his car and got evicted.

Iglesias stuck to his guns. He struggled on the circuit in the San Gabriel Valley, L.A. and Inland Empire and made a name for himself. With his signature Hawaiian shirt and infectious smile, Iglesias built a formidable fan base. It was increased when he appeared on Nickelodeon's *All That* with Nick Cannon. In 2006 he was finalist on *Last Comic Standing*, but got eliminated for smuggling in a Blackberry against the rules and not for comedy related reasons. Other standup shows he performed on were *Premium Blend, Comedy Central Presents, Live at Gotham* and *Just for Laughs*.

Gabriel Iglesias has had a fine film career (*El Matador, Magic Mike, A Haunted House 2, Magic Mike XXL*), television (*My Wife and Kids*) and a healthy Internet presence. He loves to do voice-over work and he's had the pleasure on *Family Guy, The Emperor's New School, Planes, The Nut Job, El Americano: The Movie, The Book of Life, Norm of the North, The High Fructose Adventures of Annoying Orange* and *Blazing Samurai*.

Over the course of his career, Iglesias has released three albums and scored big with his specials, *Gabriel Iglesias: I'm Not Fat ... I'm Fluffy, Hot and Fluffy Aloha Fluffy: Parts 1 and 2.* Comedy Central is the home of his highly acclaimed show, *Gabriel Iglesias Presents Stand Up Revolution.* His reality show on Fuse TV is entitled, *Fluffy Breaks Even.*

https://youtu.be/mrZMAnsqZWU

✳ ✳ ✳

JULY 18, 2003

BAD BOYS II – RELEASED BY COLUMBIA PICTURES!

The sequel to the blockbuster action-comedy of the same name once again stars Will Smith and Martin Lawrence. Directed by Michael Bay and produced by Jerry Bruckheimer, the film continues the adventures of detectives Marcus Burnett (Lawrence) and Mike Lowrey (Smith). It's been eight years since their last outing and this time the mission is to stop the flow of ecstasy into Miami.

The movie is chucked full of action and almost everything else. There's the KKK, Russian gangsters, Haitian gangsters, kidnapping, buttocks shooting, ecstasy ingesting, a busted pool, S.W.A.T., and a secret love connection between Smith and Gabrielle Union (secret because Lawrence doesn't know about it and Union is his baby sister).

Bad Boys II co-starred Theresa Randle, Joe Pantoliano, Jon Seda, Henry Rollins, Michael Shannon and John Salley. Though the critics gave it one star, thumbs down and a middle finger, *Bay Boys II* grossed practically twice as much as the original. On a budget of $130 million Bad Boys II made $273,339,556 worldwide *and* was nominated for "Outstanding Supporting Visual Effects in a Motion Picture" at the 2nd Annual Visual Effects Society Awards.

https://youtu.be/RCjbkORhw84

✳ ✳ ✳

July 18, 1980

Cheech & Chong's Next Movie – Released by Universal Studios!

D irected by Tommy Chong, this is the duo's follow up to their hit *Up in Smoke*. In this one Cheech & Chong star again as stoners, but with a more disjointed plot; which is fine because you should be high when you watch their movies anyway.

The loose story centers around seeking the ultimate high. Yeah. Cheech works at a movie studio during the day while Chong gets high. Cheech gets fired, but gets a date so he needs Chong to get lost for a while. Chong doesn't like that idea, but a constructive way to keep him occupied shows up with the Red situation. Cheech's play cousin, Red, got kicked out of a motel and needs somebody to come swoop him up. It would be beneficial because he has a suitcase full of weed. It's weed the motel clerk tried to unknowingly confiscate for back pay, but he gets into a twist with the cops he called and gets arrested himself. They end up at a brothel and get kicked out for disturbing the hoes. Next thing you know they're abducted by aliens and brought aboard their spaceship. Cheech missed his date because he slept through it and Chong returns from his space adventure in time to share space coke with Cheech and the world as they ride off on a giant blunt. Told you, you needed to be high.

Cheech & Chong's Next Movie featured the talents of Paul Reubens, Phil Hartman, Evelyn Guerrero, Faith Minton, Edie McClurg, Sy Kramer, Rita Wilson, Cassandra Peterson and Michael Winslow. Produced by Howard Brown, *Cheech & Chong's Next Movie* grossed $41,675,194 at the box office.

https://youtu.be/RslItmJlPcY

✳ ✳ ✳

JULY 20, 1962

Carlos Alazraqui (l) (Instagram)

CARLOS ALAZRAQUI – BORN IN YONKERS, NEW YORK!

Best known for his role as Deputy James Garcia on the Comedy Central series *Reno 911*, Alazraqui got his start in show business competing in open mic contest in the mid-80s while attending Cal State University Sacramento. When he won the San Francisco International Comedy Competition after four years of working stand-up, Alazraqui took his prize money and moved to Los Angeles.

Alazraqui is regarded in the industry as a consummate voice-over artist; having served as the voice of the Taco Bell Chihuahua in the popular series of commercials and Nestor in *Happy Feet*. His massive list of animated credits include Bobbi Fabulous on *Phineas and Ferb*, Rocko and Spunky on *Rocko's Modern Life*, Mr. Crocker and Juandissimo Magnifico on *The Fairly Odd Parents*, Winslow T. Oddfellow and Lube on *CatDog*, Lazlo and Clam in *Camp Lazlo*, Grandpapi Rivera in *El Tigre: The Adventures of Manny Rivera*, Mr. Weed on *Family Guy* (which Alazraqui hated leaving due to the surprising and untimely death of the character) as well as voices on *Angry Beavers*, *KaBlam*, *Cow and Chicken* and *I am Weasel*. He was the original voice of *Spyro* in the first game in the *Spyro Dragon series*. He also voices multiple characters in the Disney film *Inside Out*.

Industry insiders say Alazraqui's natural voice has no hint of any accent. They also state that his Scottish accent is the best ever even though he came from Argentine parents. He uses many dialects and accents in his stand-up act and tours regularly. He's appeared on *The Hollywood Squares* and the spin-off *Reno 911 Miami!* Carlos Alazraqui is currently voicing Tio Tortuga in the Disney show, *Sheriff Callie's Wild West*.

https://youtu.be/pZX_0RngJGA

✳ ✳ ✳

JULY 21, 1974

Steve Byrne (l) w/ Bill Burr (Instagram)

STEVE BYRNE – BORN IN FREEHOLD, NEW JERSEY!

Most stand-up comedy records are ridiculous. There's one where some comedian went over 40 hours allegedly doing stand-up (without eating or using the bathroom, huh?). Leads you to believe he did material for an hour, maybe two and talked for the other 38 with a few laughs smattered about to so you could call it comedy. But really?! Well, Steve Byrne's record in enviable for any comic. He did 13 sets in one night. You can pull that off in New York, but nobody had before Steve Byrne or after. He even filmed it in the documentary, *13 or Bust* to make sure nobody would mistake the feat for urban legend.

Byrne has shown obsessive behavior as a comedian. Besides, club hopping a lucky 13 times before Lon Chaney's hair receded back into his pores, the Korean/Irishman likes to work … a lot. He has one half hour Comedy Central special and four one-hour Comedy Central specials. Byrne showed up on the *Tonight Show with Jay Leno* nine times, was featured on television's *The Real Wedding Crashers,* and made appearances on *@midnight, Tough Crowd with Colin Quinn, Chappelle's Show, Jimmy Kimmel Live!, Last Call with Carson Daly, Premium Blend, Good Morning America* and *Comic View* on BET.

Byrne is also a festival darling. He's been the feature act at Montreal's Just For Laughs Festival, HBO's US Comedy Arts Festival, the TBS Very Funny Comedy Festival in Chicago and Toronto as well the CanWest Comedy Fest in Vancouver.

Steve Byrne has been seen in the films, *Four Christmases, Couples Retreat* and *The Goods: Live Hard, Sell Hard.* In 2012, Byrne co-created,(along with Rob Long) the hit TBS sitcom, *Sullivan & Son.* He stars in it as well. He's been on several USO tours to entertain US troops abroad, a number of national comedy tours and keeps doing sets on plenty of stages around the world (and breaking somebody's record we're sure).

https://youtu.be/TY5ur_IA-Pk

✳ ✳ ✳

JULY 21, 1989

DO THE RIGHT THING – RELEASED BY UNIVERSAL PICTURES.

This acclaimed film is one of director Spike Lee's best. Besides being a mainstay on most critic's top film list *Do the Right Thing* won three Best Film Awards, three Best Director Awards, four Best Supporting Actor Awards (three for Danny Aiello, one for Ossie Davis) and awards for Best Screenplay (Lee), Best Musical Score (Bill Lee, Spike's father), Best Actress (Ruby Dee), Best Cinematography (Ernest Dickerson), Best Editing (Barry Alexander Brown) and Best Song ("Fight the Power"). Lee wrote, produced, stars in and directed this motion picture that the U. S. Library of Congress designated as 'culturally significant' and that AFI ranked as the top film of 1989.

The story is about a day in the life of a Brooklyn neighborhood on one of the hottest days of the year. When it's hot tensions flare and in this multi-racial area that's a given. Mookie (Spike Lee) is a pizza delivery guy who's 25 years old living with his sister and has a child by his girlfriend who he does not live with. He works for Italians who have varying relationships with him. The dad tolerates him, one of the sons hates him and the other thinks he's cool. Mookie just wants to get out of the shop and be given the freedom to lollygag on his deliveries.

The tensions of this tale begin when one of the longtime residents (Giancarlo Esposito) finally notices there are no pictures of black people of the Wall of Fame at the pizzeria, only Italians in that Italian eatery. This is unacceptable and a protest is mounted with followers equalling two. No matter, the tension reaches a climax when the protesters demand a change of the wall or they will shut the pizzeria down. The owner (Aiello) has had enough of black agitators and loud boom-box music (which one of the protesters,

Radio Raheem (Bill Nunn) carries with him all the time and blasts) so Aiello curses them out with racial epithets and destroys the boom-box. This act of defiance causes Radio Raheem to immediately wrap his fingers around Aiello's neck and to choke him; that is until the police arrive and administer the chokehold on Radio Raheem, killing him in front of a slew of witnesses. Panicked, the cops load Raheem's lifeless body into their squad car and speed off. This leaves Aiello and his two sons at the whim of the mob, but before any further violence can take place on humans, Mookie throws a trash can through the pizzeria window, starting a spontaneous riot and causing violence to be committed on a building. The next morning when the smoke clears the pizzeria has been demolished, but Aiello and his sons survived. Mookie and Aiello bury an uneasy hatchet for it's time to rebuild, not only a restaurant, but racial relationships in the neighborhood. They both know that one will be easier to re-erect than the other.

Do The Right Thing was a resounding success. Besides, critical acclaim it scored big with the viewing public. On a budget of $6 million, it had a box office take of $37.3 million. The cast consists of Robin Harris, Steve White, Paul Benjamin, Frankie Faison, John Turturro, Richard Edson, Joie Lee, Bill Nunn, Roger Guenveur Smith, Steve Park, Frank Vincent, John Savage, Samuel L. Jackson with Martin Lawrence and Rosie Perez in their film debuts.

https://youtu.be/gLYTObRhcSY

✱ ✱ ✱

JULY 21, 1952

George Wallace (George Wallace Collection)

GEORGE WALLACE – BORN IN ATLANTA, GEORGIA!

Wallace got his break in comedy while working as a salesman for an advertising agency. One of his clients opened a comedy club and suggested Wallace try stand-up. So, in 1977 George Wallace hit the stage as Reverend Dr. George Wallace, decked out in a preacher's robe and an improvised act that was an immediate smash. Wallace, the New York comic was on his way.

Wallace moved to the West Coast in 1978. He got a job writing for *The Redd Foxx Show*, but after one year returned to the stage. He became a regular at the Comedy Store and went on the road opening for acts that included Diana Ross, George Benson, Smokey Robinson and Donna Summers.

In 1995 George Wallace was named the Best Male Stand-up Comedian at the American Comedy Awards. He was a regular on *The Tom Joyner Morning Show* before partnering with Isaac Hayes on radio in New York. He's had his own HBO special and appeared regularly on the late-night talk show circuit. He was voted number 93 in Comedy Central's Top 100 Greatest Stand-Ups of All Time. He's played in films such as *Batman Forever*, *The Ladykillers*, *The Wash*, *Things Are Tough All Over*, *A Rage in Harlem*, *Postcards from the Edge*, *Punchline* and *Think Like a Man Too*.

2003 saw a new beginning in the career of Wallace. He started headlining the Flamingo Resort and Casino in Las Vegas, Nevada. In no time he became known as "The New Mr. Vegas." He produced and marketed the show himself and is so popular in the desert town that he considered running for mayor.

https://youtu.be/lF4Jsewy13E

* * *

JULY 22, 1964

John Leguizamo 2008 (Public Domain)

JOHN ALBERTO LEGUIZAMO – BORN IN BOGOTA, COLUMBIA!

John Leguizamo decided to become funny at an early age. Once his family moved from Columbia to New York (Queens, Jackson

Heights) when he was four years old, making John first generation immigrant in a tough neighborhood, he knew he had to do something to keep from getting beat up every day. Making people laugh keeps a foot out of your butt so in high school he'd write comedy bits and test them on classmates; endearing himself to many who might protect "the funny guy" when fights would break out.

Once out of high school Leguizamo studied theater at Tisch School of Arts at NYU. He dropped out to become a stand-up comic. That phase began in 1984 on the New York club circuit; two years later he was on TV (*Miami Vice*). He's appeared in scores of films including *Casualties of War, Die Hard, Hangin' with the Homeboys, Regarding Henry, Romeo + Juliet, Spawn, The Pest, To Wong Foo Thanks for Everything Julie Newmar, Moulin Rouge, The Happening, Chef, Empire, Executive Decision* and *Night Owl*. In 1992 his role in the critically panned *Super Mario Bros* got him better comedy parts and his role in *Carlito's Way* earned Leguizamo better dramatic parts.

There seemed to be no end to Leguizamo's talents. He's lent his voice to the *Ice Age* franchise as Sid the Sloth. He created his own sketch show for FOX called *House of Buggin,* which lampooned Latin life in America. Leguizamo released his memoirs in 2006 entitled *Pimps, Hos, Playa Hatas and All the Rest of my Hollywood Friends: My Life*. He describes it as a brutally frank journey through his career and a candid look at celebrities he's worked with; covering their homophobia, diva tendencies, sexism and sugar daddy syndromes. He adapted it into a one-man play and presented it as *Klass Klown* to a successful, award winning run. He then renamed it and published it as a graphic novel in 2015 called *Ghetto Klown*; paralleling that one-man show for which it is loosely named, including all the self-confessional insecurities, self-doubt and anxieties

In 1991 his Off-Broadway production, *Mambo Mouth* won Leguizamo an Obie and an Outer Critics Award. His 1993 presentation, *Spic-O-Rama* won him a Drama Desk Award and four Cable ACE Awards (for the HBO version) as well as a Drama Desk Award in 1998 for *Freak*. HOLA (Hispanic Organization of Latin Actors) presented John Leguizamo with the Rita Moreno Award for Excellence in 2008 and he was given the Made in New York Award from New York City in 2011.

https://youtu.be/DFL6RKTeJk8

∗ ∗ ∗

JULY 23, 1972

Marlon Wayans (Humor Mill Magazine)

MARLON WAYANS – BORN IN NEW YORK, N Y!

His first film role was in brother Keenan's movie *I'm Gonna Git You Sucka*. He played a pedestrian. His career though, was far from that. Between 1992-1993, Wayans worked alongside siblings, Keenan, Damon, Kim, and Shawn on the Wayans' created, produced and dominated, *In Living Color* on FOX. It was during this time he was considered to play Robin in *Batman Returns*, but a character heavy script put a hold on that idea. He was later formally signed to play the Boy Wonder in *Batman Forever*, but when Tim Burton was replaced with Joel Schumacher, Wayans was cut out. Chris O'Donnell got to put on the nipply costume. Wayans still gets paid for that contract.

Despite minor setbacks, Marlon Wayans kept it going. He and Shawn jumped over to the WB and from 1995-1999 they starred in their own sitcom, *The Wayans Bros*. After the turn of the century, Marlon Wayans co-wrote and produced the first two *Scary Movies* along with brother, Shawn). They collaborated again in *White Chicks, Little Man* and *Dance Flick*.

In *Requiem for a Dream*, Marlon displayed his dramatic chops. In 2009 he showed he had a flair for action in *G. I. Joe: The Rise of Cobra*. He's appeared in *A Haunted House, A Haunted House 2* and *The Heat*. He's a partner on an online site to expose urban comedy, *What the Funny*. He created the competition show, *Funniest Wins* for TBS, produced the Nickelodeon cartoon, *Thugaboo* and toured with the family in "The Wayans Brothers Tour."

https://youtu.be/Y6rqCHPKiTg

∗ ∗ ∗

JULY 24, 1992

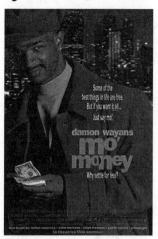

MO' MONEY – RELEASED BY COLUMBIA PICTURES!

This action comedy is the classic formula of Boy Meets Girl. Boy Wants to Impress Girl. Boy Steals Credit Cards. In this version Damon Wayans is the guy out to win over the heart of Stacey Dash. In his quest he and his cinematic brother (real life brother Marlon Wayans) use his insider job in the mailroom at a big-time credit card firm to rip off dead people in an identity theft scam to the tune of whatever will make him look good in the eyes of the superficial Dash. The fact he's a con man anyway makes the task a lot easier on his conscience. They're dead!

Along the way there's a series of seemingly unrelated murders committed by a bigshot played by John Diehl. They become very related when Wayans (Damon) is forced to kill Diehl to protect himself from being killed by Diehl's hitman and to rescue Marlon who was kidnapped by Diehl. In the end all's well that ends well. Marlon is safe and Damon is happy that he finally gets Stacey Dash before she reveals the fact she's a rapid Republican.

Directed by Peter MacDonald from a Damon Wayans script, *Mo' Money* also featured Joe Santos, Harry J. Lennix, Garfield, Rondi Reed, Quincy Wong, Mark Beltzman, Evan Lionel Smith, Kevin Casey, Larry Brandenburg, Alma Yvonne, Matt Doherty, Richard E. Butler and Bernie Mac, in his film debut.

Mo' Money was shot on a budget of $15 million and grossed $40,277,006 at the box office.

https://youtu.be/Y2_aNbKtWJg

✳ ✳ ✳

JULY 25, 1997

GOOD BURGER – RELEASED BY PARAMOUNT PICTURES.

Nickelodeon Movies partnered with Tollin/Robbins Productions to adapt this popular sketch from the series, *All That* into this feature film. Starring the comedy duo of Kenan Thompson and Kel Mitchell, *Good Burger* stayed true to the format of a dysfunctional fast food stand with an even more motley crew in charge.

The film version kicks off with Thompson wrecking his mother's car while on summer vacation. The problem is compounded by the fact the other vehicle to get damaged belonged to his teacher, played by Sinbad. A deal is struck. If Thompson pays for the repairs, Sinbad won't tell his mama. Thus, Thompson finds himself getting a summer job at Good Burger and there he meets a blissfully ignorant employee played by Mitchell. His character is so stupid he doesn't know he's sitting on a gold mine in the form of a secret sauce he invented that makes the Good Burger burgers the best burgers in town. However, the rival food chain, Mondo Burger knows how good they are and plot to steal the secret sauce recipe.

Once Thompson figures out it was Mitchell who accidently caused the car accident in the first place he leverages that bit of info to force Mitchell to sign over 80% of his secret sauce invention to his new "business partner." So they're partners not only in the invention, but also in the looney bin when the manager of Mondo Burgers has them committed while he continues to try to pilfer the thing that makes Good Burgers so doggone good. His Mondo Burgers already have a secret ingredient that makes them extremely and obscenely huge (an illegal substance of course), but tasting better wouldn't hurt.

The thing is no crazy house can hold sane nuts so Thompson and Mitchell escape and break into Mondo Burgers, and discover just how crooked they are. Following a series of mishaps, Thompson and Mitchell expose Mondo Burger's manager and save the day. Mondo Burger is destroyed by its own illegal additive and Good Burger goes back to being the neighborhood's meat-patty monopoly.

Good Burger also stars Abe Vigoda, Carmen Electra, Jan Schweiterman, Shar Jackson, Dan Schneider, Ron Lester, Lori Beth Denberg, Josh Server, Linda Cardellini with a cameos by Shaquille O'Neal, George Clinton, Robert Wuhl and Marques Houston.

On a budget of $8.5 million, *Good Burger* grossed an impressive return of $23.7 million at the box office.

https://youtu.be/rVTw5LK1zsQ

* * *

July 26, 1974

Bill Cosby and Sidney Poitier in *Uptown Saturday Night* (Instagram)

***Uptown Saturday Night* – Released by Warner Bros!**
Directed by Sidney Poitier, this classic comedy is the first in a trilogy that included *Let's Do It Again* (1975) and *A Piece of The Action* (1977). All three films starred Poitier and Bill Cosby. This outing also co-starred Harry Belafonte as Geechie Dan Beauford.

The story revolves around a robbery. Poitier plays a straight arrow working man with a lottery ticket who's on a two week vacation. Cosby is his wilder side-kick who talks him into going to Madam Zenobia's nightclub. Next thing they know robbers have everybody stripping naked and stealing everything not down their throats. Unfortunately for Poitier his wallet wasn't down his throat and it held the winning lottery ticket; which he now has to get back, with the help of Cosby of course. That's when the real fun starts.

This film features some of Black Hollywood's most enduring legends. Richard Pryor plays a con man who gets busted right after taking their money to crack the case. Harold Nicholas of the dancing Nicholas brothers plays Little Seymour Pettigrew, a diminutive gangster with a bodyguard named Big Percy. Flip Wilson is a reverend. Roscoe Lee Browne is a congressman, and Paula Kelly is pretty much Paula Kelly, but they called her Leggy Peggy. Other cast members include Rosalind Cash, Calvin Lockhart, Lee Chamberlin and Lincoln Kilpatrick.

Uptown Saturday Night was an immediate success. Written by Richard Wesley and Poitier, the film was produced by First Artists and Melville Tucker. The budget was $3,000,000 and the box office take was $6.7 million.

https://youtu.be/T8N43cc4VG4

* * *

JULY 27, 1933

Stu Gilliam (top) w/ Hilly Hicks in *Roll Out*, 1973 (Public Domain)

STU GILLIAM – BORN IN DETROIT, MICHIGAN!

Back in the day, kids would dream about running away from home and joining the circus. Stu Gilliam actually did it. He hadn't thought about it too long because he was only 14 when he packed up and got gainful employment as a ventriloquist. He rolled with the elephants and clowns for years before he started doing casinos and night clubs.

A two-year stint fighting the Korean War put things on hold for a moment, but not much. Gilliam kept on throwing his voice with a slab of wood on his lap to entertain the troops. When the bullets stopped flying he flew home and got on the chitlin circuit. He traveled the nation, culminating in the Apollo Theater (the pinnacle of the chitlin circuit of black venues), but non-black facilities were out of the question in the 1950s and 60s; especially in the South. It wasn't until the Playboy club began to book Gilliam that he was able to perform in front of mixed and sometimes all white crowds.

Mainstream acceptance opened the doors of Hollywood for Gilliam. He was seen on *The Ed Sullivan Show, Playboy After Dark* and *The Dean Martin Show*. He guest-starred on *Get Smart* as a double agent who was really white. He was a regular on *Rowan & Martin's Laugh-In*. Gilliam was everywhere you looked: *Good Morning World, Julia, Love American Style,* and if you didn't see him you heard his voice. Gilliam had a steady gig as the voice of Curl Neal starting in 1970 with *Harlem Globe Trotters* and *The New Scooby Doo Movies* in '72. He also was heard in *Houndcats* and was the announcer in *The Mack*.

Then in 1973 he was cast in the CBS sitcom, *Roll Out,* set in World War II. It was about supply drivers and had an ensemble cast that included Hilly Hicks, Mel Stewart and Darrow Igus. It was up against ratings powerhouse, *The Odd Couple* and *Roll Out* did just that after one season.

No biggie. Gilliam went right back to work: *Farewell My Lovely, Dr Black Mr. Hyde, No Deposit No Return, Quincey M. E., Brothers, Return From Witch Mountain, What's Happening, Harris & Company, B J & the Bear, The Apple Dumpling Gang Rides Again* and then of course his gig as Curly Neal in the series *The Super Globetrotters* in 1979.

Stu Gilliam, the juvenile runaway circus act, appeared in most of the major TV shows in his era. In the 1980s he was prolific: *The Misadventures of Sheriff Lobo, The Devil and Max Devlin, Herbie, the Love Bug, Small& Frye, Off the Wall, Gimme a Break, Wildside, Murder She Wrote, Simon & Simon* and *The Law & Harry McGraw*. Then 90s came and the output slowed, highlighted by *Life Stinks* and *Meteor Man*.

Whatever! Gilliam was a performer, so he performed. He went back on the road, converted to the Baha'i Faith in his 40s, got married in 2007 when he was in his 70s and died in the Czech Republic at the age of 80. The big top tent-of-comedy known as Stu Gilliam officially folded on October 11, 2013.

https://youtu.be/y5DOYWruMeA

* * *

JULY 27, 2007

WHO'S YOUR CADDY? – RELEASED BY WEINSTEIN!

The maiden voyage flick for Our Stories Films studio was a commercial and critical flop, but carries the distinction of being former-president, Bill Clinton's favorite comedy. Known as a rip-off of the classic, *Caddyshack, Who's Your Caddy?* is a who's who of pop culture figures of the era. The fast-paced romp starts rapper, Big Boi as a rapper who only wants to be admitted into a private country club, but when the hoity toity board refuse him due to cultural reasons he outsmarts them. The rapper buys property that includes the 17th hole of the oh so precious golf course. Negotiations are a waste of time. The upper-crust boys want nothing to do with him and will go to Hell and back before allowing his kind to mix with their kind. Well, then Hell it is.

The film co-stars Faizon Love, Tony Cox, Terry Crews, Jeffrey Jones, Lil Wayne, Sherri Shepherd, Andy Milonakis, Jesper Parnevik, Bruce Bruce, James Avery, Finesse Mitchell, Garrett Morris, Tamala Jones, Lawrence Hilton-Jacobs, Susan Ward and directed by Don Michael Paul. Tracey Edmonds, Kia Jam and Arnold Rifkin produced the film that made $2.76 million it's opening weekend for a total gross of $5,713,425. Too bad it cost $7 million.

https://youtu.be/fT0hv_GgeME

* * *

JULY 28, 2000

THE NUTTY PROFESSOR II: THE KLUMPS – RELEASED BY UNIVERSAL PICTURES!

This Eddie Murphy vehicle is a sequel to the 1996 film, *The Nutty Professor*, which was a remake of the 1963 Jerry Lewis film of the same name. In this edition Sherman Klump (Murphy in make-up) is a genius still, but we get to spend more time with his family who are not. However, they are all played brilliantly by Murphy, who also plays Sherman's alter ego, Buddy Love (Murphy without make-up).

The plot has Sherman discovering a formula for the fountain of youth. To complicate things, Buddy Love steals it and tries to sell it. Through DNA extraction Sherman is losing his brain cells and Buddy is on the loose as a separate entity from Sherman. With help from his assistant and his fiancé, played by Janet Jackson, Sherman regains his brain cells and dispenses with Buddy Love.

Eddie Murphy played eight roles in this film. Comedians, Wanda Sykes, Larry Miller and Chris Elliot are featured as well as Richard Gant, Anna Marie Horford, Freda Payne and Jamal Mixon. Though most critics panned the film for what they considered gross and lowbrow comedy, they overall praised Murphy for his versatility and talent. Critic legend, Roger Ebert, on the other hand, loved it – calling it "very funny" and "nothing less than amazing." Obviously many ticket buyers felt the same way.

On a budget of $84 million, *The Nutty Professor 2: The Klumps* grossed $123.3 million domestically and $43 million abroad.

https://youtu.be/iB25eDhWImc

* * *

JULY 28, 2005

NICK CANNON'S *WILD 'N OUT* – DEBUTED ON MTV!

This long running, on and off sketch comedy, improv series features up & coming comedians as well as seasoned vets. Hosted by its creator, Nick Cannon, *Wild 'N Out* is a ratings champion and holds the record for MTV2's biggest premiere.

The basic premise is two teams are pitted against each other in a series of improvisational games. One squad is captained by Cannon and the other by the celebrity guest, who also usually performs the show's musical number. Examples of the games are:

Let me Holla: Squad members use pick-up lines on a girl and good ones get a bell.

Turn up for what: When the audience replies, "Turn up for what?" the comedian must have a funny line or it's crickets.

Got props: Use props in a wrong scenario and your squad gets a buzzer and not a bell.

Remix: Gives each squad a chance to show off their ability to remix a song or nursery rhyme. The audience picks the winner of this round.

The audience also picks the winner of "**R and Beef**" where the audience also suggests the problem.

In "**Pie or Die**" squad members get custard to the mug if they use a word incorrectly in a freestyle rap.

Talking Spit forces members to hold water in their mouth while opposite squad members try to make them laugh.

In the game "**Family Reunion**" squad members introduce audience members as family members and of course the ones with most laughs wins the round.

Eat That Ass Up is a competition to see who can do a given dance the best.

Plead the Fifth has the captains in a cage answering questions posed by the opposing squad. If the captain doesn't or can't answer the question they can plead the fifth, but the more you punk out the less chance of winning. At the end the winning captain gets the championship belt.

Coming in at a half hour running time, *Wild 'N Out* has been called a hip hop version of *Whose Line Is it Anyway?*, launching and enhancing the careers of Corey Holcomb, Affion Crockett, DeRay Davis, Spanky Hayes, Kevin Hart, Dominique, Bruce-Bruce, Cedric the Entertainer, Earthquake, Jess Hilarious, Luenell, Brandon T. Jackson, Loni Love, Lil Duval, Sommore, Orlando Jones, Katt Williams, Mike Epps, Charlie Murphy, Deon Cole, King Bach, "DC" Young Fly, Karlous Miller, Chaunte Wayans, Billy Sorrells, Nate Jackson, Michael Blackson, Rip Michaels and more. Musical artists and athletes included Lil Jon, Kelly Rowland, Three 6 Mafia, Big Boi, Warren Sapp, Fat Joe, Sean Paul, Bobby Brown, Common, Serena Williams, E-40, Marques Houston, Amar'e Stoudemire, Joe Budden, Method Man, Nate Dogg, Snoop Dogg, Redman, Mariah Carey, Big Daddy Kane, Rick Ross, Nelly, T. I., Ne-Yo, Wiz Khalifa, Young Jeezy, Akon, Chris Paul, Jermaine Dupri, Da Brat and 2 Chainz.

https://youtu.be/Z8R8JjPxXgs

JULY 31, 1992

BÉBÉ'S KIDS – RELEASED BY PARAMOUNT PICTURES!

The brainchild of comedian, Robin Harris, the animated comedy was produced by Reginald Hudlin and Hyperion Pictures after Harris' death in 1990. Based on a routine from his stand-up act, *Bebe's Kids* tells the story of some bad kids and the trials and tribulations of a wannabe boyfriend forced to deal with them to score points with his potential lady.

Robin meets Jamika at a funeral and before he dies he wants some of that. He wants her so bad he gets talked into taking her and her son out to Fun World to get acquainted. The problems start to stack up when Robin goes to pick up Jamika and her son and there are three other kids there. They're Bebe's Kids and Bebe is nowhere to be seen, but she did leave a few bucks for the kids; a very few. Oh well, if Robin wants some Jamika he has to survive one little day. Off to Fun World they go.

Bebe's Kids reputation proceeds them. The guards at Fun World warn them they'll be watched. Doesn't matter – they go off anyway; running off and destroying everything in sight. It doesn't help that Robin's ex-wife is at Fun World, too. She and her weight challenged side kick try to put salt in Robin's game, but get smacked down with a barrage of mama jokes. Jamika warms up to Robin. Meanwhile Jamika's son gets no love from Bebe's Kids as they run amok, get caught by security, escape and recruit other amusement park-going kids to be menaces too. There's a trail with Lincoln and Nixon, a fully demolished Fun World and a trip to Las Vegas that ends with Bebe's Kids begin spotted and the gamblers fleeing for their lives. Best of all there's a live action clip of legendary (for good reason) Robin Harris doing stand-up comedy.

A predominately black cast voices the film, including Faizon Love (the voice of Harris), Vanessa Bell Calloway, Nell Carter, Myra J, John Witherspoon, George Wallace, Tone Loc and Marques Houston. Directed by Bruce W. Smith with a screenplay by Reginald Hudlin, Bebe's Kids made $8,442,162 at the domestic box office. Even though the critics disliked it and it came in #7 its opening weekend, audiences came to embrace the film as a cult classic. In 1994 it was adapted into a video game on Super Nintendo. Later *Bebe's Kids* was released on DVD in October of 2004, but was discontinued in March 2008.

https://youtu.be/QmqphjqWyd4

✳ ✳ ✳

AUGUST

THIS DAY IN COMEDY...

August 1, 1957

Taylor Negron (l) w/ Ray Walston in *Fast Times at Ridgemont High*

Brad Stephen "Taylor" Negron – Born.

Negron exited the womb in Glendale, California. He was of Puerto Rican descent and showed early signs of talent. His initiation into comedy came at the Comedy Store while he was in high school. Negron became an extra and did game shows to gain exposure. Negron was a hustler. He worked as Lee Strasberg's assistant briefly in a work-study program and for Lucille Ball during her stint as a guest teacher at a college.

Taylor Negron gained traction. He appeared in some of the major film comedies of his era: *Fast Times at Ridgemont High, Easy Money* (w/Rodney Dangerfield), *Punchline* (Tom Hanks), *Nothing but Trouble* (Chevy Chase), *Stuart Little* (Michael J. Fox), *Angels in the Outfield* (Christopher Lloyd), *Call Me Claus* (Whoopi Goldberg), *Bio-Dome* (Pauly Shore) and others. He was also in demand for sitcoms, guest starring on *Fresh Prince of Bel Air* (Will Smith), *Curb Your Enthusiasm* (Larry David), *My Wife and Kids* (Damon Wayans), *Friends, Seinfeld* and *That's So Raven* among others. In his last role he worked on *The Comedians* along with Billy Crystal and Josh Gad.

Negron was a talented artist. Beyond acting and stand-up he was an accomplished writer. He penned the successful production, *The Unbearable Lightness of Being Taylor Negron – A Fusion of Story and Song,* which was met with rave reviews. Negron wrote other produced plays and published several comedy essays (*Dirty Laundry* (Phoenix Books) and *Love West Hollywood: Reflections of Los Angeles* (Alyson Books). He was a contributing blogger and a painter. His artwork was displayed in solo exhibitions in prestigious venues such as Los Angeles' Laemmle Royal Theater and the Hotel de Ville Lifestyle.

Taylor Negron had long suffered from liver cancer when he succumbed in Los Angeles, California at the age of 57 on January 10, 2015.

https://youtu.be/tuENFR-9phU

✳✳✳

AUGUST 3, 2001

RUSH HOUR 2 – RELEASED BY NEW LINE CINEMA!

This sequel to the 1998 smash hit starring Chris Tucker and Jackie Chan has them reprising their roles as Detective Carter and Inspector Lee respectively. In this installment they find themselves in Hong Kong mixed up with the Asian Triads and a counterfeiting scam.

The plot unfolds with Tucker on vacation visiting Chan. His plans for a little R & R are derailed when a bomb goes off at the United States Consulate General killing two undercover custom agents. Chan is put on the case which is personal because of Ricky Tan, now a leader of the Triads, who Chan had long suspected had a role in the killing of his father, a former police officer. This distresses Tucker, who wants nothing to do with working a case. He's on vacation.

Things get complicated when the US and Hong Kong authorities fight over legal jurisdiction. Regardless the action ensues as Tucker's room is bombed, Ricky Tan is shot and Tucker and Chan go to Los Angeles to work the case.

Of course behind every great crime there is a rich white man (according to Tucker) and this one's is L.A., hotel billionaire, Steven Reign. With the help of an ex-con, Tucker and Chan track a load of counterfeit $100 bills back to Reign. They get knocked out and transported to Las Vegas where they attempt to find the engraving plates. It's discovered that Ricky Tan faked his death. Tan stabs Reign, who tries to back out of the deal and admits to Chan that he killed his father. Of course, this forces Chan to kick Tan out of a window and fall to his death. Chan and Tucker escape a bomb explosion. The film wraps up with the duo heading to New York to blow some of the money Tucker won at the casino.

Directed by Brett Ratner, Roger Birnbaum and Jonathan Glickman with music by Lalo Schifrin, *Rush Hour 2* was met with critically mixed reviews. Despite that, the live-action comedy is the highest grossing live-action martial arts film of all time, taking in $347,325,802 on a $90 million budget.

https://youtu.be/QCr8beTJsws

***

AUGUST 4, 1941

Paul Mooney (Comedy Hall of Fame Archives)

PAUL MOONEY (PAUL GLADNEY) – BORN IN SHREVEPORT, LA!

His first role as a performer came in the form of ringmaster with the Gatti-Charles Circus, where he wrote and told jokes. This led to his writing for Richard Pryor and such comedy classics as the race routine between Pryor and Chevy Chase on *Saturday Night Live*, Pryor's live stand-up concert films and comedy albums. They also co-wrote together on Redd Foxx's *Sanford & Son* and Mooney served as head writer for Pryor's NBC sketch show, *The Richard Pryor Show*, where Mooney was also casting director and introduced to the public Robin Williams, John Witherspoon, Sandra Bernhard, Marsha Warfield and Tim Reid.

Paul Mooney has acted in many memorable comedy films. He was in *Hollywood Shuffle, Which Way is Up?* and *Bustin Loose*. Mooney played Sam Cooke in *The Buddy Holly Story* and Junebug in Spike Lee's *Bamboozled*.

Mooney's influence has spanned generations. He was the head writer for *In Living Color* on FOX and created Homie the Clown. He was Negrodamus (a parody of Nostradamus) on *Chappelle's Show*, where he made outrageous and hilarious predictions to questions such as "Why do white people love Wayne Brady?" Negrodamus' answer: "Because Wayne Brady makes Bryant Gumbel look like Malcolm X."

Paul Mooney's career has been laced in controversy. From the time he called Black mayor of Los Angeles, Tom Bradley, "Uncle Tom Bradley" at a city function, to the time he ran Tracee Ellis Ross out of the showroom at the BET Comedy Awards following a typical Mooney rant about Ross' mother, Diana's DUI arrest and the mountain climbing death of Ross' step-father, Arne Naess Jr., to the time he was yanked from the Apollo Theater stage for talking about then president George W. Bush and his mama. Paul Mooney does no tongue biting.

Mooney is legendary for his stance on race. He wrote the book, *Black is the New White*. He released the comedy albums, *Race* and *Master Piece*. He did the DVD *Know Your History: Jesus Is Black; So Was Cleopatra*. He was even indirectly involved in the Michael Richard's N-Word revelation when Richards snapped on Black patrons at the Laugh Factory in 2006. Mooney publicly swore off ever using the word again; (a pivotal word in his act) and forgave Michael Richards for using it. Mooney himself has slipped and used it but must be given an E for effort.

https://youtu.be/jl_YXYbtksk

✳✳✳

AUGUST 5, 1976

The cast of *What's Happening!!* 1976 (Instagram)

WHAT'S HAPPENING!! – PREMIERED ON ABC!

Originally slated as a summer series, the sitcom received good ratings and returned in November of 1976 as a regular series. It was based on the Eric Monte film, *Cooley High*.

What's Happening!! was produced by Saul Turtletaub, Bernie Orenstein and Bud Yorkin following his split from partner, Norman Lear. The cast consisted of acting veteran, Mabel King (Mama), comedy powerhouse, Shirley Hemphill (Shirley), renowned pop-locker, Fred "Rerun" Berry (Rerun) and thespians, Ernest Thomas (Raj), Haywood Nelson (Dwayne) and Danielle Spencer (Dee).

The sitcom revolved around three teenage friends and their light-hearted antics in Watts. Never getting too heavy on social commentary, most of the problems were universally adolescent: getting girls, after school jobs and how to keep up their grades. Raj, an aspiring writer still lives with his divorced mother and wise cracking sister. His two best buddies (one overweight, the other over-shy) meet him regularly at the local café for shakes and fries and the only shots heard are back-firing buckets. Fat jokes are swapped between Rerun and Shirley, catch phrases and signatures laughs are doled out and there was always the threat that Dee would tell Mama. So, it's all good in the hood.

What's Happening!! boasted a cavalcade of talent. Besides the principle cast, Thalmus Rasulala, Lee Chamberlin, Debbi Morgan and Greg Morris were recurring characters. The Doobie Brothers, Chip Fields, Theodore Wilson, Wolfman Jack and Tim Reid made guest starring appearances.

What's Happening!! aired its last episode on April 28, 1979. It was only in the top 10 its second season, but still managed to inspire the spin-off, *What's Happening Now!!*, which ran from 1985-1988 and featured most of the original cast and a young Martin Lawrence.

https://youtu.be/Ef6U_XwfYNY

✳✳✳

AUGUST 6, 1993

THE METEOR MAN – RELEASED BY METRO-GOLDWYN-MAYER!

This superhero comedy was written, directed by and stars Robert Townsend as the title character, who gains his powers after a meteor crashes into him and puts him in the hospital. Townsend starts off as a peaceful school teacher living in a gang infested neighborhood in Washington, DC, but one night he's had enough. He tries to stop some thugs from attacking an old lady only to find himself turning tail and running for his own life. That's when the meteor gets him; when he emerges from hiding in a dumpster. Townsend heals miraculously and leaves the hospital with a variety of superpowers, such as flight, strength and the ability to gain a book's knowledge by his mere touch and talk to animals.

The Meteor Man cleans up his hood, but there's a downside to his abilities – they wear off. Soon he's just another victim of the gangs again, but this time they know his secret identity and he's a marked man. Fortunately for him the local bum also got a chunk of the meteor and when the moment is right the bum spills it into the street and this sets up the climactic battle between the neighborhood gang lord and The Meteor Man. Of course The Meteor Man wins, but not before inspiring the community to fight its own battles just before he loses his limited powers for the last time.

The Meteor Man is populated with comedians, rappers, singers and actual actors. It co-stars Marla Gibbs, Eddie Griffin, James Earl Jones, Sinbad, Robert Guillaume, Don Cheadle, Big Daddy Kane, Naughty by Nature, Cypress Hill, Nancy Wilson, Luther Vandross, John Witherspoon, Roy Fegan, Frank Gorshin, Biz Markie, Faizon Love, Tiny Lister, Wallace Shawn, Another Bad Creation and Bill Cosby as the bum.

The film spawned 6 comic books from Marvel Comics and grossed $8,016,708 domestically from a $30 million budget.

https://youtu.be/njP6YczRgsA

✳ ✳ ✳

August 7, 1839

Sam Lucas, 1911 (Public Domain)

Sam Lucas (born Samuel Mildmay Lucas or Samuel Lucas Milady) – Born in Washington Court House, Ohio!

Sam Lucas began his career as a black-faced minstrel in 1858. His parents were freed former slaves and young Sam took advantage of his enviable position during the Civil War and gained employment where there was pay, and not the fate his Southern counterparts experienced on plantations. Lucas worked as a barber while practicing guitar and vocals.

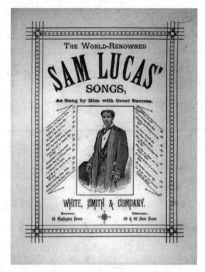

The diligence paid off. Sam Lucas was a minstrel pioneer. As a composer he was one of the first Black men to fuse established white songs with African-American rooted musical devices. He would sing his subversive tunes on stages and riverboats and as minstrelsy grew so did the stature of Sam Lucas. He became a celebrity not only for his music, but also for his comedic portrayals of the characters he sang about; sad, pitiful, downtrodden personalities, but ones with hope. Black people the way white people wanted to see them back then, minus the hope part.

Sam Lucas is recognized as the first Black man to play Uncle Tom in *Uncle Tom's Cabin* on stage and in film. The latter was his last work. Due to his comedy versatility as well as musically and dramatically, Lucas came to be known as the "Grand Old Man of the Negro Stage." From 1871-1879 he traveled throughout the country with various minstrel troupes including a tour in Havana, Cuba. Once he left minstrelsy Lucas performed in vaudeville.

Musical dramas and comedies were fine, but blackface paid the bills and after a play or two Lucas was back to smearing on burnt cork, and working with the best in the field. In 1876 he toured with Sprague's Georgia Minstrels. His fellow performers were black faced legends Billy Kersands and James Bland. This was authentic black minstrelsy. Most of the time whites played black roles. For instance, Lucas signature role as Uncle Tom had traditionally been played by Caucasian actors in blackface. Lucas' casting in 1878 changed all that. Unfortunately, the production was a flop.

Lucas went back to blackface. He also composed; lyrics and songs more militant than those of most Black writers of the time. He wrote of remembering freedom and the joyful memory of the day he was set free. During this period Lucas grew tired of minstrelsy and yearned for something new. The 1890 production of Sam T. Jack's *The Creole Show* gave him that opportunity. It was an all-Black production; one where he met and married his wife. They traveled together on stages in variety houses and vaudeville. He distanced himself from minstrelsy even further in 1898 when he did Bob Cole's *A Trip to Coontown.* It was the first black production to use black writers, director and producers. It truly was all-Black and devoid of minstrelsy.

Artistically the top of the 20th Century was good for Lucas. He worked under the direction of famed ragtime composer, Ernest Hogan from 1905-06. In 1907 he worked again for Bob Cole when the team of Cole & Johnson staged the musical comedy, *The Shoe Fly Regiment.* Once that ended Lucas jumped into another one: *The Red Moon* playing the part of – a barber. He was a member of the theatrical club, The Frogs and starred in films. One of his movies was the never finished *Lime Kiln Field Day* in 1913. (It was preserved by the Library of Congress in 2014). In 1914 he revived his role as Uncle Tom with decidedly better results for the film version. The stumbling block was Lucas' health. He'd suffered liver disease for many years and then he contracted pneumonia while filming and died soon afterwards on January 5, 1916.

https://youtu.be/6HeoN5Ynn4k

✳ ✳ ✳

AUGUST 8, 1986

SHE'S GOTTA HAVE IT – RELEASED BY ISLAND PICTURES.

This first film written and directed by Spike Lee, starred Tracy Camilla Johns, Tommy Redmond Hicks and John Canada Terrell. Ernest Dickerson was the cinematographer and S. Epatha Merkerson appeared as a doctor.

The film is about the sexual exploits of a freak in Brooklyn. She has 3 boyfriends who possess three distinctly different personalities. While Jamie (Hicks) is a nice guy and Greer is vain pretty boy, Mars (Spike Lee) is a goof-off, but a funny one. Nola (Johns) is running it like a man and that's the way she likes it. Too bad for the guys, who each want her for himself and only him.

Shot in 12 days on a budget of $175,000 and grossing $7,137,502, *She's Gotta Have It* was heralded by The New York Times as ushering in the independent film movement of the 1980s. It was also a departure from the Blaxploitation images of blacks in major motion pictures; economically and socially. The characters in this Lee maiden voyage are buppies not pimps, hos and hustlers.

She's Gotta Have It won Spike Lee multiple awards. At the 1986 Cannes Film Festival – "Award of the Youth" Foreign Film, Spike Lee won. At the 1986 Los Angeles Film Critics Awards – "New Generation Award," Spike Lee won and he also won Best First Feature at the 1987 Independent Spirit Awards.

https://youtu.be/Pd9oTGr_1DA

* * *

AUGUST 10, 1968

Rickey Smiley (Instagram)

BRODERICK "RICKEY" SMILEY – BORN IN BIRMINGHAM, AL!

The first prank call was made from Providence, Rhode Island in 1884. This was eight years after Alexander Graham Bell invented the telephone and 84 years before Rickey Smiley sprung from the womb. That call was morbid in nature, involving the prankster calling undertakers to bring candles, freezers and coffins for persons alleged to be dead. Upon learning this was all a ruse the local authorities set out to track down this mischievous abuser of the new technology. Point is – Rickey Smiley did not invent prank calls, but he became the face of it.

Starting out as a stand-up comedian, Smiley made a reputation for character driven comedy with stage personalities such as Lil Darryl and Miss Bernice. His live performances consisted of the multi-talented Smiley telling jokes, playing keyboard and launching into various alter egos to the delight of his packed crowds. His versatility was recognized by an executive at BET and Smiley not only got a showcasing spot, but landed a hosting position on the station's comedy insititution *Comic View* in 2000.

Television was a good fit for Smiley. He appeared on *Def Comedy Jam, Showtime at the Apollo, Snaps, Uptown Comedy Club, Comic Escape* and on *The Nashville Network*. He even got his own sitcom, *The Rickey Smiley Show* and *Rickey Smiley for Real,* a reality show about … wait for it …

Rickey Smiley. Fans of the *Friday* film series might also remember Smiley as a thieving Santa Claus the the third installement, *Friday After Next*.

All that was fine, but it was radio that was tailor made for Smiley's brand of ad-libbing expertise. He parlayed his Dallas, Texas based radio antics and signed a deal with Syndication One, taking *The Rickey Smiley Morning Show* nationwide. With that move the country got a liberal dose of Lil Darryl, the fella with a club foot who wasn't all right in the head; Bernice Jenkins, the Bible thumper who'd have thumped you in the head with her Bible; Rufus, a hip-hop gangsta; Buford, the redneck from Bama and an assortments of miscreants assaulting the phone lines to create havoc in the lives of unsuspecting targets.

Smiley was prolific. He'd call and ask for church members to be prayed for, looking for his daddy, looking for his girlfriend and he even returned to the roots of prank calls when Smiley called out claiming he was a funeral home employee who 'd fallen asleep in one of the caskets and they buried him alive. Would the person on the call please come to the cemetery and dig up all the graves until they found him?

https://youtu.be/rJnk1qT9eG0

✳✳✳

AUGUST 12, 1911

Cantinflas (Public Domain)

CANTINFLAS (MARIO FORTINO ALFONSO MORENO REYES) – BORN IN MEXICO CITY!

Cantinflas grew up in Tepito. A pioneer of cinema in Mexico, he was famed for portraying poor peasants and became identified as a national treasure. Referred to as "The Charlie Chaplin of Mexico" Cantinflas had a mammoth film career in his homeland and a successful one in Hollywood as well; winning a Golden Globe for Best Actor in the David Niven vehicle, *Around the World in 80 Days*. Chaplin himself called

Cantinflas the best comedian alive. However, his influence extended beyond entertainment as an outspoken advocate for the impoverished, leading to strides in the struggle to combat union corruption.

Cantinflas was raised in a tough part of town. His quick wit was his survival mechanism and he took that comic personality to work in the circus. Initially he tried to be the next Al Jolson, putting on blackface, but it didn't feel right to him so he played with a variety of characters until hitting onto the street dweller with the distinctive moustache. It was also under that circus tent that he got the name Cantinflas. It was a nonsensical moniker to hide the fact he was a performer from his parents. His folks thought such a profession was disgusting. Well, the trick must've worked because he went from the circus tent to theater to movies.

Cantinflas was a political activist. During his career he was president of the National Association of Actors; the Mexican Writer's Guild. Cantinflas was also the first secretary general of the Independent Film Worker's Union. Once retired he contributed heavily to charities to help the unfortunate and children.

In America it was the language barrier that prevented Cantinflas from receiving greater recognition. When *Around the World in 80 Days* was shown in English speaking countries David Niven was billed as the star. Cantinflas was the star everywhere else; giving him international heft and making him the top paid actor of his era.

Unfortunately, that era ended and Cantinflas, like many performers before and after, suffered backlash. His follow up American star vehicle, *Pepe* was dead on arrival and his once beloved Mexican peasant, *el pelado*, came to be viewed as a stereotypical embarrassment. Critics attacked him professionally and politically. They said he was a danger to Mexican society, a bourgeois puppet and a transgressor of gender roles. Whereas defenders saw him as a verbal innovator, a pious Catholic and a kind philanthropist.

Cantinflas died of lung cancer on April 20, 1993 in Mexico City. He'd been a lifetime smoker. His body lay in state for three days and thousands of mourners attended his funeral to pay their respects in the rain. He had his own production company, a star on the Hollywood Walk of Fame and did animated voices to educate children. He had songs written about him and his name became part of slang. He is credited with the rise in Chicano theater and spearheading the golden era of Mexican films. Even the US Senate had a moment of silence to mark his passing. Not bad for a comic.

https://youtu.be/BBMYa_GodTE

✳ ✳ ✳

AUGUST 12, 1974

Affion Crockett (Humor Mill Magazine)

AFFION CROCKETT – BORN IN FAYETTEVILLE, NC!

Crockett does a lot and is a lot. Besides, all the slashes behind his name the former Soul Train dancer is part Chinese Trinidadian, a world traveler before most kids see a globe (thanks to being raised in an Army family) and an entertainer with an actual degree and this one is best of all – in business. All of that might explain the out-of-the-blue success of Affion Crockett.

Seems everybody liked him. He was liked when he worked on the road with headlining acts and he was the feature having to drive them all around (which he did most times without complaint). People liked him when he did *Def Comedy Jam, Wild 'N Out, Black-ish, Curb Your Enthusiasm, A Haunted House 1 & 2, Soul Men, Welcome Home Roscoe Jenkins, 50 Shades of Black, Robot Chicken, Pixels* and *The Wedding Ringer.* They liked him when he released his comedy album, *Watch the Clone.* Jamie Foxx even liked this talented guy well enough to executive produce Crockett's first show, *In the Flow with Affion Crockett* for the FOX network and we're sure it won't be the last time Crockett is liked.

https://youtu.be/L6j6gpEhSZU

✱✱✱

AUGUST 12, 1974

Arj Barker (Domain.com)

ARJ BARKER (ARJAN SINGH) – BORN IN SAN FRANCISCO!

Besides being half-Indian and half-European, there's nothing halfway about Barker. He started a stand-up career right out of high school, wasting no time in getting his own room started. Once he honed his skills, he made the rounds. Barker appeared on Comedy Central's *Premium Blend, Late Night with Conan O'Brien, The Glass House* and got to host *Comedy Central Presents* a few times and did a voice for the animated series, *Shorties Watchin' Shorties* on where else – Comedy Central. He was even bold enough to jump ship and take a role on HBO's *Flight of The Conchords*. There was also an Off-Broadway play he co-wrote and starred in with Doug Benson.

Barker was running in stride. It was Hollywood that was out of step. He'd landed the lead on a proposed NBC sitcom, but the show's creator decided he wanted the part and replaced Arj with himself. Ha! The sitcom never aired, but Arj looked at other options. He moved to Melbourne, Australia where he'd been successful years before at the Melbourne International Comedy Festival.

Arj Barker has released two albums and eight DVDs.

https://youtu.be/tuTrrK48t_g

✳✳✳

AUGUST 13, 1999

Steve Martin and Eddie Murphy

BOWFINGER – RELEASED BY UNIVERSAL STUDIOS!

Produced by Brian Grazer and directed by Frank Oz, this comedy starring Eddie Murphy and Steve Martin is the story of a broke filmmaker, Bobby Bowfinger (Martin) shooting a film using major Hollywood star, Kit Ramsey (Murphy) without his knowledge or cooperation. On a budget of $2,184, Martin assembles his motley crew to film his epic, "Chubby Rain," a tale of alien takeover. Heather Graham plays a fresh-off-the-bus starlet screwing her way to the middle with Murphy in a duel role as the spoiled star and his goofy, slobbering twin brother, Jiff, used as an on camera double when the star Murphy disappears into the bosom of his cult-like religious organization, MindHead.

Bowfinger's plan is working up until his climatic last scene. Murphy the star comes out of hiding long enough to be caught up in a wild chase involving members of Martin's pack of actors. The finale takes place at an observatory with Murphy prompted to say the big line, "Gotcha suckas." Instead, the MindHead uppers shut down the films' production. All looks lost until some B-Roll footage of Murphy the star exposing himself to the Laker Girls gives Martin leverage to get his movie released without any criminal action. The premiere is packed and the flick is a hit spawning a pairing of Martin and the goofy brother Murphy in a cheap martial arts movie.

Written by Steve Martin, *Bowfinger* was a critical success, receiving generally favorable reviews. The budget was $55 million taking in $98,625,775.

https://youtu.be/9cb5Ka9SqGM

✳ ✳ ✳

AUGUST 14, 1987

DISORDERLIES – RELEASED BY WARNER BROS.

This comedy stars the rap group the Fat Boys as the title characters hired to protect a rich old guy (Ralph Bellamy) by his nephew (Anthony Geary) who actually wants the old guy dead so he can get his money. Of course, the Fat Boys thought they were given the assignment because they're competent orderlies, not bunglers who will surely have the old man die on their watch. But once they find out the plot they make it a point to protect moneybags against any possible danger. Not only do they protect him, their foolishness makes him healthier.

Disorderlies was directed by Michael Schultz and produced by George Jackson, Michael Jaffe, Doug McHenry and Joseph E. Zynczak. It co-stars Tony Plana, Helen Reddy, Marco Rodriguez, Sam Chew Jr, Ray Parker Jr and Robert V. Barron. The worldwide box office was $10,348,437.

http://youtu.be/FMXsRArwlk0

✳✳✳

AUGUST 15, 1956

Aida Pierce (l), w/Alejandra Procuna and Joel Moraguer

AIDA PIERCE – BORN IN ACAPULCO!

Raised in Mexico City where she studied acting, Aida began her career on stage in the Mexican productions of plays like *Peter Pan* and *Jesus*

Christ Superstar. This led to a contract with Televisa. Filmed in Mexico City, Pierce found herself featured in one comedy and musical variety show to another. She started out at Televisa in 1981 and didn't leave that home base of steady employment until 2012.

She also worked in film. She made her debut in 1985's *Los rockeros del barrio* and racked up an impressive resume before diving heavily back into television and stand-up personal appearances. She didn't return to the big screen for 20 years.

Televisa kept Pierce working. In 1986 she joined the cast of *Cosas de casados* and *El hospital de la risa*; featured in two shows simultaneously. Besides comedy and variety shows she also appeared frequently in tele-novelas, playing a wide range of characters and popping up on other's series as her popular characters. She was the go-to girl when it came to portraying newlywed wives.

In 1996 she gained the distinction of being the first comedian to pose naked in the Mexican edition of *Playboy.* Within the United States her work is widely seen on Univision and Telemundo and after leaving Televisa (due to ageism and a lack of roles) Pierce toured throughout Mexico as a stand-up (she writes her own material and sings in her show) and was a radio personality.

In 2007 Aida Pierce was inducted into "Paseo de las Luminarias" (Mexico's Hollywood Walk in Fame).

https://youtu.be/p1y2rNiH8bs

***

AUGUST 16, 1891

Eddie Green (seated 2nd from the left) w/ cast of "Duffy's Tavern," 1945 (Public Domain)

EDDIE GREEN – BORN IN BALTIMORE, MARYLAND!

Eddie Green had an illustrious career that spanned the mediums. During his decades as an entertainer, Green appeared in a silent film, headlined on Broadway, starred in one of the first talking motion pictures in 1929 (*Sending a Wire*), headlined at the Apollo Theater and composed the seminal hit, "A Good Man is Hard to Find" which has been performed by Frank Sinatra (in the film, *Meet Danny Wilson*), Bessie Smith, Louis Prima, Sophie Tucker, Cass Daley, Marion Harris and many more. It has also been showcased in the film *Bessie* (2015) on HBO as well as network television's *Here's Lucy* and *The Carol Burnett Show*.

Green's filmography includes motion pictures with Louis Armstrong, Hattie McDaniel, Louise Beavers, Lena Horne, Moms Mabley, Fats Waller, Eddie "Rochester" Anderson and James Baskette. His best-known movies were both in 1939 – *Dress Rehearsal* (which he also produced, as well as 1940's *Come Midnight*) and *What Goes Up* (which Green wrote and directed, along with the 1949 short, *Mr. Adam's Bomb*).

On radio, Green carried his name with him as Eddie, the Waiter on *Duffy's Tavern*. However, on the iconic *Amos 'n Andy*, he had to run with another moniker as Stonewall, the Lawyer. He lived a bigtime life and had bigtime friends, like Adam Clayton Powell, Jr., Mantan Moreland, Clarence Muse and Nat King Cole's wife, Maria.

Eddie Green died in Los Angeles, California on December 19, 1950 at the age of 59.

In 2016 a detailed biography, *Eddie Green: The Rise of an Early 1900s Black Entertainment Pioneer* was published by his daughter, Elva Diane Green. It took the Bronze Medal at the INDIES Book of the Year Awards, ensuring that the legacy of Eddie Green lives on.

https://youtu.be/1jEkBvM2ta4

AUGUST 18, 2000

The Original Kings of Comedy – Bernie Mac, Cedric the Entertainer, D L Hughley and Steve Harvey (Instagram)

THE ORIGINAL KINGS OF COMEDY – RELEASED BY PARAMOUNT!

Directed by Spike Lee this game changing comedy concert film starred comedians D.L. Hughley, Steve Harvey, Cedric the Entertainer and Bernie Mac. Before its premiere three of the four were on TV shows; two self-titled. After the premiere all parties were millionaires, stars and had TV shows.

Shot over two nights (February 26th & 27th 2000) at Charlotte, North Carolina's Charlotte Coliseum, *The Original Kings of Comedy* was a culmination of a successful tour (Actually the second leg. The first had Guy Torry as host and no D.L. Hughley) which had surprised industry types, but left African-American audiences who'd eagerly anticipated this combination in stitches. The performances showed each headlining comic at his best as well as their behind-the-scenes antics back stage, around town and on the basketball court.

Steve Harvey was MC; a role made for his quick wit and grounded style. He curses, pokes fun at audience members and sings. D.L. Hughley is up next with bits about Black families, the difference of Black people and White people and ghetto games. Cedric the Entertainer talks about the anger of a potential Black president (pre-Barack Obama) regarding sexual indiscretion. He also dives head on into routines about sports, ghetto life, migration, growing up and Jamaican music. The show is topped off by Bernie Mac who riffs on the joys of disciplining children in crude, blunt terms and about his sex life and decreased desire for lengthy sessions. The pivotal bit was one about raising his sister's kids and how he dealt sternly with them. The truth was Bernie Mac had no sister, but the routine was perfect to build a show around and *The Bernie Mac Show* was born.

The formula spawned a number of spin-offs: *The Queens of Comedy, The Original Latin Kings of Comedy, The Kims of Comedy, The Comedians of Comedy, The Killers of Comedy* and *The Blue Collar Tour.* This brainchild of producer, Walter Latham, *The Original Kings of Comedy* was nominated for an NAACP Image Award and a Chicago Film Critics Association Award. Shot on a budget of $3 million the film grossed $38,182,790 domestically.

https://youtu.be/JAa2gANm4KM?list=PLPOcHz8TDKe3bYIW83EzUYJ5uvtOiSqt3

AUGUST 19, 1994

BLANKMAN – RELEASED BY COLUMBIA PICTURES!

Directed by Mike Binder and co-written and starring Damon Wayans, this superhero spoof tells the story of a clueless repairman living in the hood and almost getting killed in it. Wayans has to have his grandmother slaughtered by local hoodlums to realize he's not in a good neighborhood. Instead of moving he decides to become a crime fighter like his idol, Batman. He invents gadgets to help him in his quest to clean up the city and puts on a costume complete with a mask to hide his identity and a bullet proof chest, but not head.

Wayans has a brother, played by David Alan Grier, who works as a news cameraman and films his brother in action, hoping this alter-ego will help him psychologically get over the murder of their grandmother. It does just the opposite. Wayans thinks just because he dresses like a superhero he's equipped to do superhero things and becomes a marked man. He calls press conferences that are ignored and at one point gets the mayor killed in a bomb defusing situation that goes wrong. That's when the city turns against "Blankman" forcing Wayans to abandon his antics, get a job at McDonald's and live a typical life (if you consider working at McDonalds typical).

Too bad Wayans made this decision so late in the game. Blankman made some enemies while he reigned and the same crime kingpin (Jon Polito) that killed his grandmother is now calling him out. If Blankman doesn't show up that kingpin will kill the object of Blankman's affections, a female news reporter (bet you didn't see that one coming) played by Robin Givens. This once again forces David Alan Grier to get involved. He dons the crime fighter suit of "Blankman's sidekick, "The Other Guy," and goes into action with Blankman. Problem is "The Other Guy" is not bulletproof (which he doesn't know) and he gets shot (or should I say wounded?).

The story wraps itself up as Blankman comes to the rescue, the crime boss is defeated and our semi-hero gets the girl.

Blankman also features Arsenio Hall, Tony Cox, Jason Alexander, Lynne Thigpen, Harris Peet, Christopher Lawford and Nick Corello. Its box office take was $7,941,977.

https://youtu.be/GSFaU4cN-qI

✳ ✳ ✳

AUGUST 20, 2010

Brandon T. Jackson, Naturi Naughton and Bow Wow

LOTTERY TICKET – RELEASED BY WARNER BROS. PICTURES!

Rapper Bow Wow (formerly Lil Bow Wow) stars in this comedy about a lottery winner pursued by everybody in his ghetto neighborhood. His friend (Brandon T. Jackson) and grandmother (Loretta Devine) are the only people who know he has the winning ticket for $370 million, but has to wait over the Fourth of July holiday before being able to cash it in, but before you know it the entire neighborhood knows and everybody wants some. A girl who previously rejected him now wants to be his baby's mama.

The local loan shark wants to assure Bow Wow's friendship by "loaning" him $100,00 to have a good time. Everybody has an I-need-money-story.

The downside is the community bully (Gbenga Akinnagbe) thinks Bow Wow snitched on him for stealing some sneakers at Bow Wow's job at Foot Locker. So now he has to look over his shoulder. The truth is Bow Wow's original dream was to come up with his own line of sneakers. By the end of the movie that dream is realized as he and his real girl (Naturi Naughton) and his boy take his helicopter to his sneaker factory.

Lottery Ticket was directed by Erik White and produced by Matt Alvarez from a screenplay by Abdul Williams. It co-starred Keith David, Ice Cube, Charlie Murphy, Leslie Jones, Teairra Mari, Terry Crews, Jason Weaver, T-Pain, Bill Bellamy and Mike Epps. The worldwide gross was $24.7 million from a budget of $17 million.

https://youtu.be/N2u5JvA5sCs

* * *

AUGUST 22, 1997

Chris Tucker and Charlie Sheen

MONEY TALKS – RELEASED BY NEW LINE CINEMA!

Starring Chris Tucker and Charlie Sheen, this action-comedy debuted at #2 its opening weekend. Tucker starred as a small-time hustler exposed by Sheen's TV reporter. After being arrested and shackled to a master criminal for transport, Tucker finds himself marked for murder once all prisoners and guards are killed by the criminal's men during their rescue of their boss. Tucker escapes death and the chase is on to get him. Meanwhile he's trying to get the stash of diamonds he overheard the criminal discuss.

Tucker is forced to reunite with Sheen, who lost his job for violence against his boss, and hide out. Instead of hiding he seeks out the diamonds with the help of Sheen's rich soon-to-be father-in-law at a car show where the gems are stashed. Tucker avoids death some more and by the end gets the diamonds, but sacrifices them to stay alive and get the bad guys caught.

Directed by Brett Ratner, *Money Talks* grossed $48 million worldwide from a budget of $25 million.

https://youtu.be/tsrM0BY-WbI

***

AUGUST 22, 1982

Aparna Nancherla (Instagram)

APARNA NANCHERLA – BORN IN WASHINGTON, DC!

Here's a girl who likes to move around. Before arriving on the planet as a full-blown human being, Nancherla's parents moved from Hyderabad in India to the United States. Then she moved from Washington DC to Amherst, Massachusetts to study psychology at Amherst College. When she graduated she moved back to Washington DC, but decided she wanted to be a stand-up comedian so Nancherla moved to Los Angeles only to move to New York to be a comedy writer. That gig scribing for *Totally Bias with W. Kamau Bell* lasted until the show was canceled and then characteristically, Nancherla moved over to write for *Late Night with Seth Meyers*.

Variety placed Nancherla on its list of "Top 10 Comics to Watch in 2016." She didn't disappoint. Her resume boasts guest appearances (*Inside Amy Schumer, Crashing Conan, The Meltdown with Jonah and Kamail*), recordings (her album, *Just Putting it out There*), web series (*Your Main Thing* with John Early, *Womanhood* with Jo Firestone), podcasts (co-host *Blue Woman Group*), and voice-overs (*BoJack Horseman, Master of None, Steven Universe*).

Now how's that for moving around?

https://youtu.be/qWvIuJLwuFY

***

August 24, 1973

Dave Chappelle (Public Domain)

David Khari Webber "Dave" Chappelle – Born in Washington, DC!

Known as the "King of the Pilots," Chappelle began his career in New York. After getting booed at the Apollo Theater, (known for booing comedians), he decided he had the courage to stay in comedy. He honed his craft in New York and made his film debut at age 19 in Mel Brook's *Men in Tights*, a parody of the Robin Hood legend. Other notable films roles included *The Nutty Professor, Con-Air, Blue Streak, Undercover Brother* and *You've Got Mail.*

In 1998 Chappelle co-wrote the cult classic film, *Half Baked* along with collaborator, Neal Brennan. The hit stoner flick helped establish the professional relationship of the two. They went on to create and pen, *Chappelle's Show*, the first iconic sketch comedy show of the 21st Century. Up until that eventual success Chappelle had presented many pilots to the networks. They were either rejected or tampered with after initial shooting. One, *Buddies*, made it to air on ABC, but instead of his original co-star and friend, Jim Breuer being on the show, Breuer was fired and replaced by an actor who Chappelle shared no chemistry. That show was canceled after five episodes. They had shot thirteen. After this experience he shot another pilot and ended up accusing a network of racism after they insisted on adding white characters that rang untrue for the project. At this point Chappelle considered leaving show business. Then came a chance to do a show for struggling cable network, Comedy Central.

Chappelle's Show got everybody's attention. It dealt with social and racial issues so hilariously that controversial actor, Charlie Sheen ruptured a hernia laughing at an episode and had to be taken to the hospital. His employers at CBS thought his absence from his own show, *Two and a Half Men* was drug related and fired Sheen. Maybe drugs were involved, but it was mainly Chappelle.

Chappelle's Show produced skits such as the "Niggar Family," about a white family with a non-white sounding name, "The Blind Racist," where a Blind black man lives as a white supremacy leader; "The Racial Lottery," where races claim who they want, most notably Wu Tang Clan being newly identified as Asian. He poked fun at Oprah, Prince, Rick James and Wayne Brady (the latter two made guest appearances) and anything else that could be clowned. Besides, sketches (not Chappelle's favorite form of comedy) the show also featured musical acts and the work of fellow comedians, Charlie Murphy, Dominique, Paul Mooney, Bill Burr and Donnell Rawlings.

In 2005 Chappelle abruptly left the show. Though his DVD had reached record proportions and Chappelle was offered 50 million dollars by Comedy Central, he didn't like the direction and felt he was being laughed at instead of with by a white crew member. This uncomfortable feeling made him flee to South Africa to get his priorities in order. Upon his return he was compelled to explain his position on shows like *Oprah* and *Inside the Actor's Studio*. Meanwhile Comedy Central aired the sketches (Titled "*The Lost Episodes*") Chappelle had shot for the aborted 3rd season against his creative wishes and that relationship was formerly severed.

Dave Chappelle produced *Dave Chappelle's Block Party* featuring musical artists (Kanye West, The Roots, Erykuh Badu, Mos Def, Jill Scott, Dead Prez), highlighted by a surprise reunion of the Fugees. In 2006 he turned 3 million into 11.7 million when he released, *Block Party All-Stars featuring Dave Chappelle* through Universal's Rogue Pictures.

Dave Chappelle's professed first love is stand-up and he's done hour-long comedy specials for HBO (*Killing Them Softly*) as well as Showtime (*For What It's Worth*) and multiple releases for Netflix. Other comedians praise him as one of the best ever and Chappelle made many unannounced appearances in comedy venues before going back on the road in 2013.

He is ranked #43 on Comedy Central's list of "100 Greatest Stand-Ups of All Time."

https://youtu.be/ofnSojq-vqI

* * *

August 25, 1996

The cast of 'The Steve Harvey Show' (Instagram)

The Steve Harvey Show – Premiered on the WB!

Created by Winifred Hervey, produced by Brillstein-Grey and with music by Patrice Rushen, *The Steve Harvey Show* was a flagship program for the new WB network. It consistently led the station in ratings and established Harvey and co-star, Cedric the Entertainer as viable television personalities. Taking place in a high school setting, the sitcom dealt with many issues affecting the youth of the era.

Harvey played a former middling funk musician who once fronted a middling funk singing group that consisted of Ron Isley, Don D.C. Curry and Jonathan Slocomb. They were a two-hit wonder and now Harvey's a music teacher at his old high school, but is forced to also instruct the drama and art departments because of school budget cutbacks. This puts him in direct contact with a variety of offbeat kids with even more wacky antics and also gives Harvey the opportunity to lend his life expertise to help them on their own life journeys.

The Steve Harvey Show also featured the talents of Wendy Raquel Robinson, Terri J. Vaughn, Merlin Santana, William Lee Scott, Tracy Vilar, Netfa Perry, Lori Beth Denberg and Ariyan A. Johnson. Recurring characters included The Lady of Rage, Dorien Wilson, Kenan Thompson and Kel Mitchell.

The majority of the episodes were directed by the legendary Stan Lathan. It aired its series finale on February 17, 2002 having garnered multiple NAACP Image Award nominations culminating in four wins for

Cedric the Entertainer for Outstanding Supporting Actor in a Comedy Series, four wins for Steve Harvey for Outstanding Lead Actor in a Comedy Series, three wins for the show and three wins for Terri J. Vaughn for Outstanding Supporting Actress in a Comedy Series.

https://youtu.be/E90fiWGl2Kk

✳✳✳

AUGUST 25, 1991

The cast of *Roc*

ROC – PREMIERED ON FOX!

The sitcom about a garbage man starred Charles S. Dutton as the title character and Ella Joyce as his wife Eleanor. A confirmed cheap skate, Roc gathered stuff on his garbage route to adorn his surroundings. His retired father Andrew, (Carl Gordon) stays with them and so does his musician brother, Joey (Rocky Carroll), who owes Roc money.

Roc was innovative. After its first season it broadcast all the second season shows live. They would deal with current events including the 1992 Presidential election and came just short of announcing the election results. No show had been broadcast live since the 1950s. This was mainly possible because all the principals were trained stage actors who'd worked together many times before in August Wilson productions.

A sitcom, *Roc* mixed comedy with heavy, dramatic social commentary. Gang influence, drug use and vigilantism were recurring topics. Another thing recurring on *Roc* were a slew of top-notch talent. Over its three seasons appearances were made by Jamie Foxx, Heavy D, Tone Loc, and a slew of others.

Not surprisingly, *Roc* was a hit in Black households, but ranked low in the Nielsen ratings. Its top ranking was #71 in season two and dipped as low as # 102 with a 5.10 rating in season three. However, it was critically acclaimed and received an Emmy nomination and a NAACP image Award win for Charles S. Dutton for Outstanding Actor.

Roc was cancelled May 10, 1994.

https://youtu.be/iPvBPQcip0g

***

AUGUST 26, 1996

Malcolm Jamal Warner and Eddie Griffin

MALCOLM & EDDIE – PREMIERED ON UPN!

Eddie Griffin and Malcolm-Jamal Warner star in this sitcom as a tow trucker owner and a buppie sharing an apartment and a business. Griffin always gets them into trouble. He's a hustler; a one man towing operation trying desperately to expand. But like most good friendships they always have each other's back to get them out of every mishap.

The show is set in Kansas City, Missouri. During its run the two partners come into some money and buy their building. This investment includes Eddie's garage and a bar. They convert the bar into a sport bar and most of the show's action takes place there, but of course trouble is always right around the corner.

Produced by Jeff Franklin Productions and TriStar Television, Malcolm & Eddie featured comedians Tommy Davidson and Freez Luv as supporting cast members. The sitcom received a pair of nominations for acting and excellence in production design. It aired its final episode on May 22, 2000.

https://youtu.be/_9yAdEoTezM

***

AUGUST 26, 2015

The cast of *The Carmichael Show*

THE CARMICHAEL SHOW – PREMIERED ON NBC!

In this sitcom, comedian, Jerrod Carmichael stars in a fictional version of his own family and life. Co-created by Ari Katcher, Willie Hunter and Nicholas Stoller, the series is set in Charlotte, North Carolina. Carmichael's TV clan consist of his mother (Loretta Devine), father (David Alan Grier), brother (Lil Rel Howery) and his brother's estranged wife (Tiffany Haddish). Carmichael and his girlfriend (Amber Stevens West) now live together and that dynamic as well as the familial ones drive the engine of the show.

The critically acclaimed comedy has been recognized for tackling contemporary issues in an honest, fresh and creative fashion. *The Carmichael Show* airs 13 episodes per season and in its second season received award nominations from the NAACP and GLAAD (even though it has no regular LGBT character in the cast).

https://youtu.be/UCMqqnW0fw8

✳✳✳

AUGUST 27, 1992

The cast of 'Martin' - Tommy Ford, Tisha Campbell, Martin Lawrence, Carl Anthony Payne II and Tichina Arnold (Instagram)

MARTIN– PREMIERED ON FOX!

C reated by Martin Lawrence, Topper Carew and John Bowman, the timing was impeccable. As the fledgling FOX network grew, *Martin* grew right along with it and was a consistent ratings champ for them.

Starring Martin Lawrence as a Detroit radio station DJ and later a public access television host, the sitcom showcased his talent and wide array of characters weekly. Lawrence played Mama Edna, his own mother complete with moustache; his ghetto girl neighbor, Sheneneh with too many weaves and too much back talk for Martin's liking; the pot-bellied security guard, Ol Otis; gold-tooth sporting, Jerome, the pimp from the bygone era; snotty-nosed, Roscoe, the little boy who Lawrence plays by standing on his knees with shoes at the end; Dragonfly Jones, the martial arts instructor who gets beaten up by his students; Bob, the white surfer, redneck who is Gina's boss; Elroy, the mechanic who claims he was the Godfather of Black Surf Music and King Beef, Martin's favorite Blaxploitation superstar with a penchant for dancing under any harrowing circumstance.

Martin was popular with all age groups. It had catchphrases ("Get to Steppin"). It had funny writing. It had a perfectly balanced cast. Tisha Campbell co-starred as Martin's college educated (and knowing it) girlfriend (and later wife) Gina. Tommy Mikal Ford played Martin's childhood, job unknown, buddy, Tommy. Tichina Arnold was Gina's friend and Martin's non-friend and verbal sparring partner, Pam. Carl Anthony Payne II had the role of Martin's other diaper buddy Cole, not-too-smart with a thing for the big girls, but a man with a steady job cleaning jets at the airport. The common theme being Martin's friends love him but he's an inconsiderate, self-centered, arrogant kind of guy and not too in touch with his feelings. In other words, he talks too much trash and always has to eat it.

The show was on top of FOX's heap for five seasons. It had a talented supporting cast including Reginald Ballard as Bruh Man from the fifth flo, who'd climb through Martin's window to fetch whatever he needed. Tracy Morgan as Hustle Man who once tried to sell Martin and his friends fried pigeon on a branch when they were snowed in and starving. Garrett Morris was Martin's cheap boss, Stan at the radio station. Comedians Charlie Murphy, John Witherspoon, Laura Hayes, Lawanda Page, David Alan Grier, Roxanne Reese, Kim Coles and rapper Yo-Yo had recurring roles.

Martin won a number of awards. It was recognized with a People's Choice Award for Best Comedy Series and Acting (Lawrence: Best Actor; Marla Gibbs: Best Supporting Actress) and an NAACP Award to Tisha Campbell for Best Actress. The show's longevity was cut short in 1996 when a lawsuit was brought by Tisha Campbell for sexual harassment against Lawrence and the show's producers. The studio settled and the final season was completed with neither co-stars making any contact. The show went off the air May 1, 1997.

https://youtu.be/7ODcB_77HZU

✳ ✳ ✳

AUGUST 28, 1996

The cast of "The Jamie Foxx Show"

THE JAMIE FOXX SHOW – PREMIERED ON THE WB!

The semi-autobiographical sitcom showcased Foxx's talents as a singer, musician, actor and comedian. Foxx plays Jamie King, an aspiring entertainer who moved from Terrell, Texas (Foxx's real-life hometown) to Los Angeles to become a star. To provide an income while he chases his dream he works at his Aunt Helen (Ellia English) and Uncle Junior's (Garrett Morris) struggling hotel.

Foxx finds a comedic foil in the person of hotel accountant, Braxton P. Hartnabrig (Christopher B. Duncan). He's an uptight brother who finds Jamie's style not to his liking. They provide comic relief with each encounter sliding in verbal jabs whenever possible. The love life portion is covered by co-worker Francesca "Fancy" Monroe (Garcelle Beavais). At first it was Jamie liked her and she didn't care, but eventually they start dating and become engaged.

The Jamie Foxx Show was never a ratings king. Then again the WB was not a big ratings gathering network. It was relatively new when this sitcom hit the air, but the show aired for 5 seasons and helped resurrect the career of Garrett Morris after his 1994 near-fatal shooting.

The sitcom and Foxx received multiple award nominations during its run with Foxx winning the NAACP Image Award for Outstanding Actor in a Comedy Series in 1998. The last episode of *The Jamie Foxx Show* was broadcast on January 14, 2001.

https://youtu.be/IXnnBfwyzlY

✳✳✳

AUGUST 29, 1993

The Cast of *Living Single*

LIVING SINGLE – PREMIERED ON FOX!

The popular sitcom ranked among the top five shows in African-American households during its entire five season run. It not only beat out competitors on rival networks, but was even viewed more than its stablemates, *Martin* and *New York Undercover*.

Produced by Yvette Lee Bowser and Warner Bros. Television, *Living Single* centered on the relationship of six friends living in a Brooklyn brownstone. Queen Latifah played Khadijah, the workaholic editor and publisher of Flavor magazine. Her roommates are her cousin, Kim Coles, the sweet, but dingy aspiring actress, Synclaire and her childhood buddy Regine, (Kim Fields), a boutique buyer/gold-digger with a heart. If only Regine could find a rich man to marry the world would be perfect. The quartet is rounded out by Maxine, played by Erika Alexander. Max doesn't live with them. She's Khadijah's friend from their days at Howard University and an attorney who stops by constantly to raid their refrigerator, gobble up their food and fill them in on the events of her exciting days in court. In another apartment lives Kyle (T.C. Carson), a stockbroker and Overton (John Henton), the maintenance man for the building, who were friends since their early days in Cleveland, Ohio.

You practically needed a scorecard to keep up with the various involvements. Kyle always talked trash to Maxine and vice versa until they finally hooked up and discovered they liked it; to the point that when Kyle got an assignment in London, England he asked Maxine to go with him. She turned him down to her regret later. However, by series end they got back together. Overton and Synclaire were more obvious with theirs. They ended up married. Regine finally got a man of semi-means in the person of Dexter Knight (Don Franklin). Even Khadijah found love with an old acquaintance; a grown man still going by the name "Scooter."

Living Single had an impressive list of recurring characters. Kim Fields real life mother, Chip played her TV mom. Heavy D played her friend. J. Anthony Brown played Overton's uncle and Isaiah Washington was a lover of Khadijah's.

Their list of guest stars was even more significant. Sports stars made appearances: Jerome Bettis, Grant Hill, Evander Holyfield, Cris Carter, Kareem Abdul-Jabbar, Jim Brown, Alonzo Mourning, Bobby Bonilla, Cedric Ceballos, Desmond Howard and Deion Sanders. Musical artists, TLC, Cece Winans, Gladys Knight, Monica, Naughty By Nature, Tone Loc, Brian McKnight and Chaka Khan showed up. Blaxploitation legends like Melvin Van Peebles, Ron O'Neal and Antonio Fargas had roles. Comedians were omnipresent: Flip Wilson, Marsha Warfield, Jack Carter, Bobcat Goldthwait, Gilbert Gottfried, Rosie O'Donnell and John Witherspoon as well as practically the entire cast of NBC's *A Different World* minus Lisa Bonet and TV's "Superman" (Dean Cain) and "Robin" (Burt Ward).

The series received multiple nominations for acting with a 1998 Image Award win for Erika Alexander for Outstanding Actress and one for the show for Outstanding Comedy Series.

Living Single had its series finale on January 1, 1998.

https://youtu.be/jnD2mdaxUAo

✳✳✳

AUGUST 29, 1977

Aida Rodriguez (The Aida Rodriguez Collection)

AIDA RODRIGUEZ – BORN IN BOSTON, MASSACHUSETTS!

Rodriguez was taken to the Dominican Republic soon after her birth. From there she studied English at Florida State University before getting into modeling, getting married, getting divorced and becoming a driven comedienne. Rodriguez kept a busy schedule as a personal appearance performer who's toured with Kim Coles and many others.

Aida Rodriguez was also a busy actress. Her filmography began in 2006 in the role of Ida in *Black Woman's Guide to Finding a Good Man*. She also appeared in *The Adventures of Umbweki* and *Bailando* (2007), *The Greatest Song* and *Fotonovela* (2008), *The Rub* (2009) and *Braniacs In La Land* (2010). Rodriguez appeared on *Stand Up and Deliver* in 2013 and in 2014 Aida Rodriguez gained national prominence as a competitor on NBC's *Last Comic Standing* hosted by J. B. Smoove with Keenan Ivory Wayans, Roseanne Barr and Russell Peters serving as judges. Though she did not win (that was Rodman), Rodriguez received rave critiques both from the panel and audience (where it matters).

https://youtu.be/dtfK2DT819U

***

AUGUST 30, 1953

Robin Harris (The Andre Lavelle Collection)

ROBIN HUGHES HARRIS – BORN IN CHICAGO, ILLINOIS!

Discovered by ventriloquist, Richard Sanfield (of Richard & Willie) washing cars for a rental agency, Harris was encouraged by the recording and touring artist to consider comedy. Harris gained experience opening for Sanfield and auditioned to be a regular at Hollywood's World-Famous Comedy Store in 1980. Owner, Mitzi Shore told him his act was "too Black" and so he went to where that was an asset not an insult. He was approached by then struggling promoter, Michael Williams and a partnership was formed. On September 5, 1985 Williams opened the first Black comedy club in Los Angeles, The Comedy Act Theater and Harris was his host.

The club became the place to be on Thursday – Saturday and Harris was the man to see. His old school style and rapid-fire insults (he talked about patrons on the way up the stairs to the bathroom and on the way back down as well as anybody wearing something dumb or saying something stupid) and ad-libs (not to mention signature routines; most famous being Bebe's Kids) made him the talk of Los Angeles and soon Hollywood. Major Black celebrities would talk about Harris during so many outings with their non-Black reps that those reps wanted to see him. When they were told he didn't perform in Hollywood (the usual showcase city) the industry types made caravan trips down to the hood to see *him*. And what they saw made dollar signs jump in their eyes.

Robin Harris was soon in the movie making business. He debuted in Keenan Ivory Wayans, *I'm Gonna Git You Sucka*. He played Kid's (of Kid 'n Play) father, Pops, in the original *House Party* (he was nominated for Best Supporting Actor by the Independent Spirit Awards). He appeared briefly in Eddie Murphy's *Harlem Nights*. His next role and some say his most memorable was as Sweet Dick Willie in Spike Lee's *Do the Right Thing*. Harris was part of a trio of bench sitters commenting on what goes on in the neighborhood. The only thing missing was the dominoes. He was then seen in Lee's *Mo' Better Blues*, starring Denzel Washington and Wesley Snipes playing the part of night club comedian, Butterbean.

Television also came calling. Harris was pegged to be the host of HBO's *Def Comedy Jam*. It was rumored CBS had a show in the works to star Harris and fellow L.A. comedy mainstay, Reynaldo Rey. There was also the film *The Last Boy Scout* to co-star Harris and Bruce Willis, but on March 18, 1990 the avalanche of a career ended. Robin Harris died of a heart attack after a sold-out show at Chicago's Regal Theater. He was only 36 years old, but he spawned what came to be known as the Urban Comedy Boom.

https://youtu.be/tX1VpzvEyYE

* * *

AUGUST 31, 1971
Chris Tucker (*Comedy the Magazine*)

CHRIS TUCKER – BORN IN ATLANTA, GEORGIA!

Tucker woodshedded his comedy briefly in Atlanta comedy clubs such as Atlanta's Comedy Act Theater before moving to Los Angeles to pursue a career. Following a disappointing result at the Bay Area Black Comedy Competition, *Def Comedy Jam* talent scout, Bob Sumner cornered Tucker and told him he felt the comedian had been robbed by the judges. He also told him he'd be on HBO the next season – first show of the new season – first slot. Tucker left an indelible impression. With high energy and a likability that translated, Tucker passed his audition before a national audience.

The stand-up comedian was now an in-demand talent and made a rapid succession of films. His debut was a small part in Robert Townsend's *The Meteor Man* followed by playing Johnny Booze in *House Party 3* where he picked up his first of many award nominations for Best Comedic Performance. Next up was his signature role as Smokey, the lovable weedhead out to make the day of his fired friend Craig (Ice Cube) a good day in the runaway hit *Friday*. That was followed up by *The Fifth Element* with Bruce Willis; a flamboyant role Tucker initially had reservations about how to portray. The end result was a performance praised by critics. He appeared in *Panther, Dead Presidents, Jackie Brown* and co-starred with Charlie Sheen in 1997's *Money Talks*. And then came *Rush Hour.*

The first *Rush Hour* martial arts action comedy paired Tucker and Jackie Chan as diverse styled officers of the law: one a motor-mouthed LAPD detective and the other an inspector from Hong Kong. The hilarious combination spawned two sequels and the films were so well received internationally that the franchise made Tucker the highest paid co-star ($20 million for *Rush Hour 2* and $25 million for *Rush Hour 3)* in Hollywood history.

Tucker's influence extended beyond the silver screen. Socially he was friends with superstar, Michael Jackson and appeared in his video. Politically he traveled with other friend, former US President, Bill Clinton. Tucker returned to stand-up in 2011 and in 2012 he was featured in the highly acclaimed film, *Silver Linings Playbook* along with Bradley Cooper, Jennifer Lawrence and Robert DeNiro. The cast won the Broadcast Film Critics Association Award for Best Cast.

https://youtu.be/bk1s9Nu_Lkw

✳ ✳ ✳

SEPTEMBER

THIS DAY IN COMEDY...

September 1, 1995

(The Guy Torry Collection)

The Birth of Phat Tuesdays – Hollywood, California!

Since the discovery of legendary urban comedian, Robin Harris and the Comedy Act Theater in 1988, the suits of Hollywood had been going down to the hood to find up & coming Black comedians. The 1992 L.A. Riots changed all that. Once flickering flames dotted the landscape and smoke billowed through the skies south of Wilshire, those same suits decided that if talent wanted to be seen they better come up to Hollywood like in the old days. Better safe than have your head bashed in like Reginald Denny.

A shutdown of career opportunities bothered Guy Torry. He had just recently gotten into the West Coast swing of comedy, following in the footsteps of older brother, Joe, not to have it snatched away by something as mundane as civil unrest. Though he himself was making inroads and getting work he didn't want to see anybody short changed. He had an idea to bring the hood to Hollywood. So, without any business, management or room running experience, Guy Torry approached the management of the Comedy Store and asked for a Black night; an evening to expose the now underserved segment of talent Hollywood still wanted to see. They agreed and in 1995 Phat Tuesday was born.

The birth took place in the cramped quarters known as the Belly Room. Guy was taking over from another comedian, Dante, who'd had achieved moderate success in the upstairs 90-seater doing a mainstream show, but had supposedly seen that room run its course. Guy came in doing a Black show and his 4-week trial run turned into a decade long marathon. After 9 months the crowds had blown up to Main Room capacity (400 seats) and Torry got a once a month – first Tuesday of the month shot on the big floor. In no time he had that platform every week and his nights were the place to be.

Phat Tuesday not only brought out the industry with their entourages looking for fresh comedy meat, but all the other meat in town as well. There were working girls and hustling guys, wanna be's and never-trieds. The room was always packed with celebrities, athletes, models, porn stars, politicians and regular old folks. The Comedy Store couldn't have been happier. Why not? They were making money by the buckets (with raised liquor prices and increased entry fees over the other mainstream nights).

The audience was also getting riches; that's because Guy was a task master when it came to the talent. He knew the tradition of the Comedy Store and its history. Guy knew the club was once Ciro's, the hottest night club in Hollywood in the 50s and 60s and the place Sammy Davis Jr. was discovered by the mainstream. He knew all the other top shelf icons who had graced that hallowed stage throughout the years, and he was intent on living up to that legacy. Guy took this historic opportunity seriously and he was determined to have the comedians take it just as seriously. There was no B Game at Phat Tuesday. If you didn't bring your A-Game, Guy would never let you play there again. Nothing personal.

Phat Tuesday was the place deals were made. The eager, yet trying to be blasé L.A. audience, were treated to the best Black comedy had to offer. The comics who were what the industry were looking for got that look and that movie, TV or touring deal. Of course, comedians became more cut throat than usual when they knew bigshots were in the house and Guy would get hit up with requests for guest spots. That wasn't the way he ran Phat Tuesday. The crowd got the comedians that were booked. Guy knew how he wanted his shows to flow. It wasn't about favors, bribes or the offering of coochie. If you weren't on the list or weren't funny enough to be on the lists you could keep your little coochie. Guy was about the integrity of his night.

Guy was also a host who got his look. The renamed Phat Tuesday (The Guy Torry Comedy Show) afforded him a weekly showcase and Hollywood took notice. Guy appeared in sitcoms, films and toured with the Original Kings of Comedy (on their first leg as the host before D.L. Hughley came aboard). He produced live specials for Magic Johnson, Martin Lawrence, The L.A. Clippers and others and had a reputation for excellence. So, with the vast career opportunities and the increasing demands of running a successful show, Guy Torry said good-bye to the biggest night in comedy history in the year 2005. He passed the torch then sat back and watched the phenomenon he created continue to shine; though without quite the amber hot glow he brought to it.

https://youtu.be/EICMJuHidZU

✳✳✳

September 1, 2012

Comediennes: Laugh Be A Lady (The Littleton Collection)

COMEDIENNES: LAUGH BE A LADY – PUBLISHED BY APPLAUSE!

This historical milestone thoroughly explores the genre of females in comedy from the 10th century to modern day. Authored by Darryl & Tuezdae Littleton (comedienne, Lady Tuezdae) with an introduction by Thea Vidale, this "herstory" chronicles the evolution of that humor through scores of interviews conducted with veteran female performers from all mediums, as well as Tuezdae's own experiences as a comedienne.

Like many art forms, female comedy got its start in the church and expanded to stage, radio, film, and television. Comedic legends are not only detailed in biographies but discussed by their peers. Talents such as Loni Love, Nora Dunn, Kym Whitley, Felicia Michaels, Dominique, Adele Givens, Monique Marvez, Luenell, Sara Contreras, Simply Marvalous, Aida Rodriguez, Miss Laura Hayes, Ajai Sanders, Cocoa Brown, Melanie Comarcho, Shayla Rivera, Alycia Cooper and many other working professionals gave their insights and pay tribute to the genre and its practitioners.

Comediennes: Laugh be a Lady became an automatic classic based on its subject matter. It's been used a source material for other publications as well as documentaries on the topic of comedy; ethnic and otherwise. This comprehensive book established its presence in libraries, universities and other academic institutions.

https://youtu.be/jIipEuaC9J0

✳ ✳ ✳

September 2, 1971

Katt Williams, 2007 (Comedy Hall of Fame Archives)

MICAH SIERRA 'KATT' WILLIAMS – BORN IN CINCINNATI, OHIO!

Raised in Dayton and declared a genius from school officials, Williams ran away from home as an early teen and joined a carnival. He learned the tricks of entertainment traveling and experimenting; transitioning his road act into clubs and eventually settling in Inglewood, California where he gained attention hosting the Hollywood Park Casino; known as comedian Katt in the Hat.

Williams's high energy delivery, distinctive voice and diminutive size made him stand out in the packed field of standup comedians. After several television appearances (*NYPD Blue, BETs Comic View, The Tracy Morgan Show*) he distinguished himself with the public in *Friday After Next* and was now Money Mike, the hyper co-proprietor of the fashion boutique, "Pimps & Hoes." Behind the scenes, Williams had united fellow actors Terry Crews and K D Aubert to strengthen their small parts to be as funny as possible and it worked so well those parts were expanded and the trio stole the movie. He next was seen in *Dumb and Dumberer: When Harold met Lloyd, Repos* and his well-received special, *Katt Williams Live: Let A Playa Play*.

However, it was the HBO special *Pimp Chronicles Part 1* that put Williams on the mainstream radar. Decked out in a green suit he was reminiscent of a mischievous leprechaun bouncing around the huge stage riffing; dropping catchphrases like, "This nigga right here" and climaxing with a sweat drenched deriding of Michael Jackson and his love of children. The show had everybody talking the next day and Williams had cemented himself as a must-see concert act.

Katt Williams was present in all mediums. He was featured as himself in the video game, *Grand Theft Auto IV*. He played Bobby Shaw on the Damon Wayans / Tisha Campbell sitcom, *My Wife & Kids*. He roasted Flavor Flav on Comedy Central. He did voice-over work for

Aaron McGruder's cartoon, *The Boondocks* playing A Pimp Named Slickback and the voice of Seamus in *Cats & Dogs: The Revenge of Kitty Galore*. Williams did improv on *Nick Cannon's Wild N Out* and recorded rap tunes with rappers (Dipset).

His notable film performances included *Norbit* (where Eddie Griffin had to convince the producers Williams was hilarious; give him some lines and Williams proved Griffin was no liar); *American Hustle* (his hybrid follow up to *Pimp Chronicles 1*, where the first part of the film shows Williams and his openers, Luenell Campbell, Melanie Comarcho and Red Grant traveling to their gig and the second portion the concert footage of Williams) and *First Sunday* (he played a heterosexual choir director).

Williams 2008 *It's Pimpin, Pimpin* national tour grossed $50 million. Following that 100 plus dates 6-month marathon Katt Williams formally retired from entertainment. He popped up in a couple of films (*The Obama Effect* and *Scary Movie 5*) but stayed relatively inactive in show business until his return in 2012 with a tour and the special *Kattpacalypse*.

Multiple legal problems and run-ins with the police plagued Williams come back prompting him to retire once again. This was short lived (3 days) and he returned to the road for his *"Growth Spurt"* Tour followed up with another culminating in his HBO special, *Priceless: After Life*, directed by Spike Lee.

However, whenever it seemed like Williams had abandoned his demons, like a groundhog he was counted on to misbehave around the holidays. There were more run-ins with police, photographers, disgruntled employees, adolescent wrestlers and various store and shop owners who met with the wrath of the Katt. Diehard fans of his comedy and fans of comedy period, were relieved to see him get his reprieve in the form of an Emmy Award win for a guest-starring appearance on the Donald Glover show, *Atlanta*. That was in 2018. Let's see what happens next.

https://youtu.be/ZCzCseQKWaw

∗ ∗ ∗

September 3, 1902

Mantan Moreland in *The Trap* – 1946 (Public Domain)

Mantan Moreland – Born in Monroe, Louisiana!

The adolescent runaway joined a minstrel show in 1910. By 1920 Moreland was a veteran performer of vaudeville, Broadway and had toured Europe. His film debut took place in a "race film" (which he did many), but it wasn't long before Hollywood beckoned and he was signed to Monogram Pictures and a co-starring contract to play in action pictures opposite Frankie Darro then transitioned into the role of detective Charlie Chan's chauffer, Birmingham Brown.

In a career that included appearances in over 300 films, Moreland chiefly appeared as shoe-shine boys, waiters and porters. Mantan's physical trembling and eye bulging whenever danger was about earned him a reputation as a premier big screen funnyman. He also worked the Apollo Theater with partner, Ben Carter and was known for the routine called the Incomplete Sentence where Moreland played straight man. It involved the two comedians cutting each other off in mid-sentence in an attempt to top the other one. "Say, did you see…?" "Saw him just yesterday… didn't look so good." When Carter died in 1946 Mantan found other partners to fill the void, such as Nipsy Russell.

Work began to dry up for Moreland in the 1950s with the rise of the Civil Rights Movement and Hollywood's forced re-assessment of Black images. Moreland along with others were considered negative stereotypes to be avoided. In 1953 he hosted a short-lived variety show on TV called *Club Mantan*, but as I said it was short lived. In 1957 he appeared in a Black production of Samuel Beckett's *Waiting for Godot* as Estragon (Gogo) on Broadway to rave reviews, but it didn't matter. The industry was soured on Moreland's kind.

One bright spot in that decade was in 1955 when Shemp Howard of the Three Stooges died (unless you were a Howard). There was serious talk of replacing Shemp with Mantan, but obviously that was only "serious" talk. Even though Shemp Howard himself had suggested Moreland would be a good replacement Stooge if the need ever arose after working with him in a film; and even though surviving partners Moe Howard and Larry Fine discussed it with an interested Morleland after Shemp's passing, Columbia Studios wanted a white guy and the prissy Joe Besser was brought in according to Moe Howard, who considered Besser a pain and wished they'd gone with Mantan to reinvigorate the Stooges in their waning years.

So, it was back to the chitlin circuit for Moreland. He recorded a few XXX party records; one where he popularized a bit called "Ain't My Finger" (the routine revolves around two people in bed and one says to the other to stop playing and "get your finger away from my butt," at which the other replies "I ain't playing and that ain't my finger.") The gag was so popular it was sampled by the Beastie Boys and reference on the animated show *Archer*, but mostly it was just a lot waiting for something to happen for Mantan.

It got to the point where in 1959, Moreland made an apology for what he'd done. Going on record he stated he would "never play another stereotype, regardless of what Hollywood offers. The Negro, as a race, has come too far in the last few years for me to dash his hopes, dreams, and accomplishments against a celluloid wall, by making pictures that show him to be a slow-thinking, stupid dolt.... Millions of people may have thought that my acting was comical, but I know now that it wasn't always so funny to my own people."

This apology also didn't matter. His career languished for decades. Mantan suffered a stroke in the early 60s, but survived and found whatever work available in a slight resurgence as older generations began to forgive and the newer generation had no knowledge. He was seen in TV commercials and a couple of low-budget horror films, but the resurgence was not to last. On September 28, 1973 Mantan Moreland died of a cerebral hemorrhage.

https://youtu.be/6bIyMBSx5Qo

✳ ✳ ✳

SEPTEMBER 4, 1960

Damon Wayans (c) awards big checks; Sheryl Underwood and Andre Lavelle are on the right
(The Andre Lavelle Collection)

DAMON KYLE WAYANS, SR. – BORN IN HARLEM!

In 1982 Damon Wayans began his career in stand-up comedy. In 1984 he made his first film appearance as a hotel employee offering Eddie Murphy bananas in *Beverly Hills Cop*. In 1985 Wayans was cast as a featured performer on *Saturday Night Live* for NBC. This lasted for a year. He was fired for changing a skit; playing his cop character gay instead of straight. By 1990 he was on *In Living Color* a sketch comedy show on FOX showcasing the talents of his brothers Keenan Ivory and Shawn Wayans as well as sister, Kim.

On *In Living Color* Wayans created an arrayed of memorable characters. There was Whiz (Homeboy Shopping Network), Homey D. Clown, Blaine Edwards (Men on Film), Handi-Man, Reverend Ed Cash and Anton Jackson. Wayans also did impressions of Louis Farrakhan, Little Richard and Babyface. He was the co-creator and a performer. He stuck around for two seasons and then Wayans was off to make movies.

Damon Wayans starred in a succession of hit films. He played in *The Last Boy Scout* with Bruce Willis, *Major Payne, The Great White Hype* with Samuel L. Jackson, *Blankman, Mo' Money* with Stacey Dash, *Hollywood Shuffle, Bulletproof* with Adam Sandler and *Celtic Pride*, just to name a handful.

Despite cinematic fame, Wayans never strayed too far from television. He produced the animated series, *Waynehead* for FOX in 1996. It lasted one season due to poor ratings. From 1997-1998 Wayans produced the short-lived drama, *413 Hope St.* starring Richard Roundtree. He starred in *Damon* in 1998 for FOX and wrote a book about family in 1999 called *Bootleg*. From 2001-2005 Damon Wayans starred in the ABC sitcom, *My Wife and Kids*. In 2006 he produced the Showtime sketch show, *The Underground* and in 2011 he wrote a novel about the *Red Hat Society*. He retired from stand-up in 2015 and in 2016 took the role of Roger Murtaugh in the TV version of *Lethal Weapon*.

Wayans has received numerous award nominations (four for acting and directing *In Living Color*; four International Press Academy's "Golden Satellite Award") and won the 2002 People's Choice Award for Favorite Male Performer for his work on *My Wife and Kids*.

https://youtu.be/57HPG4OYrM0

✳✳✳

SEPTEMBER 4, 1974

THAT'S MY MAMA – DEBUTED ON ABC!

Theresa Merritt was the title character of this short-lived sitcom. Co-starring Clifton Davis as her son, the show centered on the situations of a mother who wants her bachelor son to settle down and have a family. Stop running around with young, willing, nubile females who want nothing but to have fun. Time to get serious; not getting any younger talk. For crying out loud – the man was 26 years old. He worked at the barbershop he inherited from his daddy. He had two fun-loving buddies: Earl, the mailman (played by Ed Bernard for the first two episodes and then taken over by Teddy Wilson) and Junior, the neighborhood town crier (Ted Lange). Davis' character had everything a man in his mid-20s could want so naturally his mother felt it was time to mess it all up with marriage.

That's My Mama was set in Washington, DC. Besides, the aforementioned cast the show also featured Lynne Moody as Davis' little sister (later played by Joan Pringle) as well as DeForest Covan and Jester Hairston as local barbershop fixtures, Wildcat and Josh. An attempt was made to spin-off some of the characters after the original went off the air, but the pilot entitled, *That's My Mama Now!!* never made it to the programming schedule phase and the idea inspired by the success of the revived *What's Happening!!* (*What's Happening Now!!*), would be nothing more than a notion.

That's My Mama ran for only 39 episodes due to low ratings. It aired its last show on Christmas Eve, December 24, 1975.

https://youtu.be/fjiH2jdTe34

✳ ✳ ✳

SEPTEMBER 5, 1985

Kim Tavares, Annie McKnight, Melanie Comarcho at The Comedy Act Theater, circa 1990
(*Comedy the Magazine*)

THE COMEDY ACT THEATER OPENED!

Struggling music promoter, Michael Williams was frustrated with the business. One night to break the monotony he went to a club with a friend and saw his future. A comedian named Robin Harris was on stage wreaking and convulsing the room with laughter. When Harris departed the stage, Williams stepped to him. How would Harris like to host an all-Black comedy club? Having recently been snubbed by Comedy Store owner, Mitzi Shore for being "too Black" this sounded like a golden opportunity. Harris asked where this club was. Williams had to tell him he didn't know yet. He had just come up with the idea when he saw Harris.

That brainstorm didn't take long to materialize. Soon Williams was telling Harris to report to a small storefront on Crenshaw Boulevard in what was then known as South Central L. A. or to some Leimert Park. The opening night featured many established Black comedians. Robert Townsend was there along with Sinbad, Myra J, a Wayans or two and several other comics. Attendance was decent, but the word spread and it wasn't long before the store front could not contain the wave of people trying to make their way inside for this new party.

The new location of The Comedy Act Theater was right around the corner on 43rd east of Crenshaw in the Regency West building owned by "Mr. Calloway" father of actress Vanessa Bell-Calloway. Business boomed and celebrities spilled out of the woodwork. Everybody was there to see the cash cow, Robin Harris.

Harris made the Comedy Act Theater the legend it became. His onstage antics were the stuff people talked about the next day and throughout the weekend. It became the place to be on Thursday through Saturday. With an old school style, rapid-fire insults and bull's eye ad-libs made him the talk of Los Angeles and soon Hollywood. Industry types made caravan trips down to the hood to see *him* and it wasn't long before Robin Harris was in movies; adding even greater cache to this hot night spot.

Williams expanded his original vision. He opened another Comedy Act Theater in Atlanta. It was a success; taking the fledgling career of Jamie Foxx to "must see" status and introducing the South to up-and-comer, Chris Tucker. Then Williams went for a trifecta and founded the Comedy Act Theater in Chicago. That's when Williams' fortune started to turn. The Chicago spot was an initial success, but Chicago was a comedy town and making inroads into the territory of the already established Black favorite, All Jokes Aside was no small task. In this case it was an impossible one and Williams had his first defeat in comedy. The club closed.

When Harris died on March 18, 1990 of a sudden heart attack many thought the L.A. club was doomed. That first Thursday after the funeral only fifteen patrons attended the show. So the search was on for a new host to re-ignite the public's imagination. Many of the regular comedians had auditions in front of live audiences, but none were Robin and that's what the club needed; a comic who engaged the audience. While most on the younger comedians feared the challenge, St. Louis transplant, Joe Torry saw it as an opportunity to establish himself. So he raised his hand at the right time and got the gig. Then just like Harris he was off to Hollywood. Those returning industry types liked what they saw and Torry had a film career.

Next up to bat as host was D.L. Hughley. He went the same route as Harris and Torry. His shoulder was tapped for bigger things and he followed the beckoning finger to fame. Speedy gave it a shot as did Keith Morris, but after Hughley the interest began to wane. The club had no consistent anchor and the crowds thinned. Michael Williams was diagnosed with cancer and hospitalized. Few thought he would survive, including Williams so he left the club to be run by family who in his absence did their best, but pretty much ran it into the ground.

Atlanta's Comedy Act Theater also closed due to family mismanagement. Michael Williams beat his cancer and returned to the fray, but it was all too late. His empire had all but crumbled and by the mid-90s the original Comedy Act Theater on 43rd was nothing more than a memory, but what a glorious memory it will remain.

https://youtu.be/VeBG1BY_jPQ

✳✳✳

September 6, 1958

Michael Winslow – Born in Spokane, Washington!

Billed as the "Man of 10,000 Sound Effects," Michael Winslow's skill is reproducing realistic sounds with his voice. This talent was developed at the Lisa Maile School of Acting, Modeling and Imaging. As a military brat he had few human friends, but plenty of noises to keep him company. Winslow would while away the hours imitating barnyard critters, motors, weather sounds, musical instruments, jungle beasts, record players, artillery, household appliances and all other forms of racket. A no-brainer, Winslow scraped together enough money performing in night clubs to move to Hollywood.

Winslow's big break came on the *Gong Show* where he mystified the audience. His first film (he did over 40) was *Cheech & Chong's Next Movie*, but it was in the *Police Academy* films and television show that he gained fame playing Sgt. Larvelle "Motor Mouth" Jones. He dropped the album *I*

Am My Own Walkman and was featured in the Mel Brook's parody to Star Wars, *Spaceballs*. In the Brooks film, Winslow did all the sound effects; saving the film money. He hosted a film appreciation series for television, did commercials and toured as a motivational speaker.

Michael Winslow is foremost an innovator. Besides being a world-renowned stand-up performer, he created Apps based on his sound effects. His iPhone and iPad Touch has ThatsKungFu which gives Winslow's kung fu effects when swung. NoizeyMan is just what it sounds like; Winslow with a slew of sounds he created– noisy ones. He developed a mobile game for iOS and provided all the sound effects for the game and has been known to anonymously lend out his voice for other projects.

https://youtu.be/NAv1o9C9qow

***

SEPTEMBER 7, 1967

Leslie Jones (2nd from left) w/Cookie Hull, D'Militant and Mike Britt during Katt Williams' "It's Pimpin, Pimpin Tour," 2008 (The Littleton Collection)

LESLIE JONES – BORN IN MEMPHIS, TENNESSEE.

Starting off life as a much-traveled U S Army military brat, Jones' beloved father suggested she play basketball due to her height. This led to a scholarship at Chapman University. She later transferred to Colorado State to follow her coach who had made the switch. Over the course of her academic career she studied law, business accounting, computer science and communications (she was a radio DJ at Chapman). At one point she even considered playing basketball overseas.

Like many comics, Jones was goaded into the world of stand-up by a well-meaning friend who signed her up for the "Funniest Person on Campus" competition in 1987. She won and made her way to L.A. where she performed in clubs such as Maverick Flats, The Comedy Act Theater and The Comedy Store. However, it wasn't long before Jones felt she was on

317

a treadmill and going nowhere, but getting "exposure." At the suggestion of Dave Chappelle and others she packed up and headed for New York where comedy was more about the nuts and bolts of the craft as opposed to the glitz and glamour. She got damn good, but that didn't prevent her from being ahead of her time. She returned to the West Coast better than ever, but following some bad press on the Hollywood circuit and as Jamie Foxx's opening act, Jones packed up again and went into semi-retirement.

Leslie Jones was virtually off the comedy circuit for an astounding three years. A career killer for most, she gained perspective and when she came back this time she had a fire in her belly that only the stage could extinguish. In 2008 she was the feature of the biggest money-making comedy tour in North America, Katt Williams' It's Pimpin, Pimpin Tour along with Simply Cookie and D'Militant. Jones won rave reviews and appeared at Montreal's Just for Laughs Comedy Festival and the Aspen Comedy Festival. In 2010 Showtime broadcast her one-hour special, *Problem Child*.

In 2013, at the urging of SNL alumni Chris Rock, Jones was hired by show creator, Lorne Michaels as a writer for the long running NBC comedy institution *Saturday Night Live* to quiet down some of the talk of a lack of diversity on not only the network, but that program in particular. Jones parlayed a writing spot into a featured spot in 2014 and that into being the season's breakout performer. She broke even more new ground by being the oldest cast member of the show. Apparently time was on her side. Chris Rock cast her in his film *Top Five*, which prompted Judd Apatow and Amy Schumer to pen a part for her in Schumer's starring 2015 vehicle, *Trainwreck*.

Before you knew it she had been cast as one of the four principles for the all-female reboot of the comedy classic, *Ghostbusters* (along with Kate McKinnon, Melissa McCarthy and Kristen Wiig). Jones was on top of the world, but with seemingly overnight success comes haters and hers made their presence known on Twitter. Spewing racially hateful remarks about Jones only made the public and industry embrace her even more. She became the poster girl for all those who were sick and tired of cyber-bullies. NBC even flew her to the 2016 Summer Olympics in Rio as a goodwill correspondent, prompted by her enthusiastic tweets for America's athletes and their returned love of her fandom and support.

Besides her breakout movie performance in *Ghostbusters*, Leslie Jones has appeared in the films *National Security, A Guy Thing, Repos, Something Like a Business, Lottery Ticket, House Arrest, We Are Family, Masterminds* and *Sing*.

https://youtu.be/rDThNoeDeh4

* * *

SEPTEMBER 7, 1961

Don "DC" Curry eating in a place with no screen door (Comedy the Magazine)

DON "DC" CURRY – BORN IN DENVER, COLORADO!

This son of a preacher man is a comic's comic and an audience's dream. With a comedic style where one joke overlaps the next Curry's crowds don't have enough time to catch their breaths much less swill down their two drinks from the minimum. He's one of the best comedians of his generation and a consistent draw making personal appearances worldwide.

Don "DC" Curry introduced himself to the world as a professional baseball player. Once that successful career ran its course Curry turned to the construction business where it was even mo money, mo money, mo money. Then one day he woke up in his pile of dough and decided to climb the comedy mountain and plant his flag.

Curry won the coveted Bay Area Black Comedy Competition in 1995 then became the fourth host of BET's *Comic View* in 1996 (following D.L. Hughley, Cedric the Entertainer and Sommore) after beating out a half dozen other comedians in a televised comedy competition. He was featured in ABCs *Grace Under Fire* (the Brett Butler sitcom) for two seasons until the show was canceled due to the antics of its star. Curry played Uncle Elroy Jones (John Witherspoon's sex-crazed brother) in the Ice Cube franchise *Next Friday* and *Friday After Next,* did voice-overs on *The Boondocks* and made numerous guest appearances on sitcoms.

Oh, and did we mention how damn funny he is?

https://youtu.be/nglA9-1C_9o

✳ ✳ ✳

SEPTEMBER 8, 1940

Willie Tyler and Lester, 1969 (Public Domain)

WILLIE TYLER – BORN IN RED LEVEL, ALABAMA!

Raised in South East Detroit, Michigan, Tyler got introduced to the public in 1972 on the NBC hit show, *Rowan & Martin's Laugh-In*. From that launching pad Tyler and his dummy Lester have worked in practically every medium. If you could watch it or hear it – they did it.

In the 80s they were big. Every sitcom needed a ventriloquist and his dummy to guest star otherwise you just can't call yourself a real sitcom. Willie Tyler & Lester got it in. They appeared in *The Parent "Hood, What's Happening Now!!*, and *The Jeffersons*. They've been pitchmen for McDonalds and Toyota. They did game shows: *The Match Game* and *Family Feud*. They did variety shows: *The Flip Wilson Show, The Statler Brothers Show* and *The Hollywood Palace*. They served as host of the Saturday morning children's anthology series, *The ABC Weekend Special*. The duo even managed to squeeze films into their schedule. Willie without Lester appeared in *Coming Home* with Jon Voight in 1978. He was also in *For Da Love of Money*.

You name it – they were on it: T*he White Shadow, Pacific Blue* and *Frank McKlusky*. Willie was himself at the BET Comedy Awards in 2004 and the first ventriloquist to appear on *Late Night with David Letterman* on Ventriloquist Week (who did you expect?)

https://youtu.be/kCZ0M8KFL1o

✳ ✳ ✳

SEPTEMBER 8, 1993

The cast of *Thea* (Instagram)

THEA – PREMIERED ON ABC!

This sitcom made history because it was the first to star and be named after a Black comedienne. Thea Vidale was that comedienne. On the show she was Thea Turrell, a Houston, Texas supermarket worker home-based cosmetologist. Her porch was her station and there was no booth rent. Besides the two jobs she had four kids. That's why she needed the two jobs. Ratings were strong out of the box but declined steadily until by the end of its only season, *Thea* was #43 in the ratings. ABC pulled the plug after 19 episodes aired.

Besides having the historical significance of its racial first, *Thea* was like a who's who of unknown future household names. Grammy Award winning singer, Brandy Norwood was featured on the show. It was her first sitcom. Comedienne, Yvette Wilson was a regular and so was Countess Vaughn. Years later all of them would star (Brandy) and be featured in *Moesha* for UPN. Comedians, Miguel Nunez, Jr. (*Life*) and Blake Clark (*Community*) were also in the cast, along with Jason Weaver (singer J-Weav), Cleavant Derrick (*Sliders*), Arvie Lowe, Jr. (*Lizzie McGuire*), Venus Demilo Thomas (*Sister, Sister*), Dennis Burkley (*Sanford*), Marcus T. Paulk (*Moesha*) and the future Miss Regina "Piggy" Grier in the form of Wendy Raquel Robinson (*The Steve Harvey Show*) playing Thea's baby sister.

Thea received a Young Artist Awards nomination for Outstanding Youth Ensemble in a Television Series. It aired its last episode on February 16, 1994.

https://youtu.be/sWsRKlhIhbI

***

SEPTEMBER 9

Melanie Comarcho (Humor Mill Magazine)

MELANIE COMARCHO – BORN!

Hughes Aircraft must've been a lot of laughs on the assembly line while Comarcho was working there and plenty quiet when she left. Thanks to a friend daring her to try out stand-up comedy and thanks to the enthusiastic audience that first performance, Comarcho was convinced that standing up with a microphone suited her better than standing up with aircraft parts.

She wasted no time in developing her skills on the L.A. comedy circuit: The Comedy Act Theater, Maverick Flats, Birdland West, Tilly's Terrace and the Savoy. She was on the early Katt Williams national mega-tours along with Red Grant and Luenell. Those shows were so successful the quartet capitalized and appeared in the concert film road picture, *American Hustle* together.

Comarcho also gained the reputation of being the perennial opening act. She knew how to rouse crowds and get her laughs without stepping on the toes of the headliner. Plus, she wasn't greedy like most openers. Stars with their name on the ticket don't want to have to worry about being comedically knifed in the back by used up premises and crowds with the energy sucked out of them. So, everybody wanted her: Williams, Chris Tucker, Martin Lawrence, Maxwell and Tank just to name a few.

Naturally, getting paid well to stand on stage delivering explosive material in her signature go-go boots was cool, but Melanie Comarcho's also an actress and filmmaker. She's appeared in *Money Talks, 3 Strikes, The Jamie Foxx Show, With or Without You, First Sunday, Hair Show, Woman Thou Art Loosed, Everybody Hates Chris, Customer Service Sucks, The Sarah Silverman Program, Christmas in Compton, Busted,* and in 2012 Melanie Comarcho got her pet project, *Boosters,* shot and released. She wrote the screenplay and produced it all the way down the line. She also wrote for *Last Comic Standing, The Funny Spot* and *the 36th NAACP Image Awards.*

Comarcho starred in the comedy documentary, *Hello,* dropped a comedy CD, entertained US military troops overseas and never missed a chance to rock an audience.

https://youtu.be/0pcTKjFFuSY

***

SEPTEMBER 9, 1972

FAT ALBERT AND THE COSBY KIDS – PREMIERED ON CBS!

The Saturday morning cartoon favorite was created, produced and starred the voice of Bill Cosby. It was based on Cosby's childhood memories. There were lessons to be learned in each episode and Cosby appeared in live action form at the top and bottom of each show to drive the point home on the lessons. If that didn't do it Fat Albert and his chums singing about the lesson in a junkyard with slapped together instruments as an additional recap should've done it.

The characters first appeared in Cosby's standup act in the routine, "Buck, Buck" on his 1967 album, *Revenge.* The stories were so popular Cosby got together with animators, Ken Mundie and Amby Paliwoda for what he thought would be a onetime shot animated special for NBC, *Hey, Hey, Hey, It's Fat Albert* in 1969. Jazz great, Herbie Hancock wrote and performed the score. The special was a hit. However, the network felt it was too educational and declined the offer to place it in their Saturday morning line-up of shows. NBC was not attempting to smarten up kids on the weekends. Cosby and crew took their approach to CBS and they gave it a passing grade.

Apparently CBS was not only enamored by helping to develop young minds, but also by the colorful and vibrant characters. Fat Albert was the moral compass of the gang and was pretty athletic for an overweight kid. Mushmouth was an early example of a kid speaking Ebonics. Dumb Donald wore a stocking knit cap over his head, leaving only the eyes exposed and he wore it no matter what type of weather it was. Old Weird Harold had beady eyes. Rudy was sharp of dress, but dull of perception. It was usually his cockiness that got the gang into trouble. The rest were Bill, Cosby's younger version and his brother Russell, who Bill was always trying to save from trouble and of course Bucky, who had an overbite.

Fat Albert & the Cosby Kids lasted 12 years on CBS. After its initial run it spent another season in first-run syndication and produced three holiday specials for Halloween, Christmas and Easter. In 1989 the series was rerun on NBC on Saturday mornings and on USA Network. It ranked #12 out of a list of the 50 greatest cartoon characters of all time and earned Cosby a Doctor of Education. There was even talk about bringing it back for future generations. This talk came from Cosby himself on Facebook in 2013, but then a year or so later circumstances from the past stepped into the Cosby universe and no other word was mentioned about this revival.

https://youtu.be/y6KtbO-YfD0

* * *

SEPTEMBER 10, 1922

Our Gang w/Matthew 'Stymie' Beard (l), Pete, the Pup and Bobby Hutchins in *School's Out*, 1930
(Public Domain)

OUR GANG/LITTLE RASCALS – RELEASED BY PATHE EXCHANGE!

The shorts known for their groundbreaking view of racial equality featured children acting as children naturally behave; free of bigotry. Five black characters were featured over the years: Sunshine Sammy, Pineapple, Farina, Stymie and Buckwheat. Nothing like that had been filmed before then and now its common place. Created by producer, Hal Roach, the adventures of a group of poor kids was hilarious and insightful. He got the idea after auditioning a child actress for a film who was overly made-up and too rehearsed. It struck Roach as unnatural behavior for a child. Then he looked out of his window into a lumberyard where a bunch of neighborhood kids were playing with sticks. The littlest kid had the biggest stick and refused to relinquish it. This gave Roach the dynamics for a comedy series.

Our Gang was never stagnant. When the series began they were silent short films. Roach had attempted to produce a series of shorts centering on the adventures of a little Black boy, Sunshine Sammy, but theater owners were resistant and only one short was ever shown. So Roach just fused Sunshine Sammy into the "Our Gang" series. The actor who played Sunshine Sammy, Ernie Morrison, was under contract to Roach and was actually the first Black in Hollywood history to have a long-term studio contract. In 1927 Roach took the series from Pathe and gave it to MGM Studios for distribution. *Our Gang* started talking in 1929 soon after the sound revolution in films. In 1938 *Our Gang* was sold to MGM (for roughly $400,000 by today's money) because Roach could no longer afford to produce them himself. Theaters were cutting back on shorts.

The series went through a few name changes too since its inception. It was also known as *The Little Rascals* or *Hal Roach's Rascals*. In 1955 the shorts were packaged under the name *Little Rascals* for television syndication. In 1963 Hal Roach Studios sold the rights to Charles King who used the profits from a new TV deal to form King World Productions, one of the largest syndicators in television history.

The *Our Gang* comedies were simply fun entertainment. The kids did not act like little adults. Their dialogue was as a child would speak. No wise cracks. No innuendos. Just plain pre-adolescent verbiage and antics. The boys had a club devoted to hating women, but since they're boys they would still fall for them. They had soap box derbies with homemade racers. And whenever money got too tight, they put on a show and took in dough from the other poor kids.

One reason the child actors were so natural was because of director Frank McGowan. Even though scripts were written by writers such as Frank Capra, Leo McCarey and Walter Lantz – the kids never saw them. Instead, McGowan would explain the scene to the children before shooting and prompted them to ad-lib. When McGowan left in 1933 (due to a culmination of exhaustion from directing child actors) subsequent directors altered that approach; especially because all the shorts were in sound and things had to make sense.

Over 40 child actors worked on the Our Gang/Little Rascals series. The most famous characters over the years were Sunshine Sammy (Ernie Morrison), Pineapple (Eugene Jackson), Farina (Allen Hoskins), Joe Cobb, Mickey Daniels, Jackie Cooper, Stymie (Matthew Beard), Norman "Chubby" Chaney, Spanky (George McFarland), Alfalfa (Carl Switzer), Darla (Darla Hood), Buckwheat (Billie Thomas), Porky (Eugene Lee), Froggy (Billy Laughlin), Butch (Tommy Bond), Waldo (Darwood Kaye) and Mickey (Robert Blake). There were imposters claiming to have been part of the *Our Gang*. One man even appeared on an ABC news magazine show saying he had been Buckwheat, but when the real Spanky stepped forward to refute the claim the real Buckwheat's family was able to sue ABC for negligent reporting. Everybody wanted to be in the *Our Gang*. Even Mickey Rooney and Shirley Temple tried out, but didn't make it past the audition phase.

The series went until 1944 after the quality slipped due to MGMs lack of experience filming these types of shorts. Altogether the series produced 220 shorts and one feature length film, *General Spanky* (which was a box office disappointment and no other *Our Gang* features were ever made). A tragedy is that even though the children through the years were popular icons and did commercials and print ad product endorsements in character, they never received any further compensation other than the salary they were paid to shoot the shorts. In most cases that was either $40 per short or $200 for the senior child actors. That was it.

In 1937 *Our Gang* won an Academy Award for Best Short Subject.

https://youtu.be/j4Rb2fpPb_0

✳ ✳ ✳

SEPTEMBER 10, 1925

Wildman Steve *Eatin' Ain't Cheatin!!!* (Laff Records)

WILDMAN STEVE – BORN IN MONTICELLO, FLORIDA!

By most written accounts the Wildman was a great guy. He was a family man who at one time lived in a house on 73rd Street in Los Angeles with his three sons, wife and daughter with a little duplex in the back which housed non-family tenants. Then he would leave that urbanized Norman Rockwell setting to hit the clubs and curse like a fleet of sailors.

Gallon grew up in Waterbury CT. He got his stage name during his successful career as a radio DJ on WILD radio in Boston. His comedy sprung from his work as MC for R & B concerts on behalf of the station; giving him the opportunity to work with James Brown, the Temptations and Nat King Cole. It gave him a real gauge of what an audience of those times were ready to tolerate and embrace.

Wildman Steve released 15 recordings between 1969-1993 and appeared in several films *(Ain't That Just Like a Honky, Petey Wheatstraw, The Guy from Harlem)*. *The Six Thousand Dollar Nigger* was his only starring role. Despite his abilities and grassroots following he never tried to appeal to the mainstream. He kept it real as they say. Kept it real dirty, nasty and raw over the course of a 40-year career and when he passed on September 1, 2004 an original voice that's been ripped off countless times by lesser talents was silenced.

https://youtu.be/FkrI3-F16VI

✳ ✳ ✳

SEPTEMBER 10, 1990

The cast of 'The Fresh Prince of Bel-Air' (Instagram)

THE FRESH PRINCE OF BEL-AIR – PREMIERED ON NBC!

Based on the real-life shenanigans of record producer, Benny Medina while he lived with the Gordy Family (as in Berry Gordy), this sitcom plays on the street kid in the rich environment theme. On the show, Will Smith has the lead role as Will, a Philadelphian who was in a basketball game that got out of hand and the ramifications spooked his mother (Vernee Watson) to the point of relocating him to safe Bel-Air to live out the rest of his youth with his well-off relatives. The question arises of why

327

didn't his mother horn in on the opulent lifestyle as well? But there was never an episode that answered such a query.

Once Will was nestled securely in the bosom of his uncle Phil (James Avery), Aunt Viv (Janet Hubert-Whitten, who was replaced by Daphne Maxwell-Reid after season one) and his naïve and street dumb cousins, Hillary (Karyn Parsons), Carlton (Alfonso Ribeiro) and Ashley (Tatyana M. Ali) he managed to find every way possible to live it up; despite the watchful eye of the wise cracking butler, Geoffrey (Joseph Marcell). The sitcom took his real-life rapper sidekick, Jazzy Jeff and made him a recurring character and occasionally had the duo perform. Will Smith had been a Grammy Award winning rapper who blew his first fortune and this show was a comeback vehicle. He wrote the theme song along with QDIII (Quincy Jones' son) and the show was produced by the senior Jones.

The Fresh Prince of Bel-Air was a ratings and awards winner. It won AS-CAP's Film and Television Music Award's Top TV Series in 1994; Image Awards for Outstanding Supporting Actor in a Comedy Series for Alfonso Ribeiro in 1996 and for Outstanding Youth Actress for Tatyana M. Ali in 1997 and Kids' Choice Award for Favorite TV Actress in 1996; the 1994 TP de Oro Award for Best Foreign Series; the Young Artist Awards for Best Performance by an Actor Under Ten won by Ross Bagley two years running in 1995 and 1996 well as that organization's Best New Family Television Comedy Series in 1991 and the Young Star Award won by Tatyana M. Ali for Best Performance by a Young Actress in a Comedy TV Series in 1997.

https://youtu.be/rCOjDwbP-e4

✳✳✳

SEPTEMBER 11, 2000

The Cast of *Girlfriends*

GIRLFRIENDS – PREMIERED ON UPN!

Executive Producer, Kelsey Grammer presented one of the highest rated sitcoms among African-Americans. *Girlfriends* starred Tracee Ellis

Ross, Golden Brooks, Persia White and Jill Marie Jones. The relationships of this quartet was in constant flux throughout the series run.

Ross played Joan; a character who had problems with life's relationships and ended her friendship with Jill Marie Jones character, Toni after she failed to appear at Toni's custody battle hearing. Maya (Golden Brooks) is straight out of Compton. She was a married mother and extremely religious. She was also an author and the girlfriend who criticizes Joan for being so ego-driven. Lynn (Persia White) is the bohemian of the group. She's more sexually liberated and was known to have orgies, one-night stands and short-term boyfriends. Toni, on the other hand, considered herself the cute one of the group and initially looked down on Maya, but eventually accepted her friendship. Toni married a white man for a year and had a child by him then moved to New York so their daughter could see her father.

The show also had a male anchor, William, (Reggie Hayes). He was so jealous of Joan at one point that he got married to someone he didn't love just to beat Joan to the alter. He comes to his senses and gets a divorce and realizes that he loves Joan. They kindle a short-term relationship, but William has his hands full. He becomes a sperm donor for his biological sister and her same-sex partner and when the child is born William considers him his nephew/son.

Girlfriends featured a wide array of guest stars, many from the world of music. Donnie McClurkin, Angie Stone, Chante Moore, Common, Erykah Badu, Isaac Hayes, Jill Scott, Kelly Rowland and Master P were featured. Prominent comedians such as Mo'Nique, Joe Torry, Sandra Bernhard and Katt Williams also made appearances.

The sitcom garnered NAACP Acting Awards for cast members, Tracee Ellis Ross and Reggie Hayes over the course of its run and an award for Best Writing for a Comedy Series. After a move to the CW the show aired its final episode on February 11, 2008.

https://youtu.be/_PJB450ZMYI

* * *

September 12, 1987

Showtime at The Apollo – Premiered!

Produced at the Apollo Theater in Harlem, New York, the variety series featured live musical performances and comedy as well as its legendary Amateur Night. The latter portion had been an Apollo mainstay for over 70 years along with "Sandman" who'd literally sweep off contestants who the audience booed. The original "Sandman" was Howard Sims and when he died he was replaced by C.P. Lacey. Contestants would rub the Apollo log made from the "Tree of Hope" for good luck.

The show had a number of hosts: Bill Cosby, Rick Aviles, Sinbad, Mark Curry, Steve Harvey, Mo'Nique, Whoopi Goldberg and Rudy Rush. Anthony Anderson and Kiki Shepherd served as co-hosts. It was an ideal place to toughen up any act. If you were appreciated by the blunt New York crowd you were met with a wave of applause and cheering. If you bombed with them it was boos and a hasty exit for you. Either way, they made up their minds about an act quickly.

Produced by Bob Banner with Percy Sutton and directed by Don Weiner, *Showtime at the Apollo* aired its last original broadcast on May 24, 2008 having aired 1,093 episodes. It was nominated for the NAACP Image Award for "Outstanding Variety Series/Special" four times and won in 1991.

https://youtu.be/6a01XbHrgA8

* * *

SEPTEMBER 13, 1977

THE RICHARD PRYOR SHOW – PREMIERED ON NBC!

Industry insiders questioned putting the notoriously raw comedian on at 8:00 PM during the primetime family hour so it was no surprise when the show was cancelled rapidly. Richard Pryor, one of the greatest comedians of all time was never known for being "family-friendly" and his four-episode run illustrated why. There was the opener that had Pryor naked and his genitals blurred out as he proclaimed the network had taken nothing from him. He had a skit where he was a rocker and shot up all his white fans. Even his roast, where his cast members sliced him with cutting barbs was none too cozy. The hour-long show dealt with gay issues, political issues, religious issues and everything his time slot considered taboo.

Pryor had a great cast to help him pull off his madness. Thanks to his writer/talent coordinator, Paul Mooney top notch-unknown talent was recruited: Robin Williams, Marsha Warfield, Sandra Bernhard, John Witherspoon, Tim Reid, Vic Dunlop and Edie McClurg.

Produced by Burt Sugarman, it was a spin-off of a special Pryor had done for the network in May of 1977. They wanted to capitalize on that hit, but with all the censorship, Pryor quickly became disenchanted with network television's working realities and walked away. The last episode aired October 4, 1977.

https://youtu.be/IoHxBmstE-I

✳ ✳ ✳

SEPTEMBER 13, 1974

Freddie Prinze (r) w/ Tony Orlando on *Chico and the Man* 1976 (Public Domain)

CHICO AND THE MAN – PREMIERED ON NBC!

With theme music provided by Jose Feliciano, comedy team Cheech and Chong were the inspiration for this first sitcom in a Latin setting. Show creator, James Komack watched the duo for months and once he'd wrapped his brain around a show from two of their bits ("The Old Man in the Park" and "Pedro and Man") he approached them with his pitch. They turned him down. They were in movies and TV just didn't appeal to them so Komack revamped his idea to be about a young Chicano and an old WASP.

Komack cast hot young Latin stand-up Freddie Prinze as Chico and seasoned stage and screen veteran, Jack Albertson as Ed Brown, The Man. Brown ran a struggling garage in East L. A. and Chico needed a job. Even though Brown does business around Latins he doesn't like them and uses racial slurs whenever he gets a chance. This was not good for business, but Chico sees the old guy just needs to grow with the changing times and forces himself onto Brown by cleaning his garage, and showing he's not your typical lazy Chicano stereotype. As time progresses Brown starts to like Chico even though he would deny it if asked. That was the dynamic of this break-away hit, which also featured Della Reese, Scatman Crothers and Ronny Graham.

Chico and the Man debuted and stayed in Nielsen's Top 10 for its first two seasons. It probably would've remained there had Prinze not committed suicide on January 28, 1977 at the age of 22. The comedian was struggling with drug addiction and depression and shot himself in the head. He was taken off of life support on January 29th of that same year. Instead of cancelling the show, the producers made a lame attempt to say that Chico had gone to Mexico to be with relatives and an even lamer attempt to replace him. They tried a 12-year-old kid, brought in singer Charro and towards the end, an 18-year-old adopted niece. None of the new characters caught fire and so ratings steadily declined and *Chico and The Man* was cancelled and aired its final episode on July 21, 1978.

https://youtu.be/zwwyvLjDU3M

***

SEPTEMBER 13, 2002

BARBERSHOP – RELEASED BY METRO GOLDWYN-MEYER!

The title says it all. For 102 minutes you'll laugh at the daily antics that go on in a Black barbershop. It could be any shop. This one just happens to be in Chicago. Instead of your barber and his crew this "staff" consists of Ice Cube and Cedric the Entertainer. Cube inherited the shop from his father and Cedric is the old man of the shop. Since business isn't popping off fast enough for Cube (who has a child on the way and bills standing in the way), he sells the barbershop to a local gangster (Keith David). Not long after, Cube reconsiders that move while trying to figure out how to tell the other barbers and then realizing how much the shop is a major part of their lives and that of the community. So, he attempts to buy the shop back only to discover the gangster has upped the price. The figure to buy it back is double. After a series of mishaps and illegalities, Cube gets the barbershop back and the criminals go to jail.

Directed by Tim Story and produced by George Tillman, Jr., Robert Teitel and Mark Brown, *Barbershop* co-starred Anthony Anderson, Sean Patrick Thomas, Lahmard Tate, Deray Davis, Troy Garity, Jazmin Lewis and introduced Eve and Michael Ealy. Jalen Rose had a cameo as Jalen Rose and on a budget of $12 million *Barbershop* grossed $77, 063,924, with this original version spawning two sequels, a spin-off (*Beauty Shop*) and a television series (starring Omar Gooding in the Ice Cube role).

https://youtu.be/k721dRb2Hmc

✳ ✳ ✳

September 14, 1994

Cast of *All-American Girl* (Instagram)

ALL-AMERICAN GIRL – PREMIERED ON ABC!

This is a textbook example of a show where there was absolutely no truth in advertising. The pitch to the public was that this vehicle starring Korean-American comedienne, Margaret Cho was said to be based on her stand-up act. That was lie #1. Then came big lie #2: They said *All-American Girl* was a show about a Korean-American family. Outside of Cho, nobody and I mean nobody was Korean, not the directors, producers, writers and definitely not the actors. They were Asian, all right; plenty of Chinese and Japanese to spare, just no Koreans and as shocking as this news may sound – there is a difference. Authentic Koreans watching the show couldn't understand what the hell the actors faking Korean were talking about.

The only truthful part was that it was the first sitcom to star an Asian female. However, they didn't say much about that. The producers were too busy retooling the show to sell it properly. They kept tweaking the premise of the show from Cho living with her parents in the house, to living in their basement to moving out and living with three men – without explanation. They fired cast members and attempted to find ways to spin-off other shows from a show that obviously wasn't working itself. They didn't like her weight and round face, so she starved herself in an effort to appear like the Margaret Cho they had in mind; the fictionalized version. The result was major kidney problems for the real version. They told her she wasn't Asian enough and brought in an Asian consultant to Asian-her-up. That failed so they fired the Asian cast and moved her in with white guys then told her she was too Asian. All this led to the show being canceled after one season on March 15, 1995.

https://youtu.be/T1ilTtCg5tg

✳ ✳ ✳

SEPTEMBER 14, 1992

Host, Lester Barrie (r) during Comic View taping, circa 1999 (Comedy the Magazine)

COMIC VIEW – PREMIERED ON BET!

Created by producer Curtis Gadson, this poor man's *Def Comedy Jam* began as a showcase for comedians nationwide featuring in-studio performances as well as those shot across the country and inserted as "The Comic Cam." The first host was D.L. Hughley, who liberally used the audience; picking on select members to clown between introductions filmed at the Normandie Casino showroom in Gardena, California. After a 64-show successful season, the show returned as a comedy competition featuring three competitors per episode with the winner of each placed in contention to become the next season's host. The first winner of that competition was a then unknown Cedric, the Entertainer. Subsequent hosts were Sommore, Don "DC" Curry, Montanna Taylor, Gary Owen (the only white host on this Black comedy format), Lester Barrie, Rickey Smiley, Bruce-Bruce, Arnez J, J. Anthony Brown, Sheryl Underwood and later Kevin Hart (*Comic View One Mic Stand*) and a returning Sommore would host reboots of the program after its initial run.

The competition portion for *Comic View* stayed intact once introduced for several seasons, but other aspects came and went. The aforementioned "Comic Cam" was a one season wonder as was the playful banter and flirting of host, Cedric the Entertainer and his comedy foil, Miss Laura Hayes in a kitchen setting during season three. The kitchen remained in season four, but this time Miss Laura was being courted by writer/producer/comedian, D'Militant in the absence of Cedric. This unrequited love dynamic was also changed for the next two seasons when Gadson created a comedy soap opera starring Miss Laura called *Nuthin But a Woman* (later retitled *The Blackberry Inn*). The ongoing story of Laura owning a hotel and her wacky staff was inserted at the end of competition segments and featured comedian/impressionist Dante as well as Bo P, D'Militant (Darryl Littleton), Ada Luz Pla, Mailon Rivera, L. Anthony Ramos, Cheryl Francis Harrington, Charlene Blaine and narrated by Angelique Perrin.

Once *The Blackberry Inn* was forced out after two seasons, *Comic View* returned to a showcase format. During one season if comedians weren't deemed funny, comic strip bubbles were placed over their heads with disparaging remarks and crickets were heard. The program also saw changes in location during its run (Atlanta, Miami, New Orleans). It holds the distinction of being recorded in Louisiana one week prior to Hurricane Katrina.

https://youtu.be/aAYYBb-i93o

✱✱✱

SEPTEMBER 14, 1985

The cast of *227*

227 – PREMIERED ON NBC!

This Marla Gibbs sitcom was based on a play written by Christine Houston. Gibbs had starred in that play in Los Angeles. On the stage the setting was Chicago in the 1950s. By the time it arrived on television the setting was Washington, DC in the 1980s. The character was the same though. Mary Jenkins was a gossipy housewife with a quick wit and talent for trouble. Her husband, Lester (Hal Williams) was a hard-working man with more things to do than keep her out of it.

Mary and Lester lived in an apartment building with their boy-crazy daughter, Brenda (Regina King). They had a man-crazy neighbor, Sandra (Jackee Harry) and a nosy neighbor, Pearl (Helen Martin). Pearl has a grandson (Curtis Baldwin) and he brings out the cougar in Sandra, who dates him at one point. Another friend is Rose (Alaina Reed Hall) who becomes the landlord of the building after the old and I mean old landlord dies. They all also had a mailman named Ray (Reynaldo Rey) who knew what everybody was doing.

Everybody gossips and bickers and then end up laughing at what it was they were bickering about. That was on the show. Behind the scenes egos were clashing as Jackee's character was getting more play than Gibbs' based on increased popularity. The only solution was to give Harry her own show. The pilot was shot. It was named *Jackee* and it was rejected. Harry did not return to *227* as her full-time character, but made cameos until the show aired its last episode on May 6, 1990.

Other cast members on *227* included Kia Goodwin, Countess Vaughn, Paul Winfield, Toukie Smith, Barry Sobel, Kevin Peter Hall and Stoney Jackson. Many of them were brought in to increase ratings. That failed and the show that once enjoyed the second best ratings (behind *The Cosby Show*) of any African-American sitcom during that decade was eventually canceled. However, during its run *227* received numerous award nominations and won the BMI TV Music Award and an Emmy Award in 1987 for Outstanding Supporting Actress in a Comedy Series (Jackee Harry).

https://youtu.be/NQtVcgfDjmA

✻ ✻ ✻

September 14, 1969

The Bill Cosby Show – Premiered on NBC!

The Bill Cosby Show was the first time an African-American starred in a self-titled sitcom. It was also the first time Cosby worked on TV alone. He'd made his breakthrough in the ground-breaking action series, *I Spy*, co-starring alongside Robert Culp. *The Bill Cosby Show* was also unique because it did not employ the use of a laugh track. Cosby felt the home audience was smart enough to know where the jokes were and didn't need the producers to give them blatant hints. Risky, for prior to this, it had been awhile since 1950s shows such as *The Trouble with Father* and *The Beulah Show* had tried the no frills formula.

The Bill Cosby Show shot for realism. The series focused on the life of Cosby's character, Chet Kincaid, a high school PE instructor in Los Angeles, California. Chet's a bachelor with an eye for the ladies, but who still manages to help people out who he's not trying to date. The episodes dealt with broader lessons and not just quick solutions to challenges. Being in a high school allowed the writers to delve into universally relatable situations. Cosby would often find himself moderating disputes between teachers and students, students and students and of course teachers and teachers.

Cosby himself drew in little known veteran talents as well as legendary super-stars. During its two-season run, *The Bill Cosby Show* featured the likes of Moms Mabley and Mantan Moreland (as Cosby's aunt and uncle), Rex Ingram, Lillian Randolph (as Cosby's mother), Henry Fonda, Don Knotts, Dick Van Dyke, DeWayne Jessie, John Marley, Elsa Lanchester, Cicely Tyson, Tom Bosley, Wally Cox, Antonio Fargas, Isabel Sanford, Mike Farrell and Lou Gossett.

The show's theme song, "Hikky Burr" was written by Quincy Jones and Cosby and "sung" by the latter. Though no critical darling, viewers loved it, keeping the sitcom ranked high in the Nielsen ratings week after week until its series finale on March 21, 1971.

https://youtu.be/9gh0r1xVkgI

***

SEPTEMBER 14, 1987

The cast of *Frank's Place*

FRANK'S PLACE – PREMIERED ON CBS!

TV Guide ranked this comedy-drama as #3 on the list of shows that were "Cancelled Too Soon" and the public agreed. This brainchild of CBS executive, Gregg Maday based loosely on his childhood experiences, *Frank's Place* starred Tim Reid as Frank Parrish, a well-off Brown University professor who inherits his family's New Orleans restaurant. It's his intent to sell it, but when Frank goes back to Louisiana to make the deal the resident chef puts a spell on him. Next thing Frank knows, his life in Rhode Island has gone down the tubes and with few options, he returns to New Orleans, rolls up his sleeves and gets to work learning how to run a restaurant. He also picks up some life lessons from the locals on black heritage, culture and class system.

Created by Hugh Wilson and executive produced by Wilson and Reid, *Frank's Place* co-starred Daphne Maxwell Reid, Tony Burton, Virginia Capers, Charles Lampkin, Robert Harper and Lincoln Kilpatrick. The show was filmed on single camera format and used no laugh track (a rarity for televised comedies).

Frank's Place was cancelled and aired its last episode on March 22, 1988. It got the last laugh, though. The short-lived series was nominated for an Emmy for Outstanding Comedy Series and a Golden Globe for Best Television Series. It won Emmys for Outstanding Writing in a Comedy Series (Hugh Wilson), Outstanding Sound Mixing and Outstanding Guest Performer (Beah Richards). It was also awarded the Humanitas Prize, The NAACP Image Award and the Viewers for Quality Television

Award for Best Actor (Tim Reid) as well as the Television Critics Association Award for Outstanding Achievement in Comedy. Ha!

https://youtu.be/G5_mlLamnm0

***

SEPTEMBER 15, 1918

Nipsey Russell on 'Match Game' (Instagram)

JULIUS "NIPSEY" RUSSELL – BORN!

The Atlanta, Georgia native attained fame as a favorite at the Apollo Theater. He was also noted for his frequent appearances as a panelist on game shows, where he was known for his improvisational poems. He was seen regularly on *To Tell the Truth, Match Game, Password, Pyramid* and *the Hollywood Squares* and known by other celebrity panelists as the "poet laureate."

After returning from the Army as a medic following the end of World War II, Russell found his true calling while working as a carhop. He'd make his customers laugh and got paid more money for doing it. We call it being tipped. Russell saw it as a future career. He began performing in night clubs and was soon discovered. By the mid-1950s he had partnered with Mantan Moreland and one of their more popular routines was the "interrupted sentence" originated by Moreland and former partner, Ben Carter.

Russell performed on *The Ed Sullivan Show*. Being seen on that variety program was always a boost for any act and Russell was no exception. That appearance got him a role in the sitcom *Car 54 Where Are You?* He was co-host of *The Les Crane Show*, co-star of *Barefoot in the Park* and was constantly co-signing on *The Dean Martin Celebrity Roast*. He made "party albums" and was the Tin Man in the film, *The Wiz*.

A mainstream favorite, Russell worked throughout his career. He played Las Vegas with Sergio Franchi. He bounced from one sitcom guest starring spot to the next and whatever game show they could come up with. In 1964 Russell earned the distinction of being the first Black panelist regular on the game show, *Missing Links*. He'd shot two game show pilots, but neither was picked up by a network. Russell popped up on *Late Night with Conan O'Brien* frequently and gained a new following. Then on October 2, 2005 at the tender age of 87 Nipsey Russell passed away from stomach cancer.

https://youtu.be/2Qu7grnu0Sk

***

SEPTEMBER 15, 1970

Rodney Perry (Rodney Perry Collection)

RODNEY PERRY – BORN IN CHICAGO, !

Raised in Monroe, Louisiana, Perry got his start in comedy in grade school. He was an antsy child always running off at the mouth and causing distractions. So, his teacher made a deal with him. If little Rodney could be quiet for a full day she'd let him perform and tell jokes to the class. He did and discovered his calling. He found himself hosting school talent shows and acting as MC at sporting events. The bug continued biting when he did two stints in the Navy. Once he got out Perry moved to the Bay Area of California to hone his craft. He was going to call himself, "Rodney, the Entertainer" until one night he turned on his television and discovered a guy by the name of Cedric had already copped that moniker. So "Rodney Perry" it would remain as he made his way to Hollywood by way of Inglewood.

Perry was part of the new wave of comedians who got sharp and were ready for their close-up right before the urban comedy boom hit. He had a family and so odd jobs were part of his journey until one day while at the VA an amputee asked Perry why he was doing menial work to make ends meet when he should be living out his dream. The money couldn't have been much worse. Perry took that and started hustling any kind of comedy gig he could find. He did all the requisite shows of the era: *Def Comedy Jam, Comic View, Laffapalooza, 1ˢᵗ Amendment* and *Comic's Unleashed*. He was the warm-up act for Kym Whitley's show *Oh, Drama*. He was co-host of *Bill Bellamy's Who's Got Jokes* for TV-One and received the national notoriety he'd been seeking as the co-host of BETs *The Mo'Nique Show'*; the late-night talk show that ran from October 5, 2009 – August 16, 2011.

Bounce-TV was also good to Perry. He became the comedy face of the up & coming broadcast station. Perry hosted their comedy show, *Off the Chain*. He had the number one comedy special on Bounce as well as a recurring role on their popular, *Family Time*.

The observational comedian has toured extensively and hosted the radio show *Rodney Perry Live*. Perry has also been featured in the films, *Johnson Family Reunion, The Last Laugh* with Tony Rock and the Tyler Perry (no relation) motion picture, *Madea's Big Happy Family* and others.

https://youtu.be/lR7Jj147AOE

***

SEPTEMBER 15, 1978

UP IN SMOKE – RELEASED BY PARAMOUNT PICTURES!

This film by stage and recording duo Cheech and Chong is recognized as the first "stoner comedy." The story centers around two potheads with a band and an insatiable need for weed. One (Tommy Chong) is given an ultimatum by his parents; get a job or get shipped off to military school. The other just wants to get high. After beating a drug bust when they're discovered on the side of the road high as kites, their quest for more marijuana ensues. This journey takes them to the cousin of Cheech (Tom Skerritt), a Vietnam vet who has a flashback as the cops raid his house; to Tijuana to attend a wedding of relatives after his East L.A. kin called the INS on themselves to get a free trip over there and back to California, in a truck made, unbeknownst to them, entirely of marijuana resin (in a fiberglass-like form).

Most of the time our heroes are being tracked down by inept Sgt. Stedenko (Stacy Keach). He and his minions get close, but are thwarted time and time again by the weed fumes emanating from the truck that get the police high and distracted. The climax occurs when Cheech and Chong win the Battle of the Bands as their weedmobile spews THC smoke into the venue and gets the whole audience high.

Directed by Lou Adler, *Up in Smoke* also featured the talents of Strother Martin, Edie Adams, Mills Watson, June Fairchild, Zane Buzby, David Nelson and Ellen Barkin. On a budget of $2 million the film grossed $44,364,244 at the box office.

https://youtu.be/FAaTp_WCREw

* * *

SEPTEMBER 16, 1993

THE SINBAD SHOW – PREMIERED ON FOX!

This sitcom starred comedian, Sinbad as a foot-loose-and-fancy- free bachelor who adopts two issue-ridden orphans (Erin Davis, Ray J). If he doesn't they'll be split up. Can't have that, so Sinbad steps up and he helps them solve their problems, like relationships, pilfering, school, teenager life, the opposite sex, loyalty, inner-racial racism, cock-blocking, baby-sitter drama, life, etc., etc., etc.

Sinbad's character designs video games and gets plenty of disrespect from the Ray J, but he knows it's only because he's protective of his younger sister, who likes, Sinbad and doesn't want to go to another foster home. Sinbad's buddy, Clarence (T.K. Carter) pops in to impart very little knowledge, mainly because he knows none. The show also featured Nancy Wilson and Hal Williams, with theme music by Chuck Brown.

The Sinbad Show was cancelled on April 21, 1994, after one season, with two shows left unaired. There was controversy when Civil Rights Leader and former presidential candidate, Jesse Jackson protested the cancellation as racially motivated. He cited the fact *Roc, South Central* and *In Living Color* were all cancelled the same season. FOX said it was low ratings. Race had nothing to do with it. Nevertheless, the sitcom did receive nominations Erin Davis (Young Artist Awards) and Sinbad (Nickelodeon Kids' Choice Awards).

https://youtu.be/-pfQJF2LP5Q

* * *

SEPTEMBER 16, 1977

LaWanda Page and Teddy Wilson in *Sanford Arms*

SANFORD ARMS – PREMIERED ON NBC!

The truth is if you'd taken a vacation that lasted over a month you'd have missed this sitcom altogether. *Sanford Arms* was a spin-off of NBC's popular show, *Sanford and Son*. That show starred Redd Foxx and Demond Wilson as the title characters who owned a junkyard. It was a hilarious sitcom and a ratings hit. However, after six seasons and much behind-the- scenes drama, Redd Foxx left *Sanford and Son* and went over to ABC to do a variety show. This left Demond Wilson to hold down the fort. He wanted more money than they were willing to offer for his hold down and so he left as well. *Sanford and Son* would now have to be renamed and retooled.

The first mistake made with *Sanford Arms* (after Norman Lear stepped down as executive producer and became a mere consultant) was keeping the name Sanford. Without Foxx or Wilson there was no Sanford on the premises. The storyline had the two Sanfords move to Arizona due to Fred's failing health. They sold their place; including a rooming house next door to one of Fred's old army buddies that we never heard of, Phil. Bubba was still around (as a bellhop). Aunt Esther was still around (to help Phil) and so was Grady (now married), but audiences didn't care about those characters if they weren't going back and forth with Fred Sanford and they cared even less about Phil trying to make a rooming house in Watts into a hotel in Watts.

Sanford Arms was canceled abruptly on October 14, 1977 after four episodes aired.

https://youtu.be/FJG2DGNl00c

✳✳✳

SEPTEMBER 17, 1968

Diahann Carroll as "Julia"

JULIA – PREMIERED ON NBC!

This oatmeal-bland sitcom lacked a lot of things. It didn't have a laugh track (that was added once it went into syndication). It didn't have a stereotypical Black female lead (Julia was a nurse, not a servant). It didn't have a Black male lead to go along with its female (Julia was a widow whose husband died in the Vietnam War) and it didn't have much Blackness; even though Julia was a Black woman in the late 1960s, there was no mention of riots, overwhelming social injustices or an extremely prevalent Civil Rights Movement. In other words, *Julia* was an acceptable (for the masses), middle-of-the-road slice of entertainment.

What *Julia* did have was Diahann Carroll. The talented actress/singer sold the concept of a politically passive Black woman living in a swanky high-rise apartment building with her only son, Corey (Marc Copage). She had non-Black neighbors, the Waggedorns (father, mother and two sons, one being Corey's contemporary and playmate). She had a non-Black boss, (the doctor played by Lloyd Nolan), who also had another nurse (non-Black, Lurene Tuttle) working in his aerospace office. Julia also had a couple of suiters (Black Fred Williamson and equally Black Paul Winfield), but neither relationship seemed too serious. The program also co-starred Betty Beaird, Ned Glass, Mary Wickes, Don Marshall and Michael Link.

Created by Hal Kantor, *Julia* was never a critic's darling or a show championed by the Black press, who almost unanimously stated it was an unrealistic white fantasy of a "Negro." The end result was that this initially touted sitcom that was going to break ground (because the Black lead was not a servant) suffered from declining ratings and death threats were made upon its star. Thus, the show was cancelled and its last episode aired March 23, 1971.

During its abbreviated run *Julia* received numerous nominations for editing, acting and producing. It went on to win a Golden Globe for Diahann Carroll in 1969 and in 2003 (32 years after the show was cancelled) cable station TV-Land honored *Julia* and its star with its "Groundbreaking Show" award.

https://youtu.be/ddqaFOdJ7Us

✳✳✳

SEPTEMBER 17, 1970

. Flip Wilson w/Joe Namath on *The Flip Wilson Show*, 1972 (Public Domain)

THE FLIP WILSON SHOW – PREMIERED ON NBC!

The hour-long show was the first successful variety series on network television starring a Black person. Using a Theater-in-the-Round stage format comedian, Wilson was able to display all the action to a live audience that was seated all around the stage. It seamlessly blended music and comedy skits. In its first two seasons the show was #2 in the Nielsen ratings.

Interestingly enough, there may have been no show had it not been for Redd Foxx. While making an appearance on *The Tonight Show starring Johnny Carson*, Redd was asked who the next up & coming comedian was. Without blinking Redd said, "Flip Wilson." This unselfish act led to NBC executives tracking Wilson down and offering him an unprecedented deal for television at the time. Not only would the show of this relative unknown run a full hour in primetime, Wilson would also own it. Thank you, Redd Foxx.

Though Wilson was a top-notch comedian, his most memorable comedy contribution came in the form of his alter-ego "Geraldine." The character of the sassy, wise-cracker with a boyfriend named, "Killer." It was Wilson in drag and it was hilarious. Geraldine had catchphrases: "The devil made me do it" and "What you see is what you get." Geraldine Jones flirted with everybody from football star, Joe Namath to singing idols like Ray Charles. Geraldine was so popular that after she made an appearance on the show, nobody cared if Wilson returned as a man or not. Regardless, Wilson did return as a man of many personas. He played white collar workers, blue collar workers and was famous for his character, Reverend Leroy of the Church of What's Happening Now; a con man with a Bible.

Wilson's variety show gave plenty of first-class variety. He was not only able to showcase the artistry of then little-known acts like Richard Pryor, Lily Tomlin, George Carlin, Albert Brooks and Sandy Duncan, but the show's roster of musical guests reads like a Who's Who of legends. The Flip Wilson Show featured the talents of James Brown, Aretha Franklin, Ella Fitzgerald, Stevie Wonder, Melba Moore, Lola Falana, Gladys Knight & the Pips, The Temptations, The Supremes, The Pointer Sisters and Mahalia Jackson (in one of her last public performances) as well as white performers such as The Osmonds, Roy Clark, Johnny Cash, Pat Boone and Bobby Darin. Many of the singing talent also appeared in skits with Wilson.

Wilson owned the rights to the show and moved onto his own soundstage in the fall of 1972. However, the variety genre was in decline and that along with a personal breakdown by Wilson caused the show to be cancelled. Its last episode aired June 27, 1974.

In its four-season run, *The Flip Wilson Show* was nominated for an Emmy 18 times. It won twice: Outstanding Variety Series and Outstanding Writing Achievement in Variety or Music. Wilson also won a Golden Globe Award in 1971 for Best Performance by an Actor in a Television Series.

https://youtu.be/OmJati2W7uA

✳ ✳ ✳

SEPTEMBER 18, 1971

Bobby Lee (l) at Mr. Chow's Restaurant w/Mr. Chow (Instagram)

BOBBY LEE – BORN IN SAN DIEGO, CALIFORNIA!

Lee's Korean-American parents wanted him to go into the family clothing business. He decided he had a better future working in a coffee shop. Then fate stepped in and Lee lost his position in that lucrative venue when the place shut down and he was forced to seek employment elsewhere. For Lee elsewhere meant next door and fortunately for comedy fans next door was the La Jolla Comedy Store where Lee got a job parking cars, washing dishes and showing people to their seats. It was fun, but not as much fun as stand -up comedy looked. So one amateur night he gave it a shot.

His parents didn't like Lee's new direction in life. His father even gave him the silent treatment, but that didn't matter. Soon Lee was good enough to get on the road as the opening act for attractions such as Carlos Mencia and Pauly Shore. His climb included an attention-getting performance on The *Tonight Show*. From there he put in eight seasons on the sketch comedy show, *MADtv* (2001-2009) and did the films *Pauly Shore is Dead, Harold & Kumar Go to the White Castle, Hard Breakers, Pineapple Express, A Very Harold & Kumar 3D Christmas, Kickin it Old Skool* and *The Dictator*. He toured in the Kims of Comedy, along with Ken Jeong, Steve Byrne and Kevin Shea and appeared on *The Mind of Mencia, Curb Your Enthusiasm, Animal Practice* and as a panelist on *Chelsea Lately*. Bobby Lee's done voice-overs and music videos (domestically and internationally). He's been a credit to coffee shop boys everywhere.

https://youtu.be/9tihzyQJjeM

✳✳✳

SEPTEMBER 18, 1905

Eddie "Rochester" Anderson, July 17, 1949 (Public Domain)

EDMUND LINCOLN ANDERSON ("ROCHESTER") – BORN IN OAKLAND, CALIFORNIA!

With an instantly recognizable raspy voice due to rupturing his vocal cords yelling as a paperboy in his youth, Eddie Anderson was the first Black man to be a regular cast member on radio. He worked a number of odd jobs after leaving school at age 14 to help out the family, but the lure of back stages kept tugging at him. He'd clown around with his brother, Cornelius which led to performing as a dancer in an all-Black revue on the vaudeville circuit. He got picked up and appeared in *Struttin Along* in 1923 and later *Steppin High* with Cornelius in 1924. He added comedy to his act in 1926 and then he met comedy legend, Jack Benny, the man who would change his life.

Anderson met Jack Benny by chance. They exchanged greetings, shook hands and went their separate ways. Little did Anderson imagine that he shook the hand of the man who he'd spend most of his career. When they met again Anderson was auditioning for the part of a Pullman porter in a Benny radio episode that took place on an actual train moving across country. He got the part when the shoeshine man, Oscar, at Paramount, who Benny had in mind for the part, involved his agent (yes, the shoeshine guy had an agent) who asked for $300. Benny thought this was high for 1937 and gave the role to Anderson, who was doing comedy on Central Avenue in Los Angeles. Anderson was so memorable that he was called back five weeks later to play a waiter and join the cast in a Jell-O commercial. Letters poured in and he was called in again a few weeks after that to play a guy in a financial dispute with Benny. More letters flooded the studio and Benny decided to make Anderson a cast regular. He'd be Rochester, the valet who would talk trash to his boss. That initial back talk turned into a lengthy, lucrative career.

By 1940 Anderson was the most popular character on *The Jack Benny Show* next to Benny. He was elected Mayor of Central Avenue, an honor which carried the right to speak on issues involving Blacks in that area. Anderson's platform was getting Blacks to become aviators. After he received press pushing this agenda, President Franklin Roosevelt made the same plea. Build a strong national air force.

Racial lessons were learned due to Rochester. After World War II people were more sensitive to racial bigotry. A script that had been used prior to the war was reused seven years later with disastrous results. Listeners called and wrote in how stereotypes about Negroes was unacceptable. Benny demanded that his writers remove all racial negativity from all future scripts and went on radio to compel his audience to reject racism and endorse brotherhood of the races.

Nevertheless, racism plagued the times. Anderson could not tour with the cast to entertain the troops because as a Black man he would require separate living quarters. (Yeah, right). Yet when his name was mentioned the soldiers applauded more for him than any cast member present. Stateside Benny would have to threaten to leave a hotel if they would not let Anderson stay there as well and sometimes that threat was a promise like the time in New York when the entire crew of 44 people checked out with Anderson.

Despite these indignities Eddie Anderson was the highest paid Black actor until the 1950s. He owned a sprawling estate in West Adams area of Los Angeles renamed "Rochester Circle" as well as races horses and a boxer, not to mention various businesses. In 1951 when *The Jack Benny Show* went to television Anderson went with it. He also did guest starring spots as Rochester on *The Milton Berle Show* (1953) and *Bachelor Father* (1962). *The Jack Benny Show* went off the air in 1965.

The Benny association was a major boost, but Anderson's career wasn't all Jack Benny. Anderson was in the Benny films, *Man About Town* and *Buck Benny Rides Again,* but he also co-starred with Ethel Waters and Lena Horne in the classic, *Cabin in the Sky* and appeared in the comedy film classic, *It's a Mad, Mad, Mad, Mad World* (his last screen performance). All totaled Anderson worked in over 60 motion pictures, including *Gone with the Wind* and *Jezebel.* Regardless, there was still ignorance to tolerate. One of his films, *Brewster's Millions* (1945) was banned from theaters in the South because "it presents too much social equality and racial mixture."

A complete entertainer, Eddie Anderson touched all mediums. He did game shows, provided voices for cartoons, performed comedy in night clubs and appeared on Broadway. In 1975 Anderson was elected to the Black Filmmakers Hall of Fame. On February 28, 1977 he died of heart disease in Los Angeles at the age of 71 and posthumously inducted into the Radio Hall of Fame in 2001.

https://youtu.be/NJNEE_8PcDE

***

SEPTEMBER 18, 1970

Aisha Tyler (Public Domain through clker.com)

AISHA TYLER – BORN IN SAN FRANCISCO, CALIFORNIA!

The comedy world should thank actor, Sam Rockwell of all people. If it wasn't for his parents living near Aisha Tyler's folks she would've never had the hots for him in high school and instead of taking her tail to social studies or wherever, she tailed him to his acting class and got turned onto performing.

It didn't take Tyler long to notice Hollywood loves archetype. So, Tyler took the archetype of the nerdy good looking funny Black girl and invented it. Hollywood didn't even notice they never had one and just cast her. After a few guest-starring roles she got some steady work when she hosted *Talk Soup* and *The Fifth Wheel*. Steady work seemed to suit Tyler so she got more multiple episodes in her life. She had her name on parking lot spaces for *Friends, CSI: Crime Scene Investigation, 24, Ghost Whisperer, Archer* (and it's multiple award nominations*), XIII: The Series, RuPaul's Drag Race, The Talk* (her daytime talk show and another award nomination attraction), *Talking Dead, Whose Line is it Anyway?, BoJack Horseman* and *Criminal Minds*.

Everything else she did (and there was a lot) were one-nighters. Her filmography boasts a dozen or so motion pictures. She's done her own stand-up special and hosts *Unapologetic with Aisha Tyler*. She's voiced video games (Halo: Reach and Watch Dogs), been on web series, been in music videos and published a couple of books. Aisha Tyler was a great addition to the comedy world and all we can say is – Thank you Sam Rockwell.

https://youtu.be/9xmlBR1tps4

✻✻✻

SEPTEMBER 20, 1984

THE COSBY SHOW – PREMIERED ON NBC!

This sitcom revitalized the tired formula that was a few short steps away from being declared a dinosaur and pronounced extinct. Then in swooped Bill Cosby with the perfect sitcom for the throwback Reagan Era. *The Cosby Show* brought back the type of family entertainment where the entire clan could gather around the glowing box for a half-hour of wholesome, shared laughter. The man who'd built a solid comedy career based on universal and family themes had a show about universal themes surrounded by his television family.

The Cosby Show was all about the upper-crust African-American brood, the Huxtables. The dad was a doctor. The mom, a lawyer. The kids – adorable and their suburb problems were the kind any race of kids could have, which was the point. The sitcom, like Cosby the comedian, was cultural without being racial. You don't get dubbed, "America's Dad" without reminding people of their own or an idolized version. Thus, Bill Cosby had succeeded in fooling everybody ... with a colorblind sitcom.

Created by Marcy Carsey and Tom Werner (former ABC executives) the show boasts an amiable cast. Lisa Bonet, Malcolm Jamal-Warner, Keshia Knight-Pulliam, Tempest Bledsoe and Sabrina LeBeauf (in the part originally meant for Whitney Houston, who turned it down to concentrate on being a fulltime recording artist) played the kids and Phylicia Rashad played wife Clair Huxtable. Other cast members included Joseph C. Phillips, Raven Symone, Erika Alexander and Geoffrey Owens.

The Cosby Show was a smash hit; one of the few in television history to rank #1 for five consecutive seasons. It was the gold standard for TV sitcoms thereafter and had a huge viewership on its finale (April 30, 1992). However, in November 2014 reruns were yanked from the majority of markets carrying the show in syndication based on multiple-sexual allegations against its star, Bill Cosby (who eventually went to prison). Some broadcasters even eliminated *Fat Albert & the Cosby Kids* from their schedule as well as *I-Spy* (two of Cosby's other shows from the past).

Despite efforts to wipe the program from memory based on the personal actions of its star, the collaborative product assembled by the remaining cast and technicians has a legacy that remains intact. *The Cosby Show* won six Emmys, two Golden Globe Awards, three NAACP Awards, a Peabody Award and eleven People's Choice Awards. It's received honors from *TV Guide, Entertainment Weekly, Time* Magazine *USA Today* and *Bravo*; spawned two albums, an alter ego (Dr. Hibbert) on *The Simpsons* and the spin-off following Denise Huxtable to college – *A Different World*.

https://youtu.be/wkrYOy18evY
✳ ✳ ✳

SEPTEMBER 20, 1921

Slappy White (l) w/ Redd Foxx on *Sanford and Son*, 1972 (Public Domain)

MELVIN "SLAPPY" WHITE – BORN IN BALTIMORE, MD!

White was born near the old Royal Theatre in Baltimore. At the age of ten he was dancing outside for coins and selling candy at the theater, but by the time he was 13 he had to get out of town. All that hanging out hustling money equaled too many school absences and they were going to throw him into a reform school. So White joined a traveling carnival as a tap dancer. That career didn't last long. The police got ahold of him and took him back to his parents. That also didn't last long. White had been bitten by the show-biz bug and was terminally diseased. He was going to be a performer.

White got his nickname when a theater manager billed him and his dance partner as "Slap and Happy." He didn't get into comedy until he hooked up with Clarence Schelle in 1940. They called their act "Two Zephyrs" and appeared on *The Major Bowes Amateur Hour* as well as working with jazz greats, Lionel Hampton, Count Basie, Duke Ellington and others. They worked together for four years.

Slappy showed he was a team player when he got his second successful team pairing called "Lewis and White." They appeared with the likes of Johnny Otis, The Ink Spots and their old friends, the Count, the Duke and Hamp. They also popped up on *The Morey Amsterdam Show* on TV. However, everybody seems to remember him best for the four years he was partners with Redd Foxx from 1947-1951. Formed in Harlem, the duo toured from coast to coast with the Billy Eckstine Orchestra.

Slappy was married to Pearl Bailey at the time, but it wasn't going well. When the union commenced they were both relative unknowns, but as Bailey was getting bookings in better clubs, Slappy was still on the low-end circuit. That could put a strain on any marriage and Slappy's was no exception. So they did what any couple would under the circumstances. They got a divorce. Oddly enough Slappy worked with Pearl's brother, Bill Bailey years later in an act Slappy said should've been called, "Rev. Bill Bailey and his ex-brother-in-law."

Slappy went solo in 1951 and took a strange path to get there. He was working as a chauffeur for singer, Dinah Washington, cracking her up on jokes as he wheeled her around. One night she was running late at her engagement at the "Black Hawk" in San Francisco. She didn't want the audience to get too restless so she asked Slappy to go out on stage and be funny while she got ready. She didn't need to rush. Slappy was a hit and she hired him as her opening act.

Not only did he make Dinah Washington laugh he got her loyalty. One night Slappy made the club's owner the butt of his jokes; fine with the audience, but the white owner didn't appreciate being made fun of by a Negro and fired Slappy. He stayed fired all the way up to when Dinah said she'd leave too. Like Larry Tate (the opportunist boss on *Bewitched*), the club man did a quick rehiring job. White stayed with Washington for four years then went solo.

Slappy White gained a reputation for not using offensive material. During the civil rights movement White was more about uniting than dividing. He received a personal commendation from President Kennedy for a piece Slappy wrote and performed called "Brotherhood Creed" using one black and one white glove to demonstrate the equality between men.

Presidents seemed to love Slappy. He and his new partner, Steve Rossi performed for President Richard Nixon at the White House in 1969 and Slappy managed to do it without once hugging old Tricky Dick. White was a recurring character, Melvin, on *Sanford and Son* and remained active guest starring on various sitcoms and performing across country for the remainder of his career. In the mid-90s he was tired and in the process of retiring from acting and moving out of Los Angeles, but then Slappy White died suddenly on November 7, 1995.

https://youtu.be/sLdqVnaCBY4

✳ ✳ ✳

September 20, 2005

Tichina Arnold in *Everybody Hates Chris* (Instagram)

EVERYBODY HATES CHRIS – PREMIERED ON UPN!

The critically acclaimed sitcom was based on the teen-age years of executive producer, comedian Chris Rock (who also served as narrator). With original music by Marcus Miller and produced by Paramount. It starred Tyler James Williams (as the young Rock); Tichina Arnold as his antsy mother, Rochelle; Terry Crews as his overworked daddy, Julius; Teqwuan Richmond as Drew, the brother everybody wishes Chris was more like, and his scheming sister, Tonya, played by Imani Hakim. Everybody may not hate Chris, but they sure do get the best of him.

It's the 1980s in the Brooklyn, New York neighborhood of Bed-Stuy and Chris has the dilemma of being a Black kid in a white school; a school of more than several bigots. Of course, he has a white buddy, Greg, played by Vincent Martella, who lends moral support to Chris as much as possible, but life is still a hassle. Chris is obviously hassled at school. He brings home bad grades so he's hassled there and not just by his family, but the lowlifes that inhabit his surroundings as well. He's not a stud Black kid so it's a hassle he's not getting the girls. He's also not a money maker and that's always a hassle. Rock used a childhood friend, Kenny Montero as inspiration for many of his episodic antics.

Everybody Hates Chris reaped much praise over its four season run. It has several Emmy nominations for cinematography and costumes under its belt as well as a Golden Globe nomination for Best Television Series. The sitcom has numerous Television Critic Association, Teen Choice, Environmental Media, Satellite, People's Choice and Motion Picture Sound Editors Award nominations. The American Film Institute selected it as one of the 10 best sitcoms of 2007. That same year it won the NAACP Image Award for writing (Ali LeRoi) and Tyler James Williams won for Best Actor in a Comedy Series. In 2006 the show won the Young Artist Award for Best Family Television Series. Tichina Arnold won for Best Actress in a Comedy Series in 2006 and the show won for Best Comedy Series. *Everybody Hates Chris* aired its last episode on May 8, 2009.

https://youtu.be/2BtNVOhmx3Q

✱ ✱ ✱

September 23, 1985

Hasan Minhaj at Joint Base Andrews Washington, DC, May 5, 2016 (Public Domain)

HASAN MINHAJ – BORN IN DAVIS, CALIFORNIA!

Walter Cronkite, once America's most trusted voice in news reporting, was 47 years old when he received his first Peabody Award for excellence. Minhaj was 15 years younger when he got his, but the similarity of trustworthiness also came sooner. The United States is more of a microwave society than when Cronkite, Huntley and Brinkley dispensed information citizens believed was accurate and honest. In the 21st Century we bypass the honesty in place of even the slightest morsel of accuracy. For some reason we inherently believe Minhaj gives us that.

At a time in America's history when non-European descendants were viewed with apprehension and even fear in certain circles it's a return to rational, progressive and inclusive thinking to have vital information and perspective served to the populace by someone from an Indian Muslim household. Minhaj reminds us how intelligence takes all forms and how the message is more crucial than any preconceived notion about the messenger. However, if that messenger packs a wallop of credibility so much the better.

Hasan Minhaj was busy loading up on credibility. He was a finalist on the NBC program *Stand Up for Diversity*. It was another purveyor of truth, Chris Rock, who inspired Minhaj after watching Rock's *Never*

Scared. Fast forward past the process of working through enough material and audiences to rate opening for Gabriel Iglesias, Katt Williams and Pablo Francisco, then doing some inconsequential films and a smattering of TV guest-starring roles, Minhaj had gained the experience to go out and set his own mark. He did that when in 2014 he became a correspondent for *The Daily Show.*

Working for the faux news broadcast gave Minhaj the opportunity to voice his unique opinion and viewpoint to a captured (if they didn't change the channel) audience. He had comedy chops and crowd understanding skills, but with this gig his major in political science at the University of California, Davis would definitely come in handy. He had a grasp and frame of reference for the issues popping up well, frankly … daily and Minhaj was prepared to dissect each one.

His deft command of topics and poise landed him as host in front of the slightly judgmental crowd at the Radio and Television Correspondent's Dinner. That fearless appearance, where he chided Congress for their weak, and cowardly response to needed gun control initiatives had a lot of folks sit up and take notice. It resulted in Minhaj being booked to speak to the stiff-necked group at the 2017 White House Correspondent's Dinner, where he roasted president Donald J. Trump who was in absentia for the annual event (the first sitting president to pass since Ronald Reagan, who had a pretty valid excuse since he had been shot by a would-be assassin and hospitalized).

Following his chiding to the White House Correspondent's Dinner reporters to use due diligence and do their jobs no matter what name the "Liar in Chief" calls them, Minhaj leaped over yet another stepping stone. He adapted his successful one-person Off- Broadway show, *Homecoming King* to a Netflix stand-up comedy special, *Hasan Minhaj: Homecoming King* and had another smash hit on his hands which not only got him the coveted Peabody Award, but positioned Minhaj to get his own show where he could spew his brand, his way (within FCC boundaries of course). The aptly named *Patriot Act with Hasan Minhaj* premiered on Netflix, October 28, 2018 and the public held on for what was bound to be a ground-breaking ride.

Beyond his Peabody, Minhaj has won the MPAC Media Award, the Cchaya CDC Architects of Change Award and the International Man Trophy at the GQ India Men of the Year Awards. Stay tuned for more.

https://youtu.be/nNx5tnqD9e0

✳ ✳ ✳

SEPTEMBER 23, 1954

Charlie Barnett (l) w/ Martin Lawrence (Priscilla Clarke of PC & Associates) Source: Bob Sumner

CHARLIE BARNETT – BORN IN BLUEFIELD, WV!

Known as a comic's comic, Barnett gained notoriety as a park performer. He would gather a crowd at any New York City outdoor area, do his act and pass the hat. He was a fixture at Washington Square Park where onlookers were captivated by Barnett's quick wit and masterful style. His competing artists such as musicians, jugglers and other novelty acts all knew of Barnett's reputation and had the utmost respect for him. Dave Chappelle credits Barnett as being a mentor (at one time even discussing doing a biopic on Barnett).

However, Charlie Barnett was more than a great street performer. He was the goods. Eddie Murphy lucked up because Barnett had poor reading skills and the slot he had earned in 1980 on*Saturday Night Live* went to Murphy when Barnett skipped his follow-up audition to avoid being embarrassed. This decision plagued him for years after Murphy became a star on that show and in Barnett's slot, but as times changed so did Barnett's attitude.

Charlie Barnett had a short, but impressive career. Besides being known as the funniest comic on the East Coast, he was making a name for himself as an actor. He had a recurring role as

Charlie Barnett (r) w/Dave Chappelle (Priscilla Clarke of PC & Associates) Source: Bob Sumner

"Noogie" on the NBC hit crime drama, *Miami Vice*, working alongside Phillip Michael Thomas and Don Johnson. He appeared in the Mr. T starring vehicle *DC Cab* as well as the film *Nobody's Fool* and others. At the time of his death he was a hot commodity and very much in demand.

Unfortunately, a little-known fact outside of the industry was Barnett's addiction to heroin. This proved to be fatal when Barnett contracted the HIV virus through his abuse of the drug and died of complications of AIDS on March 16, 1996.

https://youtu.be/scipjlqqrDg

✳ ✳ ✳

SEPTEMBER 23, 2005

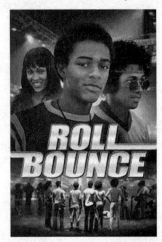

ROLL BOUNCE – RELEASED BY SEARCHLIGHT PICTURES!

A cinematic tribute to the skating craze of the late 1970s and early 80s, *Roll Bounce* stars Bow Wow as a skater, Xavier, whose life is only in harmony when he's on his wheels. His mother is dead and his father doesn't understand him; neither does his little sister. When X (Bow Wow) and his crew lose the familiarity of their neighborhood Chicago rink they're forced to skate in the upper-crust bougie part of town, only to be dissed by the local skaters; that is until a roller disco contest pits the crews against each other and life lessons are learned.

Written by former BET scribe Norman Vance, Jr. *Roll Bounce* has a cast loaded with comedians and comedy personalities. Mike Epps, Nick Cannon, Brandon T. Jackson and Charlie Murphy make up a strong supporting cast. They're assisted by acting veterans Chi McBride, Kellita Smith, Meagan Good, Jurnee Smollett, Wayne Brady and Wesley Jonathan.

Directed by Malcolm D. Lee and produced by George Tillman, Jr., Roll Bounce was made on a $10-million budget and grossed $17,500,866. Music was provided by Stanley Clarke and Niles Rodgers; featuring songs by Chaka Khan, Earth, Wind & Fire, Brooke Valentine, Fabolous, Shorty Mack, Beyonce, R. Kelly, Michelle Williams and Ray J.

Roll Bounce received several nominations for achievement in directing and acting and won the 2006 Black Reel Awards for Best Screenplay, Original or Adapted for Norman Vance, Jr.

https://youtu.be/KRbtDCxcN-M

* * *

SEPTEMBER 24, 1987

Ajai Sanders and Kadeem Hardison in Halloween episode of *A Different World*
(Ajai Sanders Collection)

A DIFFERENT WORLD – PREMIERED ON NBC!

Originally a *Cosby Show* spin-off, the sitcom became its own show. Denise Huxtable was supposed to go off to Hillman College in Virginia and viewers were meant to be exposed to life on a historically Black college. Great idea; major problems. The fact Hillman was fictional and based on Hampton University was not a problem. The fact Denise Huxtable had a white roommate (Marisa Tomei) was not a problem (many HSUs have interracial student bodies). However, the fact Lisa Bonet who played Denise Huxtable got pregnant was.

After the first season the show needed retooling. Complaints had come in that the portrayal of Hillman was inaccurate so Debbie Allen was brought in to make the show authentic. Debbie had attended Howard University (a legit HSU) and was a skillful director of actors. She took the series writers to 3 black colleges to flush out true-to-life ideas.

Since the decision had been made to have Denise Huxtable drop out of Hillman and move to Africa (so viewers would never see the "good girl's" baby bump), Allen focused the show on the new principal characters of Whitley Gilbert (Jasmine Guy) and Dwayne Wayne (Kadeem Hardison). Social issues the parent show shied from, were explored on *A Different World* such as racism, date rape, AIDS, Blacks owning slaves, the Persian Gulf War and class relations.

A Different World had a cast that remained in flux. After the first season departure of Lisa Bonet, Marisa Tomei and Loretta Devine; Cree Summers and Charnele were brought in as regulars. Dawnn Lewis and Mary Alice remained, but Sinbad and Darryl M. Bell went from recurring to main characters. Glynn Turman and Lou Myers were also given more camera time. In subsequent seasons Ajai Sanders and Jada Pinkett were signed on as recurring and later bumped up to main characters.

The sitcom was noted for accurately portraying college life, fraternity and sorority involvements and the Black experience. To help tell these stories the show featured a wide range of Black talent. Over the years, appearances were made by Kim Wayans, Jenifer Lewis, Rosalind Cash, Ron O'Neal, Phylicia Rashad, Malcolm Jamal Warner, Robert Guillaume, Bill Cosby, Patti Labelle, Diahann Carroll, Tisha Campbell, Art Evans, Lena Horne, Vanessa Bell Calloway, Richard Roundtree, Halle Berry, Roseanne Barr, Tom Arnold, Dean Cain, Whoopi Goldberg, Heavy D, David Alan Grier, Gladys Knight, Jesse Jackson, Blair Underwood and Tupac Shakur.

During its six-season run the sitcom was always in one of the top two slots with Black viewers and has been credited by many college alumni that it is that show that encouraged them to attend historically Black colleges.

A Different World had its series finale on July 9, 1993.

https://youtu.be/7a5A9h5MZlM

✳✳✳

SEPTEMBER 25, 1983

Donald Glover at the 2015 Toronto International Film Festival (Public Domain)

DONALD MCKINLEY GLOVER – BORN IN CALIFORNIA!

Raised in Stone Mountain, Georgia. Glover multi-tasked comedy and rap through his alter ego, Childish Gambino. The character released several albums (one he disowns) and won Glover two Grammy Awards for Best Rap Album and Performance. He also performs as a DJ under the name mcDJ; making many of his mixtapes available free on his website.

Glover's adeptness at humor had been recognized by classmates early on and he earned a degree in dramatic writing from New York University's Tisch School of the Arts. Then Glover took his writing skills and wrote for NBC's *30 Rock* for several seasons; making on-camera appearances as well. His stint there earned him three Writer's Guild of America Award for Best Comedy Series.

Glover showed off his acting chops as a cast member on the acclaimed NBC sitcom, *Community*. He was seriously considered for the part of Peter Parker in the *Amazing Spider-Man* before the role went to Andrew Garfield. He did, however, voice the character in the animated version, *Ultimate Spider-Man.*

The multi-talent joined the improv troupe, *Derrick Comedy*; the group that starred in the film, *Mystery Team*, and why not? They wrote and produced it. Glover has also appeared in films, *The Muppets, The To Do List, Alexander and the Terrible, Horrible, No Good, Very Bad Day, The Lazarus Effect, Magic Mike XXL, The Martian* and *Solo*, where Glover played a young Lando Calrissian. His television credits include, *Girls and Sesame Street* and he's provided voices for *Robot Chicken, Adventure Time* and *China IL.*

Glover's first stand-up special aired on Comedy Central in 2010. He toured with a show that included comedy, rap, video portions and often features guest artists. In *Atlanta*, the show he created and starred in, Glover plays the opportunist relative of a talented fledgling rapper. There'd been a feeding frenzy for *Atlanta*, with FX being chosen because Glover wanted to tour and FX said they could work around that.

Throughout his career, the highly decorated Donald Glover, has won the Rising Comedy Star Award at the Just for Laughs festival; the Comedy Awards Breakout Breakthrough Performer of the Year; Gold Derby TV Awards for Best TV Ensemble (*Community*); PAAFTJ Television Awards Best Cast in a Comedy Series (*Community*); TV Guide Awards Favorite Ensemble (*Community*); an mtvU Woodies Award for Best Video Woodie from his EP, *Kauai* and two RIAA certifications.

https://youtu.be/ioSI3KsE2_k

✳ ✳ ✳

SEPTEMBER 25, 1976

Pat Morita promo for *Mr. T & Tina* (1976) (Public Domain)

MR. T & TINA – PREMIERED ON ABC!

The extremely talented comedian/actor, Pat Morita left the ultra-successful *Happy Days* (where he played Arnold) to star in this *Welcome Back Kotter* spin-off. Career wise, not a great move, but historically it made Morita the first Asian male to star in a network sitcom. The show was about a Japanese inventor who relocates his family to Chicago from Toyko. Susan Blanchard played Tina, the take-life-as-it-comes governess hired to mind the children (June Angela, Gene Profanato) while Morita invented stuff.

Created by James Komack, this stereotypically racist turkey got put out of its misery after only 5 episodes were aired (9 were shot and you can probably get them for a grape soda and half a Snickers bar). I would mention that Ted Lange was in this debacle, but I like him too much to besmirch and sully his good name. Anyway, the reviews were horrendous, and the public was too busy watching *The Bob Newhart Show* (on CBS) or paint dry, to tune-in. Thus, *Mr. T & Tina* aired its last episode on October 30, 1976.

https://youtu.be/mKD7wu4-Iw4

✳✳✳

SEPTEMBER 27, 1947

Liz Torres in 'Phyllis', 1975 (Public Domain)

ELIZABETH LARRIEU "LIZ" TORRES – BORN IN THE BRONX!

The multi-talented Torres got her start in comedy. She'd made a low budget film in 1969 playing a whore, but that cinematic debut did not lead to a film career. Whereas being a comedienne gave her the freedom to expose her strengths when she'd hit the night club circuit (along with her buddy Bette Midler) and that's where she got noticed. Torres was seen by a scout for *"The Tonight Show"* (the version starring Johnny Carson) and invited to do a skit on the show. That did lead to other work.

Torres became a member of the Addams Family. She played Morticia in the musical version, *Addams Family Funhouse* in 1973. Guest spots ensued and by 1975 she was Julie Erskine on *Phyllis* starring Cloris Leachman. That same year she recorded a disco single, *Hustle Latino* and performed it on Dick Clark's *American Bandstand*. She had a recurring role on *All in the*

Family and co-starred with Marla Gibbs in the sitcom *Checking In* in 1981. That spin-off of *The Jeffersons* didn't last long, but no matter, Torres kept working. She appeared in *Love, American Style, Ally McBeal* and in 1990 was nominated for an Emmy for her work on *The Famous Teddy Z.*

Torres also worked in the theater. She was featured in *The Ritz, Man of LaMancha* and *A Million to Juan.* In 1993 she began working on *The John Larroquette Show,* where Torres received multiple acting nominations for her role of Mahalia Sanchez. In 1997 she found herself on CBS on the sitcom, *Over the Top.* From 2000-2007 Torres performed the role of Miss Patty LaCosta on *The Gilmore Girls.*

Liz Torres kept jobs. In between doing her own shows and her recurring parts, she was a serial guest starrer. Torres has had roles on *Desperate Housewives, Private Practice, Scandal, Devious Maids* and *Ugly Betty.*

https://youtu.be/ZINTVZ1V5vY

***

SEPTEMBER 27, 1962

Shang (r) w/ Royale Watkins at Serra's in Studio City, CA, 2009 (The Littleton Collection)

SHANG FORBES – BORN IN KINGSTON, JAMAICA!

Shang's path to comedy is a familar story. He got on stage at an open mic on a bet. He was funny and the sky opened up revealing his future. It's a typical tale, but Shang is not a typical comedian. His apocalyptic, doomsday themes are peppered with slicing attacks on politics, policy and whatever is going on at the moment.

The subversive existentialist takes full advantage of all mediums available to comedians. Making his debut at the start of the Black Comedy

Boom he appeared on *Def Comedy Jam, Laffapalooza, Loco Comedy Jam* and BETs *Comic View* multiple times as well as two half-hour comedy specials for the cable station.

Shang has made numerous guest starring appearances. He was featured on CBS's *NCIS, The Jamie Foxx Show, Zack & Cody* and *Passions* just to name a few. He's toured worldwide entertaining troops and dignitaries; debated hot button topics on *Politically Incorrect* and sparked candid dialogue as co-host and producer of BET's *Access Granted*.

Shang was a writer for *George Magazine* and a staff writer for the syndicated show, *The Newz*. His acclaimed comedy album, "SHANGRY" was a top seller on the Uproar label and is one of the most played comedy CDs on Sirius XM.

https://youtu.be/g_YSB6uV84M

✳✳✳

SEPTEMBER 27, 1986

The cast of *Amen*

AMEN – PREMIERED ON NBC!

This Carson Productions sitcom starred Sherman Hemsley and Clifton Davis. Set in Philadelphia, Hemsley plays a church deacon, who moonlights as a lawyer – or vice versa. Either way, he's not the most honest man in either profession. Actually, he's downright crooked, but gets a pass from his loving and single daughter played by Anna Maria Horsford. She loves her deacon daddy, but she loves the pastor played by Davis even more. Yeah, her father and her man-to-be don't always see things eye-to-eye, but that's their problem. During the show's run, she gets her man after pushing up on him, getting engaged, married and giving birth to a baby.

The show dealt with serious themes, but in a non-judgmental fashion. Topics such as giving birth out of wedlock, depression, suicide prevention, coveting and others were covered and mined for laughs by Hemsley and cast. The deacon is often ridiculed for his legal expertise or lack there-of. Regardless, he takes a case whenever he can and when he's not plotting something underhanded for the church.

Amen was a ratings success for NBC. It also featured the talents of Jest-er Hairston, the old guy with more sense than anybody in the church; Rosetta LeNoire as his girlfriend (and later wife); Roz Ryan and Barbara Montgomery as two church sisters of the choir; Elsa Raven as the house-keeper; Tony T. Johnson as an impressionable young boy who lives next to the deacon and Bumper Robinson as an impressionable young boy mentored by the deacon.

Amen aired its last episode on May 11, 1991.

https://youtu.be/xzCsXtln6cM

✳✳✳

SEPTEMBER 28, 2006

America Ferrera as *Ugly Betty*

UGLY BETTY – PREMIERED ON ABC!

A Columbian telenovela walks into an American studio disguised as a Mexican sitcom idea. Five years and two networks later Salma Hayek and her associates are executive producing a landmark hour-long come-dy about a plain looking young girl named Betty with no fashion sense. It wouldn't matter much, but she gets a job at a fashion magazine solely based on her plain looks. Seems the owner's son, and heir to the mag em-pire is so horny he needs a plain looking assistant to calm him down long enough to concentrate on his publishing duties. Betty is deemed plain enough; initially anyway.

The Columbian version of *Ugly Betty* (*Yo soy Betty, la fea*) revolved around the above described budding romance between two people. The American version blew up the cast like it was a Michael Bay flick. Betty had haters at the job who later became friends and haters who remained haters. It began as a hit, but once ABC tinkered with the time schedule, fans became frustrated and jumped ship causing the shows cancellation after four seasons (April 14, 2010) and establishing a solid cult following in its afterlife.

Ugly Betty starred America Ferrera as the title character. It co-starred Vanessa L. Williams, Eric Mabius, Tony Plana, Judith Light, Rebecca Romijn and Ana Ortiz. It won two Golden Globe Awards, a SAG Award, a Peabody, a Prism Award, a Gay & Lesbian Alliance Against Defamation Award, three Emmy Awards, and five NAACP Image Awards from an organization that only gives out awards to Black shows. *Ugly Betty* was not a Black show, but obviously a damn good one.

https://youtu.be/tnAWeIdIDyk

✳✳✳

SEPTEMBER 28, 1965

Joe Torry at *Def Comedy Jam 25* (Humor Mill Magazine)

JOE TORRY – BORN IN ST. LOUIS, MISSOURI!

Joe Torry is the real thing, but for the first part of his career he appeared to be a substitute. When Robin Harris, the host and draw of the Comedy Act Theater passed away suddenly, it was Torry who picked up the mantle. Nobody wanted to follow in those huge footsteps. Well, Joe Torry used to dress like a cowboy in those days and he came equipped with a pair of cowboy boots.

Then came *Def Comedy Jam*. Martin Lawrence departed the show he'd established and there was a vacancy. This time around plenty of takers were lined up, but after a few strings were pulled, Joe Torry, the show's warm-up act became the new host of the biggest cable television phenomenon in the early 1990s. Each time Torry did the job in a pressure cooker and you never saw him sweat. The suits took notice.

The work rolled in. He appeared in the films, *Poetic Justice, House Party 3, Fled, Sprung, Tales from the Hood, Exit to Eden, Back in Business, Lockdown, Commitments, The Flamingo Rising,* and more. On television the work load was similar: *ER, NYPD Blue, NCIS, Girlfriends, The King Assassin Show.* Besides, *Def Comedy Jam,* Torry flexed his stand-up muscles on *Comics Unleashed, 1ˢᵗ Amendment and Late Night with Conan O'Brien.*

The legend also lives on as he and his brother, Guy were profiled on the documentary series, *Unsung.* Huh. Like most entertainers Torry has not been free of controversy. There was a run-in with a female comic that led to charges of violence and then his support of convicted rapist and former comedy icon, Bill Cosby, not to mention Torry's acid tongue offending more than a few fans across the country who didn't necessarily like being talked about by one of the best. So, it's doubtful unsung will be the case of Joe Torry. As a matter of fact, we see the fat lady about to open her mouth right now.

https://youtu.be/ukKsiWXCqFk

✳ ✳ ✳

SEPTEMBER 29, 1970

Russell Peters in Afghanistan USO tour November 21, 2007 (Public Domain)

RUSSELL DOMINIC PETERS – BORN IN TORONTO!

Due to his Indian descent, Peters was regularly bullied in school and took up boxing to even things out. Comedy was also a great leveler of tension. Peters took up joke telling in 1989 and in 1992 he met one of his idols, George Carlin. It was that meeting that instilled an extra bit of ambition in Peters. Carlin advised the young comic to go up and perform as much as possible and wherever possible. It was that new work ethic that kicked Peters' career into that of a serious professional and got him noticed by his elders, including Carlin, who Peter's opened for on one of Carlin's last performances.

The big break for Peters came in 2004. He was the beneficiary of the latest thing known as "videos going viral." He'd shot a set on Canadian TV's "Comedy Now!" and YouTube users ate it up. Not only did they devour the 45-minute routine, they uploaded segments of his racial comedy and made sure the groups he was talking about got it. They in turn uploaded it and before long Peters was an international comedy star.

Throughout his career it's been about groundbreaking numbers. He was the first comedian to sell out Toronto's Air Canada Centre (16,000 tickets) in 2007. In 2009 he set the sales record for London's 02 Arena (16,000 tickets). His 2010 show in Australia (13,880 tickets) was the biggest stand-up comedy show in Australia's history and he did the same thing in Singapore in 2012. His DVD, *Outsourced* stayed on the National DVD charts for over a year and a half. His autobiography, *Call Me Russell* was a best-seller. For all this hard work Peters was recognized by *Forbes* Magazine as the third highest paid stand-up comedian.

Russell Peters has produced comedy for radio and hosted televised award shows (*The Juno Awards*). In 2008 he won the prestigious Gemini Award for Best Performance or Host in a Variety Program or Series. He had the 2013 Trailblazer Award bestowed upon him by the Association of South Asians in Media for his pioneering comedy contributions by a member of his culture. For the 2014 season of NBCs *Last Comic Standing* Peters served as a judge along with Keenan Ivory Wayans and Roseanne Barr. He's appeared on TV (*Mr. D, The Burn with Jeff Ross*), in films (*National Lampoon's 301: The Legend of Awesomest Maximus, My Baby's Daddy*), but mostly on stages worldwide.

https://youtu.be/INNQ8jRbMfY
✳ ✳ ✳

SEPTEMBER 29, 1976

Redd Foxx and Michael Warren

NORMAN ... IS THAT YOU? – RELEASED BY METRO-GOLD-WYN-MAYER AND UNITED ARTISTS!

Based on the hit stage play of the same name this version goes for a Black cast, not Jewish and stars Redd Foxx and Pearl Bailey. They portray the parents of fresh-out-the-closet, Norman. Well, the closet door was ajar and Redd peeked in. Foxx is an abandoned husband (his wife ran off with the brother-in-law) and to get his bearings he visits his son unannounced and pulls a Columbus of a discovery. Like most old-school fathers, Foxx tries to talk Norman (Michael Warren) into being a real man to the point of buying him a prostitute. But naturally by the end of this comedy attitudes have been adjusted, enlightenment and person-al growth have manifest and old Redd Foxx is a more tolerant man than when he arrived uninvited on the doorstep of his grown ass son.

Directed and produced by George Schlatter, *Norman ... Is That You* co-stars Dennis Dugan, Tamara Dobson, Vernee Watson-Johnson, Jayne Meadows, George Furth, Sosimo Hernandez, Sergio Aragones and Way-land Flowers.

https://youtu.be/DY77Tiwgo8o

✳ ✳ ✳

OCTOBER

THIS DAY IN COMEDY...

October 1, 1993

Malik Yoba, Leon, Doug E. Doug and Rawle D. Lewis

Cool Runnings – Released by Walt Disney Pictures!

This last film John Candy appeared in also stars Doug E. Doug, Malik Yoba, Leon and Rawle D. Lewis. The story is loosely based on the historic inclusion of Jamaicans into the sport of bobsledding at the 1988 Winter Olympics. Prior to that all bobsledding teams had hailed from locations with snow (which made it easier for them to practice), but when an 100 meter runner doesn't make the Summer Olympic games due to an on track mishap, he seeks out a former two time Gold Medalist to help him attain his dream. The difference is now the dream consists of using runners to make a bobsled go faster and possibly win a medal.

The newly formed Jamaican bobsled team find the old timer and an uneasy alliance is formed. The assembled motley crew discover their new coach was once a bigtime cheat. Other revelations dot the film as movies mixing sports, comedy and sentimentality are known to do, but they all end up gaining a greater understanding of each other as it becomes the Jamaicans and their non-Jamaican coach against all the other bobsled teams who feel superior.

With the authenticity of actual footage and fueled by a popular sound track featuring Jimmy Cliff's version of "I Can See Clearly," *Cool Runnings* was a box office hit and critical success. It debuted at #3 domestically and earned $68,856,263 in the US and Canada. In Jamaica the film made $416,771 and its total worldwide take came to $154,856,263. Not bad for a film made on a $14-million budget.

https://youtu.be/l_VMr3k152I

✳✳✳

375

October 3, 1950

Louise Beavers as *Beulah* (Public Domain)

BEULAH – PREMIERED ON ABC!

Carrying the historical distinction of being the first sitcom to star a Black female, *Beulah* got its roots on radio in 1945. At that time, it was on CBS and the original performer playing the title character, Beulah Brown, was a white man; Marlin Hurt. The guy made a living off of her. It was Hurt who invented Beulah, the housekeeper/cook for radio in 1939 for the *Hometown Incorporated* radio series. He moved her over to NBC's *Show Radio* in 1940. Hurt was Beulah in 1943 for *That's Life* and in 1944 he/she was a regular on *Fibber McGee and Molly*. Then in 1945 Hurt aka Beulah hit the big time; their own show entitled (get this) *The Marlin Hurt and Beulah Show*.

Hurt died of a heart attack in 1946. He was replaced by another white actor: Bob Corley. Corley lived, but was replaced by Hattie McDaniel in 1947. This made her the first Black actress to star on a radio show, where she doubled the show's ratings and earned $1,000 per week. When McDaniel became ill in 1952 she was replaced on radio by Lillian Randolph, who was replaced the following season by her sister, Amanda Randolph.

The show hit television in 1950 and that's when it really got confusing. "The Queen of the Kitchen" was still outsmarting her Caucasian employers by knowing how to solve problems that perplexed them, but you never knew which Beulah you were going to get. The same applied to fellow characters, Bill, her boyfriend and Oriole, her friend/maid from next door.

The first television Beulah was Ethel Waters. This also made Waters the first Black woman to star in a television show. She quit after one season saying the scripts were degrading to Black people. The next Beulah was

Hattie McDaniel; familiar with the role from her radio version. After six episodes she got sick and was replaced quickly by Louise Beavers. The reason for the rapidness was because none of McDaniel's episodes had aired. So audiences saw Ethel Waters, then Louise Beavers, then Hattie McDaniel. When McDaniel learned her situation was more serious than first considered (she was diagnosed with breast cancer), Beavers became the permanent replacement and the new Beulah.

Similar shenanigans went on with the other cast members. Initially Butterfly McQueen played Oriole under the Ethel Waters regime. When Hattie McDaniel came aboard McQueen was replaced by Ruby Dandridge, who'd played the part on radio. Dooley Wilson (Sam from *Casablanca*) became the new Bill after Percy "Bud" Harris walked citing the refusal to portray Uncle Tom in any form as the reason. Ernest Whitman was the final Bill under the Louise Beavers era.

Of course, the artistic attackers without solutions – the NAACP, jumped on the stereotypes and *Beulah's* days were numbered. The show managed to crank out 87 episodes before being shut down for good. Eighty of those episodes have been destroyed. Only seven survive along with only 21 of the radio broadcasts.

Beulah aired its last televised episode on December 23, 1952.

https://youtu.be/sQ2l_KTDcHU

✻✻✻

OCTOBER 5, 1957

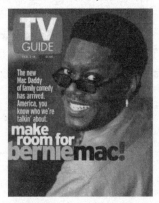

Bernie Mac (Instagram)

BERNIE MAC – BORN IN CHICAGO, ILLINOIS.

Bernie Mac was one of the most beloved comedians of his generation. Born on the South Side of Chicago, his journey to inevitable stardom took longer than most. Prior to becoming a comedian, he worked odd jobs: moving furniture and being an agent for UPS. Influenced by The Three Stooges, Redd Foxx and Richard Pryor, Mac began his own career at Chicago's Cotton Club. Following a win of the Miller Lite Comedy Competition and a bold, gutsy performance on HBO's *Def Comedy Jam* where he told a hostile audience, "I ain't scared of you muthaf**kas," Mac became da man with fans and colleagues alike.

From there the phone rang. He opened for Redd Foxx, Dionne Warwick and Natalie Cole. He was featured in small roles in sometimes equally small films (as well as classics such as *Friday*), but stole every scene he was in until it was undeniable his talent deserved greater recognition. HBO gave him the show *Midnight Mac*. He was featured in the star-studded *Ocean's Eleven* and starred in *Mr. 3000*. After the Original Kings of Comedy Tour (he shared the stage with Steve Harvey, Cedric the Entertainer and D. L. Hughley) where he proclaimed that TV was too scared to have a Bernie Mac show he got *The Bernie Mac Show* on FOX.

It seemed nothing could slow down Mac's ascent. Enter sarcoidosis. The debilitating disease which attacked his lungs and other vital organs left him in remission in 2005. It was just enough time for him to finish *Soul Men* (with Samuel L. Jackson), *Madagascar: Escape 2 Africa* and *Old Dogs* (with John Travolta and Robin Williams). All were released after his death in 2008.

Mac was #72 on Comedy Central's list of the 100 greatest standups of all time. One year before passing he spoke of retirement from stand up to concentrate on producing and films. Bernie Mac felt he'd missed too much in life and wanted to spend more time with family and friends. We know how he felt. We're missing much in our lives with the absence of Bernie Mac, who passed away by complications of pneumonia on August 9, 2008.

https://youtu.be/7JkPx0gk6LE

✳✳✳

OCTOBER 5, 1965

Ricky Harris (Humor Mill Magazine)

RICKY HARRIS – BORN IN LONG BEACH, CALIFORNIA!

Once upon a time comics would be introduced and walk up to the stage in complete silence or the tickling of a piano keyboard. That is until Ricky Harris came along. The Robin Harris protégé and Comedy Act Theater light man went up to the DJ booth one night and as soon as Robin Harris was introduced, Ricky Harris spun a record until the host made it all the way up on stage and gave a signal for the record to stop. That was the first time that had been done in comedy. The year was 1988 and Ricky Harris changed comedy intros forever.

Harris was also a beast on stage; a product of the LBC. His comedy can best be described as gangsta. It was raw, in-your-face, take-no-prisoners comedy. D. L. Hughley declared Ricky Harris to be his favorite comedian and Harris had only been at it for a few years. A few years was all it took. He was one of the first comedians known as "King of the Underground Comedians." When he graduated from the Comedy Act Theater (as the club virtually folded when founder, Michael Williams became ill) Harris found his place co-hosting HBO's *Def Comedy Jam* (along with Adele Givens and Joe Torry).

A little notoriety never hurt nobody. Harris guest-starred (*Moesha, CSI, Millennium, ER, Everybody Hates Chris*), did films (*Poetic Justice, Heat* {in a riveting scene with Al Pacino}, *Hard Rain, This Christmas, Bones, Woman Thou Art Loosed,)* short films (in the role of TaaDow in cousin Snoop Dogg's, *Murder Was the Case*), album voices (DJ EZ Dicc, Saul-T-Nutz), video game voices (*Grand Theft Auto: San Andreas*) and he produced some videos of his own.

Life was seemingly good when a health scare sidelined Harris. He was hospitalized and an outpouring of support came from the shocked comedy community. Soon Harris was back on his feet and working. For a while he'd been putting in hours as a longshoreman, but now he was doing some road gigs, some TV and film and Ricky Harris was back in the conversation. The executives and suits were bandying about his name and he was making a comeback when all of a sudden the chatter stopped.

On December 26, 2016, Ricky Harris died of a heart attack. Some say his legacy was tainted by violence at his funeral. Others would say that's the way Harris would've wanted to exit – as a pioneer; the first Black comedy funeral to make TMZ.

https://youtu.be/ELk2sN8yjJo

✳✳✳

OCTOBER 6, 2000

BAMBOOZLED – RELEASED BY NEW LINE CINEMA!

Written and directed by Spike Lee, this film is a satirical look at the world of degrading television programming. Damon Wayans plays a TV executive only his white boss doesn't like his pro-Black shows. The man, who spews Black lingo liberally because he's married to a Black woman and has half-Black kids, wants a true depiction of Black people. None of that Huxtable nonsense. So Wayans gives him a show in blackface. He's sure the idea will be rejected as ridiculous, and he'll be fired giving him the freedom to create meaningful programming elsewhere. Well, you guessed it – The Man loves the concept of tap dancing Negros and greenlights the entry immediately. Wayans is stuck.

A cast is now needed to make this travesty come alive. Tommy Davidson and Savion Glover play the two new stars of the show to be entitled, "Mantan: The New Millennium Minstrel Show." Glover (dubbed "Mantan") doesn't mind the blackface as long as he gets to tap. Davidson (dubbed "Sleep N Eat") finds it offensive and once the show airs and the entire audience is in blackface he finds it even more so. Davidson quits, but not before gaining the wrath of a militant group who can't stand cooning. So they kidnap Glover and with cameras trained on the tap dancer, assassinate him for all to see and remember. Wayans loses his mind and is shot for his crimes against humanity by his assistant played by Jada Pinkett-Smith. As he lay dying he has to watch a video left by Pinkett-Smith of degrading Black images throughout America's media history and how he has been one more brick in that building of disgust.

Bamboozled was released in a limited number of theaters and was critically panned. Budgeted at $10 million it earned $2,463,650 at the box office.

https://youtu.be/C45g3YP7JOk

✳✳✳

OCTOBER 7, 1977

A PIECE OF THE ACTION – RELEASED BY WARNER BROS!

Directed by co-star Sidney Poitier, this crime comedy is his third pairing with Bill Cosby in the trilogy that started with *Uptown Saturday Night* followed by *Let's Do It Again*. This entry is more serious in tone and less in humor.

This time the duo are thieves. Everything is rolling along fine in the world of high class robbery until a retired cop (James Earl Jones) lets them know he's got the goods on them and it's time to talk. His conversation consists of keeping his mouth shut and not sending them up the river in exchange for doing him a favor. He wants them to volunteer their time at a community youth center and help the local kids get their acts together. Naturally they don't want to do it. Naturally the kids give them a hard time and naturally they all end up liking each other in the end. The difference in this case is the kids have to help the two crooks get out of a jam from an old heist that also caught up with them.

With a soundtrack by Curtis Mayfield, *A Piece of the Action* also featured Denise Nicholas, Tracy Reed, Sheryl Lee Ralph and Ja'net Dubois.

https://youtu.be/xZmKxOvP5Bo

✳✳✳

OCTOBER 8, 1980

Nick Cannon w/ Luenell (The Campbell Collection)

NICHOLAS SCOTT "NICK" CANNON – BORN IN SAN DIEGO, CA!

Cannon got his start in comedy on his father's cable access channel in Charlotte, North Carolina. He was 11 years old and itching for more. All during high school his mother would take young Nick to various night clubs in San Diego (where she lived and Nick divided his time between his divorced parents) and he'd manage to get stage time. Even though he was underage he'd run in when his name was announced, do his set and run out the exit door, getting nowhere near the bar. This worked out fine until he graduated high school and then it was off to Hollywood.

Nick Cannon's first break came doing warm-up and making guest appearances for the show, *All That* on Nickelodeon. The teenager was the perfect fit for the youth targeted network. He soon moved from in front of the camera to behind it as well. He hosted *The Nick Cannon Show* and in 2005 produced and hosted *Wild 'N Out*, the MTV improv comedy show that made household names out of Kevin Hart, Katt Williams, Affion Crockett and Corey Holcomb. He then kept it going by jockeying to NBC to host their hit, *America's Got Talent* and created his own sketch comedy series, *Incredible Crew* featuring teenagers.

Cannon proved he was multi-faceted. He entered the world of music with his rap group, "Da G4 Dope Bomb Squad" and along with friend, Steve Groves, went on the road as an opening act. In 2001 he signed with Jive records and released an album and worked on the *Jimmy Neutron Boy Genius* film soundtrack. He established himself with the hit single, "Gigolo" with R. Kelly before forming his own label, "Can-I-Ball" Records in 2005. In 2009 he cancelled that label and replaced it with "N'Credible Entertainment"; where he collaborated with other rap artists and released a series of song parodies and a mixtape. He also did radio with a syndicated countdown show for CBS Radio.

Besides all his other endeavors and touring as a stand-up comedian, acting was also part of Cannon's empire building. Cannon has starred in a number of films including, *Drumline, Love Don't Cost a Thing, Roll Bounce* and *Goal II: Living the Dream.* He has managed Soulja Boy and Amber Rose, just to name a few and has been a multiple award nominee, winning the Nickelodeon's Kid Choice Award in 2001 for Favorite Television Actor (*The Nick Cannon Show*), The Hollywood Film Festival Award in 2006 for Ensemble of the Year (*Bobby*) and the 2012 NAACP Image Award for Outstanding Supporting Actor (*Up All Night*).

https://youtu.be/7YTBjM4jnSk

* * *

OCTOBER 9, 1972

Cocoa Brown (Humor Mill Magazine)

COCOA BROWN – BORN IN NEWPORT NEWS, VIRGINIA!

After graduating from Virginia Commonwealth University, Brown got her comedy education in clubs from the Mid-West to both coasts. She was mentored by comedy guru Fat Doctor and got her initial television exposure on *BET's Comic View, Showtime at the Apollo* and *One Mic Stand.*

Brown went on to make a fruitful living as the world's greatest extra in projects where she was identified as Woman #4, Lady Behind the Counter and Sexy Reporter. Brown has since moved up to parts where her name is near the title. She worked with Samuel L. Jackson in *Lakeview Terrace*, Nia Long in *The Single Moms Club* and Mark Wahlberg in *Ted 2*. Brown has a stand-out part as Jennifer in Tyler Perry's *For Better or Worse*. She's done soap operas (*The Young and the Restless*), sitcoms (*The Soul Man, 2 Broke Girls*) and dramas (*ER, Breaking Bad*) as well as feature length movies and a lot of touring as a national headliner.

https://youtu.be/B21IoZ1QT48
✳✳✳

OCTOBER 9, 1998

HOLY MAN – RELEASED BY BUENA VISTA PICTURES!

Starring Eddie Murphy as a smiling, happy, white robe-wearing fellow enlisted by two TV executives to help sales, Holy Man skewers the home shopping field. Jeff Goldblum is the exec out of ideas and so Kelly Preston is brought in to help him out. They don't like each other at first until they run across Murphy who somehow makes everybody feel good by the sheer will of his positive personality. Once he's seen on their low rated shopping show items start selling out and it's obvious it's because of Murphy. Soon the decision is made to give him his own show, but by the time it's set to debut Murphy's happy guy has grown weary of all the fans and attention. He's now unhappy man and in an effort to set things right Goldblum cancels the show and Murphy goes back to anonymity and happiness.

Directed by Stephen Herek, *Holy Man* was a critical failure. The film is loaded with cameos from the likes of James Brown, Betty White, Dan Marino, Soupy Sales and others, but it just didn't connect with audiences. Even Murphy blasted it publicly as being a "horrendous movie."

Holy Man grossed $12,069,719 at the domestic box office on a budget of $60 million dollars.

https://youtu.be/7e3YGlFWtDs
✳✳✳

October 11, 1975

Let's Do It Again – Released by Warner Bros!

This film is the second entry in the Poitier/Cosby trilogy of comedies. The first was *Uptown Saturday Night*. The Third – *A Piece of the Action*. Like the others this one was directed by Sidney Poitier and co-stars himself and Bill Cosby. Jimmie Walker, Calvin Lockhart, Ossie Davis, Denise Nicholas and John Amos appear, along with a cameo by George Foreman. In all the films the names of Poitier and Cosby change as do their professions.

In *Let's Do It Again*, the duo played blue-collar workers who scam to make money for their financially-strapped lodge. Poitier knows how to hypnotize and Cosby has a plan. They'll make the longshot boxer (Walker) think he's a fierce fighter, bet heavily on him winning and clean up. The scheme works like a charm until the gangsters who lost money on the plot figure it out and pay Poitier and Cosby a little visit. They want to get even. Either the two use hypnotism again to rig the upcoming title bout or the two will be out for the count. It's an offer they can't refuse, only they can't get back into Walker's training facility – security is beefed up for the new champ. So, they hypnotize the other boxer and the end result is a match that's a draw. Of course, the two buddies bet on this and the gangsters are once again on their trail.

Let's Do It Again is considered the best of the trilogy in all aspects. The music is good; with a memorable soundtrack by the Staple Singers. The critics loved it and the audiences were happy. The film grossed $11.8 million dollars on a $70,000.00 budget.

https://youtu.be/mxPCa3uFu5U

✳ ✳ ✳

OCTOBER 12, 1932

Dick Gregory – (Comedy Hall of Fame Archives)

RICHARD CLAXTON "DICK" GREGORY – BORN IN ST. LOUIS, MI!

A poor student in school, Gregory majored in running. He was a record-setting track star in the mile and half-mile events. He was so good he earned a track scholarship to Southern Illinois University Carbondale. Then his career using his feet got interrupted by the government. Uncle Sam drafted Dick Gregory into the Army in 1954. It was there that he got into comedy; winning several talent shows and getting a taste of what a career in joke-telling felt like.

Once discharged, Gregory headed back to school to finish his education, but found he lacked the same drive as before. He now noticed his instructors wanted him there to run track and couldn't care less if he ever learned a thing. So he dropped out and got into comedy full time. At least with jokes he knew where he stood. Or so he thought.

Gregory played the Black circuit in the Chicago area and opened his own comedy club in 1958. It failed and Gregory was forced to work a day job at the Post office. In the meanwhile, he became the host at the Roberts Show Club at night. Fate stepped in when white comedian, Professor Irwin Corey fell ill and Gregory was hired to substitute for him at the Playboy Club. Hugh Hefner loved what he saw and extended Gregory's run. Word caught on about this brilliant political Black comedian and the next thing you knew Gregory was invited to appear on *The Tonight Show starring Jack Paar.*

Dick Gregory refused to go on Paar's program. His good friend, big band singer, Billy Eckstine had told him not to do it because Black comics never got to sit on the couch and talk to the host; even though it was a talk show. Paar finally had to call Gregory personally and assure him he could sit on the couch and they'd have a rousing conversation, which they did. The switchboard at NBC lit up that night. It was the first time many Americans had seen a Black man and a white man in a human dialogue. Gregory became an overnight star. His salary went from $250 per week to $5,000 per night.

In the early 1960s Dick Gregory was the hottest comedian in the country – black or white. Then Martin Luther King, Jr. called and all that changed. It started with an invitation to speak at one of the marches. That turned into a devotion to the Civil Rights Movement and Gregory putting his comedy career on the back burner. It was unconscionable to him to have fans go through the hassle of going out to his show only to be told he was in jail for civil disobedience. The void he left was filled in by his protégés, Bill Cosby and Richard Pryor.

Once the Civil Rights Movement wore down Gregory dabbled in health aids. He created Dick Gregory's Bahamian Diet. He still did public speaking engagements and wrote books; his most famous being his autobiography, *Nigger.* In 1968 he ran as a write-in candidate for president of the United States. He lost, but his activism extended to women's rights, a rebuking of the Warren Commission's findings in the Kennedy Assassination, a co-authored book with conspiracy theorist, Mark Lane on the King Assassination and theories about the facts of 9/11 and other events.

Dick Gregory is #82 on Comedy Central's list of the 100 Greatest Stand-Ups of All-Time. He recorded over a dozen albums and appeared in a half-dozen films. Gregory has a star on the St. Louis Walk of Fame and is regarded in comedy circles as the first recognized Black stand-up to get big in the mainstream.

On August 19, 2017 Dick Gregory died of heart failure at Sibley Memorial Hospital in Washington DC at the age of 84.

https://youtu.be/ej5FwzhUDcM

✳ ✳ ✳

OCTOBER 13, 1965

Reginald Ballard (The Reginald Ballard Collection)

REGINALD BALLARD – BORN IN GALVESTON, TEXAS!

Known best as "Bruh-Man from the 5th Flo" on the FOX sitcom, *Martin*, Ballard got started in comedy in reverse. He'd already gotten a lot of attention from women. He'd been an all-district linebacker and received a full football scholarship to Southern Methodist University. He'd already acted; having taken theater in college and appeared in several prestigious productions. He already knew he was funny since he was on a top rated TV show and was a breakout character. As Bruh-Man, Ballard would get laughs every time he'd enter Martin Lawrence's apartment through the window for whatever reason struck his fancy, hold up four fingers and announce he was from "the fif flo."

Ballard had made films (*Lock Up, Menace II Society*) and done television (*The Bernie Mac Show, The Parkers, Sister, Sister, Crumbs*). The one thing Ballard didn't know was could he do stand-up comedy. Reynaldo Rey answered that question for him. Rey suggested to Ballard that since he had all that notoriety from being on a comedy why not parlay that into a stand-up career. He mentored Ballard; gave him pointers and directed him to places he could perform to get his feet wet. This assistance opened up a whole new career for the journeyman actor, who now tours the globe as an established stand-up comedian.

https://youtu.be/f-Qzs2Q2Z5s

✳ ✳ ✳

OCTOBER 13, 1937

Jimmy Lynch aka "The Funky Tramp," *Nigger Please!* album (Laff Records)

JIMMY LYNCH – BORN IN ACMAR, ALABAMA!

The multi-talented Lynch never slowed down which probably accounts for his alias as "Mr. Motion." In a career that started in high school performing in vocal groups, Lynch got his big break when he was doing his usual dancing in a local club and the owner needed somebody to tell some jokes. Jimmy was too young to even be in the club, much less draw attention to himself by standing on a stage with a spotlight on him. So, since it just happened to be Halloween, he dressed himself up like a bum and adopted the persona, "Funky Tramp."

The "Funky Tramp" character made Jimmy Lynch a party record star. Throughout the 60s and 70s he would sell over a million copies of his albums starting with *Tramp Time*, known for first use of the word "fuck" on a record. Lynch continued to be a filthy mouthed pioneer and is credited as being the first to also say "muthafucka" on vinyl and to lead the Black comedy record boom in the 1970s.

In a business as flakey as show business, Lynch knew how to keep the checks coming in by moonlighting as tour manager for musicians such as Bobby "Blue" Bland, ZZ Hill, Tyrone Davis, Millie Jackson, Patti LaBelle and Johnny Taylor. He also worked his thespian chops in cinematic classics with friend, Rudy Ray Moore in Dolemite flicks: *Dolemite* (1975),

The Human Tornado (1976), *Petey Wheatstraw: The Devil's Son-In-Law* (1977), *Disco Godfather* (1979) and *Dolemite Explosion* (2007). And when he wasn't in front of the camera he worked on the production staff.

Thanks to Lynch and other party record notables, Black culture moved into the arena of artists unapologetically targeting only the Black culture from comedians who put in the work on urban shows like HBO's *Def Comedy Jam* and BETs *Comic View* to rap and hip-hop talents who liberally sampled bits and pieces from recordings by Lynch and his mob.

https://youtu.be/KHwwpPM51n4
* * *

OCTOBER 14, 1952

Rick Aviles (l) and Patrick Swayze

RICK AVILES – BORN IN MANHATTAN!

The Greenwich Village night club scene was Puerto Rican, Avile's stomping ground as he worked to improve his stand-up comedy. He came up in the generation of the 1970s. and benefited from the boom of the early 1980s. His first film role was in the *Cannonball Run* in 1981. His televised claim to fame is when he hosted *Showtime at the Apollo*. Avile's other television credits include *The Carol Burnett Show* in 1991.

Rick Aviles gained notoriety in 1991 in the Patrick Swayze hit film, *Ghost*. He also appeared in *The Secret of My Success, Street Smart, Mystery Train, The Godfather Part III, Green Card, Carlito's Way* and *Waterworld*. He was the voice for a cockroach in *Joe's Apartment*.

Things were rolling along at a steady clip, but Aviles had a drug problem. Like most drug problems they eventually become a major problem. Due to his use of heroin, Aviles contracted HIV and on March 17, 1995 he died from AIDS complications.

https://youtu.be/OdaOBlYg6NQ
* * *

OCTOBER 15, 2008

CHOCOLATE NEWS – PREMIERED ON COMEDY CENTRAL!

D irected by Rusty Cundieff (*Chappelle Show*) and starring David Alan Grier, *Chocolate News* was a satirical news program aimed at the black demographic. Originally the station didn't want the show due to the negative stereotype associated with pairing the term chocolate along with black people. But once non-black actors, Martin Sheen and William Shatner intervened the show was given the okay to start production.

Chocolate News had a prime spot. It was the lead-in for the popular *Daily Show with Jon Stewart* and *The Colbert Report*. It featured Tangie Ambrose, Alphonso McAuley, Chris Tallman and Jordan Peele in sketches that were always from a black perspective and always consistently edgy and sometimes downright raw. Apparently too raw for mainstream.

Comedy Central aired the last of *Chocolate News* on December 17th of that same year after 10 episodes and the cable station made it clear on March 10, 2009 that it would not be renewing the program for a second season.

https://youtu.be/weaMWkpmnaM

OCTOBER 16, 1961

Kim Wayans (Instagram)

KIM N. WAYANS – BORN IN NEW YORK CITY, NY!

W ayans first appeared in film in 1987 (*Cathy*) and television in 1988 (*A Different World*), but it wasn't until her work on the groundbreaking FOX sketch comedy show, *In Living Color* that she got public notice. Working with a cast that included not only her siblings Keenan Ivory, Damon and Shawn, there was also Kelly Coffer, Kim Cole, Jim Carrey, Tommy Davidson, Jamie Foxx and David Alan Grier. Kim brought to life a variety of characters (Bernita Butrell, Cousin Elsee, Mrs. Brooks) and impersonations (Whitney Houston, LaToya Jackson, Tina Turner, Esther Rolle).

Once her tenure with *In Living Color* ended, Kim Wayans continued to work in television *(In the House, Criminal Minds* and as a story editor for *My Wife and Kids)*. As well as literature (she co-wrote a children's book, *Amy Hodgepodge* with her husband, Kevin Knotts). And film (among them *A Low Down Dirty Shame, Juwanna Mann* and *Pariah,* where she was nominated for Best Supporting Actress by the Black Reel Awards).

https://youtu.be/KyDMBciAihM

✳✳✳

OCTOBER 17, 1981

Cameron Esposito (r) w/ Rhea Butcher (Public Domain)

CAMERON ESPOSITO – BORN IN WESTERN SPRINGS, IL!

In high school Esposito was a breast stroker. She always swam with the current. The Mid-Westerner was a member of the Marians Society, a devout Roman Catholic organization devoted to helping their fellow man. She studied theology at Boston College and yearned to be a social worker in need-of-social-workers, Chicago. She even took social worker courses at the University of Chicago and found out quickly that Cameron Esposito did not want to be no doggone social worker.

She performed with an improv group while in Boston so she decided to give stand-up a shot. Chicago had a bustling comedy scene, a huge plus for a beginner to hold their interest and form a camaraderie with other newbies. The Lincoln Lodge was her home club for four years and she made a name for herself on the vibrant festival circuit. Next stop – TV.

Esposito kicked off her televised stand-up career with Jay Leno calling her the future of comedy when they both appeared on *The Late, Late Show with Craig Ferguson*. From there it was more exposure on *The Last Call with Carson Daly, Conan*, and a regular gig on *Chelsea Lately* with Chelsea Handler. She did some guest-starring roles, some films and toured a lot, but the main attraction to Cameron Esposito was the Cameron Esposito machine.

In a short amount of time she created a long list of branded content. She partnered with BuzzFeed Motion Pictures for a bunch of videos called "Ask a Lesbian" where she answers questions about lesbian things. She co-hosts the comedy podcast, "Put Your Hands Together" along with Rhea Butcher in front of a live audience. Their television show, *Take My Wife* went from streaming on Seeso to being broadcast on Starz. Plus, Esposito's own podcast, "Queery" is a hit with stars from Margaret Cho to Evan Rachel Wood talking the talk.

With all this fast success a lot of performers might turn over on their backs and float. Cameron Esposito, however, will most likely just keep on stroking.

https://youtu.be/xLqAx_2183I

***

OCTOBER 19, 1920

LaWanda Page and Redd Foxx at the Stars Hall of Fame in Orlando, FL, 1977 (Public Domain)

LAWANDA PAGE (ALBERTA PEALE) – BORN IN CLEVELAND, OH!

The woman who would earn the title "The Queen of Comedy" and "Queen of Black Comedy," (depending on who was doing the talking) was raised in St. Louis, Missouri. She began her career in show business dancing at the age of 15, then working small nightclubs under the title of "The Bronze Goddess of Fire"; an act where she would light cigarettes with her fingertips and eat fire. From that platform she integrated into stand-up comedy running through theaters and clubs on the so-called Midwestern "chitlin circuit."

One of her many friends on the circuit was a former schoolmate and dear friend, Redd Foxx. It was Foxx who encouraged her to go into stand-up comedy. Once she honed her skills from years of club work she moved to Los Angeles in the 1960s and joined Skillet, Leroy & Co. She had signature lines like, ""Honey, that old man couldn't keep no kinda job. That's the only man I know that ever went to the unemployment office and lost his place in line."

Page was making a name for herself on the circuit, but the circuit she was on was limited. She was doing clubs and recordings for Laff Records, but no matter how massive her reign at that level she'd always be a goldfish in a toilet bowl. So, the plan was not to keep waiting to get flushed down the tubes. Page was getting out of show business and had moved back to St. Louis to take care of her ailing mother. All that changed when she got a call from her former schoolyard buddy, Redd Foxx.

Redd was now Fred Sanford. He was going to be on NBC with his own sitcom and he wanted to work with his friends from stand-up and that meant her. She'd play the Bible thumping Aunt Esther, the sister of his deceased wife. It was truly a blessing; that is until she had to deal with the suits over at NBC.

During casting Redd had told one of the show's producers about Page. This producer was not only familiar with her reputation for being funny, but had himself caught her stage act so he needed no convincing. With that Redd called LaWanda in St. Louis and got her on the first thing smoking back to L. A. She was going to be a TV star. All she had to do was read for the part. She did and got it. Then things got foul. They loved her persona, but after a rehearsal they decided they wanted to go with a trained actress and told Redd to fire LaWanda. She was hilarious and all that, but didn't know the fundamentals of how a television sitcom was run. Foxx didn't care how it was run. If you wanted him you'd have to take her. Foxx worked with her, she learned quickly and in virtually no time Aunt Esther was one of the most popular TV characters of all time.

Everybody knew an Aunt Esther. She was pious; knew how to turn the other cheek, while simultaneously slapping yours. So maybe she'd take a zinger from Foxx and other cast members, like the time Sanford's friend Grady said, "Nice having her around, she makes the junk look so pretty." But Aunt Esther would hit back with lines like "Watch it, sucker!" her favorite catch phrase or "You old fish-eyed fool." Foxx was the star of the show, but Page was that extra reason to watch.

After brief stints on spin-offs *Sanford* and *Sanford Arms*, Lawanda Page guest starred on practically every Black sitcom on television, did cameos in hood flicks (most notably *Friday*), roasted with the best of them on the Dean Martin Roasts and remained active in comedy up until her death September 14, 2002 from complications of diabetes.

https://youtu.be/VpBjqQ1XEEE

✻✻✻

OCTOBER 21, 1982

Hari Kondabolu (r) w/ W. Kamau Bell (Instagram)

HARI KONDABOLU – BORN IN QUEENS, NEW YORK!

When his parents came from India to America, Kondabolu's father was approached by a man in Louisiana, who asked if he was Chinese. That's about the time his father decided to move them to New York. Since both his parents had been respected physicians in India they were able to get prominent positions in the medical field in The Big Apple. However, Kondabolu had no intention of following in their footsteps. He started doing comedy even before he got to college and his studies at Wesleyan University on race, culture, globalization prepared him to do material on race, culture and globalization.

Hari Kondabolu was making a name for himself as a stand-up comedian that was saying something worth listening to, but blew off those opportunities to complete his education and get his MSc. After a year he was back like he never left. He got into the alternative comedy scene and did comedy festivals (Bumbershoot Music and Arts Festival, HBO US Comedy Arts

Festival, Edinburgh Fringe Festival). TV-wise he appeared on *Jimmy Kimmel Live!*, *Conan*, *The Late Show with David Letterman*, *Live at Gotham*, *John Oliver's New York Stand-Up Show*. That was US TV. On British television he appeared on *8 Out of 10 Cats* and *Russell Howard's Good News*. He wrote for *Totally Bias With W. Kamau Bell*, had a "Comedy Central Presents" special and appeared in the film *All About Steve* (which he derides).

Kondabolu also liked to do his own thing. He's released four comedy albums. He and his brother, Ashok do a podcast titled *Untitled Kondabolu Brothers Project*. Kondabolu starred in *Manoj*, which he also wrote. It's the story of a sellout immigrant comedian and an American immigrant who despises it. Kondabolu played both parts. He also created and starred in the documentary, *The Problem with Apu*, which takes the character from *The Simpsons* cartoon and shows the stereotypical racism he experienced. This is something non-Chinese, Hari Kondabolu studied and lived.

https://youtu.be/pv7AELM1e-E

∗ ∗ ∗

OCTOBER 22, 1967

Carlos Mencia in Anchorage, Alaska, 2010 (Public Domain)

CARLOS MENCIA – BORN IN SAN PEDRO SULA, HONDURAS!

Mencia got into comedy via an open mic night at the Laugh Factory in Hollywood. From there he became a regular at the Comedy Store and got seen by the right people. He appeared on *The Arsenio Hall Show* and got the hosting job for *Loco Slam* for HBO in 1994. In 1998 he was on Galavision hosting *Funny is Funny* along with touring as part of "The Three Amigos" (with Pablo Francisco and Freddy Soto).

Carlos Mencia was drawn to hot topics. He'd slam race, politics, social issues and crime and the system meant to suppress it. Comedy Central liked that style and in 2005 he got his own sketch show, *Mind of Mencia*. It lasted three seasons and was the second highest rated show on the network on its second season.

Besides stand-up Mencia's worked as an actor. He's guest-starred on *Moesha*, *The Shield* and *The Proud Family*. His stand-up, on the other hand, has been the subject of controversy. Accused of stealing jokes, Mencia has been confronted in print and in person by Joe Rogan. George Lopez also said Mencia took material from him without permission as well as similarities to the bits of other comedians including Bill Cosby. This left a taint on Mencia's stand-up career and a strained relationship with his fellow comedians.

Regardless, Mencia won a Cable ACE Award for his second HBO Best Stand-Up Comedy special.

https://youtu.be/LeqbZYBlKA8

***

OCTOBER 22, 1976

CAR WASH – RELEASED BY UNIVERSAL PICTURES!

It's the day in the life of a Los Angeles carwash and its multi-ethnic staff. The star is Bill Duke as Abdullah, a revolutionary under suspicion for everything and Franklyn Ajaye as a man out to win a radio call-in contest and take his girl to a concert. Richard Pryor makes a cameo as a greedy media preacher. Professor Irwin Corey plays a bomber suspect and Antonio Fargas plays a proud cross-dresser. The owner's son smokes weed in the restroom and George Carlin drives a cab, searching for the whore that stiffed him.

Michael Schultz directed a Joel Schumacher script and a cast that included DeWayne Jessie, Jack Kehoe, The Pointer Sisters, Ivan Dixon, Melanie Mayron, Pepe Serna, Darrow Igus, Arthur French, Clarence Muse, Garrett Morris, Tracy Reed, Sully Boyar, Renn Woods, Brooke Adams,

Tim Thomerson, Jason Bernard, Leonard Jackson, Lorraine Gary, Richard Brestoff and Danny DeVito. With hit songs by Rose Royce and a soundtrack by Norman Whitfield, in 1977 *Car Wash* won the Technical Grand Prize and Best Music Award at the Cannes Film Festival as well as a Grammy for Best Album of Original Score.

https://youtu.be/xTwrrDANnoU

✳ ✳ ✳

OCTOBER 23, 1970

Donnell Rawlings (l) w/Dave Chappelle at Joint Base Charleston, SC, February 2, 2017
(Public Domain)

DONNELL M. RAWLINGS – BORN IN WASHINGTON, DC.

Rawlings was raised in Alexandria, Virginia and stationed in South Korea when he was in the Air Force. He learned a lot of Korean insults and used them in his comedy. Best known as a cast member on Comedy Central's *Chappelle Show*, they came in handy many times. On that sketch program Rawlings played a number of memorable characters. His most notable was Ashy Larry; a brother who looked like he'd bathed in chalk. Rawlings originated the catchphrase, "I'm rich, bitch" and was known for hitting the East Coast overused exclamation of "Son" at the end of sentences.

Dave Chappelle's show was a dream project for a comedian, but it went nightmarish when Chappelle left abruptly leaving Rawlings and Charlie Murphy to co-host the Chappelle-less Season 3, or as comedy Central billed it – *Chappelle Show: The Lost Episodes*.

As an actor, Rawlings has made numerous guest appearances. He was seen on HBO's *The Wire* as an ex-con, *Spider-Man 2* as a bystander and *The Ricki Lake Show* as a judge. Rawlings has been in music videos as well as *Guy Code, Reality Bites Back, Howard Stern* and *D L Hughley Breaks the News*. And when it came to work on radio, Rawlings did that too. The problem with the latter medium was how touchy it can be. Rawlings was fired for telling a joke about a powerful race in the entertainment industry with strong ties to Israel.

Donnell Rawlings continues to do stand-up and act.

https://youtu.be/Fdzq-GXZbk0

***

OCTOBER 25, 1971

Craig Robinson (r) w/ Mike Epps at Def Jam 25 (Humor Mill Magazine)

CRAIG PHILLIP ROBINSON – BORN IN CHICAGO!

Robinson followed in his mother's footsteps.She was a music teacher and he taught music at Horace Mann Elementary after graduating from Saint Xavier University. He got into comedy as a stand-up and improv artist through The Second City in Chicago. After doing his share of clubs with his cabaret style of performance (complete with keyboard and off-the-cuff song renderings), Robinson caught a break, got noticed and got the role as the recurring character, Darryl, on the NBC hit, *The Office*.

On television Robinson's been seen on *Arrested Development, Halfway Home, The Bernie Mac Show, Reno 911!, Friends, Eastbound & Down, LAX, Curb Your Enthusiasm*and. *Mr. Robot*. He's provided voices for *Sausage Party, Shrek Forever After, Percy Jackson: Sea of Monsters, Escape from Planet Earth, The Cleveland Show, American Dad* and *Henchmen*.

Craig Robinson's film appearances include *Pineapple Express, This is the End, Zack and Miri Make a Porno, Hot Tub Time Machine, Knocked Up, Walk Hard: The Dewey Cox Story, Peeples, Fanboys, Night at the Museum,*

Get On Up and *Morris From America*, where Robinson won the Sundance Film Festival Dramatic Special Jury Award for Individual Performance.

https://youtu.be/ojLlkhMO4Dc

✳ ✳ ✳

OCTOBER 27, 1995

VAMPIRE IN BROOKLYN – RELEASED BY PARAMOUNT!

This Eddie Murphy vehicle is about a vampire in search of his mate in of all places, Brooklyn, New York. The film co-stars Angela Bassett as the mate and Kadeem Hardison as Murphy's unwitting ghoul. John Witherspoon, Allen Payne, Zakes Mokae and Joanna Cassidy lend support. In a script from Murphy, his brother Charlie and Uncle Vernon, *Vampire in Brooklyn* was directed by horror master, Wes Craven.

Murphy has a dilemma on his hands. He has to seduce Bassett and convince her she is his true love or lose her forever. She's has no idea she's descended from vampire stock (on her daddy's side) and is living a human life blissfully as a cop. Her partner is too shy to express his feelings so Bassett is vulnerable to Murphy's advances until she finds out he's a bloodsucker and then the deal is off. Unfortunately, vampires never take the hint to leave and drastic measures always have to be employed. Murphy's case was no different. As in all vampire movies somebody's got to die.

Vampire in Brooklyn grossed $19.8 Million on a budget of $14 million.

https://youtu.be/jGdNE7yKDhE

✳ ✳ ✳

October 28, 1963

Sheryl Underwood during USO Tour in Afghanistan, December 23, 2009 (Public Domain)

SHERYL UNDERWOOD – BORN IN LITTLE ROCK, ARKANSAS!

Underwood got her initial comedic recognition as the first female finalist in the Miller Lite Comedy Search. The year was 1989 and Underwood was on a mission to succeed. She later drove from Los Angeles to New York to throw her hat in the ring as an alternate for HBO's *Def Comedy Jam,* but was out-of-luck. Everybody showed up to perform in their coveted spot, but the initiative, drive and determination was not lost on entertainment executives. Underwood performed on *Def Jam* the following season. She also impressed on BET's *Comic View* and won "Funniest Female Comedian on Comic View" award in 1994.

Sheryl Underwood was a known quantity with her peers before mainstream success. A self-admitted "sexually progressive, God-fearing, Black Republican," she hosted a male stripper/comedy show for BET's Pay-Per-View division. She toured extensively domestically and abroad, often to entertain the US military personnel (she had served in the armed forces herself). She was the co-host of BET's *Oh, Drama* and host of BET's *Comic View,* as well as *Martin Lawrence's 1st Amendment* for Starz.

Underwood has been more than a creature of television. She was featured in the Warren Beatty film, *Bulworth*; the 1998 film, *I Got the Hook Up* in the role of Bad Mouth Bessie and in 2005's *Beauty Shop.* She was a contributor on the *Tom Joyner Morning Show* and then abruptly left to join the crew of the *Steve Harvey Morning Show.* She was executive producer of the variety show, *Holla* and had her own radio show on Sirius XM called *Sheryl Underwood and Company.*

In 2011 Underwood became a talk show host. Leah Remini stepped down from her post on *The Talk* and Underwood stepped up. Along with Julie Chen, Aisha Tyler, Sharon Osbourne and Sara Gilbert, Underwood discusses controversial topics daily. Sometimes additional controversy follows these discussions like the time Underwood criticized "Black hair" and praised so-called "white hair." She also took heat for publicly blasting former Queens of Comedy, Laura Hayes, Sommore and Adele Givens. She's been under the microscope for other comments as well.

Sheryl Underwood has guest starred on *The Young and Restless* as a judge and has made numerous guest appearances as herself.

https://youtu.be/WSLmAeUr03U

✳ ✳ ✳

OCTOBER 30, 1961

Larry Wilmore (Instagram)

LARRY WILMORE – BORN IN LA COUNTY, CALIFORNIA!

Larry Wilmore is a creator. As a youth, he created an intellectual world for himself as a self-proclaimed "nerd" focused on science fiction, fantasy, science and magic. He created opportunity for himself by dropping out of his theatre studies at California State Polytechnic University, Pomona to apply what he'd learned as an actor and stand-up comedian. In the 1980s he created ways to get noticed with recurring parts on NBC's *Facts of Life* and ABC's *Sledgehammer*. In the 1990s, Wilmore created a productive lane for himself as a radio writer (*The Tom Joyner Morning Show*) and television writer (*In Living Color, Sister Sister*) and then writer/producer (*The Fresh Prince of Bel-Air, The Jamie Foxx Show, Teen Angel*).

At the turn of the century, Larry Wilmore created yet another feather for his cap – that of show creator with *The PJs* (a co-creation), *The Bernie Mac Show* and *Whoopi* (his alone). He created memorable characters in front of the camera (*The Office, I Love You Man, Dinner For Schmucks*). He even created a gig to highlight his intelligence (as Black correspondent on *The Daily Show with Jon Stewart*) and an intelligent gig (as host of *The Nightly Show with Larry Wilmore*).

In 2015 Wilmore created trouble for himself. It all started when science man Bill Nye made a segment appearance to genuinely explain the significance of the discovery of water on Mars, but instead of Wilmore's audience being enlightened, Nye was mocked by two comics on this ill-advised panel. Ricky Velez and Michelle Buteau were so busy jockeying for laughs that the joke was on the show for dumbing down its usually bright approach. Then on April 30, 2016 Wilmore performed at the White House Correspondents' Association Dinner and ended his set by looking at guest of honor, President Barack Obama (the first Black president of the United States) and saying, "Barry, you did it my nigga" before a predominantly white crowd. Al Sharpton made his displeasure known as did many in the Black and mainstream press. On August 15, 2016 Comedy Central cancelled *The Nightly Show with Larry Wilmore*.

Players play and creators create. Wilmore went on to create *Insecure* for HBO with Issa Rae and produce *Grown-ish* on the FreeForm network. He even created a punchline for this entry when his first acting role after his *Night Show* debacle was on a show called *Difficult People* playing himself.

Larry Wilmore has received scores of award nominations. He's taken home the Peabody Award, the TCA award, Teen Choice, Primetime Emmy, NAACP Image Award, Humanitas Prize and the Satellite Award (all for *The Bernie Mac Show*). Thus, Larry Wilmore created a lasting legacy for himself.

https://youtu.be/gTcZsXkCl0s

✳ ✳ ✳

ONE NIGHT ONLY!

"Got sumpin to tell you"

MOMS MABLEY

WITH

LOUIS JORDAN & HIS ORCHESTRA

LIVE AT THE APOLLO

253 WEST 125TH STREET, HARLEM

FRIDAY, NOVEMBER 23, 1961

SHOWTIME: 8:00 P.M., 10:00 P.M., AND MIDNIGHT. TICKETS: $5.00

NOVEMBER

THIS DAY IN COMEDY...

NOVEMBER 4, 1977

WHICH WAY IS UP? – RELEASED BY UNIVERSAL PICTURES!

This was Richard Pryor's first major starring role and he didn't disappoint his fans. Based on the Italian comedy, *The Seduction of Mimi*, *Which Way Is Up?* tells the story of a Black fruit picker trying to hide his mistress from his wife. Michael Schultz directed the hilarity and the laughs roll from beginning to end.

Pryor delivers a tour-de-force as three characters: the fruit picker, his daddy and the preacher who screws his wife and gets her pregnant. That happened because the fruit picker left his family (with their permission) to go to Los Angeles to pick more fruit. Of course, there are women in Los Angeles and the fruit picker meets one and falls in love with her; probably because she's fine (as played by Lonette McKee). He has to return home but takes his new family with the fine girl with him and stashes them across town. Back to that preacher. He just did what preachers do and screwed a member of his congregation who just happened to be the fruit picker's lonely wife. It all ends with the fruit picker walking up the road all by his damn self.

Which Way Is Up? was not adored by critics, but when did that ever matter when it comes to comedy? Critics who review movies for free like wit. Paying movie goers like to laugh. This flick delivers. It also delivered a cast consisting of Margaret Avery, Morgan Woodward, BeBe Drake, Otis Day, Luis Valdez, Danny Valdez and Paul Mooney.

https://youtu.be/bGyed2mG8CQ

* * *

NOVEMBER 6, 2006

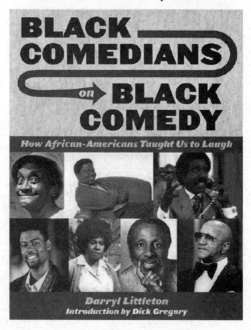

(The Littleton Collection)

BLACK COMEDIANS ON BLACK COMEDY – PUBLISHED BY HALL LEONARD CORPORATION & APPLAUSE BOOKS!

Authored by Darryl Littleton with an introduction by Dick Gregory, this historical testament chronicles the journey of Black comedy in North America. Using a combination of timeline narrative, biographies of prominent figures and interview quotes from contemporary comedians, the story is told from those who not only studied it, but made it. Over 125 pioneering legends such as Eddie Murphy, Timmie Rogers, Robert Townsend, Marla Gibbs, Arsenio Hall, Bernie Mac, Rudy Ray Moore, John Witherspoon and Chris Rock as well as this generations emerging superstars gave their insights and comedic experiences to this one-of-a-kind comedy celebration.

The story is covered from its inception in Africa. Once slaves were introduced to America, the traditions of African humor made its acquaintance as well. Innuendo, Call & Response, pantomime and other standard devices became staples of American Black comedy from the minstrel era, through Reconstruction, the Industrial Revolution, the Harlem Renaissance, the emergence of entertainment mediums; radio, film, television and the Internet, as well as the Civil Rights Movement up to the explosion of Hip Hop on the culture. Throughout it all Black comedy mirrored the society it inhabited and made sense of it for the masses.

Black Comedians on Black Comedy became an instant academic hit. Essentially a text book, it was commissioned by libraries around the globe. It went from hard cover to paperback in record time and was added to the curriculum at USC (University of Southern California). In 2007, less than a year after publication, it was adapted as a full-length documentary by Codeblack Entertainment entitled *Why We Laugh*. Directed by Robert Townsend, narrated by Angela Bassett and executive produced by Littleton and Richard Foos, the film, as did the book, uses the formula of oral history to tell not only the story of Black comedy, but explore its social and political ramifications. Andrew Young, Julian Bond, Kweisi Mfume, Maxine Waters, Elijah Cummings, Diane Watson, Michael Eric Dyson and Cornel West are just some of the politicians and academic pundits featured along with many of the most influential comedians of the modern era.

https://youtu.be/QG9_X_v5VLk

✻ ✻ ✻

NOVEMBER 9, 2009

George Lopez, 2009 (Public Domain)

LOPEZ TONIGHT – PREMIERED ON TBS!

This George Lopez hosted late night talk show appeared to be nestled in for a long run when Lopez announced its abrupt cancellation on air. That in itself was historic as was the fact Lopez was the first Mexican-American to even host a late-night talk show. The critics found Lopez's voice grating and his humor not to their liking, but his target audience didn't read or care about what "the critics" said and rewarded the show with solid ratings for its time slot. So, his demographics seemed assured and his approach was a fresh departure from the norm (yet still using the format of monologue, sketches, interviews and musical performance) with guests not usually seen on other such talk shows.

There had only been a moment of concern when rival late nighter, Conan O'Brien moved over to the cable station when his program on NBC was jeopardized by another rival, Jay Leno (with a combined $44 million payout for O'Brien and his staff). Thus, that situation seemed as though it was resolved amiably with accommodating time slots (O'Brien reluctantly took over Lopez's time slot of 11:00pm at Lopez's urging and *Lopez Tonight* then aired an hour later), but amiable was just a word journalists were using at the time. Behind the scenes, *Lopez Tonight* was in trouble and once Lopez gave his audience the bad news the show had a mere 24 hours before its final episode.

Changing to a later time slot spelled lower ratings. Lopez's audience had things to do the next day so staying up that extra hour for a few laughs *vs* getting fired for nodding off at the job was an easy decision to make and most chose to get some shut eye and keep their checks rolling in. TBS and advertisers noticed the decline and after three quarters, pulled the plug. Even though Conan O'Brien made a public acknowledgement of how much his success was based on the generosity of George Lopez, the die was cast and the party was over on August 10, 2011. *Lopez Tonight* was now just a part of late-night television history. It was an exciting moment that caught lightning in a bottle and just as quickly sparked out with the help of its creator. Within two weeks the time slot was taken over by reruns of the sitcom, *The Office* and the *Lopez Tonight* website was taken down.

https://youtu.be/cAPojR1wyGU

✳ ✳ ✳

NOVEMBER 10, 1968

Tracy Morgan (Public Domain)

TRACY MORGAN – BORN IN THE BRONX!

When Morgan first got started in comedy he wore a cap with a propeller on top of it. It was probably a reminder of when his world was spinning out of control. He dropped out of high school just a few credits shy of graduating to care for his father who was a victim of Vietnam and was dying of AIDS from a syringe. Morgan married his girlfriend and was supporting their child by trying to sell crack. The murder of a friend, who one week before told Morgan he should go into comedy, after watching him hustle money telling jokes on the street scared Morgan straight; straight into comedy and off the streets.

After putting in his time in the fast-paced New York club scene, Tracy Morgan got a gig as a regular on *The Uptown Comedy Club*. The show consisted of sketches and a guest stand-up comedy. His next check came from *Martin* for seven episodes and then from *Saturday Night Live* for seven years, where he played a wide array of characters. Then he got his own sitcom named after him where he basically played Tracy Morgan. He followed that up with another seven year stint; this time on *30 Rock*, where he once again basically played Tracy Morgan.

Things were spinning along nicely: guest-starring roles, films, an autobiography (*I am the New Black*), comedy specials. Then tragedy struck. On June 7, 2014, Morgan and members of his touring crew were fatally plowed into by a Walmart tractor-trailer, killing one member of the group, James McNair and mortally injuring the rest of the passengers, including Morgan. His ribs, legs, femur and nose were all broken and surgery was required. He was in a coma, and once out endured a lengthy rehabilitation process. It was uncovered that the Walmart driver had not gotten enough rest in between shifts and Walmart had further endangered the public by having that driver commute from his home to a distant Walmart facility to start his run versus one closer to his residence. The lawsuit against the conglomerate was settled for an undisclosed amount and Morgan returned fully to the public life on September 20, 2015 when he was overwhelmed by a mass standing ovation when he made an appearance at the Primetime Emmy Awards ceremony.

As any true artist, Morgan used the accident in his comedy. His next comedy special was entitled, *Tracy Morgan: Staying Alive*. He continued to work on the road, in films and television. He got another sitcom, *The Last OG*. So, the life of Tracy Morgan went back to spinning like a top, or at least like a propeller on top of a cap.

https://youtu.be/Q4LN9kbqK0E

✳ ✳ ✳

NOVEMBER 10, 1956

Sinbad performing for US Military on the Island of Crete in Greece, June 14, 2010
(Public Domain)

DAVID ADKINS ("SINBAD") – BORN IN BENTON HARBOR, MI!

Most young men want to be athletes. Adkins had a basketball scholarship at the University of Denver and lettered for two seasons, but he didn't want to be an athlete. He wanted to be a comedian. So, he went into the military (the perfect place to start a comedy career) and went AWOL all the time because he'd sneak off to do comedy shows. When he was finally discharged he went to Hollywood to make it big. Sinbad was almost 30-years old and living the standard life of a struggling comedian. He resided in a seedy part of town in an even seedier hotel. When he went on the road he did so on a Greyhound Bus. It was a route he strung together himself and dubbed it "The Poverty Tour." It turned out to be the number one comedy tour of that summer.

Sinbad made the conscious decision to work clean so his parents could come to his shows and be proud. He boosted their pride level when he became a finalist on CBS's hit talent showcase, *Star Search*. He was cast for the short-lived *Redd Foxx Show* on ABC, but got more lasting exposure when he landed a role in the NBC hit sitcom, *A Different World*. He spent four seasons on the show (1987-1991).

Naturally, the star comedian got the star comedian deal – his own show. *The Sinbad Show* debuted on FOX in 1993 and was gone in 1994. Featuring T.K. Carter, Sinbad admitted he never wanted a TV show in the first place and gave his self-titled sitcom very little of his efforts or talent. He wanted to do movies, but had to fulfill the television obligation of the star comedian package. Then he did films. *House Guest* with Phil Hartman (1994), *First Kid* (1996), the Arnold Schwarzenegger holiday vehicle, *Jingle All the Way* (1996) and *Necessary Roughness* (1991) were all successful.

Sinbad expanded his fan base with music. He hosted HBO's annual music specials. Acts like Earth, Wind & Fire, Kool & the Gang, Smokey Robinson, Chaka Khan and the Stylistics were the norm. There were music festivals and Sinbad shared the stage with other prominent comedians of the day. For a brief time, he hosted the Quincy Jones produced, late night talk show, *Vibe* until its foreseen cancellation. Sinbad has done cartoon voice overs, wrote a book and had his own reality show *Sinbad: it's Just Family,* but mainly he continued to tour as a top-drawing stand-up comedian.

Sinbad was ranked #78 on Comedy Central's 100 Greatest Stand-Ups of All-Time list.

https://youtu.be/5pLzfYVrboM

✳✳✳

NOVEMBER 10, 1963

Tommy Davidson – 2010 (Public Domain)

TOMMY DAVIDSON – BORN IN WASHINGTON DC!

Davidson started the marathon of life with no legs and still crossed the finish line. At 18 months old he was abandoned in the trash. The woman who rescued him was white. She took him home to her family where Davidson grew up with two white siblings, a white father and a lot of love. They formally adopted the child and he was educated in Maryland.

The year was 1986. A friend of Davidson's talked him into performing stand-up for the first time at a strip club. By 1987 Davidson was winning comedy competitions and opening up for established acts like, Pattie LaBelle, Kenny G, Starpoint, Anita Baker and Luther Vandross. Next stop was *The Arsenio Hall Show* where stars were made. That appearance led to his big break – *In Living Color.*

413

Davidson was part of a strong ensemble for the FOX sketch comedy show that initially included David Alan Grier, T'Keyah Crystal Keymah, Kelly Coffield, Jim Carrey and all the Wayans. Regardless, he made his mark with spot-on impersonations of Sammy Davis, Jr., Sugar Ray Leonard and Michael Jackson. Davidson released his stand-up recordings of *Illin in Philly* and *On the Strength* then hit the movie circuit, co-starring in *Ace Ventura: When Nature Calls, Strictly Business, Juwanna Mann, Woo and Booty Call.*

Tommy Davidson did cartoon voice-overs; TV games shows and co-hosted a travel program (*Vacation Creations*) giving away a good time to mainly white families the way a good life was given to him.

https://youtu.be/zgdkVmW7NM4

✳✳✳

November 11, 1968

Lavell Crawford (r) w/ Tommy Davidson (Humor Mill Magazine)

Lavell Maurice Crawford – Born in St. Louis, MI!

Show me a comedian and I'll show you somebody who's had issues. Lavell Crawford is no different. He almost drowned as soon as he reached double-figures. Then he father left him and the family. Surely somebody wanted to make a fuss, but Crawford's father was a body builder, and so ... Crawford was raised by his mother and two sisters.

Show me a comedian with issues and I'll show you somebody funny. Lavell Crawford is no different. He's a self-deprecating, heckler-annihilating wrecking machine. His rapid, staccato delivery punctuate each bit until his audience is convulsing and doubling over with gut wrenching laughter. Crawford developed his arsenal of bits and ab-lib fluency working comedy clubs all over the Mid-West, doing chitlin circuit tours and before long basic cable opportunities came along. He performed on BET's *Comic View* and was so good he practically became a recurring comedian. He had a likeability that he leveraged for a wider audience.

Lavell Crawford kept a full schedule of comedy commitments. He was constantly doing stand-up – televised (*Shaq All-Star Comedy Jam, Comic's Unleashed, 1st Amendment, Comedy Central Presents, Laffapalooza, Showtime at the Apollo*) and otherwise (the road - national and international). He appeared on sitcoms (*The Jamie Foxx Show, It's Always Sunny in Philadelphia, My Parents, My Sister & Me*), films (*American Ultra, The Ridiculous 6*), music videos (J-Kwon's *Tipsy*) and late-night TV (*Lopez Tonight* and *Nightly with Larry Wilmore* as correspondent and panelist). Crawford was also a *Last Comic Standing* runner-up and wrote the book, *Can a Brother Get Some Love?*

However, his big break came on AMC's hit *Breaking Bad* in the role of Huell Babineaux, body guard to bottom feeding attorney Jimmy McGill. The character was so popular it got a spin-off in the form of a video short (*Huell's Rules*). Then Crawford reprised the part again in another spin-off, *Better Call Saul*. Crawford became so busy fulfilling his dreams he had no place in his life to be overwhelmed by his personal issues. He just put them in jokes where they belong.

https://youtu.be/q543BSvlrKY

***

NOVEMBER 12, 1874

Bert Williams (r) w/ George Walker and Adah Overton Walker dancing "*The Cake Walk*" in their production, *In Dahomey* – 1903 (Public Domain)

BERT WILLIAMS – BORN IN NASSAU, THE BAHAMAS!

Williams became known as the greatest comedian of the first half of the 20th Century. Fellow Vaudevillian W. C. Fields said of Williams that he was "the funniest man I ever saw and the saddest man

I ever knew." Williams arrived at this perceived melancholy mainly due to the times in which he lived. Bert Williams was an educated, cultured man who was not born with American values; meaning he didn't have the baggage of racial injustice thrust upon him from an early age. So any undeserved slight or poor treatment was more of an affront compared to Blacks raised in the States who knew it was nothing personal. It was because you were Black.

Bert Williams defied barriers. While working with various minstrel shows on the West Coast he met his future partner, George Walker and they made history. Billed as "Two Real Coons" (so they weren't confused with many of the white minstrels billing themselves as real coons), their routine consisted of skits, funny dialogue and song-and-dance numbers. In 1896 they popularized the dance craze, The Cake Walk and simultaneously they were criticized for not being better role models. After all their stage personas were that of a slick dandy (Walker) and a dimwitted coon (Williams). This knocking of the duo was despite the fact they were always dressed immaculately and used exquisite manners when in public and in photos. Few seemed to notice their mockery of the very blackface they employed with pointed satirical jabs at the process. No matter. They were derided, whereas the truth was they became the first to move away from the broad style of minstrelsy and portray a more naturalistic, human brand of comedy. They even touched upon the divisions of class in the Black community.

Then came the 20th century. After Walker was beaten by a mob in New York following a performance (he was mistaken for a "darkie" who'd shot a cop), the duo had a string of major stage successes, most notably Son of Sam and In Dahomey (the first Black production to open on Broadway). The latter production did a command performance at Buckingham Palace in London and Williams and Walker were initiated into the Edinburgh Lodge of the Freemasons, because the Scottish weren't into discriminating racially as the Masons were in the USA. The twosome recorded hit songs in 1901 (Williams had the hit, Nobody). They did Bandanna Land where Williams introduced his signature routine, The Card Game. He pantomimed an entire poker game alone.

When Walker contracted syphilis in 1909, suffered a stroke and later died, Williams was forced to become a solo act. His first production was met with resistance from an organization known as "The White Rats," who intimidated theater owners who were sympathetic to hiring Black acts. Thus, Bert Williams did not gain the support needed to mount a successful run. He flopped and went back to vaudeville. The White Rats went right with him to protest his working. Regardless, he was too good not to hire, but the theater owners put him as secondary to a lesser headliner even though they put Williams name in larger letters to draw a crowd and lend legitimacy to their show.

Despite the persistent interference of the White Rats Williams was hired to perform in the Ziegfeld Follies in 1910. Many of the white performers threatened to quit. Owner, Flo Ziegfeld told them they'd be missed. Williams was a huge success and became the top paid act in the Follies. He recorded four songs under his new contract with Columbia Records and they were hits. He was paired with white entertainer, Leon Errol for a hilarious 20-minute routine and they became the first black and white comedy teaming. Williams was also featured in 1913 in the all-Black revue, "The Frogs," giving his Black fans who couldn't make the Follies a chance to see him.

By 1914 things were slowing down at the Follies for Bert Williams. The focus was more on the parade of beautiful girls the show featured than on comedy routines and Williams got less and less stage time. In 1918 Williams worked in Ziegfeld's secondary production known as "Midnight Frolic" and thrived in this setting because it allowed him longer stretches on stage. During that same period, he was being touted as one of the three top recording artists in the world (along with Al Jolson and Nora Bayes) shipping out 180,000 copies at a time when 10,000 was considered a major feat.

Massive success aside, Bert Williams still faced racial prejudice. Once while attempting to buy a drink at the bar of the Hotel Astor, the bartender threatened to throw him out if he couldn't pay $50 for the glass of liquid. Williams pulled out a wad of $100 bills, slapped them on the bar and demanded drinks for everyone in the establishment. Such disrespect continued all the way up to his death in 1922 from pneumonia. He had stubbornly performed while ill to save a dying show and collapsed on stage, only to say in his dressing room, "That's a nice way to die. They was laughing when I made my last exit."

Bert Williams had a World War II battleship named in his honor and was inducted posthumously into the International Clown Hall of Fame in 1996.

https://youtu.be/9xbf-pfGMmQ

* * *

NOVEMBER 13, 1955

Whoopi Goldberg (l) w/Elisabeth Hasselbeck, Sherri Shepherd and military personnel posing for photo at taping of *The View* – 2010 (Public Domain)

WHOOPI GOLDBERG (CARYN ELAINE JOHNSON) – BORN IN MANHATTAN!

Goldberg burst upon the scene in a one-woman show she creat-ed entitled *The SpookShow*. Famed director, Mike Nichols took it to Broadway and the artist who could do so many funny characters stole the town. This accomplished, she was then cast as Celie in Alice Walker's *The Color Purple* for Steven Spielberg and in 1985 became a household name. From there Whoopi was making plenty. Besides film, Goldberg had her own NBC sitcom, a late night talk show, co-produced the veteran game show, *The Hollywood Squares*, wrote books, produced plays on Broadway, did voice-overs in classic cartoons (*Lion King, Toy Story*), co-founded Comic Relief, was the first Black female to host the Academy Awards and co-hosted the ABC morning gabfest, *The View*.

By the way did I mention she won an Oscar (for *Ghost*), making her the 1st African-American stand-up comedienne to receive the award?-Goldberg understood the business she was in and how to manipulate it to her benefit, all the way down to her name change. Whoopi was a nickname associated with her for her ability to release pressure from an individual (with laughter) similar to whoopee cushions. However, she adopted the name "Goldberg' because her mother told her"Johnson" wasn't Jewish enough to make her a star. And not only did she become that, one year she was recognized as the highest paid actress of all time. Her output was tremendous by any measure. After winning the Academy Award in 1990 for *Ghost* Goldberg has appeared in no less than three films a year, every year with a high count of seven motion pictures in 1998. She did this for 20 straight years. Talk about a role model.

Race and gender were minor obstacles in her approach. From the very beginning Goldberg set her sights on what was normally not considered traditional Black casting. This sprung from one of her first experiences seeing this practice. While watching *StarTrek* as a youth she called out to her mother that there was a Black woman on TV that-was not a maid. Nichelle Nichols portrayal of Uhura on the Starship Enterprise sparked in Goldberg the desire to be all she could be. She even auditioned for the lead in the film, *The Princess Bride*, a role that requested a blond haired, blue eyed single white female. She didn't get the part, but not due to lack of trying. When she couldn't win parts meant for men she played men in parts (*The Associate*, 1996). And a whiteman at that.

Goldberg was also no stranger to controversy. Often criticized by the African-American community for dating out of her race, Goldberg married director of photography, David Claessen and divorced soon after the failure of one of her contracted films, *The Telephone*. That was her second marriage. Her first lasted 6 years, her third held on for one.

In 1995 she convinced boyfriend Ted Danson to don blackface at a Friar's Club event that got publicized and scrutinized and in 2004 she lost her SlimFast endorsement after telling an off-color joke about sitting president, George W. Bush. She's been a vocal proponent of whatever she chose to be vocal about as co-host of *The View* and never lost sight of her power in the medium. She knew she was there to entertain; to be Whoopi – and she was all that.

Whoopi took on comedic celebrities. After comedienne Kathy Griffin called Senator Scott Brown's daughters "prostitutes," Goldberg said that if anyone insulted her daughter like that "I would beat their ass." Don't look so shocked. You hired Whoopi Goldberg. As a veteran comedienne, she knew who she was, and was going to be to that audience. As one of the few entertainers to have the coveted EGOT (Emmy, Grammy, Oscar and Tony awards), she also knew her power and where things stood historically. Fundamentally – the woman knew the score and how to keep it.

https://youtu.be/Olm-eJwTpac

✱✱✱

NOVEMBER 14, 2001

THE BERNIE MAC SHOW – PREMIERED ON FOX!

Shortened to *Bernie Mac* in syndication, this sitcom was created by Larry Wilmore and based loosely on comedian, Bernie Mac's stand-up act. The premise is Mac is a married, but childless stand-up comedian. When his sister goes into rehab he takes her three kids (Vanessa, Jordan and Bryana) in and raises them old school style; with plenty of discipline and a whole lot of tough love.

The show used the device of Mac talking directly into the camera. These addresses to "America" gave Mac the opportunity to voice what was really on his mind before returning to the action of the actual show. Another opportunity was capitalized on by having Mac as a stand-up comedian. It allowed multiple unforced cameos from talents such as Don Cheadle, Chris Rock, Dom DeLuise, Angela Bassett, Billy Crystal, Ellen DeGeneres, Ice Cube, Snoop Dogg, Shaq, Hugh Hefner, Sugar Ray Leonard and Wesley Snipes. The show also featured recurring comedians, Reginald Ballard, Carlos Mencia and Anthony Anderson.

Co-starring Kellita Smith (Wanda, the wife), Dee Davis (Bryana, the youngest niece). Jeremy Suarez, (Jordan, the nephew) and Camille Winbush (Vanessa, the eldest niece), the show had behind the scenes drama which led to its demise. After a ratings decline due to stiff competition from Damon Wayans ABC sitcom, *My Wife and Kids*, executive producer, Larry Wilmore was fired. FOX didn't like the direction he was taking the show and Wilmore didn't care for the interference FOX kept implementing. The ratings continued to drop and the show was moved to follow *American Idol*. The ratings leaped back up, but that wasn't good enough for FOX, who moved it around even more. Eventually the audience grew tired of trying to find which night *The Bernie Mac Show* was on and lost interest. On April 14, 2006, FOX aired the final episode.

The Bernie Mac Show won the Emmy Award for Outstanding Writing for a Comedy Series, a Peabody Award and three NAACP Image Awards for Outstanding Comedy Series. Bernie Mac, the actor, was honored by the Television Critics Association for Individual Achievement in a Comedy and four NAACP Image Awards for Outstanding Actor in a Comedy Series (2003-2006).

https://youtu.be/_403bABOjyc

✳ ✳ ✳

NOVEMBER 17, 1989

Redd Foxx, Richard Pryor, Eddie Murphy, Desi Arnez Hines II, Reynaldo Rey rehearsing a scene from *Harlem Nights* (The Reynaldo Rey Collection)

HARLEM NIGHTS – RELEASED BY PARAMOUNT PICTURES!

Written, executive produced, and directed by Eddie Murphy, *Harlem Nights* featured practically every working veteran comedian of the era. Richard Pryor plays Murphy's surrogate father who raised him and taught him how to get over in the world of crime after young Murphy shoots a man to save Pryor. They end up running a nightclub in Depression Era Harlem where criminal activity and corruption are always lurking in plain sight. And speaking of sight, Redd Foxx plays a damn near blind partner of the duo. Robin Harris and Charlie Murphy are henchmen. Arsenio Hall is a rival gangster and Della Reese runs the hoes at their brothel. Also featured are Tommy Mikal Ford, Jasmine Guy, Berlinda Tolbert, Michael Lerner, Danny Aiello,Stan Shaw, Uncle Ray Murphy and Reynaldo Rey.

The plot revolves around Pryor being muscled in on by gangsters. He decides to retire before he has unwanted partners, but wants to make sure all his people are taken care of. So he plans a scheme for an upcoming fight and uses a call girl named Sunshine to help him carry out his plot. Sunshine was considered so sexy and fine for that time period that an Italian bagman called his surely equally Italian wife to tell her he wouldn't be coming back and to take care of the kids. That along with a series of twists and turns leave Pryor and Murphy triumphant.They get the scam money, avoid death and arrest and leave Harlem for good after screwing its underworld system.

Critics panned *Harlem Nights*. They didn't like the direction. They didn't like the screenplay. They didn't like the sets or the cinematography. They just plain didn't like it. Oh well, *Harlem Nights* opened at number one at the box office its first weekend. On a budget of $30 million it grossed a total of $60,864,870 domestically and was nominated for an Academy Award for Best Costume Design.

https://youtu.be/LuEjEZioD4I

***

NOVEMBER 18, 1970

Mike Epps (Humor Mill Magazine)

MICHAEL ELLIOT "MIKE" EPPS – BORN IN INDIANAPOLIS!

Epps got started in stand-up comedy as a teenager. By the time he was old enough to legally be in the clubs he was performing he was seasoned. He moved to Atlanta, got a job working at the Comedy Act Theater there and got more seasoned. Then he moved to Brooklyn, got on *Def Comedy Jam* and the Def Jam tour. Epps was moving up fast.

His next move was film. He got his cherry busted in 1997 under the direction of Vin Diesel in the film *Strays*. In 2000 he got his breakthrough role as Day-Day playing opposite Ice Cube in *Next Friday*, the sequel to the surprise blockbuster, *Friday*. After that he cranked them out: *3Strikes, Bait, Dr. Dolittle 2* (voice only), *How High, All About the Benjamins, Friday After Next, Malibu's Most Wanted, Guess Who, The Honeymooners, Lottery Ticket, Soul Men, Janky Promoters, The Hangover* trilogy, the *Resident Evil* films, *Welcome Home Roscoe Jenkins* and a slew of others. He did cartoon voice-overs (*The Boondocks, Open Season 2*), comedy specials(*Under Rated & Never Faded*) and plenty of TV (*Wild 'n Out, Survivor's Remorse, Being MaryJane*).

Epps also showed he had a dramatic side. In the remake of *Sparkle*, Epps played a demented drug lord and received favorable reviews from critics and audiences alike. He co-starred alongside Queen Latifah in

HBO's *Bessie*, the biopic of blues singer Bessie Smith. Once again Epps was impressive as Bessie's personal bootlegger/boyfriend. It was work like that which convinced director, Lee Daniels to cast him in the coveted role of Richard Pryor in *Is It Something I Said*, the languishing biopic of the famed and controversial comedian.

https://youtu.be/w1UJHvvA-hc

✳ ✳ ✳

NOVEMBER 20, 1956

Thea Vidale performing for troops in Iraq, 2011 (Public Domain)

THEA VIDALE – BORN IN WASHINGTON, DC!

A waitress before friends convinced her to go into comedy, Vidale became proficient working comedy clubs in Houston, Washington DC and New York. She got her break in 1989 when she appeared in the cable comedy special *Rodney Dangerfield: Opening Night at Rodney's Place* on HBO. Since she came up during a period of blatant misogyny, the neophyte powerhouse had to deal with sexist behavior from White, Black, and Latino male comics who didn't want a woman to be funnier than them. She featured for Tim Allen, Brad Garrett, Jeff Foxworthy, to name a few and they were dumbfounded that she was not headlining.

They weren't stupefied long. Soon Vidale was headlining clubs across the country and making guest appearances on every available televised stand-up show and sitcom that wanted laughter in big doses on the menu. Thea appeared on *Ellen, The Wayans Bros, The Drew Carey Show* and *My Wife & Kids*. Off camera she was opinionated and some say slightly insensitive. Whatever the case, Thea got her own show on ABC bearing her own name. This was a first for an African-American female. The sitcom *Thea* lasted one season and Vidale was back on the road where her onstage style was in-your-face and to the point.

An advocate for gay rights, Vidale made her first appearance for LGBT in 1999. It was the Philadelphia LGBT Pride Fest with comic Etta May. The city's mayor officially named the day "Thea Vidale Day" & "Etta May Day." Vidale went on to work events for the Adult Film Industry(the AVN Awards) and perform as WWE wrestler, Shelton Benjamin's mother. This latter was mock, but when Vidale experienced real life heart problems her character was written out of the charade. She acknowledged things got tough for a while professionally; from the industry and peers alike.

Vidale discovered, as many who came before her, that ageism is also a negative for a Black comedienne. She observed that the industry tries to discredit you unless you're a White male."White men get to be funny for a long time. Black men get to be funny. For some reason, women as we get older, it seems they don't want to hear what we have to say. I got a lot of sh*t to say."

https://youtu.be/6iATkh4tkU4

* * *

NOVEMBER 21, 2001

BLACK KNIGHT – RELEASED BY 20TH CENTURY FOX!

This Martin Lawrence vehicle is about a black theme park employee transported back to Merry Ole England. When Lawrence falls in the moat at his job at Medieval World, he believes he's at the rival theme park, Castle World. All the villagers look like actors to him until somebody gets their head cut off and then it gets real. Lawrence realizes he's in deep crap, but with the help of a drunken ex-knight and a chambermaid, he assumes an identity so he keeps his dome intact. Telling them he's from Florence and Normandie (South Central in the house) they assume he's a French Moor. He then calls himself Skywalker (high school nickname) and becomes the king's head of security after accidentally saving him from assassination. It's all good until Lawrence finds out the king is scum and the former queen needs to be restored to the throne. So he teaches the villagers football and wrestling moves from the future and the climactic scene finds the king overthrown.

Black Knight features Tom Wilkerson as the drunken knight. Marsha Thomason as the chambermaid. Kevin Conway as the scummy king and Vincent Regan as the scummy king's bodyguard. Daryl Mitchell is also featured. The film was shot in North Carolina, which as everybody knows, bears a striking resemblance to England.

Directed by Gil Junger, *Black Knight* was critically panned. Junger was known more as a sitcom director and it was said the film looked lazy. However, it was nominated for a Golden Reel Award for Best Sound Editing/ Music, but on a budget of $50 million dollars *Black Knight* only grossed $39,976,235 at the worldwide box office.

https://youtu.be/lw7dzS8UJ4Q

* * *

NOVEMBER 22, 2002

FRIDAY AFTER NEXT – RELEASED BY NEW LINE CINEMA!

This third installment of the *Friday* series of comedies starred Ice Cube (also the producer)and Mike Epps. The duo reprised their roles as Craig and Day-Day, respectively, two cousins out to retrieve their stolen Christmas presents. They also have the dilemma of being evicted if they don't pay their rent. They get jobs working as security at a strip mall owned by a stripmall slum lord. When a group of thugs beat the sleazy owner in retaliation to Craig and Day-Day, they're fired. So, Craig's father (John Witherspoon), the owner of the Bar-B-Que spot, rats the guy out to the Health Department. By the end Craig and Day-Day catch the thief, get their presents back and pay their rent.

Friday After Next is notable for its comedic cast. The film put Katt Williams (Money Mike) and Terry Crews (homosexual ex-con, Damon) on the map. It also featured Rickey Smiley as the thieving Santa Claus; Don "DC" Curry as Elroy, the co-runner of "Bros. BBQ"; Bebe Drake as the flirtatious Ms. Pearly, out to get a taste of Witherspoon's ribs; Maz Jobrani as the scummy mall-lord and K. D. Aubert as Donna, Money Mike's partner in "Pimps and Hoes." Also appearing are Sommore, Anna Maria Hosford and Clifton Powell.

Directed by Marcus Raboy, *Friday After Next* was made on a budget of $10 million and grossed $33,526,835.

https://youtu.be/Xdx7j-k7E7I

✳✳✳

NOVEMBER 23, 1994

A LOW DOWN DIRTY SHAME – RELEASED BY BUENA VISTA!

Written, directed and starring Keenan Ivory Wayans, this action-comedy cast him as a disgraced private detective. His agency is about to go under when he gets a cold case involving a drug lord he thought he'd killed long ago. It turns out the dealer's old girlfriend, who was also Wayans's girlfriend stole $20 million of drug money and is now being sought by the still alive drug lord. Wayans assistant, Peaches, tries to help, but ends up a hostage. To add to his troubles, his old-time partner has turned on him. By the time it's all wrapped up people are dead, but Wayans and Peaches (Jada Pinkett) find love and keep $5 million of the recovered illegal money to take a long vacation.

A Low Down Dirty Shame co-stars Charles S. Dutton as Wayans traitor partner. Salli Richardson plays the thieving girlfriend on the run and

Gregory Sierra is the police captain looking for an excuse to throw Wayans behind bars. The film also features Chris Spencer and Kim Wayans. With original music by Marcus Miller, *A Low Down Dirty Shame* was shot on a budget of $10 million and grossed $29,392,418 at the box office.

https://youtu.be/PlP9zvGr17E

✳✳✳

NOVEMBER 23, 1967

Courtney Gee (r) w/D'Militant (The Littleton Collection)

CORTNEY GEE (CORTNEY GILMORE) – BORN!

Music legend, Prince, let Cortney Gee know he'd arrived when the icon startled the young comic with such a warm greeting you'd have thought they were long lost buds. Ah, the power of TV, even if it is just basic cable. Gee was part of the wave assaulting the beach of American and English speaking homes around the world known as the Urban Comedy Boom of the late 1980s and early 1990s. Cortney Gee had established himself as a fixture at BET (Black Entertainment Television) on the stand-up competition show, *Comic View* so much so that he was practically considered furniture to be struck with the set. He was ghetto fabulous and on his way to the next level.

Cortney Gee was representative of the trajectory taken by a lot of comedians during this era. Gee had gotten good in local clubs in his beloved, Cleveland, Ohio. He'd gotten a big time West Coast manager with big time West Coast and nationwide connections. He'd been on TV (*Def Comedy Jam, 1ˢᵗ Amendment*) and toured (with Katt Williams). He traveled overseas entertaining US troops in Asia, Europe and the Middle-East. Cortney Gee received celebrity treatment at award shows and film premieres. He'd done guest-starring parts in sitcoms (*The Jamie Foxx Show*) and even landed a three book deal and had published the first (*One Hustle*) when tragedy intervened.

In 2016 Cortney Gee was diagnosed with kidney disease, slamming on the brakes and bringing his career to a screeching halt. Like many comedians he'd lived a life on the road and all that goes along with that: poor diet, inconsistent sleep, and questionable accommodations; especially on occasions when somebody said, "Let me holla atcha."

Comedy is known as a verbal laughing tonic. People feel better when they're physically moved to laugh. It also works with the ill, even if that ill person is a comedian In the case of Cortney Gee he performed whenever possible despite painful dialysis treatments and an amputation. His desire to get well and return to the stage exemplifies the unquantifiable element embedded in all comedians; the ability to let the art sustain you and prolong you. It's such an example of determination that respect must be paid.

https://youtu.be/h9e44MhNJvo

✳ ✳ ✳

DECEMBER

THIS DAY IN COMEDY...

DECEMBER 1, 1940

Richard Pryor - 1969 (Public Domain)

RICHARD FRANKLIN LENNOX THOMAS PRYOR – BORN IN PEORIA, ILLINOIS!

Known universally as the greatest comedian of the 20th Century, Richard Pryor's road to success was decidedly unconventional. Raised in a brothel and constantly abused both physically and mentally, the young man delved into self-expression as an escape from the realities of his sordid life. However, his violent upbringing followed him. While in the Army Pryor was part of a mob of Black soldiers who beat and stabbed a white soldier for laughing too hard at a section of the film, *Imitation of Life* (a movie about a Black girl passing as white). That act put him behind bars for most of his military stint.

Once free from the stranglehold of Uncle Sam, Pryor relocated in New York and began his career. It was a shaky start to say the least. He was opening for singer Nina Simone and shook so much from stage fright that the songstress had to hold him and rock him back and forth until he calmed down. She did this each night he performed.

Initially Richard Pryor was not the firebrand the public came to love. He was a Bill Cosby clone … comedy-wise. He dressed like Cos, talked like him, walked like him, had similar facial expressions and themes in material. They even did the same TV shows until one day Cosby told Pryor (who was a friend) that he had to stop imitating him. Pryor response was something to the effect of "I'm making a lot of money acting like you so I'm going to keep doing it." That attitude lasted until Pryor played the

Aladdin Hotel in Las Vegas, a town known for artistic restriction. Pryor had finally had enough of being like his watered down colleague and in 1967 he walked off the stage in the middle of his show. But before he made his exit, legend has it that Pryor stripped naked, ran into the gaming room, jumped on the table and yelled, "Blackjack!" At least that's the legend.

Richard Pryor (Public Domain)

In any case, a new Pryor had to be cultivated and so he went to Northern California. Pryor honed his personalized persona in front of Oakland and Berkeley audiences consisting of hoes, pimps, drug dealers and gangsters. He was talking the language of the people to the people and they loved it. He was cursing and talking about race and social issues. He spoke the lingo of the streets and before long the industry took notice. Pryor signed with Laff Records and recorded the seminal *Craps After Dark*. That raw-edged comedy classic led to a deal with Stax records for more money and larger distribution. He laid his hit *That Nigger's Crazy*. His name was now on everybody's lips as he jumped over to Reprise/Warner Bros. At this point Pryor was a comic's comic and despite breaching his contract with Laff (which they settled to their mutual benefit) Pryor went on to make a succession of popular albums: *Is it Something I Said?*, *Bicentennial Nigger*, *Richard Pryor: Live in Concert*, *Richard Pryor: Live on the Sunset Strip* and *Richard Pryor: Here and Now*.

Pryor was on a roll. He won an Emmy for writing and five Grammys for his albums as well as box office recognition for films such as *Lady Sings the Blues*, *The Mack*, *Car Wash*, *Which Way Is Up*, *Blue Collar*, *Greased Lightning*, *Silver Streak*, *Stir Crazy*, *Superman III* and more. He was so much in demand that NBC gave him his own sketch show. It lasted for only four episodes.Pryor was too raw for TV. Pryor also had problems. The problem was that he had a drug problem; there weren't enough drugs to keep him happy. A known cocaine addict, Pryor began a rapid decent when he dabbled with freebasing. Smoking coke in its purest form cost Pryor the lead in *History of the World, Pt. I* (replaced by Gregory Hines) and *Trading Places* (replaced with Eddie Murphy, who indirectly owes his career boost to drugs. Whereas, Pryor owed the decline of his career to them.).

Then things really hit the skids. Pryor lit himself on fire during a freebase session. This landed him in the hospital and on every news outlet.

He recovered after multiple operations, but was never the same. The man who was the first to win the Mark Twain Humor Award was just a shell of his former self. He contracted multiple sclerosis and was restricted to a wheelchair. With close friend and personal writer, Paul Mooney as his support system, Pryor continued to perform, but the audiences were more there to see the last gasp of glory.

That gasp occurred on December 10, 2005 – ten days after the great man's 65th birthday. He did something most never imagined. Richard Pryor retired at the mandatory retirement age; perhaps the only conventional thing he ever did in his life.

https://youtu.be/mmZm2HBMtTQ

DECEMBER 3, 1979

Tiffany Haddish (*Humor Mill Magazine*)

TIFFANY SARAC HADDISH – BORN IN LOS ANGELES!

Stand-up comedy is the ultimate art form for self-expression and in many cases therapeutic salvation. Tiffany Haddish utilized it for both. The offspring of a Jewish refugee father (who abandoned the family when Haddish was three years-old) and an African-American mother who was Jehovah Witness, Haddish soon found herself heaped in adult burdens. When she was eight her mother (who had remarried) was in a crippling auto accident that caused brain damage and schizophrenia. This placed the responsibility of watching her four younger siblings on the shoulders of young Tiffany. By age 12 the situation devolved to the point the family was split up and the children placed into foster homes. Haddish tried to use jokes as a means of making matters tolerable, but still found herself hospitalized with toxic shock syndrome.

Tiffany Haddish's grandmother was eventually given custody, but the ordeal of being shuffled around had taken its toll. Haddish was getting in trouble in school, yet showed signs of being artistically inclined (she won a drama competition doing a monologue from Shakespeare). Her social worker gave her a choice – either go to a comedy camp sponsored by the Laugh Factory or go into psychiatric therapy. Thus, the Laugh Factory Comedy Club became her saving grace. Mentored by established professionals she found her niche.

By 2005, Tiffany Haddish was working in front of the camera. Her first television role was on *That's So Raven* and the parts kept coming steadily from there (*My Name is Earl, It's Always Sunny in Philadelphia, The Underground, Nick Cannon's Short Circuitz, Just Jordan, Racing for Time, If Loving You Is Wrong, New Girl*). Her on-going role as Nekeisha Williams on NBC's *The Carmichael Show* established her as a scene stealer America needed to keep an eye on.

Tiffany Haddish stayed busy doing guest spots on shows such as *Chelsea Lately, Reality Bites Back, Real House Husbands of Hollywood, Funniest Wins* and she did films (*Meet the Spartans, Janky Promoters, A Christmas Wedding, School Dance, Keanu, Mad Families*) where she was good even in the ones where the same couldn't be said.

Then came 2017 – her star making year. She had the box office smash *Girls Trip*, the project that put her over the top and in everybody's conversation. In the Queen Latifah, Jada Pinkett-Smith, Regina Hall vehicle, Haddish stole everything, but the cameras. Award nominations came piling in and while lips were still flapping Haddish dropped her Showtime comedy special, *Tiffany Haddish: She Ready! From the Hood to Hollywood* and made additional history by being the first Black comedienne to host *Saturday Night Live* (she won an Emmy for it), not to mention being featured in a Jay-Z video ("Moonlight") even though we just mentioned it and releasing her first book, *The Last Black Unicorn*. In 2018 she co-starred with Kevin Hart in *Night School* and starred in her own vehicle, *Nobody's Fool* with Whoopi Goldberg.

Whereas numerous comics who find success in film and television abandon the stage, Tiffany Haddish never sacrificed the vehicle that allowed her the freedom for further success – stand-up. Besides touring, she appeared on *Bill Bellamy's Who's Got Jokes* and *Def Comedy Jam* on her ascent and regularly returns to the Laugh Factory Comedy Camp to mentor the youth who need role models and guidance just as she did.

https://youtu.be/lCIXMjZxKIA

✳ ✳ ✳

DECEMBER 3, 1961

Adal Ramones – 2005 (Public Domain)

ADAL RAMONES (ADALBERTO JAVIER RAMONES MARTÍNEZ) – BORN IN MONTERREY, NUEVO LEON!

Ramones has not been the most fortunate of entertainers. For years he suffered from heart disease requiring numerous operations. He recovered from that harrowing experience and was then kidnapped. Ramones spent a week locked in a closet, blindfolded with his feet tied and only given water. He lost 15.5 pounds. After that he caught on fire while shooting his show and was rushed to the hospital. In 2004 he needed crutches after breaking his ankle in yet another accident.

Now as far as his comedy, Ramones made his reputation with his material on Mexican social life. He's best known as the host of *Otro Rollo*, aired by Televisa and seen in 53 countries outside of Mexico (by Univision in the United States). The show featured a portion called *La pesera del amor*, where Ramones matches up a couple and they marry on live TV, with the show picking up all expenses. It was supposed to be a onetime thing, but was so popular it was added on as a regular part of the show. Who doesn't want a free honeymoon with a relative stranger who now has your last name?

Ramones received support from American artists on his program. Britany Spears kicked things off in July of 2003 and from there the Yanks kept going south. Other celebrities Ramones hosted include, Sylvester Stallone, Chris Rock, Cameron Diaz, Kevin James, Lucy Liu, Arnold Schwarzenegger, Christina Aguilera, John Leguizamo, Chayanne and others. Will Smith appeared three times. Paris Hilton stood him up.

Ramones has done dozens of voices for animation and in 2005 he was nominated for the Mexican MTV Movie Award for Favorite Actor.

https://youtu.be/Q_DPyCEnYa0

✳ ✳ ✳

DECEMBER 4, 1992

THE DISTINGUISHED GENTLEMAN – RELEASED BY BUENA VISTA!

Eddie Murphy stars in this comedy about a con man who uses the name recognition of a deceased career politician to be elected to the US Congress. After his win he tries to actually address real issues along with taking the system for all he can get. It turns out the system in Washington is even more corrupt than Murphy expected. He's being blocked by a crooked official. So after an elaborate con, Murphy exposes the trouble maker as an elected criminal and in the process exposes himself as a fraud.

The Distinguished Gentleman was directed by Jonathan Lynn. It also stars Lane Smith as the crooked politician and features Sheryl Lee Ralph, James Garner, Victoria Rowell, Charles S. Dutton, Chi McBride, Joe Don Baker and Noble Willingham.

The film was critically panned, but made $47 million at the box office and was granted the Environmental Media Award for feature film and the Political Film Society Award.

https://youtu.be/_GK1xWGYx5s

✳ ✳ ✳

DECEMBER 4, 1972

Lady Tuezdae (The Littleton Collection)

LADY TUEZDAE (LITTLETON) – BORN IN LOS ANGELES!

Lady Tuezdae has the distinction of being the first comedienne to write a book on the history of comediennes. This is just one of the first in her unconventional comedy career. Prior to gracing a stage or penning a joke she was the first female to work under the expert tutelage of the founder of the Black Stuntmen's Association, Eddie Smith.

This led her into a career behind the scenes as a respected, in-demand presence in productions including *Waist Deep, Live Free or Die Hard* and *The Last Day of Summer.* She then used her talents to ghost write material for established comedians.

In 2006 she began performing stand-up in Los Angeles, California and performed regularly at the World-Famous Comedy Store, the Laugh Factory and the Ha-Ha Comedy Club. She even found a fanbase in the motorcycle club circuit. The bikers adored her hard-hitting brand of take-no-prisoners humor and established her underground credentials.

Lady Tuezdae applied her aggressive approach to her writing. She wrote material for the Loni Love comedy special on Comedy Central which aired in May of 2010. In 2012 she co-hosted the podcast "Tuezdae's with D'Militant" with her husband, comedian, D'Militant. That same year the duo co-wrote and released her debut book, *Comediennes: Laugh Be a Lady.*

This history ("herstory") of females in comedy was an immediate hit in comedy circles and academia. The oral chronicling boasted insights from dozens of top comediennes and traced the evolution of the art from the 10th century to current day. It became a mainstay in libraries and book stores around the country.

Lady Tuezdae used this tentacle of her far-reaching talent to branch into public speaking on the lecture circuit. She currently travels the country promoting her book and female comedy.

https://youtu.be/hGus81PJU28

✳✳✳

December 5, 1968

Margaret Cho (Instagram)

Margaret Moran Cho – Born in San Francisco!

The distinction Cho holds is being the first Asian comedienne with her own sitcom. A major achievement considering Cho's culture looked down on such displays of foolishness. She was pointed in that direction as soon as Mom met Dad. Born in the late 60s, Cho was raised in San Francisco. Her father wrote joke books and owned a book store. There was a comedy club nearby and Margaret developed her act around the old hippies, drag queens, drug heads and immigrants in the area. After working universities for years, she got a break with a role on *The Golden Girls* spin-off, *The Golden Palace* then as Jerry Seinfeld's opening act.

In a profession dominated by men and few Asians of any gender – Margaret got noticed. ABC took her act and churned out, *All American Girl*. For Cho it was more like All American nightmare. The producers kept tweaking the premise of the show from Cho living with her parents in the house, to living in their basement to moving out and living with three men – without explanation. They fired cast members and attempted to find ways to spin-off other shows from a show that obviously wasn't working itself. They didn't like her weight and round face so she starved herself in an effort to appear like the Margaret Cho they had in mind; the fictionalized version. The result was major kidney problems for the real version. Then they told her she wasn't Asian enough and brought in an Asian consultant to Asian-her-up. That failed so they fired the Asian cast and moved her in with white guys then told her she was too Asian. All this led to the show being canceled after one season and Margaret Cho (the real life one), becoming an alcoholic and drug addict. If those producers had had their way she would've committed hari kari during Sweeps Week.

It took Cho awhile to pull out of her depression and addictions and resume comedy work. The show was not the only downer. She had never met with acceptance in the Korean community for her choice of profession. She was looked down upon and this naturally didn't help when her shot at worldwide success fizzled. Regardless, Cho went forward and created a fashion line of crotchless underwear for men as well as women. She wrote a new act and took her brand of race and sex humor back on the road. She also recorded and released her music.

Margaret Cho has won over a half dozen awards from GLAAD, Entertainment Weekly, the Gracie Allen Award, Lambda Legal, the National Organization for Women and the Asian Excellence Award. She mounted almost a dozen major comedy tours. She's appeared in 30 films, including *Face/Off* with John Travolta. She's guest starred in dozens of sitcoms, published two books and released nine comedy recordings.

https://youtu.be/hXRYLb1m4q4

* * *

DECEMBER 7, 1969

Patrice O'Neal (2nd from left) w/ Smokie Suarez, Eddie Bryant, Turae Gordon, an Unidentified Brother and Kevin "Damn Fool" Simpson (Eddie Bryant Collection)

PATRICE LUMUMBA MALCOLM O'NEAL – BORN!

Plucked from the womb in New York City, O'Neal grew up in Roxbury near Boston, Massachusetts. He turned down a football scholarship to study performing arts and got his start in stand-up at Estelle's Bar & Grill. It was an open mic and the year was 1992. After putting in time on the Boston circuit, O'Neal moved to New York and then Los Angeles. It turned out L.A. was not a good fit for an uncompromising, confrontational and controversial talent like O'Neal. So after trying virtually every angle to achieve success he took his act overseas; to the UK. Five months later he'd gained the respect of his British colleagues and garnered the support of the likes of Ricky Gervais.

In 2002 O'Neal returned to New York and this time, things were different. He was invited back to shoot a Showtime special. He then proceeded to get a gig on the cast of *Tough Crowd with Colin Quinn*. In 2003 O'Neal recorded a Comedy Central Presents special. He appeared on *The Apollo Comedy Hour, MTV's 2F, Assy McGee, Ed, Z Rock, Yes Dear, Arrested Development, Chappelle's Show, The Office* and as a writer for the WWE. He did animated voice-overs for Comedy Central and was a radio regular with *Opie and Anthony's Traveling Virus Comedy Tour.*

O'Neal's first hour-long acclaimed special, *Elephant in the Room* aired on Comedy Central in 2011. He had a popular podcast and was the voice of Jeffron James in the video game *Grand Theft Auto IV.* He did celebrity roasts and recorded an album. Never stagnant, Patrice O'Neal stayed active until his death from a stroke on November 29, 2011.

https://youtu.be/3gAu4x0xIGY

* * *

December 8, 1933

Flip Wilson as alter ego Geraldine Jones – 1971 (Public Domain)

Clerow Wilson, Jr., (aka Flip Wilson) – Born in Jersey City, New Jersey!

Wilson arrived on the planet during the Great Depression and his father was constantly looking for work. There were 10 siblings and Wilson's mother took poverty and near starvation as her cue to leave the family. His father couldn't handle all those kids alone and so he placed many of them in foster homes. Wilson was one of them and after bouncing around he lied about his age when he turned 16 and enlisted in the Air Force. His sense of humor soon landed Wilson an assignment working special services, traveling around entertaining other troops.

When he was discharged in the mid-50s, Wilson found work as a shill. He'd act drunk in the audience in between acts. That bit of distraction soon became his act up and down the coast of California. He later wrote a routine and found his way on stage and into the professional world of stand-up comedy. Wilson became an Apollo Theater regular and it wasn't long before he made appearances on *The Tonight Show, The Ed Sullivan Show* and *Rowan & Martin's Laugh-In* (where he became a cast regular). His Grammy Award winning comedy album, *The Devil Made Me Buy This Dress* got him noticed by the network brass and soon after Flip Wilson had his own TV show.

The Flip Wilson Show in 1970 ushered in an era of top-rated Black programming by every network. NBC gave Wilson a primetime variety slot that put him as must-see TV for Nielsen homes and the rest of America. Wilson exposed Black acts seldom seen on mainstream shows: The Jackson Five, The Temptations, Redd Foxx and others. George Carlin was one of the writers as well as on camera talent. And the talented Flip Wilson had a plethora of sketch characters; his most memorable being Reverend Leroy of "The Church of What's Happening Now" and the super popular, Geraldine Jones and her catchphrases, "The Devil made me do it" and "What you see is what you get." The public ate it up and the show earned Wilson a Golden Globe and two Emmys.

In 1974 *The Flip Wilson Show* went off the air and Wilson took a rest. He later made guest appearances on sitcoms (*Here's Lucy*) and variety shows (*The Dean Martin Show*). Wilson did films (*Uptown Saturday Night, The Fish That Saved Pittsburgh*) and a televised musical (*Pinocchio* with Sandy Duncan and Danny Kaye) before returning to TV as host of *People Are Funny* in 1984 and in a sitcom called *Charlie & Co.* in 1985. His last televised appearance was on the Queen Latifah sitcom, *Living Single* on FOX in 1993.

Flip Wilson died of liver cancer on November 25, 1998 in Malibu, CA.

https://youtu.be/0SLifea3NHQ

✳ ✳ ✳

DECEMBER 9, 1922

Redd Foxx – 1966 (Public Domain)

REDD FOXX – BORN!

Foxx stated on many occasions that he wanted to leave the world as he came in – with nothing. And he did. His journey of burning through life leaving a stack of bills and few cares started when Mary Hughes from Ellisville, Mississippi gave birth to little John Sanford in Saint Louis, Missouri. She raised him on Chicago's Southside along with his brother, Fred G. Sanford Jr. Their father Fred G. Sanford Sr. ran off when little John was four years old, so he had to grow up quick.

Show business was a profession even a kid could do. So he joined a wash-tub band and in 1939 his group, the Jump Swinging Six, performed on the *Major Bowes Amateur Hour* on radio. However, show business was also an inconsistent profession meaning taking odd jobs between gigs was the norm. In the 1940s he worked as a dishwasher, scrubbing alongside the man who would later come to be known as Malcolm X. During this period in both of their unheralded lives Malcolm Little was known as St. Louis Red and called John, Chicago Red, "the funniest dishwasher in the world." John used the "Red" part for his stage name and got the Foxx from baseball player Jimmie Foxx.

Redd avoided the draft during World War II by eating half a bar of soap. That little trick right before his physical caused him to have heart palpitations. Still performing as a musician, Redd Foxx recorded fives songs for the Savoy label in 1946. Then he decided to use his laugh making ability

Redd Foxx – 1977 (Public Domain)

and integrated into comedy. Like most Black performers, his technique got tight on the chitlin circuit and he made a lot of friends. He worked solo, but for a time partnered with Slappy White.

Redd Foxx got his big break when famed singer, Dinah Washington introduced him to Dooto Records owner, Dootsie Williams and Foxx started recording party albums. Foxx wound up recording over 50 and earning the title, "The King of the Party Records." His style was raw, uncensored and uncut. A lot of it is tame by today's standards, but totally shocking in the 1950s and 60s.

Redd Foxx was one of the first Black comedians to perform before white audiences on the Strip in Las Vegas. He did a few films, but it was his cameo in *Cotton Comes to Harlem* as a junk man that put him on the path for his defining role as Fred G. Sanford on NBC's *Sanford and Son*. It was an American version of the hit British sitcom, *Steptoe and Son*, but there was nothing British about the way Foxx did it. For one thing he hired most of his friends from the chitlin circuit, including LaWanda Page, Bubba Bexley, Slappy White (his former partner) and Leroy & Skillet. The year was 1972 and the show was a thunderous hit.

Foxx was riding high, but NBC was dragging him down emotionally by not giving him the same things his white counterpart, Carroll O'Connor (Archie Bunker) of *All in the Family* was getting. Foxx walked out when he found out O'Connor had a window in his dressing room and Redd had none. The walkout was a minor protest, but it bothered the show's producers that production had to be held up; especially since he did it more than once. Soon they grew tired of it and Redd grew tired of them growing tired, so in 1977 the show was canceled.

Never one to be idle too long Redd did a variety show, but in 1980 found himself back at NBC attempting a revival of the original named

Sanford. That didn't last long so he did what all comedians do when they're on TV hiatus – he worked clubs, mainly in Las Vegas. He went back to the boob tube in 1986 for ABC on *The Redd Foxx Show*, but it lasted only a dozen episodes. So back to Vegas he went to earn millions. Known to some as the Godfather of Comedy, he got to work with the King and Prince (Richard Pryor and Eddie Murphy respectively) along with a slew of other amazing comedians in the Murphy directed vehicle, *Harlem Nights*. So money was never the problem. It was how quick Redd would blow it to fulfill his prophecy. This got him into tax problems.

In an attempt to hold off the IRS and continue living in the life style in which he was accustomed, Redd hopped over to CBS and starred in *The Royal Family* along with old friend, Della Reese. Things were going fine until October 11, 1991, the day Foxx's long standing gag of grabbing his heart when things got stressful looking upward and saying, "This is the big one, I'm coming to join you, Elizabeth" from his *Sanford and Son* days fooled everybody on the set. His always-mock heart attack was real this time and John Sanford aka Redd Foxx died that evening at Queen of Angels Hollywood Presbyterian Medical Center.

He left one current wife and three former wives, an adopted daughter, a $3.6 million bill for the IRS and a world of fans and admirers. Oscar winner Jamie Foxx used Redd's last name as a tribute to the man. Yes, a fake name replaced another fake name as flattery. Perhaps Jimmie Foxx should've been the one flattered.

https://youtu.be/qVs8yr-1ZIY

✳ ✳ ✳

DECEMBER 9, 1987

Kountry Wayne (Instagram)

"KOUNTRY WAYNE" (WAYNE COLLEY) – BORN IN MILLEN, GA!

Kountry Wayne is prolific. He has produced over 2500 videos and has nine children (at the time this is being written). He credits being a teen-age father (age 17 when his first was born) with giving him the focus he's had in life. He and his wife, Gena run several businesses in Georgia and he's always looking to further securing his legacy. This attitude didn't come easy. After shooting his financial wad trying to promote himself in the music industry, Wayne woke up to reality that he was naturally funny and got into the laugh game, with his inspirations being Martin Lawrence and Eddie Murphy.

Wayne's own comedy career started by shooting funny content and posting them on Facebook and Instagram. His first Facebook post from October 2014 went viral and from there he was off to the races gathering new followers by the thousands weekly. Those fans took his videos from Facebook and uploaded them to YouTube and he currently has over 4 million YouTube fan followers and it keeps growing.

Kountry Wayne is constantly touring including world tours. He sells out clubs and theaters across the nation. His material is edgy, yet he doesn't curse, meaning you can buy a Kountry Wayne ticket for everybody in the family. So, what began as an Internet seed has grown into a solid stand-up career based on time and Wayne's work ethic and desire to succeed. He has even evolved from Kountry Wayne to calling himself King Kountry Wayne. Well, every king has a kingdom and King Kountry Wayne is definitely conquering his as he leverages his online popularity to obtain TV, film and commercial opportunities.

https://youtu.be/Kr_ieN4E7Jk

***

DECEMBER 11, 1967

Mo'Nique at 82nd Academy Awards – 2010 (Public Domain)

MO'NIQUE ANGELA IMES-JACKSON – BORN IN WOODLAWN, MD!

The fourth child of a drug-counselor father and engineer mother, Queen Monique Angela Imes-Jackson became an example of perseverance, strength and the ability to excel. Once her brother, Steve, directed her to her destiny by daring Monique to get on stage at an open mic comedy night and from there it was no looking back. Mo'nique put a spin on her name and a twist of being a big female comedian. Pride in her size was her mantra and she put out product and a message to have other plus size women join her crusade. After learning how to be a comic in a Baltimore comedy spot she ran, Mo'Nique starred in a movie *Phat Girlz*. She put out a cook book entitled, *Skinny Cooks Can't Be Trusted*. She parodied a Beyonce's dance number, "Crazy In Love" with other large females at the 2004 BET Awards and she made big women proud of themselves in the process. Be who you are and love you was the theme and it was long overdue.

Many were taken by surprise by her seemingly rapid ascension. Having already taped *Def Comedy Jam*, her second appearance got an unexpected two-fold jolt. The show's producers felt her choice of material did not serve her well and decided not to air it. That same night she was plucked up by *Moesha* show co-creator, Ralph Farquhar for the role of Nikki Parker, Countess Vaughn's mother on *Moesha* and the spin-off *The Parkers*.

The Parkers made Mo'Nique a household name and lowered the draw bridge to the Queens of Comedy Tour and concert film, radio ("Mo'Nique in the Afternoon"), more television (*Showtime at the Apollo, Flavor of Love Girls: Charm School, The Mo'Nique Show*), a documentary (*I Could've Been Your Cellmate*) more films (*3 Strikes, Domino, Soul Plane, Welcome Home Roscoe Jenkins*) and a gang of awards including SAG, Golden Globe, BAFTA and the coveted Academy Award for her searing performance as an abusive mother in the highly acclaimed motion picture, *Precious*.

https://youtu.be/qUsPnQj9HXQ

✳ ✳ ✳

December 11, 1978

Roy Wood, Jr. (The Roy Wood, Jr. Collection)

ROY WOOD, JR. – BORN IN BIRMINGHAM, ALABAMA!

They call him Mr. Wood! Once Roy Jr. made up his mind about something it was a waste of breath jawing on about anything else. While he was in college (Florida A&M) working as a news reporter, he blew off his mid-terms to open up for Tommy Davidson after getting bit by the comedy bug hanging around the station cracking jokes. When he graduated he got a job in Birmingham as head writer/producer of the Buckwilde Morning Show, but when they messed with his money he blew them off and bounced to Los Angeles, and started supplying Jamie Foxx's Sirius XM station with prank call bits.

Wood wasn't content. So, he started his own radio show and got top ratings until they whined about him doing a TV show, so he blew them off. He was doing his TV show, *Sullivan & Son* on TBS when the station blew the cast and crew off when the show got canceled. That's when Mr. Wood blew off any worries and got a gig as a correspondent on *The Daily Show* for Comedy Central and hit the road and airwaves as an in-demand stand-up. He's appeared on BET's *Comic View, Late Night with Seth Meyers, Late Show with David Letterman, Late Late Show with Craig Ferguson, Chelsea Lately, Conan* (a frequent visitor) and *Def Comedy Jam*. He released three prank call LPs, contributed to ESPN's *SportsNation* and hosted award shows. And all the while they called him Mr. Wood.

https://youtu.be/AnuePuVFiK8

✳ ✳ ✳

DECEMBER 12, 1980

STIR CRAZY – RELEASED BY COLUMBIA PICTURES!

This Richard Pryor/Gene Wilder comedy marks the first time a film directed by a Black director grossed over 100 million dollars. The director was Sidney Poitier and the true figure was $101,300,000 on a $10 million budget. It was the third biggest box office hit of 1980 right behind *The Empire Strikes Back* and *9-to-5*. With music by Tom Scott, *Stir Crazy* was a fun ride.

The story is about mistaken identity. Pryor and Wilder are in the entertainment business, but have soured of living in New York. So, they pack up and head to Hollywood, taking odd jobs along the way. One of those gigs is a promotion for a local hick bank. The duo dressed up like giant chickens and dance around like fools singing a silly song. When Pryor and Wilder go on their lunch break, two unsavory characters steal their chicken suits and rob the bank. When our clueless and hapless heroes return to work they're arrested and put through a hasty trial that nets them 125 years in a maximum security prison.

Life behind bars does not agree with Pryor and Wilder. Between their court appointed lawyer asking them to relax while he appeals and the guards attempting to break them down, they're ready to go. Their exit strategy makes its appearance in the form of a lucky break. The cocky warden wants to humiliate the two New Yorkers and test their manhood by having them ride the mechanical bull in his office. To the warden's surprise, as well as that of his galoot guard, Wilder can not only stay on the bull, he's a natural born rodeo star. This gets the warden to thinking. If he has Wilder ride in the upcoming annual rodeo he can finally win the big bet from the warden at the competing penitentiary.

The warden's plans fail when Wilder refuses to participate. The guards make him work until he's supposed to drop. He still won't do it. He's put in solitary confinement. No, he won't do it. Finally, he agrees as long as the warden gives him a bigger cell and lets him pick his own rodeo team. Agreed. The team is made up of the group of prisoners Pryor and Wilder have befriended and who all plan to escape during the rodeo. That plan works wonders as the huge mass murderer opens a panel for each member of the crew to slip out. Once Pryor and Wilder leave they all meet up and some of the crew head off to south of the border. As Pryor and Wilder drive off in their car the court appointed lawyer cuts them off. He got a judge to let them off with his newly submitted evidence. They're free to go on with their lives and Pryor, Wilder and the lawyer's cousin, who Wilder is now hooked up with, drive off into the sunset as the lawyer waves his good-bye.

Stir Crazy received favorable reviews. Written by Bruce Jay Friedman, the film featured the talents of Georg Sanford Brown, Franklyn Ajaye, Grand L. Bush, Jobeth Williams and Craig T. Nelson.

https://youtu.be/sU0BGb2KcmU

✳ ✳ ✳

DECEMBER 13, 1967

Jamie Foxx (Public Domain)

JAMIE FOXX (ERIC MARLON BISHOP) – BORN IN TERRELL, TX!

The multi-talented entertainer was a natural when it came to him being funny. In the second grade if the kids were good Foxx's teacher would reward them with a joke session by one of their own. Musically he was admittedly a reluctant piano student and credits his adopted grandmother's insistence for his success. His piano lessons started when he was five years old and Foxx went on to play piano in his Baptist church, lead the choir, sing in a band called "Leather and Lace" and later study classical music and composition at the United States International University. Thanks to her stability and guidance, he spent his formative years as not just a budding musician, but a top-rated student and star athlete (basketball and football, where he played quarterback and was the first in the school's history to throw for over 1,000 yards).

Then one night, Eric Bishop walked into a comedy club and he left as Jamie Foxx. The year was 1989 and it was open mic night. His date dared him to go up, he did and decided he was going to keep doing it. The name change came to assure stage time. When comedy club managers looked at sign-in lists they always tried to get as many female comics up as possible because there were less of them than males. So he adopted the name Jamie since it sounded female. The Foxx part was less strategic; merely a tribute to Redd Foxx.

Foxx cut his teeth at the Comedy Act Theater and other clubs around Los Angeles. He won competitions and got middling attention (though his talent was evident paid gigs were so infrequent he had to sleep on couches as many unknown comedians do), but it was a scheduled week long booking at Atlanta's Comedy Act Theater that changed his career. His week got held-over for weeks as lines grew around the block to see the dynamo performer: joking, singing, doing impressions and generally seducing his audiences with his unmistakable versatility. At the advice of a club promoter, he had a piano placed on stages for his act and yet another dimension was added to his presentation.

In 1991 Foxx became a cast member of the FOX network runaway hit, *In Living Color*. His signature character of Wanda, the ugly girl looking for love, catapulted him to national prominence. He had a recurring role in another FOX hit, *Roc*, and then Jamie Foxx got his own self-titled sitcom on the WB. Soon films were added to the equation (*The Truth About Cats & Dogs, The Great White Hype, Booty Call, Players Club, Held Up*) with his breakthrough in Oliver Stone's 1999 football epic, *Any Given Sunday*. Foxx played opposite acting legend Al Pacino, who after a scene cut told Foxx he was a helluva an actor. That statement played out in nominations for subsequent films, *Collateral* (Academy Award Best Supporting Actor nomination) and *Ray*, the role of musical genius Ray Charles culminating in a Golden Globe for Best Actor and an Oscar as well as a slew of other acting accolades.

On the musical front, Foxx took his cemented fame to concentrate on his initial entertainment goal: music. His collaborations with Twista, Kanye West, Ludacris and Field Mob all shot up to the top of the charts.

His Platinum certified album, *Unpredictable* debuted at #2 and went to #1 the following week. The Grammy Award winning artist released his third album, *Intuition* (his first was 1994's *Peep This*) in 2008 and produced even more hits. He not only made his own chart busters, but made frequent appearances on practically everyone else's songs; including the country group Rascal Flatts. His album *Best Night of My Life* debuted in 2010 followed by *Hollywood: A Story of a Dozen Roses* in 2015.

Besides more movies (*Jarhead, Miami Vice, Dreamgirls*), Foxx expanded his brand by moving into radio. He established "The Foxxhole" for Sirius-XM with a format of comedy and music. He's done animated voices (*Rio*), produced programming for other talents (*In the Flow with Affion Crockett*), hosted award shows (BET Awards, MTV Music Video Awards), toured (2006's The Unpredictable Tour and 2009's The Blame It Tour), had televised stand-up comedy specials (*Straight from the Foxxhole, I Might Need Security, Lost, Stolen and Leaked*) and made more movies (*The Soloist, Due Date, Horrible Bosses, The Amazing Spider-Man 2, Django Unchained, White House Down, Annie, Sleepless, Baby Driver, Robin Hood*).

A perennial award nominee, Jamie Foxx is the recipient of over two dozen acting awards and a half dozen musical honors.

https://youtu.be/6w8o0BwE9Pk

✳✳✳

December 14, 1988

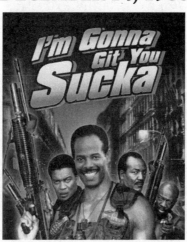

I'm Gonna Git You Sucka – **Released by United Artists!**

This acclaimed parody of Blaxploitation films was written, directed by, and starred Keenen Ivory Wayans. For this ghetto flick masterpiece, he enlisted icons from the 70s era of wacka-wacka guitars and perfectly coiffed fros. Jim Brown, Bernie Casey, Isaac Hayes, Steve James and Antonio Fargas represent the old school. Comedy actors Kadeem Hardison, Dawnn Lewis, Tony Cox, Ja'net DuBois and Anne-Marie Johnson as well as comedians Damon Wayans, Chris Rock, Robin Harris, David Alan Grier and John Witherspoon represent the new breed on the screen (as most were virtual unknowns in 1988). The movie also features Clarence Williams III, KRS-One, Marlon, Kim and Shawn Wayans, Gary Owen, Eve Plumb, Peggy Lipton, Robert Townsend and John Vernon.

The story is all about the gold. The neighborhood that returning military vet, Wayans comes back to has changed. Gone are the apple pies cooling on the window sill, little girls with pigtails playing hop scotch in the street and blue birds chirping on the branches. The place has been saturated with gold chains by the nefarious "Mr. Big." Thanks to this status-symbol-pimp, Wayans' brother OD'd from too many gold chains and thus Mr. Big must be stopped. Now! So Wayans puts together a gang to squash a mob. With names like "Slade," "Spade," "Hammer," "Slammer," "Kung Fu Joe" and "Flyguy" there's no way they can be stopped. Watch out, Whitey!

I'm Gonna Git You Sucka was met with positive reviews and was even shot as a TV pilot with many of the actors reprising their screen roles. The show didn't sell, but the OG made good. On a $3 million budget, *I'm Gonna Git You Sucka* grossed $13,030,057 at the box office.

https://youtu.be/BWNQTqMkezc

✳ ✳ ✳

DECEMBER 16, 1965

J B Smoove celebrating his 50th Birthday in style (*Humor Mill Magazine*)

J. B. SMOOVE (JERRY ANGELO BROOKS) – BORN IN PLYMOUTH, NC!

Smoove grew up in Mount Vernon, New York, then headed to Virginia where he attended Norfolk State University. There he took the route of most students, he studied hard, worked a job printing T-shirts and tinkered with model trains and he got into stand-up comedy. That's why he had to change his name from Jerry Brooks to J. B. Smoove. He looked more like a J. B. than a Jerry.

Following a memorable appearance of HBO's *Def Comedy Jam* and several high-profile tours, Smoove's explosive style of physical comedy caught the industry's eye and he became the king of the recurring characters. He had the recurring role of Leon Black on Larry David's *Curb Your Enthusiasm,* as well as roles on *Everybody Hates Chris* and *Saturday Night Live.* On the latter Smoove was also a writer.

J.B. Smoove also got to sit at the big table. He was a full cast member on the Brad Garrett / Joely Fisher sitcom, *'Til Death* on FOX. He was featured on *The Millers* for CBS. Smoove was a cast member on the sketch show, *Cedric the Entertainer Presents* and hosted the Russell Simmons stand-up series, *Stand-Up at the El Rey.*

However, Smoove's more than a creature of television. Kicking things off with 1997's *Lesser Prophets* (in the role of Chucky), Smoove was omnipresent in films; appearing in *With or Without You, Pootie Tang, Mr. Deeds, Date Night, Hall Pass, The Sitter, We Bought a Zoo, The Dictator, A Haunted House, Think Like A Man, Clear History, Top Five* and many others.

Smoove's animated personality allowed him to be used extensively. He's been a pitchman for various products. He's lent his voice to animated fare (*The Simpsons, American Dad, Smurfs 2, Black Dynamite,* and *Robot Chicken*). Smoove was instrumental in reviving the Wanda Sykes produced version of NBC's stand-up comedy competition, *Last Comic Standing.* He served as its energetic host. Smoove's one of The Replacers in the video game Call of Duty: Black-Ops II and provides the voice of Dr. Ray D'Angelo Harris, host of the Chakra Attack radio show in Grand Theft Auto V. He even transcended his own celebrity and has played versions of himself in a number of projects including Kevin Hart's reality show, *Real Husbands of Hollywood.*

In 2007 JB Smoove earned the Writers Guild of America award for Best Comedy/Variety Series and his first comedy special *JB Smoove: That's How I Dooz It* premiered on Comedy Central in 2012.

https://youtu.be/qUOmlE-O5Pg

✳ ✳ ✳

December 17, 1979

Lil Rel w/ Tiffany Haddish at Essence (Humor Mill Magazine)

Milton "Lil Rel" Howery – Born.

A native of the West Side of Chicago, The Lion's Den in East Chicago gave birth to the stand-up comedy career of Howery. He was soon proficient enough to expand his horizons and competed in NBC's *Last Comic Standing* in 2007. Turns out he liked TV and more importantly TV liked him. Howery's next televised break came on the FOX reboot of the '90's hit sketch star maker, *In Living Color*. The revival lasted less time than you could spell that word, but Howery didn't go unnoticed.

Lil Rel landed a gig at TruTV on another sketch comedy show. He wrote, produced and co-starred in *Friends of the People* in 2012. Several years later he got the breakout part he'd been looking for thanks to another young comedian.

Jerrod Carmichael was also making some noise on the comedy circuit. So much so that NBC greenlit a self-titled sitcom, *The Carmichael Show* featuring Loretta Devine and David Alan Grier as the star's parents. Howery got the part of his recently divorced brother, Robert; more affectionately known as Bobby. His ex-wife was played by another comedy sensation – Tiffany Haddish.

In 2016 he performed on his own stand-up special on Netflix. *Kevin Hart Presents: Lil Rel: RELevent* streamed nationwide and exposed Howery to yet another medium. Next was film as he played the friend and eventual hero in Jordan Peele's surprise hit of 2017 – *Get Out*. The role of TSA officer, Rod Williams earned Howery the MTV Movie & TV Award for "Best Comedic Performance." In 2018, Rel's good friend, Mr Carmichael, executive produced the sitcom *Rel* for FOX.

https://youtu.be/hS-BupiTBto

✳ ✳ ✳

DECEMBER 18, 1987

EDDIE MURPHY'S *RAW* – RELEASED BY PARAMOUNT PICTURES!

Filmed in the Madison Square Garden complex and directed by Robert Townsend this stand-up comedy concert film was Eddie Murphy's second such effort following *Delirious*, but his first with a wide theatrical release. Besides being a highly acclaimed critical and box office success, *Raw* lives up to its title and held the record of most "f**ks" (223) in film (beating out even Al Pacino's *Scarface*) until Robert DeNiro's *Goodfellas* came along several years later.

Raw opens with a sketch (featuring Tatyana Ali) of a young Eddie Murphy telling a joke and merrily cursing his way through it. That's the theme of the film as grown up Murphy emerges from behind the see-through curtain illuminating his posed silhouette. Once the earth-shaking applause dies down Murphy launches into a series of bits reflecting his station in life and show business. He talks about celebrities (Mr. T, Michael Jackson) who didn't like what he said about them in *Delirious*. He riffs on fans who didn't like his gay jokes from the same film. He clowns Bill Cosby for criticizing Murphy's act as being too scatological and how Murphy got advice from Richard Pryor to tell Cosby to shut the f**k up.

Murphy goes on during the 93 minutes to discuss his love for Pryor and his influence on young Eddie. He talks about non-English speaking people only yelling out his curse words to him; the perils of strange tail diseases and marriage; divorce and costly alimony; the need to find a sheltered woman from the bush who knows nothing about alimony; the need to keep her sheltered so American women don't hip her to alimony; the surprising fact that men cheat and women will do the same; eating burgers made by your mama as a kid and not McDonald's like the other kids; uncoordinated white people; overly-aggressive Italians and drunk relatives round out the set.

Raw was written by Eddie Murphy and Keenen Ivory Wayans (the opening sketch). Ernest Dickerson did the cinematography and the film made $50,504,655 at the box office.

https://youtu.be/YMqMKxJJYvY

✳ ✳ ✳

DECEMBER 19, 1944

Tim Reid speaking at the USDA Black History Month celebration February 16, 2012, (Public Domain)

TIMOTHY L. "TIM" REID – BORN IN NORFOLK, VIRGINIA!

Reid got into comedy as a duo. He was working for the DuPont Corporation when he met Caucasian insurance salesman, Tom Dreesen. They reluctantly partnered on an anti-drug program for local schools to try and make a difference. It was 1968 – what can I tell you? People cared about society back then. Anyway, they basically had to go around and preach about the evils of drugs. The difference with these two was they had a sense of humor. They engaged the kids with skits and stand-up. It was actually working and Tim and Tom were pleased merely being good members of the community. To them they were just helping inform the youth. That is until a kid asked them if they ever thought about being a comedy team. The thought had never crossed their minds, but now that the idea was in front of them they went for it and became the first inter-racial comedy team in American history (circa 1911 Bert Williams and Leon Errol were the first time a black and white teamed up but it was only for a 20-minute routine. They were *not* a comedy team). Tim & Tom appeared on *The Tonight Show with Johnny Carson* numerous times and toured extensively, but the country wasn't really ready to see a white man and a black man making fun of being a white man and a black man so the team dissolved after five years and Reid moved more towards comedy acting.

Tim Reid broke into television guest starring on sitcoms. He worked on *That's My Mama, Rhoda, Fernwood 2 Night, The Richard Pryor Show,* and *What's Happening*!! Then he got his big break on *WKRP in Cincinnati* in the role of ultra-cool radio disc jockey, Venus Flytrap. The CBS hit lasted for six seasons. When that show was canceled he stayed on CBS in the light-hearted detective show, *Simon & Simon* (Reid was not one of the Simon brothers). He played the part of Lieutenant Marcel "Downtown" Brown. In 1988 he starred in the critically acclaimed, *Frank's Place.* On this (CBS) program Reid had the part of a professor who inherits a restaurant in Louisiana. The realistic depiction, stellar acting and outstanding writing might not have been rewarded with longevity (the show was short-lived), but received well-deserved accolades. *Frank's Place* won Reid the "Best Actor in a Quality Series" award and an NAACP Image Award for "Outstanding Lead Actor in a Comedy Series."

Reid was always in our face. He was Ray Campbell on the Tia and Tamara Mowry sitcom, *Sister, Sister* from 1994-1999. Then he had a recurring role from 2004-2006 as William Barnett on *That '70s Show* on FOX. And when we didn't see him we still felt his touch. As a director, Reid helmed feature films as well as television programs. Going full circle from his roots, he created an after school special called *Stop the Madness*. It was an anti-drug project.

For his various outstanding and distinguished contributions over the years, Tim Reid was named to the board of directors of the American Civil War Center in 2011 and in 2014 he received an honorary doctorate from VCU.

https://youtu.be/K27f6AM2_hg

✳✳✳

DECEMBER 19, 1987

PARTNERS IN CRIME – PREMIERED ON HBO!

Fresh off the success of his hit feature film, *Hollywood Shuffle*, hot director Robert Townsend, treated the public to a comedy variety banquet. *Partners in Crime* combined sketches ("The Bold, The Black & The Beautiful," "How the West Was Won ... Maybe"), music and stand-up while introducing the world to some unsung heroes at the same time.

Directed by Townsend and Walter C. Miller, the funfest featured Robin Harris, Franklyn Ajaye, Jesse Aragon, David Alan Grier, Marlon Wayans, Anne-Marie Johnson, Tommy Davidson, Barry Diamond, Damon Wayans, Lewis Dix, Roy Fegan, Bobby Brown, Myra J, Paul Mooney, Bobby McGee, M C Hammer, Kim Wayans, Kool Moe Dee, Don Reed, Sinbad, Patrice Rushen, Keenan Ivory Wayans, Jimmy Woodard, John Witherspoon, Shawn Wayans, Stephanie Williams, Brenda Russell, Reynaldo Rey, Myreah Moore, Howard Hewett, Carl Craig and Cindera Che.

The musical director was the amazing Patrice Rushen. Townsend and Keenan Ivory Wayans served as executive producers. The episodes were released on DVD on February 2, 1991.

https://youtu.be/C3cVVUO8xjg

✳ ✳ ✳

DECEMBER 20, 1912

Ernie Morrison aka Sunshine Sammy reading *Motion Picture Magazine* in 1920 (Public Domain)

ERNEST FREDRIC "ERNIE" MORRISON ("SUNSHINE SAMMY") – BORN IN NEW ORLEANS!

Sunshine Sammy got his stage name by behaving. When a film crew member persuaded young Morrison's father to bring in the newborn for a shoot, the infant defied expectations as well as trepidations and did not cry. He was a professional right out of the womb. The film crew dubbed him "Sunshine" for making it such a cheerful day and Morrison's father threw in the "Sammy" part. Oh, he would be given other names later on, like "Little Sambo" and "Smiling Sambo," but for his maiden voyage, "Sunshine Sammy" was what Morrison responded to when summoned.

With his early reputation established, Sammy became a popular and in demand child actor. He worked opposite silent screen favorites, Harold Lloyd and Snub Pollard. From there he was signed to a long term studio contract, making Sammy the first Black actor to be signed to such an agreement (child or adult) when he put his Johnny Cochran on the dotted line for mega-producer, Hal Roach in 1919. Roach's first project for Sammy was a series of shorts about a little Black boy (surely to be an acting stretch), but the distributors wanted nothing to do with it. Only one episode was ever shown to the public. This left Roach with the dilemma of what to do with his young talent.

One afternoon Roach was casting for his *Our Gang* series about a group of kids and their antics. He'd tired of auditioning grown-up acting child thespians and took a moment to look out of his office window. Across the street in a parking lot were regular kids playing in a regular, realistic manner. They were of different races and sizes and Roach had a brainstorm. He'd rewrite his cutesy project to be more down-to-Earth and cast Sunshine Sammy in this retooled version of the proposed *Our Gang*.

Sunshine Sammy was featured in the *Our Gang* series from 1922-1924. He set the template of those other Black cast members (Alan Hoskins as "Farina," Eugene Jackson as "Pineapple," Matthew Beard as "Stymie" and William Thomas as "Buckwheat") to follow since most shorts with children were not as innovative as *Our Gang* when it came to racial harmony. Instead of Sammy being picked on and the butt of the majority of jokes, he was just one of the kids having the same fun and bouts of trouble, regardless of his race. Even when an occasional insensitive Caucasian writer would attempt to inject some racial jibes, Roach would shut it down for the most part and insist that Sammy (his protégé) was just one of the gang.

In 1924 Sammy left the *Our Gang* cast and went to work on vaudeville. He appeared in shows that also featured up & comers Abbott & Costello and that hot young comic of the day, Jack Benny. Sammy had a partner now, Sleepy Williams and they toured Australia. When they got back from their successful run, Sammy was plucked up by producer, Sam Katzman to be an East Side Kid. This would be another first for Sammy. He was the first Black kid in the *Our Gang* fledgling series. This time he would be the first and only Black cast member of the *East Side Kids,* an established and popular series of the time. Sammy played the part of "Scruno" and went all Stanislavski on them by drawing on his early experiences as a New York kid from theEast Side. He was a hit.

Sammy stayed with the *East Side Kids* for three years. He left when he was offered a chance to perform with the Step Brothers. They were a Black film and dance act and Sammy wanted in. He got his groove back right before he was drafted into the Army during World War II. When he returned he was still in demand, but not for the kind of work he wanted. He was approached to do *The Bowery Boys*, another series of shorts devoted to getting laughs from the shenanigans of young boys raised on the wrong side of the tracks. Once again Sammy would be the only Black, but this time he declined. He said he didn't like the set up. Perhaps too much-cooning was in the works.

Uncharacteristic for entertainers of his era, Morrison made a good amount of money in show business and apparently kept most of it. There were never any stories of financial hardships and in his later years he quit the glamour biz and went to work at an aircraft plant developing missiles. He occasionally would dip his toe back into the world of make believe, like in the 1970s when he appeared on the CBS hit sitcom, *Good Times*. However, he didn't make a full return to work before the cameras and after scores of projects, Morrison died of cancer in Lynwood, California on July 24, 1989.

https://youtu.be/uxD0Ke7SS6g

✳ ✳ ✳

DECEMBER 21, 2001

HOW HIGH – RELEASED BY UNIVERSAL PICTURES!

Entertainment Weekly ranked this stoner film as third in their top ten. Other mainstream critics dismissed the Dustin Lee Abraham written movie, but what do they know? It won a Stony Award in 2002. Not bad for the first feature film of director, Jesse Dylan. Starring rappers Method Man and Redman, *How High* was a celebration of smoking weed and hallucinating.

Two academic loafers get a break is the basic story. Their friend dies. So naturally they use his ashes for fertilizer and grow weed that when smoked brings forth visions of the dead friend. However, he's a spook with a purpose.

He gives his buddies all the right answers to their Finals exams which land them into Harvard University. There, they hook up with beautiful girls and-frustrate the Dean (Cain) with their free-wheeling falderal and anecdotes. It's all good until their plant is ripped off and the two are actually forced to study. When that doesn't work they dig up another dead guy, smoke his ashes, but no go. Looks like they're out of college until a truth serum experiment works and they pass their exam. It's the kind of thing that happens all the time.

How High had a number of comedy cameos. Comedians, Mike Epps, Fred Willard, Tracy Morgan and Garrett Morris are featured as well as comedic personalities, Obba Babatunde, Anna Maria Horsford, Jeffrey Jones, Lark Voorhies, Hector Elizondo, Essence Atkins, Spalding Gray, Chuck Liddell and Cypress Hill. Produced by Danny DeVito and five others *How High* was-made on a budget of $20 million and grossed $31,283,790 at the box office.

https://youtu.be/q0b0s5oZ_Pw

DECEMBER 23, 1975

Azhar Usman (3rd from left) at 2nd #laughnearminimalistfurniture show, 2016 (Instagram)

MUHAMMAD USMAN – BORN IN CHICAGO, ILLINOIS!

The off-spring of Indian parents, Usman's impressive and extensive credentials almost sound like the set-up of a good joke. "A Muslim walks into a bar and starts speaking Spanish…" "The Ayatollah of Laughter," as he's known, started his comedy career after a career as a lawyer. He banned together with Preacher Moss and Azeem Muhammad (later Mohammed Amer) to mount the comedy tour, *Allah Made Me Funny* and Usman co-wrote and produced a documentary on the tour.

Usman is a numbers man. He speaks three languages, has performed in 23 countries on five continents and has been reviewed by over 100 media outlets worldwide. He's also opened up for Dave Chappelle (who says

Usman is "untouchable") over 40 times and Georgetown University listed him as one of the "500 Most Influential Muslims." CNN did a special on him in 2008 called *America's Funniest Muslim*. Few dispute the claim. Usman's produced films, been in film (with Nia Long and Danny Glover) and been interviewed for multiple documentaries. He premiered the one-man show he wrote in Chicago and serves as an advisor to the Inner-City Muslim Action Network there, while practicing some law on the side.

https://youtu.be/gz4WrCQuNVI

***

DECEMBER 29, 1966

Mystro Clark (2nd from left) w/ Marc Howard, D'Militant and Keith Morris (The Littleton Collection)

MYSTRO CLARK – BORN IN DAYTON, OHIO!

Known as the "100% Brother," Clark got it in at the legendary Comedy Act Theater in Los Angeles in the late 1980s. In this pre-Black Comedy Boom period he was mentored by talents such as Robin Harris and Reynaldo Rey and honed a rapid fire comedic style grounded in precise visual imagery. Those writing skills served him well as a writer for the Bill Bellamy show mixing live action with advanced puppetry, *Cousin Skeeter*.

Clark was seasoned by constantly being on stage. By staying in performance shape when opportunities arose he was ready. One such career break came when Don Cornelius decided to step down as full time host of his cultural phenomenon, *Soul Train*. After trying out numerous guest hosts, the long running program's creator decided on Clark. His energetic approach gave the show new life and alerted the 1997 audience that there was a new sheriff in town and they better like him. The audience liked him enough, but unfortunately internal conflicts with the micromanaging Cornelius lead to a termination of the Clark Era in 1999, but not an end to the Clark juggernaut.

Clark could also act. He starred in the sitcom, *The Newz,* as well as *The Show, OffLimits* and *Lovespring International.* And when he wasn't working in television full time he was guest-starring on any number of sitcoms. He also did feature films. Clark was featured in the Carrot Top epic movie, *Chairman of the Board.* He co-starred with Dolph Lundgren in *Storm-Chaser* and appeared in *Shrink* with Kevin Spacey and the film *Out at the Wedding* in 2006.Other credits include hosting syndicated children's programs and releasing the comedy album, *Sexy, Funny Bastard.*

https://youtu.be/nq6J_C15rMM

✳✳✳

THE MYSTERY DATES...

Some comedy legends have birthdays that are unknown or unverifiable. This does not minimize their impact on comedy, and since we know they were born, we used this portion of the encyclopedia to recognize their contributions.

Kym Whitley (r) w/ Cookie Hull on Katt Williams' It's Pimpin, Pimpin Tour, 2008 (Littleton Collection)

KYM ELIZABETH WHITLEY – BORN IN SHAKER HEIGHTS, OHIO!

A former personal assistant to Arsenio Hall, Whitley merged into comedy without having to sleep on another comic's couch or futon. She got a huge break when she toured with the stage play, *Beauty Shop* by Shelly Garrett in 1989. In the early 90s she hit the TV circuit and guest starred her way around the channels. Whitley appeared in *Vinny and Bobby, The Parent 'Hood, Martin, Married . . . with Children, The Wayans Bros., Moesha, That's So Raven, Arli$$* and *Curb Your Enthusiasm*. She was a regular on *Sparks, Black Dynamite, Animal Practice* and *Young and Hungry* and had recurring roles on *My Brother and Me, The Parkers, Let's Stay Together* and *The Boondocks*.

Kym Whitley got into films in 1999 in *Beverly Hood*. Once in she had a succession of film roles in *Next Friday* (where off-camera Ice Cube tricked her with real liquor in a scene and not the usual iced tea), *Nutty Professor II: The Klumps, House Party 4, Baby Boy, Deliver Us from Eva, Love Chronicles, Along Came Polly, The Perfect Man, Fun with Dick & Jane, College Road Trip, I Love You, Man, Rango, Transformers, We Bought a Zoo* and more.

Whitley was the co-host of the early precursor female panel discussion shows, *Oh, Drama* on BET. She co-hosted the talk show, *The Brian McKnight Show* in 2010 and in 2013 she got her own reality show, *Raising Whitley* on Oprah Winfrey's network, OWN.

A civic minded individual, Whitley used her celebrity to raise public awareness on childhood food allergies. She co-created the T-shirt, "Don't Feed Me" for children to wear to alert caregivers of the needs of that specific child. The foods they're allergic to are printed on their shirt.

In 2004 Kym Whitley was nominated for Outstanding Supporting Actress (*Deliver Us from Eva*) by the BET Comedy Awards.

https://youtu.be/U4wWz38CDjg

✳ ✳ ✳

Simply Marvalous (Pricilla Clarke of PC & Associates) Source: Bob Sumner

SIMPLY MARVALOUS (MARVA MONCRIEFFE) – BORN IN BATON ROUGE, LA!

This woman is an unsung pioneer who established her pedigree during the Black Comedy Boom. The Louisiana native opened the doors for many female comediennes who followed, with her down-home brand of raucous humor and uncompromising style. However, it was her accessibility and ability to work a crowd in large or intimate settings that set her apart and made her a role model for her peers.

Marvalous' career was brief but left a lasting impression. She catapulted to national notoriety with her galvanizing performance on HBO's *Def Comedy Jam*. From there Marvalous became the first of the new wave to shoot a coveted HBO comedy special when receiving the opportunity to tape one was truly special. Hers was a smash hit and she followed it up with appearances in the films, *Class Act* (1992), *Country Estates* (1993) and *House Party 3* (1994). She was a huge draw around the country and had a fan base that was busting at the seams. With her catchphrase of "How yer doinnnnn?," she was the unofficial queen of comedy in the early 1990s until life stepped in and changed Marvalous' fate.

Her mother got sick and Simply Marvalous put her career on hold to return to Baton Rouge to take care of her. The illness lingered, and the comedy world kept moving. New stars were introduced to the public and those who laid the bricks for their success were soon pushed back into the recesses of memory. Marvalous returned to the big screen in 2005's *A Get2Gether*, but then fell ill herself. After a long bout she passed away on August 8, 2018 leaving a void in comedy that will never be filled.

https://youtu.be/KWdgWvw_-5k

✳ ✳ ✳

Billy Kersands (Public Domain)

BILLY KERSANDS – BORN CIRCA 1842!

Little is known about Kersands early years. Nobody even remembers when or where he was born and even if they did they're no longer around to tell us. All we know about Billy Kersands is the most important thing you can derive from knowledge of any entertainer – he was damn good. Oh, we also know that he had a big mouth. Not at he'd rat you out, but his gaping hole was his chief comedic device. He could fill it with pool balls, cups and saucers or he could contort it to get a laugh from the crowd.

Kersands only had crowds. He got into minstrelsy in the early 1860s and rode the wave of its popularity since letting Black men perform. Minstrelsy itself had begun in the 1820s, but had been exclusive to white men until the Civil War when many white minstrels went to fight making this form of entertainment now a viable profession for a Black man in America. Kersands seized the moment.

Billy Kersands was Black minstrelsy biggest star. It was said that a minstrel show without Billy Kersands was like a circus without elephants. He worked with a number or Black troupes doing tours stateside and overseas. While giving a command performance to Queen Victoria, Kersands remarked on how his mouth was so big that if it was any bigger they'd have to move his ears.

In 1885, Kersands started his own troupe. "The Kersands Minstrels" were known for their acrobatic marching band. Kersands challenged anybody to outmarch them and put up $1,000 to anyone who could. It was said that 200 pound Billy Kersand's dance, "The Virginia Essence" became the soft shoe. In 1904 he tried to do shows in the East, but Kersands loved performing in the South and the people there who made him feel at home.

Kersands was a strange mix. He played upon his dumb-coon stage persona to appease white audiences, who loved him; especially because he had big lips, etc. Then at the same time as he was being a buffoon, he'd drop anti-slavery rhetoric in his routines. He'd allude to equality when he thought nobody was listening and throw in African-American folklore. This led to an attraction that had theater owners lightening up on their segregation policies to allow more paying patrons into their midst. All thanks to a man with a big mouth who we know very little about except that his mouth shut permanently in 1915.

https://www.there is no footage of Kersands.com

J. Anthony Brown (r) w/ Damon Williams (The Damon Williams Collection)

J. ANTHONY BROWN – BORN IN COLUMBIA, SC!

The man made clothes. When kids are asked what they want to do when they grow up, Brown probably said he wanted to dress people. The future award winning comedian was a tailor who wanted to be a cloths designer. Then for some reason (probably money) he entered a talent show in his resident town of Atlanta, told some jokes he'd put together just for the occasion – and won. Hell, the club liked him so much they made him the house MC for the next two years. The only thing that broke-up that side-tracking relationship was Brown moving to Los Angeles to be a comic in the main arena.

Brown got to California and got to work. He landed a job as a writer for *The Arsenio Hall Show*, stayed there for five years then wrote for sitcoms all while lighting up L.A. comedy stages. He held court regularly weekend at Maverick's Flat on the world-renown Crenshaw Boulevard and every prominent Black comedian in the early 1990s went through that spot to perform, but also to see J. Anthony Brown destroy the stage. His reputation as a killer comedian spread quickly and the club had to do two shows a night with a line down the block waiting for the second show.

Success in entertainment was nice, but Brown was never far from a sewing machine. He still stitched together clothes while at the same time sewing together an impressive resume. In 1996 he got a radio gig working on *The Tom Joyner Morning Show* as comic relief. He popularized many of his night club bits and his hilarious song parodies. Brown was a solid attraction to the program and 20 years later he was still there. Then in 2016 he bounced over to *The Steve Harvey Morning Show* to slay to commuting-to-work audience there.

However, all these musical chairs were taking place in early hours of the day which left Brown the rest of the day to get off and he did. He not only did stand-up in clubs he blanketed the television landscape (*Def Comedy Jam, Showtime at the Apollo, Vibe, An Evening at the Improv* and *The Oprah Winfrey Show*). He got his acting on and played guest-starring roles (*Sparks, The Parkers*), recurring roles because they liked him so much the first time around (*Moesha, The Parent 'Hood, Living Single*), films (*Def Jam's How to be a Player, Drumline, Mr. 3000*) and he hosted BET's *Comic View* for two seasons.

Brown also kept his side hustles. He has his comedy club, "The J. Spot," as well as "The J. Anthony Brown Clothing Store" and of course "The J. Anthony Brown Collection" (sold outta his store). Brown is also the recipient of a NAACP Image Award and a Peabody Award.

https://youtu.be/8lby0L6OJ1Q

*** ✱ ✱ ✱

Erik Griffin (The Erik Griffin Collection)

Erik Griffin – Born in Los Angeles!

G riffin is one of those performers that has a huge hit and everybody thinks that person was an overnight success. Not likely. This guy put in the work to have a solid foundation for that hit when it came along and to make the most of it. The hit being Showtime's, Jim Carrey produced, *I'm Dying Up Here*. The hour-long dramedy uses the L. A. comedy scene of the 1970s as the backdrop to tell the story of struggling artists and dysfunctional camaraderie. Griffin plays a veteran stand-up who traded in youthful aspirations to realistically take a writing job penning for Sonny & Cher. It pays the bills, but doesn't feed the soul and he's excellent in the role.

Part of the reason Griffin brings so many layers to his work is because he's lived it. Little is publicized about his upbringing, but what is known is that he made his bones in comedy in L.A. as a regular at clubs like the Haha Café in North Hollywood. He did the audition grind and landed parts – a lot of them.

Erik Griffin had several dozen acting credits under his belt before *I'm Dying Up Here*. He was on *One Day at a Time, Mike and Dave Need Wedding Dates, Arrested Development, Daddy Knows Best, Bob's Burgers* and *Roomies*, just to name more than a few. He also showed he had comedy chops (*Comics Without Borders, Comedy-TV, The Kevin Nealon Show, Absolutely Jason Stuart, Dom Irrera Live*, etc.). He's toured, done two comedy specials (so far) and written for others. So, why would anybody think he'd have a hard time playing a seasoned comedian?

https://youtu.be/eL-2AekMdh8

✳✳✳

Bobby Law (Bobby Law Collection)

BOBBY LAW – BORN IN COLUMBUS, GA!

Law was a promoter's dream. You could hire one man and get two and sometimes three acts. He was literally a one-man show. Bobby Law, the ex-Marine with plenty of life experiences and hilarious stories was one act. He could give you 45 minutes without sweating. Women adored him because he was good looking and athletically built. Bobby Law the comedian dressed well and spoke that country accent that makes you feel like you could trust him. Here was a nice guy you could feel comfortable with so why not laugh?

Then Bobby Law had his alter ego, Uncle Cleophus Brown. Once Law left the stage to resounding applause the host would do a few minutes and introduce Cleophus, the backwoods, country gregarious character with a wild-haired wig, a raggedy grill, crotch hugging pulled up slacks, an ever present 40-ouncer and a shirt you'd have

Uncle Cleophus Brown

left in the closet during your selection process. Uncle Cleophus was loud, crude and knee-slapping funny. He had a catch phrase when someone from the audience would say, "What them girls doing to you?" Law would reply, "They jockin and jockin and jockin a brotha." He was a show-stopper and a tremendous actor because nobody in any audience ever knew it was the same guy.

If that wasn't enough talent for one live performer to have – Law was a consummate guitarist. He'd began his comedy career doing impressions in between band sets to keep the entertainment going and became a respected stand-up. That was the beauty of employing Bobby Law, with a band backing him up or all alone with just his axe, Bobby Law could smoke. The

Bobby Law, the Musician

guy could also sing. So any promoter with a limited budget, but good intensions loved Bobby Law. He was your opener, middle and closer. A veritable triple threat.

The man should've been a household name and certified legend based on his versatility and professionalism. He appeared on television (*BET's Comic View*) films (*They Love Me, Out On Parole*) and he toured internationally as a comedian and musician. However, Bobby Law was stricken with cancer and after a lengthy battle, succumbed in the Summer of 2018. His funeral was not only attended by family, friends, comedians and fellow musicians, but also by many of his fans who'd simply been members of his audience over the years. Many of them wept.

https://youtu.be/D-dD13ASD64

✳ ✳ ✳

Valued Players …

Every person who has devoted their life to comedy is important and deserves mention. *On This Day in Comedy* recognizes these vital individuals and their dedication to preserving the art form by performing in any venue where laughs are needed, hosting comedy nights, writing for comedians, sitcoms and films; hosting podcast and radio programs; entertaining on cruise ships, bringing laughter to our troops overseas, blogging, vlogging, promoting honestly, and all the other countless (and often thankless) functions that makes comedy the best art in the world and you fine folks its immortals:

A-Train, Aaron Aryanpur, Aaron Westly, AC, Ace, AD (Anthony Demmer), AD Hodge, Adam Carral, A J Jamal, Akilah Hughes, Akintunde, Al Dipmore, Ala Bama, Alex Thomas, Alexander Brown, Alexis Rhee, Alfred Robles, Algiers Diamond, Ali LeRoy, Ali Roc, Ali Siddiq, Alice Nikki Johnson, Alisha Coley, All D. Freeman, Allen Hoskins (Farina), Alley Cat (L.A.), Alley Cat (Oakland), Alvin Childress, Alycia Cooper, Amanda Seales, Ambrose Jones, Amil Johnson, Aminah Imani, Amir Kabiri, Amir Rahim, Andre Covington, Andre Lavelle, Andre Paradise, Andrew Fraser, Angel Gaines, Angel Harper, Angela Means Kaaya (Bye Felicia), Angelique Cope, Angelique Perrin, Angelo Sykes, Angie Montgomery, Annie McKnight, Anthony Armstrong, Anthony Driver, Anthony Griffin, Anthony Ramos, Anthony Stone, Arceneaux & Mitchell (Curtis Arceneaux & Norman Mitchell), Ardie Fuqua, Arlene Lopez, Armando "Pops" Cosio Jr., Arnesto, Arnez Jay, Ashia Sims, Aubrey Lyles (Miller & Lyles), Aubrey Plaza, Averell Carter, Azeem Muhammed

B Cole, B Funny, B Jones, Baratunde Thurston, Barbara Carlyle, Barbara Perez, Barry Brewer, Basial, Belinda Criddell, Ben Carter, Beny Mena, Bernard B, Bernard L Eatmon, Beth Payne, Big Boy, Big Daddie Fitz, BigDaddyWiburn, Big Head Bo Hawkins, Big Keef, Big Mo Dixon, Big Ness, Big Rome, Big Spike (Thompson), Bigg Q, Bigg Weezy, Bill Hill, Bill Santiago, Bill Torres, Billy D. Washington, Billy Sorrells, Black Boi, Black Kasper, Black Prince, Bo P (Preston Barnes), Bob Height, Bob Sumner, Bobby Brown,

Bobby McGee, Bone, Boomer Nichols, B-Phlat, Brandon Bowlin, Brandon Marshall, Brandon Paxton, Brandon T. Jackson, Brandonn Mosley, Brent B-Real, Brian Hooks, Brooklyn Mike, Bruce Jingles, B T Kingsley, Bubba Loc, Butler "Stringbeans" May, Butterbeans & Susie, Butterfly McQueen

Cain Lopez, Cam Jones, Can't Get Rite, Capone, Caramel Grai, Carl Banks, Carl Payne, Carleton D. Murrell, Carlos Oscar, Carmen Barton, Carter Gregory, Carly Carr, Casper, Cassius Creflo, Cathy Lewis, Cha Cha Sandoval, Chalant, Charles Allen, Charles Cozart, Charles Hicks, Charles Sanchez, Charles Walden, Chello Davis, Chinedu Unaka, Chloe Hilliard, Chocolate, Chris G, Chris Hester, Chris Redd, Chris Tabb, Chris Thomas, Chriss Charles, Christian Redd, Christina Payne, Christopher Brown, Christy Medrano, Chuckie Miller, Chuy Bravo, Clayton English, Clayton Thomas, Cliff Hughes, Clipperman Godboldo, Coco, Cole & Johnson, Colin 'Cya' Taylor, Comedian Job, Cookie Hull, Coolaide, Corlotta Adams, Cornell Ross, Corey D'Markus, Corey Mack, Corey "Zooman" Miller, Cory Fernandez, Cory "Showtime" Robinson, Craig Bush, Craig Capone, Craig Frazier, Cream Stew (Shinya Ueda, Teppei Arita), Crys Styles, Crystal P

Da Jester, Damon Williams, Dana Austin, Dana Point, Daniel Dugar, Dannon Green, Danny Grayson, Daran Howard, Darian Perkins, Darius Bradford, Darrel Heath, Darrell Kelly, Darren Fields, Darrow Igus, Darrell J. Carter, Darryl Black, Darryl "Doc" Carter, Darryl Lenox, Daryl Kamack, Dat Phan, Daugne Keith, David A. Arnold, Dave Edwards, Dave Johnson, Dave Tyree, David Alvarez, David Banks, David Damas, David Mann, David Raibon, Dawn Keith, DB, D. C. Erwin, Sr., D. C. Erwin, Jr., D C Young Fly, D. D. Rainbow, Dean Austin, Dean Edwards, Dean Roberts, Debi Gutierrez, Deborah Delk, Debra Terry, Debra Wilson, Dee Brooks, Del Harrison, Del Van Dyke, DeLayne, Demond Wilson, Dennis Gaxiola, Denny Live, Denzel Snipes, Derrick DT Thompson, Derrick Ellis, Derrick Fox, Derrick Mohammad, Derrick Smart, Derrick Xavier Cohen, Derrico MrComedy Cathey, Detroit Red, DeWayne, Dexter Tucker, Dezz White, Diane Corder, Dick Black, Dijon, Dillon Garcia, Dino Shorte, Dirty South, D J Pooh, D K Dudley, D'Lai, D Lo, D. Lamont Hall, Don "Bubba" Bexley, Don Garrett, Don Reed, Donald Brooks, Donald Lacy, Donald Randell, Donna Gooch, Donna Lewis, Donnell Kearney, Donte Coleman, Doo Doo Brown, Dother, Double D, Doug Starks, Doug Williams, Douglas Howington, Downtown (Hitoshi Matsumoto, Masatoshi Hamada), Downtown Tony Brown, Dr. Lou, Dread Archie, Jr., Drew Fraser, D-Rock, D-Sharpe, Dwayne Jackson, Dwayne Perkins, Dyana Ortelli

E. Green, Ebon Leggs, Eddie Bryant, Eddie Ray, Eddie Who, Edwonda White, E J Nonstop, Ella Joyce, Ellen Cleghorne, Elliot Enriquez, Emani Moore, Enns Mitchell, Eric Andre, Eric Blake, Eric Jerome Dickey, Eric Rhone, Erica Clark, Erica Vittina Phillips, Erik Clark, Erik Terrell, Ernest Hogan, Ernie G., Esau McGraw, Esther Ku, Evan Lionel, Evelyn

Faceman, Farooq, Fat Doctor, Fats Waller, Fifi Whitman, Fig, Finesse Mitchell, Fire (formerly Small Frie), Flame Monroe, Flex Alexander, Flournoy E. Miller (Miller & Lyles), Food Stamp, Foolish, Francesca Ramsey, Frank Holder, Frank Lyles, Frantz Casseus, Fred Armisen, Freddie Ricks, Fredo Davis, Freez Luv, Funny Man Pratt

Gab Spain, Garlyn Norris, Garrett Mendez, Garrett Morris, Garrick Dixon, Gary "G-Thang" Johnson, Geneva Joy Hughes, Geoff Brown, George "Lovin'" Jackson. George Perez, George Walker (Williams & Walker), George Wilborn, Gerald Kelly, Gerald "Slink" Johnson, Gerard Guillory, Gina Yashere, Glen Bullard, Gloria Bigelow, G. Mama Lee, Godfrey, Golden Brooks, Gracie Armijo, Grave Digger, Greg Grady, Greg Eagles, Greg Pittman, G Reilly, Griff, G-Rocc, Guy Betancourt

Haddie Djemal, Hadi Khorsandi, Hal Williams, Hamburger, Harold Bridges, Harry Goodspeed, Helen Martin, Henry Cho, Henry Coleman, Henry Welch, Hilly Hicks, Hodge Twins, Horatio Sanz, Hotlink, Howie Bell, Huggy Lowdown, Hunter Marvin, Hurricane Andrew

Ian Edwards, Ike Nwala, Insane Wayne, Irv Burton, Isaac Ike Smalls, Isiah Kelly, Iva LaShawn, Ivory Corley

Jack Shepherd, Jackee Harry, Jackie Fabulous, Jackie Guerra, Jada Pinkett-Smith, Jade Esteban Estrada, Jak Knight, Jamal Doman, Jamal Russell, James Bland, James Stephens III, Janelle James, Ja'net Dubois, Janet Dollar, Janet Stockdale, Jarmel Foster, Jasmine Guy, Jasper Redd, Jay, Jay Deep, Jay Ellis, Jay Lamont, Jay Pharoah, Jay Phillips, Jay Rocc, Jayson Cross, J. Derrell White, Jedda Jones, Jeff Arnold, Jeff Clanagan, Jemmerio is Jemmerio, Jenifer Lewis, Jenny Yang, Jerrold Benford, Jerry Winn, Jesse Aragon, Jessica Williams, Jessica "It's All Good" Williams, J Funny, Jig, Jimmy Thompson, JJ Ramirez, JJ Williamson, J Lew, J-Marc, Job Mixon, Joc Rivera, Joe Blount, Joe Charleston, Joe Clair, Joe Jackson, Joe Recca, Joe Wong, Joeryl Jackson, Joey Vega, Joey "J-Dub" Wells, John Henton, John Marshall Jones, John Moody, John Reed, Johnnie Flowers, Johnny Sanchez, Jonathan Slocumb, Jon Champion, Jon Laster, Jones the Comedian, Jordan Jackson, Jordan Rock, Jose Mota, Josephine Baker, Josh

Johnson, Joshua Gilyard, Joyce Coleman, Joyelle Johnson, J Renee Witherspoon, Juan Garcia, Juan Medina, Juan Villareal, Judee Brown, Junji Takada, Jus June, Justin Hires, Justine, J'Vonne Pearson

Kal Penn (Kalpen Suresh Modi), Kanesha Buss, Kara Lindsay, Kareem Green, Karel Spikes, Karen Addison, Karen Marie, Karlous Miller, Kathy Westfield, K-Dubb, K D Ringer, Keilah, Keisha Hunt, Keisha Zollar, Keith Michael Ashton, Keith Morris, Keith Robinson, Kel Mitchell, Kellita Smith, Kellye Howard, Ken Cox, Ken Sagoes, Ken Spearman, Kenan Thompson, Kenny Hill, Kenny Howell, Kenny King, Kenny Stroud, Kenney Johnson, Kente Scott, Kevin Anthony, Kevin Boseman, Kevin Davis, Kevin Robe, Kevin D. Williams, Kier Spates, Kim Holmes, Kim Tavares, Kimani Callender, King Kedar, King Khalid (Khalid Lamb), King Tink, Kirk McHenry, Kivi Rogers, Komedian KG, Kool Bubba Ice, Kool Keith, Kool Herm, Kris Atkins, Ku Egenti, Ky Nelly, Kyle Erby, Kyle Grooms, Kymedienne Fluff Puff Jackson

Lachelle, Lady Mac, Lady of Rage, Lady Roz, Lady Shamar, Lady Vain, L A Hardy, LaKisha McCullough, Lamarr Lee, Lamond Shepherd, Lamont Bonman, Lamont Ferrell, Lance Caruthers, LaRita Shelby, Larry Beyah, Larry Goodwell, Larry Omaha, LaShawn Grice, LaShonda Montgomery, LaToya Tennille, Lauren Bailey, Laurence Whyte, Lavar Walker, Lawanda Young, Layson Brooks, Jr., Leggs Coleman, Lee Ali, Lenny Henry, Leo Flowers, Leo Lawrence, Leola 'Puddin' Stafford, Leonard Reed, Leroy & Skillet, Lester Barrie, Lester Bibbs, Lewis Dix, Lionel Walton, Lisa Holly, Lite Skinned, Little G, Little JJ, L J Brown, Lonnel Harris, Lotus B, Ludo Vika, LueLue Korrell, LueLue Sutton, Luis de Alba, Luke Torres, Lydia Nicole, Lynn Dillard, Lynn Harris-Taylor

Mac Page, Mack Bootsy, Macio, Madd Marv (Marvin Thomas), Maija DiGiorgio, Malikah E, Malcolm Jamal Warner, Malik S, Manny Maldonado, Marc Howard, Marc Wilmore, Marcos Lara, Marcus Combs, Marcus King, Marcus Martin, Marcus Mason, Marcy Gutherie, Marina Franklin, Mario Joyner, Mark Christopher Lawrence, Mark Gregory, Mark Prince, Mark Reedy, Mark Viera, Mark Wheatle, Marlan Ballard, Maronzio Vance, Marquez the Greatest, Martel Green, Marvin Dixon, Marvin Hunter, Mary Alice, Mary Boyce, Mary Lindsey, Maryssa Smith, Matte, Max Amini, Maya Rudolph, Mazerati, Megan Piphus, Mel Stewart, Mel Watkins, Melvin Bender, Memphis Will, Marc B, Merlin Santana, Meshach Taylor, Micah "Bam Bam" White, Michael A. Sanford, Michael Adams, Michael Blackson, Michael, Jr., Michael Sanford, Michael Williams, Michaela Coel, Mickey Housley, Miguel Washington, Mike Bonner, Mike Britt, Mike Estime, Mike Mitchell, Mike Paramore, Mike Robles, Mike Washington, Mo Amer, Monica Floyd, Monie Jonezy, Monique Marvez, Monique Scott, Montanna Taylor, Monte Crews, Mr. Jerry Walker, Mr. Wendell, Ms. Cutnup, Ms. Pat, Ms. Woody, Murv, Myra J

Nacole Williams, Na'im Lynn, Nancy Bellany, Nard, Natalie Desselle, Nate Jackson, Nate Smith, Nell Carter, Nephew Tommy, Neshia Brathwaite, Neven Milline, Nick Moore, Nicky Sunshine, Nicole Byer, Nikki Carr, Niko, Ninety-Nine (Takashi Okamura, Hiroyuki Yabe), Niroma Johnson, Norman Vance, Jr., Nyima Funk

Ocean, Ogiyahagi, Olivia Arrington, Omar Laquon Regan, Omid Djalili, Onnie 'Lollipop' Jones, Oscar Nunez, Owen Smith

P. B. Smiley, Paul Ogata, Paul 'Smokey' Deese, Paul Varghese, Peanut (Johnson), Peanut (the other one), Percy Crews, Perry the Clown, Peyvand Khorsandi, Phoebe Robinson, Phyllis Yvonne Stickney, Pierre Edwards, Pinky Thomas, PMAN. Pooh Carter, Poochie Hammonds, Porsha Renee, Preacher Lawson, Preacher Moss (Bryant Moss), Prelow, Prescott Gilliam,

Queat Harris, Queen Aisha

Rafihna Bastos, Rain Pryor, Ralph Porter, Ramon Rivas II, Randall Park, Randi Skye, Randy Hernandez, Rasheed Thurmond, Ray Chatman, Ray Diva, Ray Grady, Real Cole, Red Grant, Redman, Regal Riser, Reggie Carroll, Reggie McFadden, Reggie Reg, Reggie Watts, Regina Ivery, Reginald D. Hunter, Reginald Turner, Rell Battle, Rene Garcia, Rene Hicks, Retha Jones, Retta, Rex Garvin, Rex Navarrete, Rich Lewis, Rich Williams, Richard and Willie, Richard Trask, Richard Villa, Rick Najera, Rick Ramos, Rick Raw, Rick Rome, Rick Sullivan, Ricky Velez, Rico Reed, RIP tha Playa, Rip Michaels, Rob Allen, Rob Love, Rob Stapleton, Rob West, Robbie Peron, Robert BFunny Flowers, Robert Johnson, Robert Joseph, Robin Montague, Robin Thede, Rodman, Rodney Bingham, Rodney Lumpins, Rodrigo Torres, Roman Murray, Ron Funches, Ron G, Ron Ramey, Rondell Sheridan, Roni Shandell, Ronnie Jordan, Rory Darvel, Rori Diggs, Rory Flynn, Rosie Tran, Roy Anthony, Roy Fegan, Roy Rice (Screw), Royale Watkins, Roz Browne, Roz Washington, Ruben Paul, Rudy Mancuso, Rudy Medina, Rudy Moreno, Rudy Rush, Ruperto Vanderpool, Rushion McDonald, Rusty Cundieff, Ryan ReAves

Sadiki Fuller, Sam Adams, Sam McDaniel, Sam Ridley, Sammy Davis, Jr., Sammy Gartner, Sammy Sammy, Sandra Valls, Sandy Brown, Sara Contreras, Sasheer Zamata, Scatman Crothers, Sco Bubble, Scoey Mitchell, Scooby, Scooter Magruder, Scott Shimamoto, Scruncho (Anthony McKinley), Sean Larkins, Sebastian Cetina, Sexy Marlo, Shady Grady, Shanel Hughes, Shante Wayans, Shaun Jones, Shaquita Griffin, Sharrie McCain, Shawn Harris, Shawn Harvey, Shawn Leveret, Shayla Rivera, Shay-Shay, Shellee Brown, Sherman Golden, Sherman Holloway, Sherry E, Shuckey Duckey, Shugga D Rosenbloom, Side 2 Side, Silk Willie Dunn the Bus Driver, Sister Quintella, Skillz Hudson, Skip Clark, Smokey Suarez, Solo, Son Tran, Sonia Denis, Sonya D, Spanky Brown, Spanky Hayes, Special K, Speedy (Donald Caldwell), Spike Davis, Stacy Hall, Stephan Caddell, Stephan GM Ford, Stephanie O, Stephon Smith, Steve Brown, Steve Flye, Steve Turner, Steve White, Steve Wilson, Stevie Mack, Stixx, Stogie Kenyatta, Straaw, Stymie Beard, SugaBear, Suli McCullough, Sully Diaz, Sunshine, Susan B. Douglas, Suzanne Suter, Sweet Baby Kita, Sydnee Washington, Sydney Castillo, Sylvia Traymore Morrison

Tacarra Williams Tai Griffin, Talentt Harris, Tamala Jones, Tangie Ambrose, Tanya Cha Cha Sandoval McMahon, Tanya Hunter, Tasha Smith, Tavaris Kelly, Tavon Patterson, Tayboo, Tayne Morano, T C Cope, Teddy Carpenter, Tehran Von Ghasri, Terry Gross, Terry Hodges, Terry Tuff, T. Faye Griffin, The Diva Rodriguez, The Lucas Brothers, The Mooney Twins (Daryl & Dwayne), Thomas Scooter Wilkerson, Thomas Ward, Tiff Money, Tiffany Mabry, Tiffany Younger, T'keyah "Crystal" Keymah, Tim Jennings, Tim Moore, Tim Murray, Tim Persons, Tim Tayag, Timberlee Hill, Timmy Hall, Tina Kim, Tito Helper, T J McGee, T K Carter, Toby Hixx, Tom Fletcher, Tom Howard, Tom Webb, Tomasina Hicks (Boomerang), Tommy Chunn, Tommy Ford, Tone Bell, Tone X, Toni Byrd, Toni Taylor, Tony Asar, Tony Baker, Tony Casillas, Tony Cox, Tony Roberts, Tony Roney, Tony Scofield, Tony Tone (Llewelyn), Tony Woods, Toogie Jackson, Tootsie Two Times, Torrei Hart, T P Hearn, T P Lucas, Travis Simmons, T Ray Sanders, Trenton Stuart Jones, Tressa Eleby, T-Rexx, TuRae Gordon, Ty Barnett, Ty Robbins, Tyler Craig, Tymal TJ Johnson, Tymon Shipp, Tyrone Burston

Unpredictable Drew, Untouchable

Vaina, Vargus Mason, Vic Dunlop, Victor Miller, Vince D, Vince Morris, Vince Royale, Vincent Cook, Vincent Molina, Viruta

Walter Franks, Wan Dexter (Marlon Thompson), Wanda Smith, Warren Brooks, Warren Hutcherson, Wassan Jackson, Wavy Davy, Wayne "BiggWeezy" Brown, Wayne Manigo, Wil Sylvince, Wiley Roberts, Will-E-Robo, Will "Spank" Horton, Will "Sweets" Morales, William "J-Dubb" Johnson, William Wilson, Willie Barcena, Willie Brown & Woody, Willie Lynch, Jr., Willis Turner. Winston Woodard, Woody & Roscoe, Wyatta (Robert Keith Wyatt)

Xazmin Garza, Xora Lou

Yamaneika Saunders, Ya Girl AP, Yvette Nicole Brown, Yvette, the Funny Lady

Zack Hoover, Zhivago, Zo, Zorba Jevon Hughes

ADULTS ONLY

REDD FOXX

WITH

COUNT BASIE
AND HIS ORCHESTRA

THE CRESCENDO NIGHTCLUB
5772 SUNSET BOULEVARD
LOS ANGELES

THURS-SUN • OCTOBER 12-15, 1961

SHOWTIME: 8:00 P.M. TICKETS: $5.00

Good For Exposure ...

Not every television show or film made it big (or was all that funny). Most were passing distractions that few remember, but they meant something in their time. Others were big, but don't necessarily qualify as ethnic just because the lead character was. Either way, we acknowledge those visual stories and their contribution to the art of laughter and understanding of the human condition.

48 HRS

A Thousand Words, All of Us, Another 48 HRS,

Baby Boy, Barbershop 2, Beverly Hills Cop, Beverly Hills Cop 2, Beverly Hills Cop 3, Big Momma's House, Big Momma's House 2, Black Dynamite, Blazing Saddles, Blue Collar, Blue Streak, Booty Call, Born in East L. A., Bring the Pain

Central Intelligence, Christmas in Compton, Class Act, College Road Trip, Come Back Charleston Blue, Cooley High, Cos, Cosby, Cousin Skeeter, Crazy Rich Asians

D C Cab, Da Block Party, Daddy Day Care, Death at a Funeral, Def Jam's How To Be A Player, Deliver Us From Eva, Diary of a Tired Black Man, Disco Godfather, Dolemite, Dolemite Explosion, Double Take, Down to Earth, Dr. Dolittle 2

Eddie

Family Matters, Fat Albert (the movie), For Da Love of Money

Ghost Dad, Girl's Trip, Good Hair, Greased Lightning,

Half & Half, Hangin' With Mr. Cooper, Head of State, Here & Now, Homeboys From Outer Space, House Party 2, House Party 3

I Think I Love My Wife, Imagine That

Janky Promoters, Johnson Family Vacation, Jumanji (the remake), Jumpin' Jack Flash, Jumping the Broom

Kingdom Come

Leonard Part 6, Leprechaun in the Hood, Little Bill, Live on the Sunset Strip, Love Don't Cost a Thing, Love Thy Neighbor

Madea Goes to Jail, Madea's Big Happy Family, Madea's Witness Protection and all the rest of the Madeas, Master of None, Me & the Boys, Meet Dave, Metro, Mr. 3000

National Security, Night School, Nobody's Fool, Nora's Hair Salon, Norbit

One on One

Petey Wheatstraw: The Devil's Son-In-Law, Phat Girlz, Pootie Tang, Putney Swope

Ride Along 2, Rush Hour 1 & 2

Senseless, Showtime, Silver Streak, Sister Act, Sister Act 2, Smart Guy, Soul Men, South Central, Sprung, Still Smokin, Strictly Business

Taco Shop, Tales From the Hood, Talkin Dirty After Dark, The 6th Man, The Adventures of Pluto Nash, The Brothers Garcia, The Cosby Mysteries, The Diary of Desmond Pfeiffer, The Great White Hype, The Haunted Mansion, The Honeymooners, The Human Tornado, The Inkwell, The Monkey Hustle, The New Bill Cosby Show, The Parkers, The Princess & the Frog, The Proud Family Movie, The Redd Foxx Show, The Return of Dolemite, The Royal Family, The Wash, Things Are Tough All Over, Think Like A Man, Think Like A Man 2, Tiana, Tortilla Soup, Trading Places, True Colors

Uncle Drew, Uncle P, Universal Remote

Watermelon Man, Welcome Home, Roscoe Jenkins, White Chicks, Who Made the Potato Salad?, Woo

You Can Tell 'Em I Said It, You So Crazy

In Conclusion...

S imilar to the old segue, "Before I go I'm still not leaving," the exploration of ethnic comedy is over for now because we're at the end of this book, but ethnic comedy is not going anywhere. Like the various people that comprise it the art is a survivor, an innovator and an organic and enriching part of our lives. It's ever evolving, with new pioneers cracking surprisingly fertile turf and creating fresh legends for generations we haven't imagined.

Truth is, comedy never needed to be logged. A jokes is a joke. Does it matter who wrote it or popularized it? Does it matter that we honor and pay respects to people who poured their hearts and souls into making others happy in times of personal turmoil and strife? What difference does it make that many of those laugh-makers are obscure figures we'll never brag about; who lost their families, standing in their communities and their health in the pursuit of somebody else's happiness – so what? Well, when you put it that way you're damn right it matters. Heroes stand on the shoulders of all those discarded on the heap, of those who didn't get written about; the ones who aspired to be those few we lionize. That's who books are written for – that majority who needs to be reminded what the art offers and the sacrifices inherent to it.

Let this encyclopedia encourage knowledge seekers to read biographies and if they don't exist – to write them. There's an excellent book on the great Jewish and predominantly mainstream comedians called *The Comedians*, by Kliph Nesteroff. It's a fantastic journey through the history of that segment of the craft and was an inspiration for this volume to be scribed. So, this way everybody gets to go to the party. Let the truly knowledgeable supplant the segregated labels we require in our times to be simply "comedy." Let them cast off the prefixes of Black, Latin, Asian, Middle Eastern or Native American and rely on the universal and binding title "'comedy" as not racially motivated but motivated by the purity of a joke. Nobody's saying the joke can't be racial, but a good racial joke can be laughed at by anybody, not just the member of a club they didn't choose. Leave the parceling out of comedic sub-groups to money grubbing, short-sighted club owners and show promoters.

Once we've become educated as a mass, the need to isolate and maintain one's artistic heritage will be pointless; those artists and events will belong to all of us. So, the next collection of tomes should be about just comedy without need for overdue recognition. Those in the future should be perplexed by this strange compartmentalization of art and innocently ask, "What is ethnic humor?" That will be a long-awaited punchline to a gag set up by societal arrested development. To paraphrase one of our comedy benefactors, when that day happens, that will be a good day.

Until then accept this tribute to those wonderful souls who made our lives so much better and whose deeds we gratefully recognize.

HUMOR MILL'S LISTS

HUMOR MILL'S TOP 100 COMEDY MOVIES OF ALL-TIME

1. Uptown Saturday Night
2. Coming to America
3. Harlem Nights
4. Trading Places
5. Let's Do it Again
6. Which Way is Up?
7. Friday
8. Up in Smoke
9. Blazing Saddles
10. Life
11. The Nutty Professor
12. Stir Crazy
13. Beverly Hills Cop
14. 48 HRS
15. Rush Hour
16. Car Wash
17. Half Baked
18. Soul Men
19. Do the Right Thing
20. I'm Gonna Git You Sucka
21. Hollywood Shuffle
22. Bowfinger
23. Bad Boys
24. Beverly Hills Cop 2
25. Norbit
26. Boomerang
27. Madea Goes to Jail
28. Sextuplets
29. Fist Fight
30. Big Momma's House
31. Born in East L. A.
32. Don't be a Menace in South Central While Drinking Your Juice in the Hood
33. Black Dynamite
34. Friday After Next
35. House Party
36. How High
37. The Nutty Professor 2: The Klumps
38. Barbershop
39. School Daze
40. Crazy Rich Asians
41. Welcome Home, Roscoe Jenkins
42. Girls Trip
43. The Ladies Man
44. Disorderlies
45. National Security
46. Cheech & Chong's Next Movie
47. Central Intelligence
48. D.C. Cab
49. Putney Swope
50. The Big Sick
51. Money Talks
52. The Wash
53. Dr. Dolittle
54. White Chicks
55. The Players Club

56. *I Got the Hook Up*

57. *Pootie Tang*

58. *Rush Hour 2*

59. *Undercover Brother*

60. *Little Man*

61. *Scary Movie*

62. *Still Smokin'*

63. *Big Momma's House 2*

64. *Jumanji*

65. *Blue Streak*

66. *Booty Call*

67. *Death at a Funeral*

68. *Ride Along*

69. *She's Gotta Have It*

70. *Strictly Business*

71. *Woo*

72. *Cool Runnings*

73. *Good Burger*

74. *Bad Boys 2*

75. *Nice Dreams*

76. *Def Jam's How to be a Player*

77. *B*A*P*S*

78. *Guess Who?*

79. *Major Payne*

80. *All About the Benjamins*

81. *Rush Hour 3*

82. *Next Friday*

83. *Barbershop 2*

84. *House Party 2*

85. *Night School*

86. *Watermelon Man*

87. *Distinguish Gentleman*

88. *Big Momma's House 3*

89. *Get Hard*

90. *A Thin Line*

91. *Think Like A Man*

92. *Blankman*

93. *Good Burger*

94. *Mo Money*

95. *3 Strikes*

96. *Talkin' Dirty After Dark*

97. *Are We There Yet?*

98. *Two Can Play That Game*

99. *Soul Plane*

100. *Bamboozled*

Humor Mill's Top 50 Sitcoms Of All-Time

1. *Sanford & Son*
2. *Good Times*
3. *The Jeffersons*
4. *Martin*
5. *The Bernie Mac Show*
6. *The Royal Family*
7. *The Cosby Show*
8. *What's Happening!!*
9. *Everybody Hates Chris*
10. *The Fresh Prince of Bel-Air*
11. *A Different World*
12. *The Wayans Bros*
13. *Different Strokes*
14. *Living Single*
15. *Insecure*
16. *Roc*
17. *Chico & the Man*
18. *My Wife & Kids*
19. *Black-ish*
20. *The Soul Man*
21. *Atlanta*
22. *George Lopez*
23. *Frank's Place*
24. *What's Happening Now!!*
25. *The Jamie Foxx Show*
26. *Malcolm & Eddie*
27. *Marlon*
28. *The Tracy Morgan Show*
29. *The Steve Harvey Show*
30. *Ugly Betty*
31. *The Bill Cosby Show*
32. *The Mindy Project*
33. *That's My Mama*
34. *Family Matters*
35. *227*
36. *Amen*
37. *The Carmichael Show*
38. *The Parkers*
39. *Girlfriends*
40. *Wanda at Large*
41. *Hangin With Mr. Cooper*
42. *The Parent' Hood*
43. *Moesha*
44. *Half & Half*
45. *Dr. Ken*
46. *Thea*
47. *House of Payne*
48. *The Last OG*
49. *Sister, Sister*
50. *The Hughleys*

HUMOR MILL'S TOP 25 COMEDY SPECIALS

1. Richard Pryor: *Live in Concert*

2. Dave Chappelle: *Sticks & Stones*

3. Richard Pryor: *Here & Now*

4. Chris Rock: *Bring the Pain*

5. Eddie Murphy: *Delirious*

6. Dave Chappelle: *Killin' Them Softly*

7. Eddie Murphy: *Raw*

8. Damon Wayans: *Last Stand*

9. Patrice O'Neal: *Elephant in the Room*

10. Bill Cosby: *Himself*

11. Robin Harris: *HBO Comedy*

12. Felipe Esparza: *They're Not Gonna Laugh at You*

13. Katt Williams: *Pimp Chronicles Pt 1*

14. Wanda Sykes: *I'ma Be Me*

15. George Lopez: *America's Mexican*

16. Ali Wong: *Baby Cobra*

17. Tommy Davidson: *Takin' it to D.C.*

18. Mike Epps: *Only One Mike*

19. Michael Che: *Michael Che Matters*

20. Simply Marvalous: *HBO Comedy*

21. Katt Williams: *It's Pimpin, Pimpin*

22. DeRay Davis: *How to Act Black*

23. Kevin Hart: *Irresponsible*

24. Tracy Morgan: *Staying Alive*

25. D L Hughley: *Contrarian*

HUMOR MILL'S TOP 25 COMEDY ALBUMS OF ALL-TIME

1. Richard Pryor: *Live on the Sunset Strip*

2. Richard Pryor: *That Nigger's Crazy*

3. Dick Gregory: *The 2 Sides of Dick Gregory*

4. Richard Pryor: *Bicentennial Nigger*

5. Eddie Murphy: *Comedian*

6. Bill Cosby: *Why is There Air?*

7. Franklyn Ajaye: *Don't Smoke Dope, Fry Your Hair*

8. Richard Pryor: *Are You Serious?*

9. Moms Mabley: *The Funniest Woman in the World*

10. Pigmeat Markham: *Here Comes the Judge*

11. Redd Foxx: *Uncensored*

12. Chris Rock: *Bigger & Blacker*

13. Patrice O'Neal: *Mr. P*

14. Cheech & Chong: *Big Bambu*

15. LaWanda Page: *Pipe Layin' Dan*

16. George Lopez: *Tall, Dark & Chicano*

17. Aziz Ansari: *Intimate Moments for a Sensual Evening*

18. Freddie Prinze: *Looking Good*

19. Chris Rock: *Never Scared*

20. Franklyn Ajaye: *I'm a Comedian, Seriously*

21. Flip Wilson: *The Devil Made Me Buy This Dress*

22. Dick Gregory: *In Living Black & White*

23. Godfrey Cambridge: *Them Cotton Pickin' Days is Over*

24. Marsha Warfield: *I'm A Virgin*

25. Richard Pryor: *Wanted: Richard Pryor Live in Concert*